Secrets of the
JavaScript Ninja

JOHN RESIG
BEAR BIBEAULT

MANNING

SHELTER ISLAND

Manning Publications Co.　　Development editors: Jeff Bleiel, Sebastian Stirling
20 Baldwin Road　　　　　　　Technical editor: Valentin Crettaz
PO Box 261　　　　　　　　　　Copyeditor: Andy Carroll
Shelter Island, NY 11964　　　　Proofreader: Melody Dolab
　　　　　　　　　　　　　　　Typesetter: Dennis Dalinnik
　　　　　　　　　　　　　　　Cover designer: Leslie Haimes

ISBN: 978-1-933988-69-6
Printed in the United States of America
2 3 4 5 6 7 8 9 10 – MAL – 18 17 16 15 14 13

brief contents

contents

preface

When I started writing *Secrets of the JavaScript Ninja* years ago, in early 2008, I saw a real need: there were no books providing in-depth coverage of the most important parts of the JavaScript language (functions, closures, and prototypes), nor were there any books that covered the writing of cross-browser code. Unfortunately, the situation has not improved much, which is surprising.

More and more development energy is being put into new technologies, such as the ones coming out of HTML5 or the new versions of ECMAScript. But there isn't any point to diving into new technologies, or using the hottest libraries, if you don't have a proper understanding of the fundamental characteristics of the JavaScript language. While the future for browser development is bright, the reality is that most development needs to make sure that code continues to work in the majority of browsers and for the majority of potential users.

Even though this book has been under development for a long time, thankfully it is not out of date. The book has been given a solid set of revisions by my coauthor, Bear Bibeault. He's made sure that the material will continue to be relevant for a long time to come.

A major reason why this book has taken so long to write is the experience upon which I was drawing for the later chapters on cross-browser code. Much of my understanding of how cross-browser development happens in the wild has come from my work on the jQuery JavaScript library. As I was writing the later chapters on cross-browser development, I realized that much of jQuery's core could be written differently, optimized, and made capable of handling a wider range of browsers.

Perhaps the largest change that came to jQuery as a result of writing this book was a complete overhaul from using browser-specific sniffing to using feature detection at the core of the library. This has enabled jQuery to be used almost indefinitely, without assuming that browsers would always have specific bugs or be missing specific features.

As a result of these changes, jQuery anticipated many of the improvements to browsers that have come during the past couple years: Google released the Chrome browser; the number of user agents has exploded as mobile computing has increased in popularity; Mozilla, Google, and Apple have gotten into a browser performance war; and Microsoft has finally started making substantial improvements to Internet Explorer. It can no longer be assumed that a single rendering engine (such as WebKit, or Trident in Internet Explorer) will always behave the same way. Substantial changes are occurring rapidly and are spread out to an ever-increasing number of users.

Using the techniques outlined in this book, jQuery's cross-browser capabilities provide a fairly solid guarantee that code written with jQuery will work in a maximum number of browser environments. This guarantee has led to explosive growth in jQuery over the past four years, with it now being used in over 57% of the top 10,000 websites on the Internet, according to BuiltWith.com.

JavaScript's relatively unchanging features, such as code evaluation, controversial with statements, and timers, are continually being used in interesting ways. There are now a number of active programming languages that are built on top of, or compiled to, JavaScript, such as CoffeeScript and Processing.js. These languages require complex language parsing, code evaluation, and scope manipulation in order to work effectively. Although dynamic code evaluation has been maligned due to its complexity and potential for security issues, without it we wouldn't have had the CoffeeScript programming language, which has gone on to influence the upcoming ECMAScript specification itself.

I'm personally making use of all of these features, even today, in my work at Khan Academy. Dynamic code evaluation in the browser is a very powerful feature: you can build in-browser programming environments and do crazy things like inject code into a live runtime. This results in an extremely compelling way to learn computer programming and provides new capabilities that wouldn't be possible in a traditional learning environment.

The future for browser development continues to be very strong, and it's largely due to the features encapsulated in JavaScript and in the browser APIs. Having a solid grasp of the most crucial parts of the JavaScript language, combined with a desire for writing code that'll work in many browsers, will enable you to create code that's elegant, fast, and ubiquitous.

JOHN RESIG

acknowledgments

The number of people involved in writing a book would surprise most people. It took a collaborative effort on the part of many contributors with a variety of talents to bring the volume you are holding (or ebook that you are reading onscreen) to fruition.

The staff at Manning worked tirelessly with us to make sure this book attained the level of quality we hoped for, and we thank them for their efforts. Without them, this book would not have been possible. The "end credits" for this book include not only our publisher, Marjan Bace, and editor Mike Stephens, but also the following contributors: Jeff Bleiel, Douglas Pudnick, Sebastian Stirling, Andrea Kaucher, Karen Tegtmayer, Katie Tennant, Megan Yockey, Dottie Marsico, Mary Piergies, Andy Carroll, Melody Dolab, Tiffany Taylor, Dennis Dalinnik, Gabriel Dobrescu, and Ron Tomich.

Enough cannot be said to thank our peer reviewers who helped mold the final form of the book, from catching simple typos to correcting errors in terminology and code, and helping to organize the chapters in the book. Each pass through a review cycle ended up vastly improving the final product. For taking the time to review the book, we'd like to thank Alessandro Gallo, André Roberge, Austin King, Austin Ziegler, Chad Davis, Charles E. Logston, Chris Gray, Christopher Haupt, Craig Lancaster, Curtis Miller, Daniel Bretoi, David Vedder, Erik Arvidsson, Glenn Stokol, Greg Donald, James Hatheway, Jared Hirsch, Jim Roos, Joe Litton, Johannes Link, John Paulson, Joshua Heyer, Julio Guijarro, Kurt Jung, Loïc Simon, Neil Mix, Robert Hanson, Scott Sauyet, Stuart Caborn, and Tony Niemann.

Special thanks go to Valentin Crettaz, who served as the book's technical editor. In addition to checking each and every sample of example code in multiple environments, he also offered invaluable contributions to the technical accuracy of the text, located information that was originally missing, and kept abreast of the rapid changes to JavaScript and HTML5 support in the browsers.

Special thanks also to Bert Bates, who provided invaluable feedback and suggestions for improving the book. All those endless hours on Skype have certainly paid off.

John Resig

I would like to thank my parents for their constant support and encouragement over the years. They provided me with the resources and tools that I needed to spark my initial interest in programming—and they have been encouraging me ever since.

Bear Bibeault

For this, my fifth published tome, the cast of characters I'd like to thank has a long list of "usual suspects," including, once again, the membership and staff at javaranch.com. Without my involvement in JavaRanch, I'd never have gotten the opportunity to start writing in the first place, and so I sincerely thank Paul Wheaton and Kathy Sierra for starting the whole thing, as well as fellow staffers who gave me encouragement and support, including (but probably not limited to) Eric Pascarello, Ernest Friedman Hill, Andrew Monkhouse, Jeanne Boyarsky, Bert Bates, and Max Habibi.

My partner Jay, and my dogs, Little Bear and Cozmo, get the usual warm thanks for putting up with the shadowy presence who shared their home and rarely looked up from his keyboard except to curse Word, or one of the browsers, or anything else that attracted my ire while I was working on this project.

And finally, I'd like to thank my coauthor, John Resig, without whom this project would not exist.

about this book

JavaScript is important. That wasn't always so, but it's true now.

Web applications are expected to give users a rich user interface experience, and without JavaScript, you might as well just be showing pictures of kittens. More than ever, web developers need to have a sound grasp of the language that brings life to web applications.

And like orange juice and breakfast, JavaScript isn't just for browsers anymore. The language has knocked down the walls of the browser and is being used on the server in engines such as Rhino and V8, and in frameworks like Node.js.

Although this book is primarily focused on JavaScript for web applications, the fundamentals of the language presented in part 2 of this book are applicable across the board.

With more and more developers using JavaScript, it's now more important than ever that they grasp its fundamentals, so that they can become true ninjas of the language.

Audience

This is *not* your first JavaScript book. If you're a complete novice to JavaScript, or you only understand a handful of statements by searching the web for code snippets, this is not the book for you. Yet.

This book is aimed at web developers who already have at least a basic grasp of JavaScript. You should understand the basic structure of JavaScript statements and how they work to create straightforward on-page scripts. You don't need to be an advanced user of the language—that's what this book is for—but you shouldn't be a rank novice.

You should also have a working knowledge of HTML and CSS. Again, nothing too advanced, but you should know the basics of putting a web page together.

If you want some good prerequisite material, grab one of the popular books on JavaScript and web development, and then tackle this one. We can recommend *JavaScript: The Definitive Guide* by David Flanagan, *JavaScript: The Good Parts* by Douglas Crockford, and *Head First JavaScript* by Michael Morrison.

Roadmap

This book is organized to take you from an apprentice to a ninja in four parts.

Part 1 introduces the topic and some tools we'll need as we progress through the rest of the book.

Part 2 focuses on JavaScript fundamentals: aspects of the language that you take for granted but aren't really sure how they work. This may be the most important part of the book, and even if it's all you read, you'll come away with a much sounder understanding of JavaScript, the language.

In part 3, we dive into using the fundamentals that we learned in part 2 to solve knotty problems that the browsers throw at us.

Part 4 wraps up the book with a look at advanced topics focusing on lessons learned from the creation of advanced JavaScript libraries, such as jQuery.

Let's take a brief look at what each chapter will cover.

Chapter 1 introduces us to the challenges that we face as writers of advanced web applications. It presents some of the problems that the proliferation of browsers creates, and suggests best current practices that we should follow when developing our applications, including testing and performance analysis.

Chapter 2 discusses testing, taking a look at the current state of testing and test tools. It also introduces a small but powerful testing concept, the assert, which will be used extensively throughout the remainder of the book to make sure that our code does what we think it should be doing (or sometimes to prove that it doesn't!).

Armed with these tools, chapter 3 begins our foray into the fundamentals of the language, starting, perhaps to your surprise, with a thorough examination of the *function* as defined by JavaScript. Although you might have expected the *object* to be the target of first focus, it's a solid understanding of the function, and JavaScript as a functional language, that begins our transformation from run-of-the-mill JavaScript coders to JavaScript ninjas!

Not being done with functions quite yet, chapter 4 takes the fundamentals we learned in chapter 3 and applies them to problems we face in creating our applications. We'll explore recursion—not only for its own sake, but because we can learn a lot more about functions through scrutinizing it—and we'll learn how the functional programming aspects of JavaScript can be applied to not only make our code elegant, but also more robust and succinct. We'll learn ways to deal with variable argument lists, and ways to overload functions in a language that doesn't natively support the object-oriented concept of method overloading.

One of the most important concepts you can take away from this book is the subject of chapter 5: closures. A key concept in functional programming, closures allow us to exert fine-grained control over the scope of objects that we declare and create in our programs. The control of these scopes is the key factor in writing code worthy of a ninja. Even if you stop reading after this chapter (but we hope that you don't), you'll be a far better JavaScript developer than when you started.

Objects are finally addressed in chapter 6, where we learn how patterns of objects can be created through the `prototype` property of the function, and we'll learn how objects are tied to functions for their definitions—one of the many reasons we discussed functions first.

Chapter 7 focuses on the regular expression, an often-overlooked feature of the language that can do the work of scores of lines of code when used correctly. We'll learn how to construct and use regular expressions and how to solve some recurring problems elegantly, using regular expressions and the methods that work with them.

Part 2 on language fundamentals closes out with chapter 8, in which we learn how timers and intervals work in the single-threaded nature of JavaScript. HTML5 promises to bring us relief from the confines of the single thread with *web workers*, but most browsers aren't quite there yet, and virtually all of the existing JavaScript code depends upon a good understanding of JavaScript's single-threaded model.

Part 3 opens with chapter 9, in which we open the black box of JavaScript's runtime code evaluation. We'll look at various ways to evaluate code on the fly, including how to do so safely and in the scope of our choosing. Real-world examples, such as JSON evaluation, metalanguages (a.k.a. domain-specific languages), compression and obfuscation, and even aspect-oriented programming, are discussed.

In chapter 10, we examine the controversial `with` statement, which is used to shorten references within a scope. Whether you are a fan or detractor of `with`, it exists in a lot of code in the wild, and you should understand it regardless of whether you think it's the bomb or an abomination.

Dealing with cross-browser issues is the subject of chapter 11. We examine the five key development concerns with regard to these issues: browser differences, bugs and bug fixes, external code and markup, missing features, and regressions. Strategies such as feature simulation and object detection are discussed at length to help us deal with these cross-browser challenges.

Handling element attributes, properties, and styles is the focus of chapter 12. While the differences in how the various browsers handle these aspects of elements are slowly converging over time, there still exists a number of knotty problems that this chapter describes how to solve.

Part 3 concludes in chapter 13 with a thorough investigation of event handling in the browsers and ways to create a unified subsystem that handles events in a browser-agnostic manner. This includes adding features not provided by the browsers, such as custom events and event delegation.

In part 4 we pick up the pace and delve deeply into advanced topics taken from the heart of JavaScript libraries such as jQuery. Chapter 14 discusses how DOM manipulation APIs can be constructed to manipulate the Document Object Model at runtime, including the Gordian knot of injecting new elements into the DOM.

Finally, in chapter 15, we discuss how CSS selector engines are constructed and the different ways in which they parse and evaluate selectors. Not for the faint of heart, this chapter, but it's a worthy final test of your ninja-hood.

Code conventions

All source code in listings or in the text is in a `fixed-width font like this` to separate it from ordinary text. Method and function names, properties, XML elements, and attributes in the text are also presented in this same font.

In some cases, the original source code has been reformatted to fit on the pages. In general, the original code was written with page-width limitations in mind, but sometimes you may find a slight formatting difference between the code in the book and that provided in the source download. In a few rare cases, where long lines could not be reformatted without changing their meaning, the book listings contain line-continuation markers.

Code annotations accompany many of the listings, highlighting important concepts. In many cases, numbered bullets link to explanations that follow in the text.

Code downloads

Source code for all the working examples in this book (along with some extras that never made it into the text) is available for download from the book's web page at www.manning.com/SecretsoftheJavaScriptNinja.

The code examples for this book are organized by chapter, with separate folders for each chapter. The layout is ready to be served by a local web server, such as the Apache HTTP Server. Simply unzip the downloaded code into a folder of your choice and make that folder the document root of the application.

With a few exceptions, most of the examples don't require the presence of a web server at all and can be loaded directly into a browser for execution, if you so desire.

All examples were tested in a variety of modern browsers (as of mid-2012), including Internet Explorer 9, Firefox, Safari, and Google Chrome.

Author online

The authors and Manning Publications invite you to the book's forum, run by Manning Publications, where you can make comments about the book, ask technical questions, and receive help from the authors and other users. To access and subscribe to the forum, point your browser to www.manning.com/SecretsoftheJavaScriptNinja and click the Author Online link. This page provides information on how to get on the forum once you are registered, what kind of help is available, and the rules of conduct in the forum.

Manning's commitment to our readers is to provide a venue where a meaningful dialogue between individual readers and between readers and the authors can take place. It's not a commitment to any specific amount of participation on the part of the authors, whose contribution to the book's forum remains voluntary (and unpaid). We suggest you try asking the authors some challenging questions, lest their interest stray!

The Author Online forum and the archives of previous discussions will be accessible from the publisher's website as long as the book is in print.

About the cover illustration

The figure on the cover of *Secrets of the JavaScript Ninja* is captioned "Noh Actor, Samurai," from a woodblock print by an unknown Japanese artist of the mid-nineteenth century. Derived from the Japanese word for *talent* or *skill*, Noh is a form of classical Japanese musical drama that has been performed since the 14th century. Many characters are masked, with men playing male and female roles. The samurai, a hero figure in Japan for hundreds of years, was often featured in the performances, and in this print the artist renders with great skill the beauty of the costume and the ferocity of the samurai.

Samurai and ninjas were both warriors excelling in the Japanese art of war, known for their bravery and cunning. Samurai were elite soldiers, well-educated men who knew how to read and write as well as fight, and they were bound by a strict code of honor called Bushido (The Way of the Warrior), which was passed down orally from generation to generation, starting in the 10th century. Recruited from the aristocracy and upper classes, analogous to European knights, samurai went into battle in large formations, wearing elaborate armor and colorful dress meant to impress and intimidate. Ninjas were chosen for their martial arts skills rather than their social standing or education. Dressed in black and with their faces covered, they were sent on missions alone or in small groups to attack the enemy with subterfuge and stealth, using any tactics to assure success; their only code was one of secrecy.

The cover illustration is from a set of three Japanese prints owned for many years by a Manning editor, and when we were looking for a ninja for the cover of this book, the striking samurai print came to our attention and was selected for its intricate details, vibrant colors, and vivid depiction of a ferocious warrior ready to strike—and win.

At a time when it is hard to tell one computer book from another, Manning celebrates the inventiveness and initiative of the computer business with book covers based on two-hundred-year-old illustrations that depict the rich diversity of traditional costumes from around the world, brought back to life by prints such as this one.

about the authors

John Resig is the Dean of Computer Science at Khan Academy and the creator of the jQuery JavaScript library. jQuery is currently used in 58% of the top 10,000 websites (according to BuiltWith.com) and is used on tens of millions of other sites, making it one of the most popular technologies used to build websites and possibly one of the most popular programming technologies of all time.

He's also created a number of other open source utilities and projects, including Processing.js (a port of the Processing language to JavaScript), QUnit (a test suite for testing JavaScript code), and TestSwarm (a platform for distributed JavaScript testing).

He is currently working to take Computer Science education a step further at Khan Academy, where he's developing Computer Science curriculum and tools to teach people of all ages how to program. Khan Academy's goal is to create excellent educational resources that are freely available for all to learn from. He's working to not just teach people how to program, but to replicate the initial spark of excitement that every programmer has felt after writing their first program.

Currently, John is located in Brooklyn, NY, and enjoys studying Ukiyo-e (Japanese woodblock printing) in his spare time.

Bear Bibeault has been writing software for over three decades, starting with a Tic-Tac-Toe program written on a Control Data Cyber supercomputer via a 100-baud teletype. Because he has two degrees in Electrical Engineering, Bear should be designing antennas or something; but since his first job with Digital Equipment Corporation, he has always been much more fascinated with programming.

Bear has also served stints with companies such as Lightbridge Inc., BMC Software, Dragon Systems, Works.com, and a handful of other companies. Bear even served in the U.S. Military, teaching infantry soldiers how to blow up tanks—skills that come in handy during those daily scrum meetings.

Bear is currently a Software Architect for a leading provider of household gateway devices and television set-top boxes.

Bear is the author of a number of other Manning books: *jQuery in Action* (first and second editions), *Ajax in Practice*, and *Prototype and Scriptaculous in Action*, and he has been a technical reviewer for many of the web-focused "Head First" books by O'Reilly Publishing, such as *Head First Ajax*, *Head Rush Ajax*, and *Head First Servlets and JSP.*

In addition to his day job, Bear also writes books (duh!), runs a small business that creates web applications and offers other media services (but not wedding videography—*never, ever* wedding videography), and helps to moderate CodeRanch.com as a "marshal" (very senior moderator).

When not planted in front of a computer, Bear likes to cook *big* food (which accounts for his jeans size), dabble in photography and video, ride his Yamaha V-Star, and wear tropical print shirts.

He works and resides in Austin, Texas, a city he dearly loves except for the completely insane drivers.

Part 1

Preparing for training

This part of the book will set the stage for your JavaScript ninja training.

In chapter 1, you'll learn what we're trying to accomplish with this book, and we'll lay the framework for the environment in which JavaScript authors operate.

Chapter 2 will teach you why testing is so important and give you a brief survey of some of the testing tools available. Then we'll develop some surprisingly simple testing tools that you'll use throughout the rest of your training.

When you're finished with this part of the book, you'll be ready to embark on your training as a JavaScript ninja!

Enter the ninja

This chapter covers

- A look at the purpose and structure of this book
- Which libraries we'll look at
- What is "advanced" JavaScript programming?
- Cross-browser authoring
- Test suite examples

If you're reading this book, you know that there's nothing simple about creating effective and cross-browser JavaScript code. In addition to the normal challenges of writing clean code, we have the added complexity of dealing with obtuse browser differences and complexities. To deal with these challenges, JavaScript developers frequently capture sets of common and reusable functionality in the form of JavaScript libraries.

These libraries vary widely in approach, content, and complexity, but one constant remains: they need to be easy to use, incur the least amount of overhead, and be able to work across all browsers that we wish to target.

It stands to reason, then, that understanding how the very best JavaScript libraries are constructed can provide us with great insight into how our own code can be constructed to achieve these same goals. This book sets out to uncover the techniques and secrets used by these world-class code bases and to gather them into a single resource.

In this book we'll be examining the techniques that were (and continue to be) used to create the popular JavaScript libraries. Let's meet those libraries!

1.1   *The JavaScript libraries we'll be tapping*

The techniques and practices used to create modern JavaScript libraries will be the focus of our attention in this book. The primary library that we'll be considering is, of course, jQuery, which has risen in prominence to be the most ubiquitous JavaScript library in modern use.

jQuery (http://jquery.com) was created by John Resig and released in January of 2006. jQuery popularized the use of CSS selectors to match DOM content. Among its many capabilities, it provides DOM manipulation, Ajax, event handling, and animation functionality.

This library has come to dominate the JavaScript library market, being used on hundreds of thousands of websites, and interacted with by millions of users. Through considerable use and feedback, this library has been refined over the years—and continues to evolve—into the optimal code base that it is today.

In addition to examining example code from jQuery, we'll also look at techniques utilized by the following libraries:

- Prototype (http://prototypejs.org/)—The godfather of the modern JavaScript libraries, created by Sam Stephenson and released in 2005. This library embodies DOM, Ajax, and event functionality, in addition to object-oriented, aspect-oriented, and functional programming techniques.
- Yahoo! UI (http://developer.yahoo.com/yui)—The result of internal JavaScript framework development at Yahoo! and released to the public in February of 2006. Yahoo! UI (YUI) includes DOM, Ajax, event, and animation capabilities in addition to a number of preconstructed widgets (calendar, grid, accordion, and others).
- base2 (http://code.google.com/p/base2)—Created by Dean Edwards and released in March 2007. This library supports DOM and event functionality. Its claim to fame is that it attempts to implement the various W3C specifications in a universal, cross-browser manner.

All of these libraries are well constructed and tackle their target problem areas comprehensively. For these reasons, they'll serve as a good basis for further analysis, and understanding the fundamental construction of these code bases will give us insight into the process of world-class JavaScript library construction.

But these techniques aren't only useful for constructing large libraries; they can be applied to all JavaScript coding, regardless of size.

The makeup of a JavaScript library can be broken down into three aspects:

- Advanced use of the JavaScript language
- Meticulous construction of cross-browser code
- The use of current best practices that tie everything together

We'll be carefully analyzing these three aspects in each of the libraries to gather a complete knowledge base we can use to create our own effective JavaScript code.

1.2 Understanding the JavaScript language

Many JavaScript coders, as they advance through their careers, may get to the point where they're actively using the vast array of elements comprising the language, including objects and functions and (if they've been paying attention to coding trends) even anonymous inline functions. In many cases, however, those skills may not be taken beyond fundamental levels. Additionally, there's generally a very poor understanding of the purpose and implementation of *closures* in JavaScript, which fundamentally and irrevocably exemplify the importance of functions to the language.

JavaScript consists of a close relationship between objects, functions, and closures (see figure 1.1). Understanding the strong relationship between these three concepts can vastly improve our JavaScript programming ability, giving us a strong foundation for any type of application development.

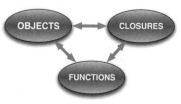

Figure 1.1 JavaScript consists of a close relationship between objects, functions, and closures.

Many JavaScript developers, especially those coming from an object-oriented background, may pay a lot of attention to objects, but at the expense of understanding how functions and closures contribute to the big picture.

In addition to these fundamental concepts, there are two features in JavaScript that are woefully underused: timers and regular expressions. These two concepts have applications in virtually any JavaScript code base, but they aren't always used to their full potential due to their misunderstood nature.

A firm grasp of how timers operate within the browser, all too frequently a mystery, gives us the ability to tackle complex coding tasks such as long-running computations and smooth animations. And a sound understanding of how regular expressions work allows us to simplify what would otherwise be quite complicated pieces of code.

As another high point of our advanced tour of the JavaScript language, we'll take a look at the with statement in chapter 10, and the divisive eval() method in chapter 9—two important, but controversial, language features that have been trivialized, misused, and even condemned outright by many JavaScript programmers.

> **NOTE** Those of you who have been keeping track of what's moving and shaking in the web development world will know that both of these topics are controversial and are either deprecated or limited in future versions of JavaScript.

But as you'll likely come across these concepts in existing code, it's important to understand them, even if you have no plans to use them in future code.

By looking at the work of some of the best JavaScript coders, we'll see that, when used appropriately, advanced language features allow for the creation of some fantastic pieces of code that wouldn't be otherwise possible. To a large degree, these advanced features can also be used for some interesting metaprogramming exercises, molding JavaScript into whatever we want it to be.

Learning how to use advanced language features responsibly and to their best advantage can certainly elevate our code to higher levels, and honing our skills to tie these concepts and features together will give us a level of understanding that puts the creation of any type of JavaScript application within our reach. This foundation will give us a solid base for moving forward, starting with writing solid, cross-browser code.

1.3   *Cross-browser considerations*

Perfecting our JavaScript programming skills will take us far, especially now that JavaScript has escaped the confines of the browser and is being used on the server with JavaScript engines like Rhino and V8 and libraries like Node.js. But when developing browser-based JavaScript applications (which is the focus of this book), sooner rather than later, we're going to run face first into *The Browsers* and their maddening issues and inconsistencies.

In a perfect world, all browsers would be bug-free and would support web standards in a consistent fashion, but we all know that we most certainly don't live in that world.

The quality of browsers has improved greatly as of late, but they all still have some bugs, missing APIs, and browser-specific quirks that we'll need to deal with. Developing a comprehensive strategy for tackling these browser issues, and becoming intimately familiar with their differences and quirks, is just as important, if not more so, than proficiency in JavaScript itself.

When writing browser applications or JavaScript libraries to be used in them, picking and choosing which browsers to support is an important consideration. We'd probably like to support them all, but limitations on development and testing resources dictate otherwise. So how do we decide which to support, and to what level?

An approach that we can employ is one loosely borrowed from an older Yahoo! approach that was called *graded browser support*. In this technique, we create a browser support matrix that serves as a snapshot of how important a browser and its platform are to our needs.

In such a table, we list the target platforms on one axis, and the browsers on the other. Then, in the table cells, we give a "grade" (A through F, or any other grading system that meets our needs) to each browser/platform combination. Table 1.1 shows a hypothetical example of such a table.

Note that we haven't filled in any grades. What grades you assign to a particular combination of platform and browser is entirely dependent upon the needs and requirements of your project, as well as other important factors, like the makeup of

Table 1.1 A hypothetical "browser support matrix"

	Windows	OS X	Linux	iOS	Android
IE 6		N/A	N/A	N/A	N/A
IE 7, 8		N/A	N/A	N/A	N/A
IE 9		N/A	N/A	N/A	N/A
Firefox				N/A	
Chrome					
Safari			N/A		N/A
Opera					

the target audience. We can use this approach to come up with grades that measure how important support for the platform/browser is, and combine that info with the cost of that support to try to come up with the optimal set of supported browsers. We'll be exploring this in more depth in chapter 11.

As it's impractical to develop against a large number of platform/browser combinations, we must weigh the costs versus the benefits of supporting the various browsers. Any such analysis must take into account multiple considerations, the primary of which are

- The expectations and needs of the target audience
- The market share of the browser
- The amount of effort necessary to support the browser

The first point is a subjective one that only your project can determine. Market share, on the other hand, can frequently be measured using available information. And a rough estimate of the effort involved in supporting each browser can be determined by considering the capabilities of the browsers and their adherence to modern standards.

Figure 1.2 shows a sample chart that represents information on browser usage (obtained from StatCounter for August 2012) and our personal opinions on the cost of development for the top desktop browsers.

Charting the benefit versus cost in this manner shows at a glance where we can put our effort to get the most "bang for the buck." Here are a few things that jump out of this chart:

- Even though it's relatively a lot more effort to support Internet Explorer 7 and 8 than the standards-compliant browsers, they still have a large market share, which makes the extra effort worthwhile if those users are an important target for our application audience.
- IE 9, having made great strides towards standards compliance, is easier to support than previous versions of IE, and it's already making headway into market share.

- Supporting Firefox and Chrome is a no-brainer, because they have a large market share and are easy to support.
- Even though Safari has a relatively low market share, it still deserves support, as its standards-compliant nature makes its cost small. (As a rule of thumb, if it works in Chrome, it'll likely work in Safari—pathological cases notwithstanding.)
- Opera, though it requires no more effort than Safari, can lose out on the desktop because of its minuscule market share. But if the mobile platforms are important to you, mobile Opera is a bigger player; see figure 1.3.
- Nothing really need be said about IE 6. (See www.ie6countdown.com.)

Things change pretty drastically when we take a look at the mobile landscape, as shown in figure 1.3.

Of course, nothing is ever quite so cut-and-dried. It might be safe to say that benefit is more important than cost, but it ultimately comes down to the choices of those in the decision-making process, taking into account factors such as the needs of the market and other business concerns. But quantifying the costs versus benefits is a good starting point for making these important support decisions.

Also, be aware that the landscape changes rapidly. Keeping tabs on sites such as http://gs.statcounter.com is a wise precaution.

Another possible factor for resource-constrained organizations is the skill of the development team. While the primary reason for building an app is its use by end users, developers may have to build the skills necessary to develop the application to meet the end users' needs. Such considerations need to be taken into account during the cost analysis phase.

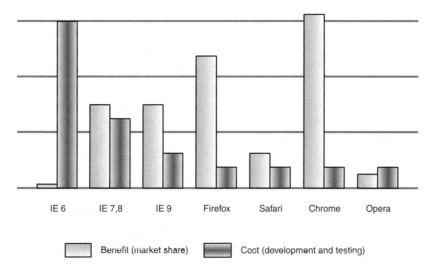

Figure 1.2 Analyzing the cost versus the benefit of supporting various desktop browsers indicates where we should put our effort.

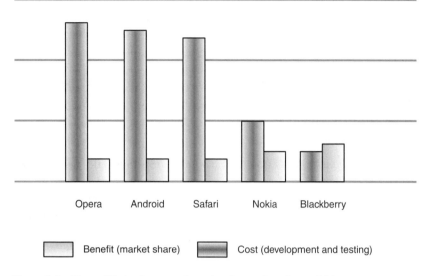

Opera   Android   Safari   Nokia   Blackberry

☐ Benefit (market share)   ▨ Cost (development and testing)

Figure 1.3 The mobile landscape, where development costs are fairly even, comes down to usage statistics.

The cost of cross-browser development can depend significantly on the skill and experience of the developers, and this book is intended to boost that skill level, so let's get to it by looking at current best practices.

1.4 Current best practices

Mastery of the JavaScript language and a grasp of cross-browser coding issues are important parts of becoming an expert web application developer, but they're not the complete picture. To enter the big leagues, you also need to exhibit the traits that scores of previous developers have proved are beneficial to the development of quality code. These traits, which we'll examine in depth in chapter 2, are known as *best practices* and, in addition to mastery of the language, include such elements as

- Testing
- Performance analysis
- Debugging skills

It's vitally important to adhere to these practices in our coding, *and* frequently; the complexity of cross-browser development certainly justifies it. Let's examine a couple of these practices.

1.4.1 Current best practice: testing

Throughout this book, we'll be applying a number of testing techniques that serve to ensure that our example code operates as intended, as well as to serve as examples of how to test general code. The primary tool that we'll be using for testing is an `assert()` function, whose purpose is to assert that a premise is either true or false.

The general form of this function is

```
assert(condition, message);
```

where the first parameter is a condition that should be true, and the second is a message that will be displayed if it's not.

Consider this, for example:

```
assert(a == 1, "Disaster! a is not 1!");
```

If the value of variable `a` isn't equal to 1, the assertion fails, and the somewhat overly dramatic message is displayed.

Note that the `assert()` function isn't an innate feature of the language (some languages, such as Java, provide such capabilities), so we'll be implementing it ourselves. We'll be discussing its implementation and use in chapter 2.

1.4.2 *Current best practice: performance analysis*

Another important practice is performance analysis. The JavaScript engines in the browsers have been making astounding strides in the performance of JavaScript itself, but that's no excuse for us to write sloppy and inefficient code.

We'll be using code such as the following later in this book for collecting performance information:

```
start = new Date().getTime();
for (var n = 0; n < maxCount; n++) {
  /* perform the operation to be measured *//
}
elapsed = new Date().getTime() - start;
assert(true,"Measured time: " + elapsed);
```

Here, we bracket the execution of the code to be measured with the collection of timestamps: one before we execute the code and one after. Their difference tells us how long the code took to perform, which we can compare against alternatives to the code that we measure using the same technique.

Note how we perform the code multiple times; in this example, we perform it the number of times represented by `maxCount`. Because a single operation of the code happens much too quickly to measure reliably, we need to perform the code many times to get a measurable value. Frequently, this count can be in the tens of thousands, or even millions, depending upon the nature of the code being measured. A little trial-and-error lets us choose a reasonable value.

These best-practice techniques, along with others that we'll learn along the way, will greatly enhance our JavaScript development. Developing applications with the restricted resources that a browser provides, coupled with the increasingly complex world of browser capability and compatibility, makes having a robust and complete set of skills a necessity.

1.5   *Summary*

Here's a rundown of what we've learned in this chapter:

- Cross-browser web application development is hard, harder than most people would think.
- In order to pull it off, we need not only a mastery of the JavaScript language, but a thorough knowledge of the browsers, along with their quirks and inconsistencies, and a good grounding in standard current best practices.
- While JavaScript development can certainly be challenging, there are those brave souls who have already gone down this tortuous route: the developers of JavaScript libraries. We'll be distilling the knowledge demonstrated in the construction of these code bases, effectively fueling our development skills and raising them to world-class level.

This exploration will certainly be informative and educational—let's enjoy the ride!

Arming with testing and debugging

This chapter covers

- Tools for debugging JavaScript code
- Techniques for generating tests
- Building a test suite
- How to test asynchronous operations

Constructing effective test suites for your code is always important, so we're going to discuss it now, before we go into any discussions on coding. As important as a solid testing strategy is for *all* code, it can be crucial for situations where external factors have the potential to affect the operation of your code, which is *exactly* the case we're faced with in cross-browser JavaScript development.

Not only do we have the typical problems of ensuring the quality of the code, especially when dealing with multiple developers working on a single code base, and guarding against regressions that could break portions of an API (generic problems that all programmers need to deal with), but we also have the problem of determining if our code works in all the browsers that we choose to support.

We'll further discuss the problem of cross-browser development in depth when we look at cross-browser strategies in chapter 11, but for now, it's vital that the importance of testing be emphasized and testing strategies defined, because we'll be using these strategies throughout the rest of the book.

13

In this chapter, we're going to look at some tools and techniques for debugging JavaScript code, for generating tests based upon those results, and for constructing a test suite to reliably run those tests.

Let's get started.

2.1   Debugging code

Remember when debugging JavaScript meant using `alert()` to verify the value of variables? Well, the ability to debug JavaScript code has dramatically improved in the last few years, in no small part due to the popularity of the Firebug developer extension for Firefox.

Similar tools have been developed for all major browsers:

- Firebug—The popular developer extension for Firefox that got the ball rolling. See http://getfirebug.org/.
- IE Developer Tools—Included in Internet Explorer 8 and later.
- Opera Dragonfly—Included in Opera 9.5 and newer. Also works with mobile versions of Opera.
- WebKit Developer Tools—Introduced in Safari 3, dramatically improved as of Safari 4, and now available in Chrome.

There are two important approaches to debugging JavaScript: logging and breakpoints. They're both useful for answering the important question, "What's going on in my code?" but each tackles it from a different angle.

Let's start by looking at logging.

2.1.1   Logging

Logging statements (such as using the `console.log()` method in Firebug, Safari, Chrome, IE, and recent versions of Opera) are part of the code (even if perhaps temporarily) and are useful in a cross-browser sense. We can write logging calls in our code, and we can benefit from seeing the messages in the consoles of all modern browsers.

These browser consoles have dramatically improved the logging process over the old "add an alert" technique. All our logging statements can be written to the console and be browsed immediately or at a later time without impeding the normal flow of the program—something not possible with `alert()`.

For example, if we wanted to know what the value of a variable named x was at a certain point in the code, we might write this:

```
var x = 213;
console.log(x);
```

The result of executing this statement in the Chrome browser with the JavaScript console enabled would be what you see in figure 2.1.

Older versions of Opera chose to go their own way when it came to logging, implementing a proprietary `postError()` method. If logging in those older versions is

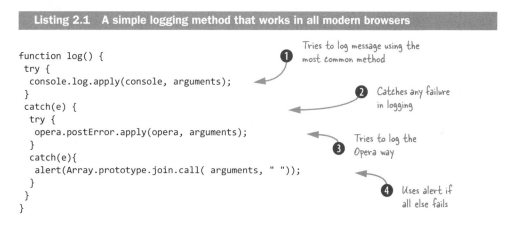

Figure 2.1   Logging lets us see the state of things in our code as it's running.

necessary, we can get all suave and implement a higher-level logging method that works across all browsers, as shown in the following listing.

NOTE   If you aren't dealing with outdated versions of Opera, you can forgo all this and just use `console.log()`.

Listing 2.1   A simple logging method that works in all modern browsers

```
function log() {
 try {
  console.log.apply(console, arguments);
 }
 catch(e) {
  try {
   opera.postError.apply(opera, arguments);
  }
  catch(e){
   alert(Array.prototype.join.call( arguments, " "));
  }
 }
}
```

❶ Tries to log message using the most common method

❷ Catches any failure in logging

❸ Tries to log the Opera way

❹ Uses alert if all else fails

TIP   If you're curious, a more comprehensive version of listing 2.1 is available at http://patik.com/blog/complete-cross-browser-console-log/.

In listing 2.1, we first try to log a message using the method that works in most modern browsers ❶. If that fails, an exception will be thrown that we catch ❷, and then we can try to log a message using Opera's proprietary method ❸. If both of those methods fail, we fall back to using old-fashioned alerts ❹.

NOTE   Listing 2.1 uses the `apply()` and `call()` methods of the JavaScript `Function()` constructor to relay the arguments passed to *our* function to the logging function. These `Function()` methods are designed to help us make precisely controlled calls to JavaScript functions, and we'll be seeing much more of them in chapter 3.

Logging is all well and good for seeing what the state of things might be while the code is running, but sometimes we'll want to stop the action and take a look around.

That's where breakpoints come in.

2.1.2 Breakpoints

Breakpoints are a somewhat more complex concept than logging, but they possess a notable advantage over logging: they halt the execution of a script at a specific line of code, pausing the browser. This allows us to leisurely investigate the state of all sorts of things at the point of the break. This includes all accessible variables, the context, and the scope chain.

Let's say that we have a page that employs our new log() method, as shown in the next listing.

Listing 2.2   A simple page that uses the custom `log()` method

```html
<!DOCTYPE html>
<html>
  <head>
    <title>Listing 2.2</title>
    <script type="text/javascript" src="log.js"></script>
    <script type="text/javascript">
      var x = 213;
      log(x);
    </script>
  </head>
  <body>
  </body>
</html>
```

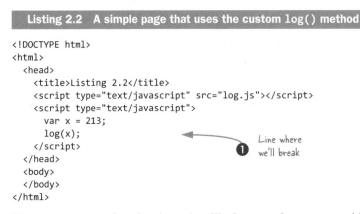

❶ Line where we'll break

If we were to set a breakpoint using Firebug on the annotated line ❶ in listing 2.2 (by clicking on the line number margin in the Script display) and refresh the page to cause the code to execute, the debugger would stop execution at that line and show us the display in figure 2.2.

Note how the rightmost pane allows us to see the state within which our code is running, including the value of x. The debugger breaks on a line *before* the

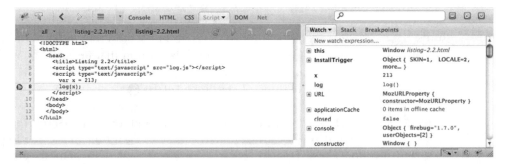

Figure 2.2   Breakpoints allow us to halt execution at a specific line of code so we can take a gander at the state.

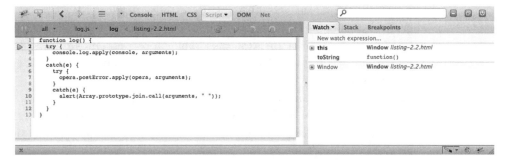

Figure 2.3 Stepping into a method lets us see the new state in which it executes.

breakpointed line is actually executed; in this example, the call to the log() method has yet to be executed.

If we were trying to debug a problem with our new method, we might want to *step into* that method to see what's going on inside it. Clicking on the "step into" button (the left-most gold arrow button) causes the debugger to execute up to the first line of our method, and we'd see the display shown in figure 2.3. Note how the displayed state has changed to allow us to poke around the new state in which the log() method executes.

Any full-featured debugger with breakpoint capabilities is highly dependent upon the browser environment in which it's executing. For this reason, the aforementioned developer tools were created; otherwise, their functionality wouldn't be possible. It's a great boon and relief to the entire web development community that all the major browser implementers have come on board to create effective utilities for allowing debugging.

Debugging code not only serves its primary and obvious purpose (detecting and fixing bugs), but it also can help us achieve the current best-practice goal of generating effective test cases.

2.2 *Test generation*

Robert Frost wrote that good fences make good neighbors, but in the world of web applications, and indeed any programming discipline, good tests make good code. Note the emphasis on the word *good*. It's quite possible to have an extensive test suite that doesn't really help the quality of our code one iota if the tests are poorly constructed.

Good tests exhibit three important characteristics:

- *Repeatability*—Our test results should be highly reproducible. Tests run repeatedly should always produce the exact same results. If test results are nondeterministic, how would we know which results are valid and which are invalid? Additionally, reproducibility ensures that our tests aren't dependent upon external factors issues like network or CPU loads.

- *Simplicity*—Our tests should focus on testing one thing. We should strive to remove as much HTML markup, CSS, or JavaScript as we can without disrupting the intent of the test case. The more we remove, the greater the likelihood that the test case will only be influenced by the specific code that we're testing.

- *Independence*—Our tests should execute in isolation. We must avoid making the results from one test dependent upon another. Breaking tests down into the smallest possible units will help us determine the exact source of a bug when an error occurs.

There are a number of approaches that can be used for constructing tests, with the two primary approaches being *deconstructive tests* and *constructive tests*:

- *Deconstructive test cases*—Deconstructive test cases are created when existing code is whittled down (deconstructed) to isolate a problem, eliminating anything that's not germane to the issue. This helps us to achieve the three characteristics listed previously. We might start with a complete website, but after removing extra markup, CSS, and JavaScript, we'll arrive at a smaller case that reproduces the problem.

- *Constructive test cases*—With a constructive test case we start from a known good, reduced case and build up until we're able to reproduce the bug in question. In order to use this style of testing, we'll need a couple of simple test files from which to build up tests, and a way to generate these new tests with a clean copy of our code.

Let's look at an example of constructive testing.

When creating reduced test cases, we can start with a few HTML files with minimum functionality already included in them. We might even have different starting files for various functional areas; for example, one for DOM manipulation, one for Ajax tests, one for animations, and so on.

For example, the following listing shows a simple DOM test case used to test jQuery.

Listing 2.3 A reduced DOM test case for jQuery

```
<script src="dist/jquery.js"></script>
<script>
  $(document).ready(function() {
    $("#test").append("test");
  });
</script>
<style>
  #test { width: 100px; height: 100px; background: red; }
</style>
<div id="test"></div>
```

To generate a test, with a clean copy of the code base, we can use a little shell script to check out the library, copy over the test case, and build the test suite, as shown here:

```
#!/bin/sh
# Check out a fresh copy of jQuery
git clone git://github.com/jquery/jquery.git $1
# Copy the dummy test case file in
cp $2.html $1/index.html
# Build a copy of the jQuery test suite
cd $1 && make
```

Saved in a file named gen.sh, the preceding script would be executed using this command line,

```
./gen.sh mytest dom
```

which would pull in the DOM test case from dom.html in the Git repository.

Another alternative is to use a prebuilt service designed for creating simple test cases. One of these services is JS Bin (http://jsbin.com/), a simple tool for building a test case that then becomes available at a unique URL—you can even include copies of some of the most popular JavaScript libraries. An example of JS Bin is shown in figure 2.4.

Figure 2.4   A screenshot of the JS Bin website in action

Once we have the tools and knowledge needed to create test cases, we can build test suites around cases so that it becomes easier to run these tests over and over again. Let's look into that.

2.3   *Testing frameworks*

A test suite should serve as a fundamental part of your development workflow, so you should pick a suite that works particularly well for your coding style and your code base. A JavaScript test suite should serve a single need: displaying the results of the tests, making it easy to determine which tests have passed or failed. Testing frameworks can help us reach that goal without having to worry about anything other than creating the tests and organizing them into suites.

There are a number of features that we might want to look for in a JavaScript unit-testing framework, depending upon the needs of the tests. Some of these features include the following:

- The ability to simulate browser behavior (clicks, keypresses, and so on)
- Interactive control of tests (pausing and resuming tests)
- Handling asynchronous test timeouts
- The ability to filter which tests are to be executed

An informal survey attempting to determine which JavaScript testing frameworks people used in their day-to-day development yielded results that were quite illuminating. Figure 2.5 depicts the disheartening fact that a lot of the respondents don't test at all. In the wild, it's easy to believe that the percentage of non-testers is actually higher.

> **NOTE** The raw results, should you be interested, can be found at http://spreadsheets.google.com/pub?key=ry8NZN4-Ktao1Rcwae-9Ljw&output=html.

Another insight from the results is that the vast majority of script authors who do write tests use one of four tools, all of which were pretty much tied in the results: JsUnit, QUnit, Selenium, and YUI Test. The top ten "winners" are shown in figure 2.6.

This is an interesting result, showing that there isn't any one definitive preferred testing framework at this point. But even more interesting is the number of one-off frameworks that have relatively few users, as can be seen in figure 2.6.

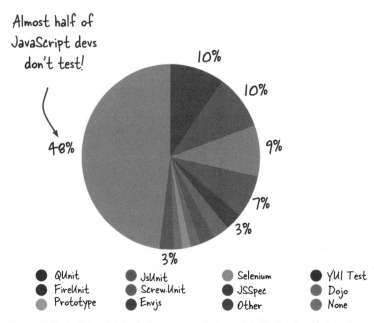

Figure 2.5   A dishearteningly large percentage of JavaScript developers don't test at all!

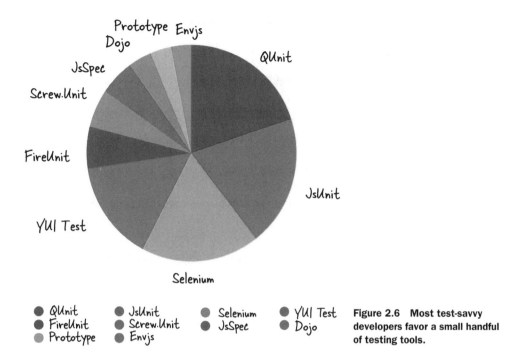

Figure 2.6 **Most test-savvy developers favor a small handful of testing tools.**

It should be noted that it's fairly easy for someone to write a testing framework from scratch, and that's not a bad way to gain a greater understanding of what a testing framework is trying to achieve. This is an especially interesting exercise to tackle because, when writing a testing framework, we'd typically be dealing with pure JavaScript without having to worry much about cross-browser issues. Unless, that is, you're trying to simulate browser events, and if you are, good luck! (Although that *is* something we'll be tackling in chapter 13.)

According to the results depicted in figure 2.6, a number of people have come to this same conclusion and have written a large number of one-off frameworks to suit their own particular needs. But while it's possible to write a proprietary unit-testing framework, it's likely that you'll want to use something that's been prebuilt.

General JavaScript unit-testing frameworks tend to provide a few basic components: a test runner, test groupings, and assertions. Some also provide the ability to run tests asynchronously. Let's take a brief look at some of the most popular unit-testing frameworks.

2.3.1 QUnit

QUnit is the unit-testing framework that was originally built to test jQuery. It has since expanded beyond its initial goals and is now a standalone unit-testing framework. QUnit is primarily designed to be a simple solution to unit testing, providing a minimal, but easy to use, API.

QUnit's distinguishing features are as follows:

- Simple API
- Supports asynchronous testing
- Not limited to jQuery or jQuery-using code
- Especially well-suited for regression testing

More information can be found at http://qunitjs.com.

2.3.2 YUI Test

YUI Test is a testing framework built and developed by Yahoo! and released in October of 2008. It was completely rewritten in 2009 to coincide with the release of YUI 3. YUI Test provides an impressive number of features and functionality that's sure to cover any unit-testing case required by your code base.

YUI Test's distinguishing features are as follows:

- Extensive and comprehensive unit-testing functionality
- Supports asynchronous tests
- Good event simulation

More information is available at http://developer.yahoo.com/yui/3/test/.

2.3.3 JsUnit

JsUnit is a port of the popular Java JUnit testing framework to JavaScript. While it's still one of the most popular JavaScript unit-testing frameworks around, JsUnit is also one of the oldest (both in terms of the code base age and quality). The framework hasn't been updated much recently, so for something that's known to work with all modern browsers, JsUnit may not be the best choice.

More information can be found at www.jsunit.net/.

2.3.4 Newer unit-testing frameworks

According to information on the JUnit main page, the Pivotal Labs team is now focused on a new testing tool named Jasmine. More information is available at http://pivotallabs.com/what/mobile/overview.

Another testing tool to be aware of is TestSwarm, a distributed, continuous-integration testing tool, originally developed by John Resig and now part of Mozilla Labs: https://github.com/jquery/testswarm/wiki.

Next, we'll take a look at creating test suites.

2.4 The fundamentals of a test suite

The primary purpose of a test suite is to aggregate all the individual tests that your code base might have into a single unit, so that they can be run in bulk, providing a single resource that can be run easily and repeatedly.

To better understand how a test suite works, it makes sense to look at how a test suite is constructed. Perhaps surprisingly, JavaScript test suites are really easy to construct. A functional one can be built in only about 40 lines of code.

One would have to ask, though, "Why would I want to build a new test suite?" For most cases, it probably isn't necessary to write your own JavaScript test suite. There are already a number of good-quality suites to choose from (as already shown). But building your own test suite can serve as a good learning experience, especially when looking at how asynchronous testing works.

2.4.1 The assertion

The core of a unit-testing framework is its assertion method, usually named `assert()`. This method usually takes a value—an expression whose premise is *asserted*—and a description that describes the purpose of the assertion. If the value evaluates to true, and in other words is "truthy," the assertion passes; otherwise it's considered a failure. The associated message is usually logged with an appropriate pass/fail indicator.

A simple implementation of this concept can be seen in the next listing.

Listing 2.4 A simple implementation of a JavaScript assertion

```html
<html>
  <head>
    <title>Test Suite</title>
    <script>

      function assert(value, desc) {
        var li = document.createElement("li");
        li.className = value ? "pass" : "fail";
        li.appendChild(document.createTextNode(desc));
        document.getElementById("results").appendChild(li);
      }

      window.onload = function() {
        assert(true, "The test suite is running.");
        assert(false, "Fail!");
      };
    </script>

    <style>
      #results li.pass { color: green; }
      #results li.fail { color: red; }
    </style>
  </head>

  <body>
    <ul id="results"></ul>
  </body>
</html>
```

❶ Defines assert() method

❷ Executes tests using assertions

❸ Defines styles for results

❹ Holds test results

The function named `assert()` ❶ is almost surprisingly straightforward. It creates a new `<li>` element containing the description, assigns a class named `pass` or `fail`, depending upon the value of the assertion parameter (`value`), and appends the new element to a list element in the document body ❹.

The test suite consists of two trivial tests ❷: one that will always succeed, and one that will always fail.

Style rules for the `pass` and `fail` classes ❸ visually indicate success or failure using colors.

This function is simple, but it will serve as a good building block for future development, and we'll be using this assert() method throughout the book to test various code snippets, verifying their integrity.

2.4.2   *Test groups*

Simple assertions are useful, but they really begin to shine when they're grouped together in a testing context to form *test groups*.

When performing unit testing, a test group will likely represent a collection of assertions as they relate to a single method in our API or application. If you were doing behavior-driven development, the group would collect assertions by task. Either way, the implementation is effectively the same.

In our sample test suite, a test group is built in which individual assertions are inserted into the results. Additionally, if any assertion fails, then the entire test group is marked as failing. The output in the next listing is kept pretty simple—some level of dynamic control would prove to be quite useful in practice (contracting/expanding the test groups and filtering test groups if they have failing tests in them).

> **Listing 2.5   An implementation of test grouping**

```
<html>
  <head>
    <title>Test Suite</title>
    <script>

      (function() {
        var results;
        this.assert = function assert(value, desc) {
          var li = document.createElement("li");
          li.className = value ? "pass" : "fail";
          li.appendChild(document.createTextNode(desc));
          results.appendChild(li);
          if (!value) {
            li.parentNode.parentNode.className = "fail";
          }
          return li;
        };
        this.test = function test(name, fn) {
          results = document.getElementById("results");
          results = assert(true, name).appendChild(
              document.createElement("ul"));
          fn();
        };
      })();

      window.onload = function() {
        test("A test.", function() {
          assert(true, "First assertion completed");
          assert(true, "Second assertion completed");
          assert(true, "Third assertion completed");
        });
        test("Another test.", function() {
          assert(true, "First test completed");
          assert(false, "Second test failed");
```

```
        assert(true, "Third assertion completed");
      });
      test("A third test.", function() {
        assert(null, "fail");
        assert(5, "pass")
      });
    };
  </script>
  <style>
    #results li.pass { color: green; }
    #results li.fail { color: red; }
  </style>
</head>
<body>
  <ul id="results"></ul>
</body>
</html>
```

As can be seen in listing 2.5, the implementation is really not much different from the basic assertion logging. The one major difference is the inclusion of a `results` variable, which holds a reference to the current test group (that way the logging assertions are inserted correctly).

Beyond simple testing of code, another important aspect of a testing framework is the handling of asynchronous operations.

2.4.3 *Asynchronous testing*

A daunting and complicated task that many developers encounter while developing a JavaScript test suite is handling asynchronous tests. These are tests whose results will come back *after* a nondeterministic amount of time has passed; common examples of this situation are Ajax requests and animations.

Often the handling of this issue is over-engineered and made much more complicated than it needs be. To handle asynchronous tests, we need to follow a couple of simple steps:

1 Assertions that rely upon the same asynchronous operation need to be grouped into a unifying test group.
2 Each test group needs to be placed on a queue to be run after all the previous test groups have finished running.

Thus, each test group must be capable of running asynchronously.

Let's look at an example in the next listing.

Listing 2.6 A simple asynchronous test suite

```
<html>
  <head>
    <title>Test Suite</title>
    <script>
      (function() {
        var queue = [], paused = false, results;
        this.test = function(name, fn) {
          queue.push(function() {
            results = document.getElementById("results");
```

```
      results = assert(true, name).appendChild(
          document.createElement("ul"));
      fn();
    });
    runTest();
  };
  this.pause = function() {
    paused = true;
  };
  this.resume = function() {
    paused = false;
    setTimeout(runTest, 1);
  };
  function runTest() {
    if (!paused && queue.length) {
      queue.shift()();
      if (!paused) {
        resume();
      }
    }
  }

  this.assert = function assert(value, desc) {
    var li = document.createElement("li");
    li.className = value ? "pass" : "fail";
    li.appendChild(document.createTextNode(desc));
    results.appendChild(li);
    if (!value) {
      li.parentNode.parentNode.className = "fail";
    }
    return li;
  };
})();
window.onload = function() {
  test("Async Test #1", function() {
    pause();
    setTimeout(function() {
      assert(true, "First test completed");
      resume();
    }, 1000);
  });
  test("Async Test #2", function() {
    pause();
    setTimeout(function() {
      assert(true, "Second test completed");
      resume();
    }, 1000);
  });
};
</script>
<style>
  #results li.pass {
    color: green;
  }

  #results li.fail {
    color: red;
  }
</style>
```

```
  </head>
  <body>
    <ul id="results"></ul>
  </body>
</html>
```

Let's break down the functionality exposed in listing 2.6. There are three publicly accessible functions: test(), pause(), and resume(). These three functions have the following capabilities:

- test(fn) takes a function that contains a number of assertions—assertions that will be run either synchronously or asynchronously—and places it on the queue to await execution.
- pause() should be called from within a test function and tells the test suite to pause executing tests until the test group is done.
- resume() unpauses the tests and starts the next test running after a short delay designed to avoid long-running code blocks.

The one internal implementation function, runTest(), is called whenever a test is queued or dequeued. It checks to see if the suite is currently unpaused and if there's something in the queue, in which case it'll dequeue a test and try to execute it. Additionally, after the test group is finished executing, runTest() will check to see if the suite is currently paused, and if it's not (meaning that only asynchronous tests were run in the test group), runTest() will begin executing the next group of tests.

We'll be taking a closer look at delayed execution in chapter 8, which focuses on timers, where we'll examine in depth the details relating to delaying the execution of JavaScript code.

2.5　Summary

In this chapter, we've looked at some of the basic techniques related to debugging JavaScript code and constructing simple test cases based upon those results:

- We examined how to use logging to observe the actions of our code as it's running, and we even implemented a convenience method that we can use to make sure that we can successfully log information in both modern and legacy browsers, despite their differences.
- We explored how we can use breakpoints to halt the execution of our code at a certain point, allowing us to take a look around at the state in which the code is executing.
- We then turned to test generation, defining and focusing on the attributes of good tests: *repeatability*, *simplicity*, and *independence*. The two major types of testing, *deconstructive* and *constructive* testing, were examined.
- We also presented some data regarding how the JavaScript community uses testing, and we briefly surveyed existing test frameworks that you might want to explore and adopt, should you want to use a formalized testing environment.

- Building upon that, we introduced the concept of the assertion, and we created a simple implementation that will be used throughout the remainder of this book to verify that the code does what we intend it to do.
- Finally, we looked at how to construct a simple test suite capable of handling asynchronous test cases. Altogether, these techniques will serve as an important cornerstone to the rest of our development with JavaScript.

We are now equipped to begin training. Take a short breather and then proceed to the training arena, where the first lesson may not be on the subject that you would expect it to be!

Part 2

Apprentice training

Now that you're mentally prepared for training and you're armed with the basic testing tools that we developed in the previous section, you're ready to learn the fundamentals of the JavaScript tools and weapons available to you.

In chapter 3, you'll learn all about the most important basic concept of JavaScript: no, not the object, but the *function*. This chapter will teach you why understanding JavaScript functions is the key to unlocking the secrets of the language.

Chapter 4 continues our in-depth exploration of functions—yes, they are important enough to warrant multiple chapters—showing how functions can be used to solve the challenges and problems that we face as web developers.

Chapter 5 takes functions to the next level with training on closures—probably one of the most misunderstood (and even unknown) aspects of the JavaScript language.

Object fundamentals are the subject of your training in chapter 6, with particular focus on how the blueprint of objects is determined by its prototype. This chapter will teach you how the object-oriented nature of JavaScript can be exploited.

From there, your training heads into deeper territory, with a thorough examination of regular expressions in chapter 7. You'll learn that many tasks that used to take reams of code to accomplish can be condensed to a mere handful of statements through the proper use of JavaScript regular expressions.

Your apprentice training then completes with chapter 8's lessons on how timers work, including lessons on the single-thread model that JavaScript employs. You'll learn how to not let it best you, and also how to use it to your advantage.

Functions are fundamental 3

In this chapter we discuss

- Why understanding functions is so crucial
- How functions are *first-class* objects
- How the browser invokes functions
- Declaring functions
- The secrets of how parameters are assigned
- The context within a function

You might have been somewhat surprised, upon turning to this part of the book dedicated to JavaScript fundamentals, to see that the first topic of discussion is to be *functions* rather than *objects*.

We'll certainly be paying plenty of attention to objects (particularly in chapter 6), but when it comes down to brass tacks, the main difference between writing Java-Script code like the average Joe (or Jill) and writing it like a JavaScript ninja is understanding JavaScript as a *functional language*. The level of the sophistication of all the code you'll ever write in JavaScript hinges upon this realization.

If you're reading this book, you're not a rank beginner and we're assuming that you know enough object fundamentals to get by for now (and we'll be taking a look at more advanced object concepts in chapter 6), but *really* understanding functions in JavaScript is the single most important weapon you can wield. So important, in fact, that this and the following two chapters are going to be devoted to thoroughly understanding functions in JavaScript.

Most importantly, in JavaScript, functions are *first-class objects*; that is, they coexist with, and can be treated like, any other JavaScript object. Just like the more mundane JavaScript data types, they can be referenced by variables, declared with literals, and even passed as function parameters.

The fact that JavaScript treats functions as first-class objects is going to be important on a number of levels, but one significant advantage comes in the form of code terseness. To take a sneak-peek ahead to some code that we'll examine in greater depth in section 3.1.2, consider this imperative code (in Java) that performs a collection sort:

```
Arrays.sort(values,new Comparator<Integer>(){
  public int compare(Integer value1, Integer value2) {
    return value2 - value1;
  }
});
```

Here's the JavaScript equivalent written using a functional approach:

```
values.sort(function(value1,value2){ return value2 - value1; });
```

Don't be too concerned if the notation seems odd—you'll be an old hand at it by the end of this chapter. We just wanted to give you a glimpse of one of the advantages that understanding JavaScript as a functional language will bring to the table.

This chapter will thoroughly examine JavaScript's focus on functions and give you a sound basis on which to bring your JavaScript code to a level that any master would be proud of.

3.1   *What's with the functional difference?*

How many times have you heard someone moan, "I hate JavaScript"?

We're willing to bet that nine times out of ten (or perhaps even more), this is a direct consequence of someone trying to use JavaScript as if it were another language that the lamenter is more familiar with, and that they're frustrated by the fact that it's *not* that other language. This is probably most common with those coming to JavaScript from a language such as Java, a decidedly nonfunctional language, but one that a lot of developers learn before their exposure to JavaScript.

Making matters even worse for these developers is the unfortunate naming choice of *Java*Script. Without belaboring the history behind that naming decision, perhaps developers would have fewer incorrect preconceived notions about JavaScript if it had retained the name *LiveScript* or been given some other less confusing name. Because JavaScript, as the old joke depicted in figure 3.1 goes, has as much to do with Java as a hamburger has to do with ham.

Figure 3.1   JavaScript is to Java as hamburger is to ham; both are delicious, but they don't have much in common except a name.

TIP For more information on how JavaScript got its name, see http://en .wikipedia.org/wiki/JavaScript#History, http://web.archive.org/web/200709 16144913/http://wp.netscape.com/newsref/pr/newsrelease67.html, and http:// stackoverflow.com/questions/2018731/why-is-javascript-called-javascript-since-it-has-nothing-to-do-with-java. If you follow these links, they indicate that the intent was to identify JavaScript as a *complement* to Java, rather than something that shared its characteristics.

Hamburgers and ham are both foods that are meat products, just as JavaScript and Java are both programming languages with a C-influenced syntax. But other than that, they don't have much in common and are fundamentally different right down to their DNA.

NOTE Another factor that plays into some developers' poor initial reaction to JavaScript may be that most developers are introduced to JavaScript in the browser. Rather than reacting to JavaScript, *the language,* they may be recoiling from the JavaScript bindings to the DOM API. And the DOM API ... well, let's just say that it isn't going to win any *Friendliest API of the Year* awards. But that's not JavaScript's fault.

Before we learn about how functions are such a central and key concept in JavaScript, let's consider *why* the functional nature of JavaScript is so important, especially for code written for the browser.

3.1.1 *Why is JavaScript's functional nature important?*

If you've done any amount of scripting in a browser, you probably know all that we're going to discuss in this section, but let's go over it anyway to make sure we're all using the same vernacular.

One of the reasons that functions and functional concepts are so important in JavaScript is that the function is the primary modular unit of execution. Except for the inline script that runs while the markup is being evaluated, all of the script code that we'll write for our pages will be within a function.

NOTE Back in the Dark Ages, inline script was used to add dynamism to pages via `document.write()`. These days, `document.write()` is considered a dinosaur and its use isn't recommended. There are better ways to make pages dynamic, such as the use of server-side templating, client-side DOM manipulation, or a healthy combination of both.

Because most of our code will run as the result of a function invocation, we'll see that having functions that are versatile and powerful constructs will give us a great deal of flexibility and sway when writing our code. We'll spend the rest of this chapter examining just how the nature of functions as first-class objects can be exploited to our great benefit.

Now, that's the *second* time we've used the term "first-class object," and it's an important concept, so before we go on, let's make sure we know what it really means.

FUNCTIONS AS FIRST-CLASS OBJECTS

Objects in JavaScript enjoy certain capabilities:

- They can be created via literals.
- They can be assigned to variables, array entries, and properties of other objects.
- They can be passed as arguments to functions.
- They can be returned as values from functions.
- They can possess properties that can be dynamically created and assigned.

Functions in JavaScript possess all of these capabilities and are thus treated like any other object in the language. Therefore, we say that they're *first-class* objects.

And more than being treated with the same respect as other object types, functions have a special capability in that they can be *invoked*.

That invocation is frequently discharged in an *asynchronous* manner, so let's talk a little about why that is.

THE BROWSER EVENT LOOP

If you've done any programming to create graphical user interface (GUI) desktop applications, you'll know that most are written in a similar fashion:

- Set up the user interface
- Enter a loop waiting for events to occur
- Invoke handlers (also called *listeners*) for those events

Programming for the browser is no different, except that our code isn't responsible for running the event loop and dispatching events; the browser handles that for us.

Our responsibility is to set up the handlers for the various events that can occur in the browser. These events are placed in an event queue (a FIFO list; more on that later) as they occur, and the browser dispatches these events by invoking any handlers that have been established for them.

Because these events happen at unpredictable times and in an unpredictable order, we say that the handling of the events, and therefore the invocation of their handling functions, is *asynchronous*.

The following types of events can occur, among others:

- Browser events, such as when a page is finished loading or when it's to be unloaded
- Network events, such as responses to an Ajax request
- User events, such as mouse clicks, mouse moves, or keypresses
- Timer events, such as when a timeout expires or an interval fires

The vast majority of our code executes as a result of such events. Consider the following:

```
function startup(){
  /* do something wonderful */
}
window.onload = startup;
```

Here, we establish a function to serve as a handler for the load event. The establishing statement executes as part of the inline script (assuming it appears at the top level and not within any other function), but the wonderful things that we're going to do *inside* the function don't execute until the browser finishes loading the page and fires off a load event.

In fact, we can simplify this to a single line if we like. Consider this:

```
window.onload = function() { /* do something wonderful */ };
```

(If the notation used to create the function looks odd to you, be assured that we'll be making it crystal clear in section 3.2.)

Unobtrusive JavaScript

The approach of assigning a function, named or otherwise, to the onload property of the window instance may not be the way that you're used to setting up a load handler. You may be more accustomed to using the onload attribute of the <body> tag.

Either approach achieves the same effect, but the window.onload approach is vastly preferred by JavaScript ninjas as it adheres to a popular principle known as *unobtrusive JavaScript*.

Remember when the advent of CSS pioneered the moving of style information out of the document markup? Few would argue that segregating style from structure was a bad move. Unobtrusive JavaScript does the same thing for *behavior*, moving scripts out of the document markup.

This results in pages having their three primary components—structure, style, and behavior— nicely partitioned into their own locations. Structure is defined in the document markup, style in <style> elements or external style sheets, and behavior in <script> blocks or external script files.

You won't see any script embedded into document markup in the examples in this book, unless it's to make a specific point or to vastly simplify the example.

It's important to note that the browser event loop is *single-threaded*. Every event that's placed into the event queue is handled in the order that it's placed onto the queue. This is known as a *FIFO list* (first-in, first-out), or perhaps a *silo* to the old-timers. Each event is processed in its own "turn," and all other events have to wait until the current event's turn is over. Under no circumstances are two handlers executing simultaneously in separate threads.

Think of a line at the bank. Everyone gets into a single line and has to wait their turn to be "processed" by the tellers. But with JavaScript, there's only *one* teller window open! So the customers only get processed one at a time, as their turn comes. All it takes is one person, who thinks it's appropriate to do their financial planning for the fiscal year while they're at the teller's window (we've all run into them!), to gum up the whole works.

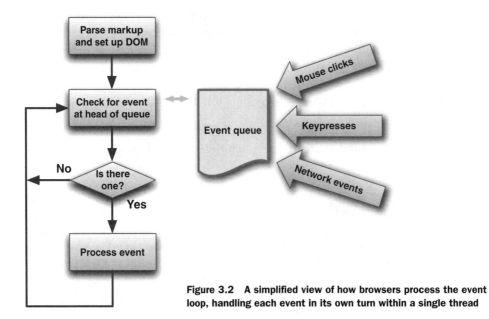

Figure 3.2   A simplified view of how browsers process the event loop, handling each event in its own turn within a single thread

We'll explore this execution model, and ways of dealing with its challenges, in great depth in chapter 8.

A vastly simplified overview of this process is shown in figure 3.2.

This concept is central to on-page JavaScript, and it's something we'll see again and again throughout the examples in this book: code is set up in advance in order to execute at a later time. Except for inline setup code, the vast majority of the code that we place onto a page is going to execute as the result of an event (as part of the "Process event" box in figure 3.2).

It's important to note that the browser mechanism that puts the events *onto* the queue is external to this event loop model. The processing necessary to determine when events have occurred and to push them onto the event queue doesn't participate in the thread that's *handling* the events.

For example, when the end user waves the mouse around on the page, the browser will detect these motions and push a bunch of mousemove events onto the event queue. The event loop will eventually come across these events and trigger any handlers established for that type of event.

Such event handlers are examples of a more general concept known as *callback functions*. Let's explore that very important concept.

THE CALLBACK CONCEPT

Whenever we set up a function to be called at a later time, whether by the browser or other code, we're setting up what is termed a *callback*. The term stems from the fact that we establish a function that some other code will later "call back" into at an appropriate point of execution.

Callbacks are an essential part of using JavaScript effectively, and we're about to look at a real-world example of how callbacks are used. But it's a tad complex, so before we dive into it, let's strip the callback concept completely naked and examine it in its simplest form.

We'll see callbacks used extensively as event handlers throughout the remainder of this book, but event handlers are just one example of callbacks; we can even employ callbacks ourselves in our own code. Here's an illuminating example of a completely useless function that accepts a reference to another function as a parameter and calls that function as a callback:

```
function useless(callback) { return callback(); }
```

As useless as this function is, it helps us demonstrate the ability to pass a function as an argument to another function, and to subsequently invoke that function through the passed parameter.

We can test our useless function with this code:

```
var text = 'Domo arigato!';
assert(useless(function(){ return text; }) === text,
        "The useless function works! " + text);
```

Here, we use the `assert()` testing function that we set up in the previous chapter to verify that the callback function is invoked and returns the expected value, which is in turn returned as the useless value. The result is shown in figure 3.3.

That was really, really easy. And that's because JavaScript's functional nature lets us deal with functions as first-class objects.

Now let's consider a not-so-useless example and compare it with using callbacks in a nonfunctional language.

3.1.2 Sorting with a comparator

Almost as soon as we *have* a collection of data, odds are we're going to need to sort it in some fashion. And as it turns out, we're going to need a callback in order to do anything but the most simple of sort operations.

Let's say that we have an array of some numbers in a random order: 213, 16, 2058, 54, 10, 1965, 57, 9. That order might be just fine, but chances are that, sooner or later, we're going to want to rearrange them into some sorted order.

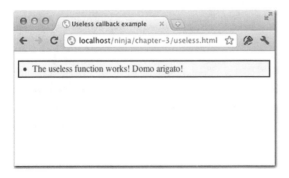

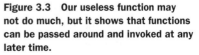

Figure 3.3 Our useless function may not do much, but it shows that functions can be passed around and invoked at any later time.

Both Java and JavaScript provide a simple means to sort arrays into ascending order. Here it is in Java:

```
Integer[] values = { 213, 16, 2058, 54, 10, 1965, 57, 9 };
Arrays.sort(values);
```

Here's the JavaScript version:

```
var values = [ 213, 16, 2058, 54, 10, 1965, 57, 9 ];
values.sort();
```

> **NOTE** We're not *picking* on Java—really, we're not. It's a fine language. We're just using Java as the crutch here because it's a good example of a language *without* functional capabilities, and one that lots of developers coming to JavaScript are familiar with.

There are some minor differences between the implementations of sorting in these languages—most notably, Java supplies a utility class with a static function, whereas JavaScript provides the capability as a method on the array itself—but both approaches are straightforward and easy to understand. But if we decide we want a sorting order *other* than ascending—something as simple as descending, for example—things start to diverge rather markedly.

In order to allow us to sort the values into *any* order we want, both languages let *us* provide a comparison algorithm that tells the sort algorithm how the values should be ordered. Instead of just letting the sort algorithm decide what values go before other values, *we'll* provide a function that performs the comparison. We'll give the sort algorithm access to this function as a callback, and it will call it whenever it needs to make a comparison. The concept is similar in both languages, but the implementations couldn't be more different.

In nonfunctional Java, methods can't exist on their own and can't be passed as arguments to other methods. Rather, they must be declared as members of an object that *can* be instantiated and passed to a method. Therefore, the `Arrays.sort()` method has an overload that accepts an object containing the comparison method that it will call as a callback whenever a comparison needs to be made. This object and its method must conform to a known format (Java being strongly typed), so an interface needs to be defined. In this case, the Java library provides the following interface (in general cases, you may need to define your own):

```
public interface Comparator<T> {
  int compare(T t, T t1);
  boolean equals(Object o);
}
```

A novice Java developer might create a concrete class that implements this interface, but to make a fair comparison, we're going to assume a fair level of Java savvy-ness and use an inline anonymous implementation. A usage of the `Arrays.sort()` static method to sort the values in descending order could look like the following code:

```
Arrays.sort(values,new Comparator<Integer>(){
  public int compare(Integer value1, Integer value2) {
    return value2 - value1;
  }
});
```

The compare() method of the inline Comparator implementation is expected to return a negative number if the order of the passed values should be reversed, a positive number if not, and zero if the values are equal, so simply subtracting the values produces the desired return value to sort the array into descending order.

The result of running the preceding code is the re-sorted array:

```
2058, 1965, 213, 57, 54, 16, 10, 9
```

That wasn't overly complicated, but it did involve a fair amount of syntax, especially if you include the declaration of the required interface, to perform an operation that's fairly simple in nature.

The wordiness of this approach becomes even more apparent when we consider the equivalent JavaScript code that takes advantage of JavaScript's functional capabilities:

```
var values = [ 213, 16, 2058, 54, 10, 1965, 57, 9 ];
values.sort(function(value1,value2){ return value2 - value1; });
```

No interfaces. No extra object. One line. We simply declare an inline anonymous function that we directly pass to the sort() method of the array.

The functional difference in JavaScript allows us to create a function as a stand-alone entity, just as we can any other object type, and to pass it as an argument to a method, just like any other object type, which can accept it as a parameter, just like any other object type. It's that "first-class" status coming into play.

That's not even remotely possible in nonfunctional languages such as Java.

> **NOTE** There's a strong possibility that functional aspects will be added to Java in Java 8 as "lambda expressions," but for now, Java isn't a functional language. If you like Java, but want something with more functional capabilities, you might try Groovy. It's a JVM language that brings functional capabilities to a very Java-like language, and it has been gaining traction lately (thanks to the Grails web framework).

One of the most important features of the JavaScript language is the ability to create functions anywhere in the code where an expression can appear. In addition to making the code more compact and easy to understand (by putting function declarations near where they're used), this feature can also eliminate the need to pollute the global namespace with unnecessary names when a function isn't going to be referenced from multiple places within the code.

But regardless of how functions are declared (much more on this in the upcoming section), they can be referenced as values and be used as the fundamental building blocks for reusable code libraries. Understanding how functions, including anonymous functions, work at their most fundamental level will drastically improve our ability to write clear, concise, and reusable code.

Now let's take a more in-depth look at how functions are declared and invoked. On the surface it may seem that there's not much to the acts of declaring and invoking functions, but there's actually a lot going on that we need to be aware of.

3.2   *Declarations*

JavaScript functions are declared using a *function literal* that creates a function value in the same way that a numeric literal creates a numeric value. Remember that, as first-class objects, functions are values that can be used in the language just like other values, such as strings and numbers. And whether you realize it or not, you've been doing that all along.

Function literals are composed of four parts:

1   The function keyword.
2   An *optional* name that, if specified, must be a valid JavaScript identifier.
3   A comma-separated list of parameter names enclosed in parentheses. The names must be valid identifiers and the list can be empty. The parentheses must always be present, even with an empty parameter list.
4   The body of the function, as a series of JavaScript statements enclosed in braces. The body can be empty, but the braces must always be present.

The fact that the function name is optional may come as a surprise to some developers, but we've seen ample examples of just such *anonymous functions* in the previous section. If there's no need for a function to be referenced by its name, we don't have to give it one. (Sort of like the joke about cats: *why give a cat a name if it's not going to come when called?*)

When a function is named, that name is valid throughout the scope within which the function is declared. Additionally, if a named function is declared at the top level, a property using the function name is created on window that references the function.

And lastly, all functions have a property named name that stores the function's name as a string. Functions with no name still possess this property, set to the empty string.

But why *say* all that when we can *prove* it? We can write tests to assert that what we've said about functions is true. Examine the following code.

> **Listing 3.1   Proving things about the way that functions are declared**

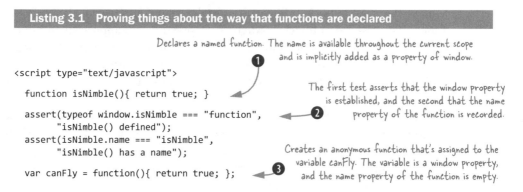

Declares a named function. The name is available throughout the current scope and is implicitly added as a property of window. **1**

The first test asserts that the window property is established, and the second that the name property of the function is recorded. **2**

Creates an anonymous function that's assigned to the variable canFly. The variable is a window property, and the name property of the function is empty. **3**

```
<script type="text/javascript">

  function isNimble(){ return true; }

  assert(typeof window.isNimble === "function",
      "isNimble() defined");
  assert(isNimble.name === "isNimble",
      "isNimble() has a name");

  var canFly = function(){ return true; };
```

```
        assert(typeof window.canFly === "function",
               "canFly() defined");
        assert(canFly.name === "",
               "canFly() has no name");

        window.isDeadly = function(){ return true; };

        assert(typeof window.isDeadly === "function",
               "isDeadly() defined");

        function outer(){
            assert(typeof inner === "function",
                   "inner() in scope before declaration");
            function inner(){}
            assert(typeof inner === "function",
                   "inner() in scope after declaration");
            assert(window.inner === undefined,
                   "inner() not in global scope");
        }

        outer();
        assert(window.inner === undefined,
               "inner() still not in global scope");

        window.wieldsSword = function swingsSword() { return true; };

        assert(window.wieldsSword.name === 'swingsSword',
               "wieldSword's real name is swingsSword");

    </script>
```

④ Tests that the variable references the anonymous function and that the name property is set to the empty string (not null).

⑤ Creates an anonymous function referenced by property of window.

⑦ Defines an inner function inside the outer function. Tests that inner() is able to be referenced before and after its declaration and that no global name is created for inner().

Tests that the property ⑥ references the function. We could also test that the function has an empty name property here.

⑧ Tests that outer() can be referenced in the global scope, but that inner() can't.

The variable that we assign a function to has nothing to do with its name; that's controlled by what we actually name the function in its literal.

In this test page, we declare globally scoped functions in three different ways:

- The isNimble() function is declared as a named function ❶. This is likely the most common declaration style that most developers have seen. That will change as you progress through this book.
- An anonymous function is created and assigned to a global variable named canFly ❸. Because of JavaScript's functional nature, the function can be invoked through this reference as canFly(). In this respect, it's *almost* functionally equivalent (no pun intended) to declaring a named function named "canFly", but not quite. One major difference is that the function's name property is "", not "canFly".
- Another anonymous function is declared and assigned to a window property named isDeadly ❺. Again, we can invoke the function through this property (window.isDeadly() or simply isDeadly()), and this is again *almost* functionally equivalent to a named function named "isDeadly".

Throughout the example, we placed assertions that verify that what we said about functions is true, the results of these tests being shown in figure 3.4.

The test proves the following:

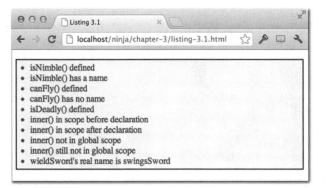

Figure 3.4   Running our test page shows that all those things that we said about functions are true!

- That `window.isNimble` is defined as a function. This proves that named functions are added as properties to `window` ❷.
- That the named function `isNimble()` has a `name` property that contains the string "isNimble" ❷.
- That `window.canFly` is defined as a function, proving that global variables, even those containing functions, end up on `window` ❹.
- That the anonymous function assigned to `canFly` has a name property consisting of the empty string ❹.
- That `window.isDeadly` is defined as a function ❻.

NOTE   This is far from a complete test set of *everything* that we said about functions so far. How would you extend this test code to assert the suppositions for the declared functions?

Then comes the time to test nonglobal functions. We create a function, appropriately named `outer()`, in which we'll test our assertions regarding functions declared in a non-global scope ❼. We declare an inner function named `inner()`, but before it's declared, we assert that the function is in scope. This tests our assertion that a function is available throughout the scope within which it's declared, even when forward-referenced.

Then we declare the function, check that it's within scope inside the function, and check that it isn't within the global scope.

Finally, we execute the inner test and once again assert that the inner function didn't creep its way out into the global scope ❽.

These concepts are very important, as they lay down the foundations for the naming, flow, and structure that functional code provides, and they begin to establish the framework through which we employ functional programming to our great benefit.

The point we made with the inner function ❽—namely, that the function is forward-referenceable within the outer function—may have you wondering: "When we declare a function, what scope is that function available within?" It's a good question and one that we'll answer next.

3.2.1 *Scoping and functions*

When we declare a function, not only do we need to be concerned with the scope within which that function is available, but also with what scopes the function itself *creates* and how declarations within the function are affected by those scopes.

Scopes in JavaScript act somewhat differently than in most other languages whose syntax is influenced by C; namely, those that use *braces* ({ and }) as block delimiters. In most such languages, each block creates its own scope; not so in JavaScript!

In JavaScript, scopes are declared by *functions*, and not by blocks. The scope of a declaration that's created inside a block isn't terminated (as it is in other languages) by the end of the block.

Consider the following code:

```
if (window) {
  var x = 213;
}
alert(x);
```

In most other languages, one would expect the scope of the declaration for x to terminate at the end of the block created by the `if` statement, and for the alert to fail with an undefined value. But if we were to run the preceding code in a page, the value 213 would be alerted because JavaScript doesn't terminate scopes at the end of blocks.

That seems simple enough, but there are a few nuances to the scoping rules that depend upon what is being declared. Some of these nuances may come as a bit of a surprise:

- Variable declarations are in scope from their point of declaration to the end of the function within which they're declared, regardless of block nesting.
- Named functions are in scope within the entire function within which they're declared, regardless of block nesting. (Some call this mechanism *hoisting.*)
- For the purposes of declaration scopes, the global context acts like one big function encompassing the code on the page.

Once again, instead of just saying it, we're going to *prove* it. Take a look at the following code snippet:

```
function outer(){

  var a = 1;

  function inner(){ /* does nothing */ }

  var b = 2;

  if (a == 1) {
    var c = 3;
  }

}
outer();
```

In this code, we declare five items: an outer function named outer(), a function inside that named inner(), and three numeric variables inside the outer function named a, b, and c.

To test where the various items are in scope—and, perhaps more importantly, where they aren't—we'll intersperse a block of tests throughout this code. We'll put the same block of tests, with one test for each of these declarations, at strategic places in the code. Each test asserts that one of the items we're declaring is in scope (except for the first, which isn't a test at all, but just a label that will help keep the code and output more readable).

This is the test block:

```
assert(true,"some descriptive text");
assert(typeof outer==='function',
    "outer() is in scope");
assert(typeof inner==='function',
    "inner() is in scope");
assert(typeof a==='number',
    "a is in scope");
assert(typeof b==='number',
    "b is in scope");
assert(typeof c==='number',
    "c is in scope");
```

Note that in many circumstances, some of these tests will fail. Under normal circumstances, we'd expect our asserts to always pass; but in this code, which is only for demonstration, it suits our purposes to show where the tests pass and where they fail, which directly corresponds to whether the tested item is in scope or not.

Listing 3.2 shows the completely assembled code, omitting the repeated test so that we can see the forest for the trees. (Wherever the test code has been removed, we show the comment /* test code here */ so you'll know where the test code appears in the actual page file.)

Listing 3.2   Observing the scoping behavior of declarations

Runs the test block before we've defined anything at all. All our tests assert that each item is in scope, so all but the tests for items that can be forward-referenced will fail. As such, only the top-level function outer() is in scope at this point. See figure 3.5 (or better yet, run the code in your browser so that you don't have to flip pages as much) to verify that all tests but that for outer() fail.

```
<script type="text/javascript">

    assert(true,"|----- BEFORE OUTER -----|");
    /* test code here */

    function outer(){
    assert(true,"|----- INSIDE OUTER, BEFORE a -----|");
    /* test code here */

        var a = 1;
```

Runs the test block inside function outer() but before anything else has been declared. The outer() function is still in scope as is the inner() function, which is defined within the outer() function. Functions can be forward-referenced, but not variable declarations, so all other tests fail.

```
        assert(true,"|----- INSIDE OUTER, AFTER a -----|");
    /* test code here */

    function inner(){ /* does nothing */ }

    var b = 2;

        assert(true,"|----- INSIDE OUTER, AFTER inner() AND b -----|");
    /* test code here */

    if (a == 1) {
        var c = 3;
        assert(true,"|----- INSIDE OUTER, INSIDE if -----|");
        /* test code here */
    }

        assert(true,"|----- INSIDE OUTER, OUTSIDE if -----|");
    /* test code here */

    }
    outer();

    assert(true,"|----- AFTER OUTER -----|");
    /* test code here */

</script>
```

Runs the test block inside outer() and after the variable a has been declared. Test results show that a has been added to the scope at this point.

Runs test code after inner() and b have been declared. Testing shows that b has been added to the scope. The fact that inner() was declared at this point is moot. Its scope extends back to the beginning of the containing function, and its declaration certainly doesn't remove it from the scope.

Runs tests inside if block after variable c has been declared in that block. Tests show that all items are in scope at this point.

Runs test code inside outer() but after if block has been closed. Tests show that all items are in scope, even c, although the if block within which it was declared is closed. Unlike most other block-structured languages, variable declarations extend from the point of declaration to the end of the function, crossing any block boundaries.

Runs tests in the global scope after outer() has been declared. Once again, only outer() is in scope because the scope of anything declared within outer() is confined to within it.

Running this code results in the display shown in figure 3.5.

As expected, there are many failures because not all of the items are in scope at every position where we placed the block of tests.

Of particular note, see how the declaration of inner() is available (*hoisted*) throughout the entire outer() function, whereas the numeric variables a, b, and c are only available from their point of declaration to the end of outer(). This clearly shows that function declarations can be forward-referenced within their scope but variables can't.

Also take particular note of how the closing of the if statement block within which c is declared doesn't terminate the scope of c. Variable c, despite being nested in a block, is available from its point of declaration to the end of outer(), just like the variables not defined in a nested block.

The scopes of the various declared items are graphically depicted in figure 3.6.

PONDER THIS Now that you understand a bit about scope, you should be able to answer the following question: rather than cutting and pasting the block of tests over and over again, why did we not create one function to hold them and call it as needed?

(And no, we're not going to give you the answer.)

Now that we've seen how functions are declared, let's take a look at how we can invoke them.

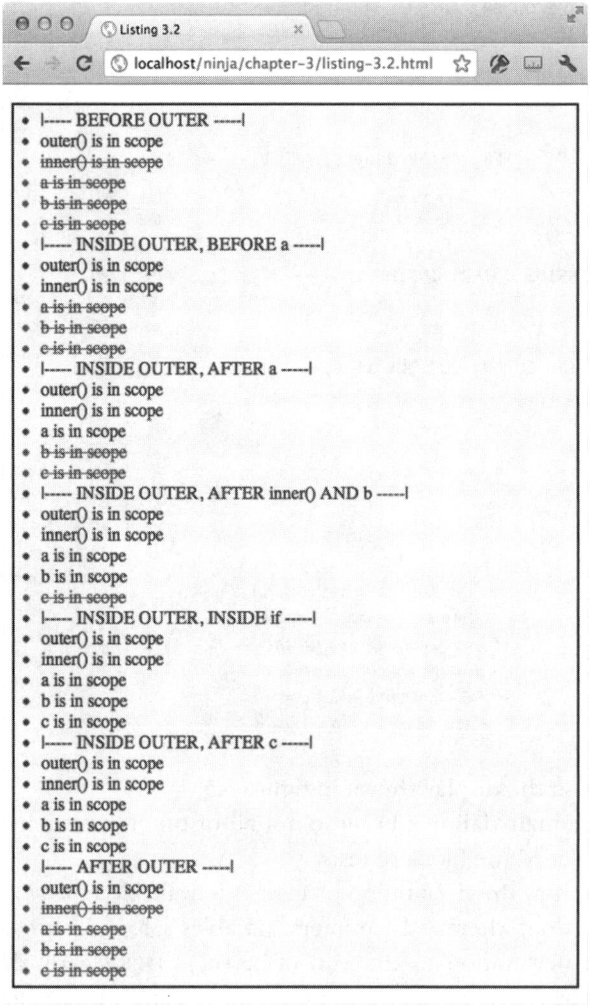

Figure 3.5   Running our scope tests clearly shows where the declared items are in scope and where they aren't.

3.3   *Invocations*

We've all called JavaScript functions, but have you ever stopped to wonder what really happens when a function is called? In this section, we'll examine the various ways that functions can be invoked.

As it turns out, the manner in which a function is invoked has a huge impact on how the code within it operates, primarily in how the this parameter is established. This difference is much more important than it might seem at first. We'll examine it within this section and exploit it throughout the rest of this book to help elevate our code to ninja level.

There are actually four different ways to invoke a function, each with its own nuances:

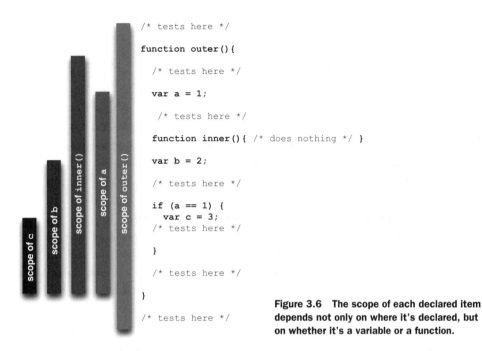

```
/* tests here */

function outer(){

  /* tests here */

  var a = 1;

   /* tests here */

  function inner(){ /* does nothing */ }

  var b = 2;

  /* tests here */

  if (a == 1) {
    var c = 3;
    /* tests here */

  }

  /* tests here */

}

/* tests here */
```

Figure 3.6 The scope of each declared item depends not only on where it's declared, but on whether it's a variable or a function.

- As a function, in which the function is invoked in a straightforward manner
- As a method, which ties the invocation to an object, enabling object-oriented programming
- As a constructor, in which a new object is brought into being
- Via its `apply()` or `call()` methods, which is kind of complicated, so we'll cover that when we get to it

For all but the last of these approaches, the function invocation operator is a set of parentheses following any expression that evaluates to a function reference. Any arguments to be passed to the function are included inside the parentheses as a comma-separated list.

For example:

```
expression(arg1,arg2);
```

Before we take a close look at those four ways of making our functions execute, let's examine what happens to the arguments that are to be passed to the invocations.

3.3.1 *From arguments to function parameters*

When a list of arguments is supplied as part of a function invocation, these arguments are assigned to the parameters specified in the function declaration in the same order that each was specified. The first argument gets assigned to the first parameter, the second argument to the second parameter, and so on.

If there is a different number of arguments than there are parameters, no error is raised; JavaScript is perfectly fine with this situation and deals with it as follows:

- If more arguments are supplied than there are parameters, the "excess" arguments are simply not assigned to parameter names.

  For example, let's say that we have a function declared as

  ```
  function whatever(a,b,c) { ... }
  ```

  If we were to call it with `whatever(1,2,3,4,5)`, the arguments, 1, 2, and 3 would be assigned to a, b, and c, respectively. Arguments 4 and 5 are unassigned to any parameters.

  We'll see in just a bit that even though some arguments aren't assigned to parameter names, we still have a way to get at them.

- If there are more parameters than there are arguments, the parameters that have no corresponding argument are set to undefined.

  For example, if we were to call the `whatever(a,b,c)` function with `whatever(1)`, parameter a would be assigned the value 1, and b and c would be set to undefined.

And, very interestingly, all function invocations are also passed two implicit parameters: arguments and this.

By *implicit*, we mean that these parameters aren't explicitly listed in the function signature, but they're silently passed to the function and are in scope within the function. They can be referenced within the function just like any other explicitly named parameter.

Let's take a look at each of these implicit parameters in turn.

THE ARGUMENTS PARAMETER

The arguments parameter is a collection of all of the arguments passed to the function. The collection has a property named length that contains the count of arguments, and the individual argument values can be obtained using array indexing notation; arguments[2] would fetch the third parameter, for example.

But note that we went out of our way to avoid calling the arguments parameter an array. You may be fooled into thinking that it's an array; after all, it has a length parameter, its entries can be fetched using array notation, and we can even iterate over it with a for loop. But it's *not* a JavaScript array, and if you try to use array methods on arguments, you'll find nothing but heartbreak and disappointment. Just think of arguments as an "array-like" construct, and exhibit restraint in its use.

The this parameter is even more interesting.

THE "THIS" PARAMETER

Whenever a function is invoked, in addition to the parameters that represent the explicit arguments that were provided on the function call, an implicit parameter named this is also passed to the function. The this parameter refers to an object that's implicitly associated with the function invocation and is termed the *function context*.

The function context is a notion that those coming from object-oriented languages such as Java will think that they understand—that this points to an instance of the class within which the method is defined. But beware! As we'll see, invocation as a *method* is only one of the four ways that a function can be invoked. And as it turns out, what the this parameter points to isn't, as in Java, defined by how the function is declared, but by how it's *invoked*. Because of this fact, it might have been clearer to call this the *invocation* context, but we were never consulted about the name.

We're about to look at how the four invocation mechanisms differ, and you'll see that one of the primary differences between them is how the value of this is determined for each type of invocation. And then we'll take a long and hard look at function contexts again in section 3.4, so don't worry if things don't gel right away; we'll be discussing this at great length.

Now let's see how functions can be invoked.

3.3.2 *Invocation as a function*

"Invocation as a function?" Well, of course functions are invoked as *functions*. How silly to think otherwise.

But in reality, we say that a function is invoked "as a function" to distinguish it from the other invocation mechanisms: methods, constructors, and apply/call. If a function isn't invoked as a method, as a constructor, or via apply() or call(), it's simply invoked "as a function."

This type of invocation occurs when a function is invoked using the () operator, and the expression to which the () operator is applied doesn't reference the function as a property of an object. (In that case, we'd have a method invocation, but we'll discuss that next.)

Here are some simple examples:

```
function ninja(){};
ninja();

var samurai = function(){};
samurai();
```

When invoked in this manner, the function context is the global context—the window object. We're going to refrain from writing any tests to prove this at the moment, as it'll be more interesting to do so when we have something to compare it to.

As it turns out, this concept of invoking "a function as a function" is really a special case of the next invocation type we'll talk about: invoking "as a method." But because of the implicitness of the window as the "owner" of the function, it's generally thought of as its own mechanism, and one that you've likely used again and again without much thought about what's really going on under the covers.

So let's see what this "method" stuff is all about.

3.3.3 *Invocation as a method*

When a function is assigned to a property of an object *and* the invocation occurs by referencing the function using that property, then the function is invoked as a *method* of that object. Here's an example:

```
var o = {};
o.whatever = function(){};
o.whatever();
```

OK, so what? The function is called a "method" in this case, but what makes that interesting or useful?

Well, if you come from any object-oriented background, you'll remember that the object to which a method belongs is available within the body of the method as this. The same thing happens here. When we invoke the function as the *method* of an object, that object becomes the function context and is available within the function via the this parameter. This is one of the primary means by which JavaScript allows object-oriented code to be written. (Constructors are another, and we'll be getting to them in short order.)

Contrast this with invocation "as a function," in which the function is defined on the window and called without the need to use a reference to window. Except for being able to leave off the implicit window reference, it's the same thing. The function "belongs" to window, and window is set as the function context, in the same way that object o is the function context in the above example. Even though these mechanisms look different, they're really the same.

Let's consider some test code in the next listing to illustrate the differences and similarities between invocation as a function and invocation as a method.

Listing 3.3 Illustrating the differences between function and method invocations

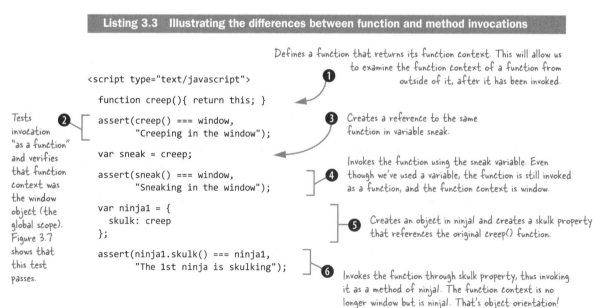

Defines a function that returns its function context. This will allow us to examine the function context of a function from outside of it, after it has been invoked. ❶

```
<script type="text/javascript">

    function creep(){ return this; }

    assert(creep() === window,
            "Creeping in the window");

    var sneak = creep;

    assert(sneak() === window,
            "Sneaking in the window");

    var ninja1 = {
        skulk: creep
    };

    assert(ninja1.skulk() === ninja1,
            "The 1st ninja is skulking");
```

Tests ❷ invocation "as a function" and verifies that function context was the window object (the global scope). Figure 3.7 shows that this test passes.

❸ Creates a reference to the same function in variable sneak.

❹ Invokes the function using the sneak variable. Even though we've used a variable, the function is still invoked as a function, and the function context is window.

❺ Creates an object in ninja1 and creates a skulk property that references the original creep() function.

❻ Invokes the function through skulk property, thus invoking it as a method of ninja1. The function context is no longer window but is ninja1. That's object orientation!

```
var ninja2 = {
  skulk: creep
};
```
⑦ Creates another object, ninja2, that also has
a skulk property referencing creep().

```
assert(ninja2.skulk() === ninja2,
       "The 2nd ninja is skulking");
```
Invokes the function as a method of ninja2,
and behold, the function context is ninja2.

```
</script>
```

Figure 3.7 shows that all our test assertions pass.

In this test, we set up a single function named `creep` ❶ that we'll use throughout the rest of the listing. The only thing that this function does is return its function context so that we can see, from outside the function, what the function context for the invocation is. (Otherwise, we'd have no way of knowing.)

When we call the function by its name, this is a case of invoking the function "as a function," so we'd expect that the function context would be the global context—in other words, the `window`. We assert that this is so ❷, and as we see in figure 3.7, this assertion passes. So far, so good.

Then we create a reference to the function in a variable named `sneak` ❸. Note that this doesn't create a second instance of the function; it merely creates a reference to the same function. You know, first-class object and all.

When we invoke the function via the variable—something we can do because the function invocation operator can be applied to any expression that evaluates to a function—we'd once again be invoking the function as a function. As such, we'd once again expect that the function context would be the `window` ❹, and it is.

Next, we get a bit trickier and define an object in variable `ninja1` with a property named `skulk` that receives a reference to the `creep()` function ❺. By doing so, we say that we've created a *method* named `skulk` on the object. We don't say that `creep()` has *become* a method of `ninja1`; it hasn't. We've already seen that `creep()` is its own independent function that can be invoked in numerous ways.

According to what we stated earlier, when we invoke the function via a method reference, we expect the function context to be the method's object (in this case, `ninja1`) and we assert as much ❻. Again figure 3.7 shows us that this is borne out. We're on a roll!

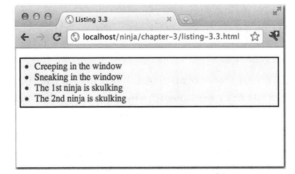

Figure 3.7   A single function, invoked in various ways, can serve as either a "normal" function or a method.

This particular ability is crucial to writing JavaScript in an object-oriented manner. It means that we can, within any method, use this to reference the method's owning object—a fundamental concept in object-oriented programming.

To drive that point home, we continue our testing by creating yet another object, ninja2, also with a property named skulk that references the creep() function ❼. Upon invoking this method through its object, we correctly assert that its function context is ninja2.

Note that even though the *same* function is used throughout all these examples, the function context for each invocation of the function changes depending upon how the function is *invoked*, rather than on how it was declared.

For example, the exact same function instance is shared by both ninja1 and ninja2, yet when it's executed, the function has access to, and can perform operations upon, the object through which the method was invoked. This means that we don't need to create separate copies of a function to perform the exact same processing on different objects—this is a tenet of object-oriented programming.

This is a powerful capability, yet the manner in which we used it in this example has limitations. Foremost, when we created the two ninja objects, we were able to share the same function to be used as a method in each, but we had to use a bit of repeated code to set up the separate objects and their skulk methods.

But that's nothing to despair over—JavaScript provides mechanisms to make creating objects from a single pattern much easier than in this example. We'll be exploring those capabilities in depth in chapter 6. But for now, let's consider a part of that mechanism that relates to function invocations: the *constructor.*

3.3.4 *Invocation as a constructor*

There's nothing special about a function that's going to be used as a constructor; constructor functions are declared just like any other functions. The difference is in how the function is invoked.

To invoke the function *as a constructor,* we precede the function invocation with the new keyword.

For example, recall the creep() function from the previous section:

```
function creep(){ return this; }
```

If we want to invoke the creep() function as a constructor, we'd write this:

```
new creep();
```

But even though we can invoke creep() as a constructor, that function isn't particularly well suited for use as a constructor. Let's find out why by discussing what makes constructors special.

THE SUPERPOWERS OF CONSTRUCTORS

Invoking a function as a constructor is a powerful feature of JavaScript, because when a constructor is invoked, the following special actions take place:

- A new empty object is created.
- This object is passed to the constructor as the this parameter, and thus becomes the constructor's function context.
- In the absence of any explicit return value, the new object is returned as the constructor's value.

This latter point is why creep() makes for a lousy constructor. The purpose of a constructor is to cause a new object to be created, to set it up, and to return it as the constructor value. Anything that interferes with that intent isn't appropriate for functions intended for use as constructors.

Let's consider a more appropriate function in the following listing—one that will set up the skulking ninjas of listing 3.3 in a more succinct fashion.

Listing 3.4 Using a constructor to set up common objects

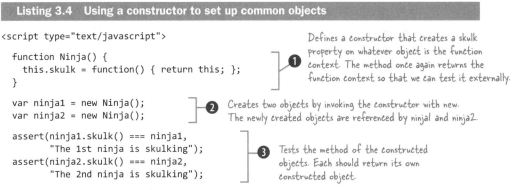

```
<script type="text/javascript">

  function Ninja() {
    this.skulk = function() { return this; };
  }

  var ninja1 = new Ninja();
  var ninja2 = new Ninja();

  assert(ninja1.skulk() === ninja1,
         "The 1st ninja is skulking");
  assert(ninja2.skulk() === ninja2,
         "The 2nd ninja is skulking");

</script>
```

❶ Defines a constructor that creates a skulk property on whatever object is the function context. The method once again returns the function context so that we can test it externally.

❷ Creates two objects by invoking the constructor with new. The newly created objects are referenced by ninja1 and ninja2.

❸ Tests the method of the constructed objects. Each should return its own constructed object.

The results of this test are shown in figure 3.8.

In this example, we create a function named Ninja() ❶ that we intend to use to construct, well, ninjas. When invoked with the new keyword, an empty object instance will be created and passed to the function as this. The constructor creates a property named skulk on this object, which is assigned a function, making that property a method of the newly created object.

The method performs the same operation as creep() in the previous sections, returning the function context so that we can test it externally.

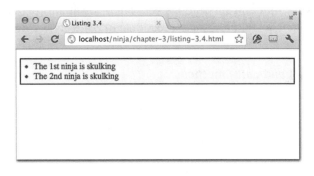

Figure 3.8 Constructors let us create multiple objects following the same pattern with a minimum of fuss and bother.

With the constructor defined, we create two new Ninja objects by invoking the constructor twice ❷. Note that the returned values from the invocations are stored in variables that become references to the newly created Ninjas.

Then we run the same tests as in listing 3.3 to ensure that each invocation of the method operates upon the expected object ❸.

Functions intended for use as constructors are generally coded differently from other functions. Let's see how.

CODING CONSIDERATIONS FOR CONSTRUCTORS

The intent of constructors is to initialize the new object that will be created by the function invocation to initial conditions. And while such functions *can* be called as "normal" functions, or even assigned to object properties in order to be invoked as methods, they're generally not very useful as such.

For example, it'd be perfectly valid to call the Ninja() function as follows:

```
var whatever = Ninja();
```

But the effect would be for the skulk property to be created on window, and for window to be returned and stored in whatever; that's not a particularly useful operation.

Because constructors are generally coded and used in a manner that's different from other functions, and they generally aren't all that useful unless invoked as constructors, a naming convention has arisen to distinguish constructors from run-of-the-mill functions and methods. If you've been paying attention, you may have already noticed it.

Functions and methods are generally named starting with a verb that describes what they do (skulk(), creep(), sneak(), doSomethingWonderful(), and so on) and start with a lowercase letter. Constructors, on the other hand, are usually named as a noun that describes the object that's being constructed and start with an uppercase character; Ninja(), Samurai(), Ronin(), KungFuPanda(), and so on.

It's pretty easy to see how a constructor makes it much easier to create multiple objects that conform to the same pattern without having to repeat the same code over and over again. The common code is written once, as the body of the constructor. In chapter 6, we'll see much more about using constructors and about the other object-oriented mechanisms that JavaScript provides that make it even easier to set up object patterns.

But we're not done with function invocations yet. There's still another way that JavaScript lets us invoke functions that gives us a great deal of control over the invocation details.

3.3.5   *Invocation with the apply() and call() methods*

So far, we've seen that one of the major differences between the types of function invocation is what object ends up as the function context referenced by the implicit this parameter that is passed to the executing function. For methods, it's the method's owning object; for top-level functions, it's always window (in other words, a method of window); for constructors, it's a newly created object instance.

But what if we wanted to make it whatever we wanted? What if we wanted to set it explicitly? What if ... well, why would we want to do such a thing?

To get a glimpse of why we'd care about this ability, we'll look a bit ahead and consider that when an event handler is called, the function context is set to the bound object of the event. We'll examine event handling in detail in chapter 13, but for now just assume that the bound object is the object upon which the event handler is established.

That's usually exactly what we want, but not always. For example, in the case of a method, we might want to force the function context to be the owning object of the method and not the object to which the event is bound. We'll see this scenario in chapter 13, but for now the question is, can we do that?

Well, yes we can.

USING THE APPLY() AND CALL() METHODS

JavaScript provides a means for us to invoke a function and to explicitly specify any object we want as the function context. We do this through the use of one of two methods that exist for every function: `apply()` and `call()`.

Yes, we said methods of functions. As first-class objects (created, by the way, by the `Function()` constructor), functions can have properties, including methods, just like any other object type.

To invoke a function using its `apply()` method, we pass two parameters to `apply()`: the object to be used as the function context, and an array of values to be used as the invocation arguments. The `call()` method is used in a similar manner, except that the arguments are passed directly in the argument list rather than as an array.

The following listing shows both of these methods in action.

Listing 3.5   Using the `apply()` and `call()` methods to supply the function context

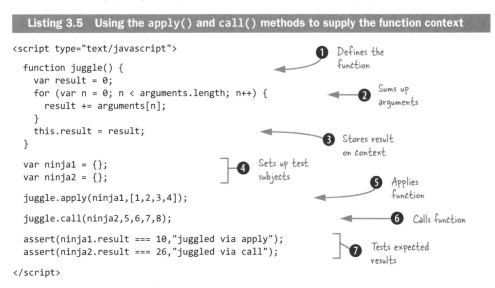

```
<script type="text/javascript">
  function juggle() {                                    ❶ Defines the
    var result = 0;                                          function
    for (var n = 0; n < arguments.length; n++) {        ❷ Sums up
      result += arguments[n];                               arguments
    }
    this.result = result;                               ❸ Stores result
  }                                                         on context
  var ninja1 = {};                                      ❹ Sets up test
  var ninja2 = {};                                          subjects
                                                        ❺ Applies
  juggle.apply(ninja1,[1,2,3,4]);                           function

  juggle.call(ninja2,5,6,7,8);                          ❻ Calls function

  assert(ninja1.result === 10,"juggled via apply");     ❼ Tests expected
  assert(ninja2.result === 26,"juggled via call");          results
</script>
```

The results are shown in figure 3.9.

In this example, we set up a function named `juggle()` ❶, in which we define juggling as adding up all the arguments ❷ and storing them as a property named `result`

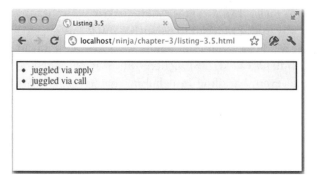

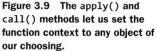

Figure 3.9   The apply() and call() methods let us set the function context to any object of our choosing.

on the function context ❸. That may be a rather lame definition of juggling, but it *will* allow us to determine whether arguments were passed to the function correctly, and which object ended up as the function context.

We then set up two objects that we'll use as function contexts ❹, passing the first to the function's apply() method, along with an array of arguments ❺, and passing the second to the function's call() method ❻, along with a number of other arguments.

Then we test ❼!

First, we check that ninja1, which was passed via apply(), received a result property that's the result of adding up all the argument values. Then we do the same for ninja2, which was passed via call().

The results in figure 3.9 show that the tests passed, meaning that we were successfully able to specify arbitrary objects to serve as function contexts for function invocations.

This can come in handy whenever it would be expedient to usurp what would normally be the function context with an object of our own choosing—something that can be particularly useful when invoking callback functions.

FORCING THE FUNCTION CONTEXT IN CALLBACKS

Let's consider a concrete example of forcing the function context to be an object of our own choosing. Let's take a simple function that will perform an operation on every entry of an array.

In imperative programming, it's common to pass the array to a method and use a for loop to iterate over every entry, performing the operation on each entry:

```
function(collection) {
  for (var n = 0; n < collection.length; n++) {
    /* do something to collection[n] */
  }
}
```

In contrast, the functional approach would be to create a function that operates on a single element and passes each entry to that function:

```
function(item){
  /* do something to item */
}
```

The difference lies in thinking at a level where functions are the building blocks of the program rather than imperative statements.

You might think that it's all rather moot, and that all we're doing is moving the for loop out one level, but we're not done massaging this example yet.

In order to facilitate a more functional style, quite a few of the popular JavaScript libraries provide a "for-each" function that invokes a callback on each element within an array. This is often more succinct, and this style is preferred over the traditional for statement by those familiar with functional programming. Its organizational benefits will become even more evident (*cough*, code reuse, *cough*) once we've covered closures in chapter 5. Such an iteration function *could* simply pass the "current" element to the callback as a parameter, but most make the current element the function context of the callback.

NOTE A forEach() method has been defined for Array instances in JavaScript 1.6 and already appears in many modern browsers.

Let's build our own (simplified) version of such a function in the next listing.

Listing 3.6 Building a for-each function to demonstrate setting a function context

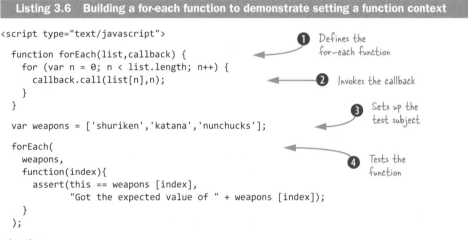

```
<script type="text/javascript">

  function forEach(list,callback) {                          ❶ Defines the
    for (var n = 0; n < list.length; n++) {                     for-each function
      callback.call(list[n],n);                               ❷ Invokes the callback
    }
  }
                                                              ❸ Sets up the
  var weapons = ['shuriken','katana','nunchucks'];              test subject

  forEach(
    weapons,                                                  ❹ Tests the
    function(index){                                             function
      assert(this == weapons [index],
             "Got the expected value of " + weapons [index]);
    }
  );

</script>
```

Our iteration function sports a simple signature that expects the array of objects to be iterated over as the first argument and a callback function as the second ❶. The function iterates over the array entries, invoking the callback function ❷ for each entry.

We use the call() method of the callback function, passing the current iteration entry as the first parameter and the loop index as the second. This *should* cause the current entry to become the function context and the index to be passed as the single parameter to the callback.

Now to test that!

We set up a simple array ❸ and then call the forEach() function, passing the test array and a callback within which we test that the expected entry is set as the function

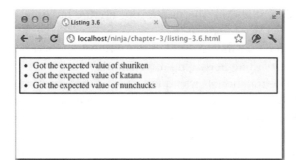

Figure 3.10   The test results show that we have the ability to make any object we please the function context of a callback invocation.

context for each invocation of the callback ❹. Figure 3.10 shows that our function works splendidly.

In a production-ready implementation of such a function, there'd be a lot more work to do. For example, what if the first argument isn't an array? What if the second isn't a function? How would you allow the page author to terminate the loop at any point? As an exercise, you can augment the function to handle these situations.

Another exercise you could task yourself with is to enhance the function so that the page author can also pass an arbitrary number of arguments to the callback in addition to the iteration index.

But given that `apply()` and `call()` do pretty much the same thing, how do we decide which to use?

The high-level answer is the same answer as for many such questions: we'd use whichever one improves code clarity. A more practical answer would be to use the one that best matches the arguments we have handy. If we have a bunch of unrelated values in variables or specified as literals, `call()` lets us list them directly in its argument list. But if we already have the argument values in an array, or if it's convenient to collect them as such, `apply()` could be the better choice.

3.4   *Summary*

In this chapter we took a look at various fascinating aspects of how functions work in JavaScript. While their use is completely ubiquitous, an understanding of their inner workings is essential to writing high-quality JavaScript code.

Specifically, within this chapter, we learned:

- Writing sophisticated code hinges upon learning JavaScript as a functional language.
- Functions are first-class objects that are treated just like any other objects within JavaScript. Just like any other object type, they can be:
  - Created via literals
  - Assigned to variables or properties
  - Passed as parameters
  - Returned as function results
  - Possess properties and methods

- Each object has a "super power" that distinguishes it from the rest; for functions it's the ability to be invoked.
- Functions are created via literals, for which a name is optional.
- The browser can invoke functions during the lifetime of a page by invoking them as event handlers of various types.
- The scope of declaration within a function differs from that of most other languages. Specifically:
  - Variables within a function are in scope from their point of declaration to the end of the function, spanning block boundaries.
  - Inner named functions are available anywhere within the enclosing function (hoisted), even as forward references.
- The parameter list of a function and its actual argument list can be of different lengths:
  - Unassigned parameters evaluate as undefined.
  - Extra arguments are simply not bound to parameter names.
- Each function invocation is passed two implicit parameters:
  - arguments, a collection of the actual passed arguments
  - this, a reference to the object serving as the function context
- Functions can be invoked in various ways, and the invocation mechanism determines the function context value:
  - When invoked as a simple function, the context is the global object (window).
  - When invoked as a method, the context is the object owning the method.
  - When invoked as a constructor, the context is a newly allocated object.
  - When invoked via the apply() or call() methods of the function, the context can be whatever the heck we want.

In all, we made a thorough examination of the fundamentals of function mechanics. In the next chapter, we'll see how we can take this functional knowledge and put it into use.

Wielding functions

4

This chapter covers

- Why anonymous functions are so important
- The ways that functions can be referenced for invocation, including recursively
- Storing references to functions
- Using the function context to get our way
- Dealing with variable-length argument lists
- Determining whether an object is a function

In the previous chapter, we focused on how JavaScript treats functions as first-class objects, and how that enables a functional programming style. In this chapter, we'll expand on how to use those functions to solve various problems that we might come across when authoring web applications.

The examples in this chapter were purposefully chosen to expose secrets that will help you to truly understand JavaScript functions. Many are simple in nature, but they expose important concepts that will be broadly applicable to the dilemmas we're bound to run into in future coding projects.

Without further ado, let's take the functional JavaScript knowledge that we now possess in our two hands and wield it like the mighty weapon that it is.

4.1   *Anonymous functions*

You may or may not have been familiar with anonymous functions prior to their introduction in the previous chapter, but they're a crucial concept we all need to be familiar with if we're striving for JavaScript ninja-hood. They're an important and logical feature for a language that takes a great deal of inspiration from functional languages such as Scheme.

Anonymous functions are typically used in cases where we wish to create a function for later use, such as storing it in a variable, establishing it as a method of an object, or using it as a callback (for example, as a timeout or event handler). In all of these situations, the function doesn't need to have a name for later reference. We'll see plenty such examples throughout the rest of this chapter and book, so don't panic if that still seems a bit strange at the moment.

If you're coming from a background of strongly typed and object-oriented languages, you may think of functions and methods as things that are rigidly defined prior to their use, that are always available, and that are always named for referencing—generally, as something very concrete and enduring. But we'll find that in functional languages, including JavaScript, functions are much more ethereal; they're frequently defined as needed, and discarded just as quickly.

The following listing shows some common examples of anonymous function declarations.

Listing 4.1   Common examples of using anonymous functions

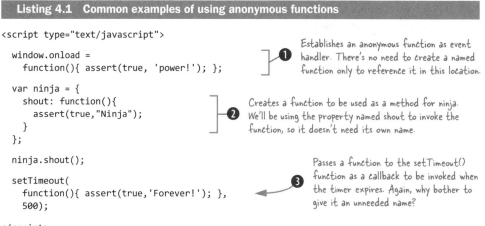

```
<script type="text/javascript">

  window.onload =
    function(){ assert(true, 'power!'); };

  var ninja = {
    shout: function(){
      assert(true,"Ninja");
    }
  };

  ninja.shout();

  setTimeout(
    function(){ assert(true,'Forever!'); },
    500);

</script>
```

❶ Establishes an anonymous function as event handler. There's no need to create a named function only to reference it in this location.

❷ Creates a function to be used as a method for ninja. We'll be using the property named shout to invoke the function, so it doesn't need its own name.

❸ Passes a function to the setTimeout() function as a callback to be invoked when the timer expires. Again, why bother to give it an unneeded name?

In listing 4.1, we do a couple of typical things.

First, we establish a function as a handler for the load event ❶. We're never going to call this function directly; we're going to let the event-handling mechanism do it for us. We could have done the same thing like this:

```
function bootMeUp(){ assert(true, 'power!'); };
window.onload = bootMeUp;
```

But why bother to create the separate top-level function with a name when it's not really needed?

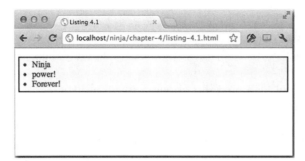

Figure 4.1 Anonymous functions can be called at various times despite not being named.

Next, we declare an anonymous function as a property of an object ❷, which we know from the previous chapter makes the function a method of the object. We then invoke the method using the property reference.

Another interesting use of an anonymous function, and one that should look familiar from the previous chapter, is its use as a callback supplied to another function call. In this example, we supply an anonymous function as an argument to the set-Timeout() method (of window) ❸, which is invoked after half a second has elapsed.

The results (after letting things run for a second or two) can be seen in figure 4.1.

Note how, in all of these cases, the functions didn't need to have a name in order to be used after their declarations. Also note our use, once again, of the assert() function with a test condition of true as a lazy man's means of emitting output. Hey, we wrote the code, why not use it?

> **NOTE** Some might think that by assigning an anonymous function to a property named shout that we give the function a name, but that's not the correct way of thinking about it. The shout name is the name of the *property*, not of the function itself. This can be proven by examining the name property of the function. Review the results of listing 3.1 in figure 3.4 (in chapter 3) to see that anonymous functions don't possess names in the same manner that named functions do.

We're going to see anonymous functions a lot in the rest of this book's code because prowess with JavaScript relies upon using it as a functional language. As such, we're going to use functional programming styles heavily in all the code that follows. Functional programming concentrates on small, usually side-effect-free, functions as the basic building blocks of application code. As we go along, we're going to see that this style is essential to the types of things we need to do in web applications.

So in addition to not polluting the global namespace with unnecessary function names, we're going to create lots of little functions that get passed around instead of large functions full of imperative statements.

Functional programming with anonymous functions will solve many of the challenges that we'll face when developing JavaScript applications. In the rest of this chapter, we'll expand on their use, and look at various ways in which they can be employed. We'll start with recursion.

4.2   Recursion

Recursion is a concept that you've probably run into before. Whenever a function calls itself, or calls a function that in turn calls the original function anywhere in the call tree, recursion occurs.

Recursion is a really useful technique for applications of all types. You might be thinking that recursion is mostly useful in applications that do a lot of math, and that's true—many mathematical formulae are recursive in nature. But it's also useful for doing things like walking trees, and that's a construct that we're likely to see popping up within web applications. We can also use recursion to develop an even deeper understanding of how functions work within JavaScript.

Let's start by using recursion in its simplest form.

4.2.1   Recursion in named functions

There are any number of common examples for recursive functions. One is the test for a palindrome—this is perhaps the "Hello world!" for recursive techniques.

The non-recursive definition of a palindrome is "a phrase that reads the same in either direction," and we can use that to implement a function that creates a reversed copy of the string and compares it to the original. But copying the string isn't an elegant solution on a number of levels, not the least of which is the need to allocate and create a new string.

By using a more mathematical definition of a palindrome, we can come up with a more elegant solution. Here's the definition:

1   A single or zero-character string is a palindrome.
2   Any other string is a palindrome if the first and last characters are the same, and the string that remains, excepting those characters, is a palindrome.

Our implementation using this definition follows:

```
function isPalindrome(text) {
  if (text.length <= 1) return true;
  if (text.charAt(0) != text.charAt(text.length - 1)) return false;
  return isPalindrome(text.substr(1,text.length - 2));
}
```

Note that the new definition, and our implementation of it, is *recursive*, because it uses the definition of a palindrome to determine if a string is a palindrome. The implementation is straightforward, and we make a recursive call, using the function's name, in the last line of the function.

> **PONDER THIS**   Our function doesn't handle text parameter values of `null` or undefined. How would you handle this? In fact, what would you return in such cases? Are non-existent strings palindromic?

Things get a bit more interesting, and a tad less clear, when we begin dealing with anonymous functions, but we'll get to that in a bit. Let's establish a really simple example of recursion that we'll build upon as we go along.

Ninjas frequently need to signal each other in code, often employing natural sounds as a cover. We're going to give our ninja the ability to chirp like a cricket, with the number of chirps encoding different messages. We'll start with an implementation using recursion via the function's name, as shown in the following listing

Listing 4.2 Chirping using a named function

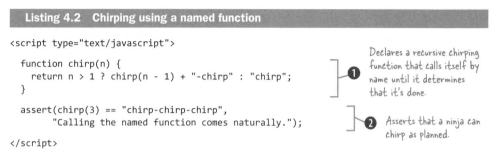

```javascript
<script type="text/javascript">

  function chirp(n) {
    return n > 1 ? chirp(n - 1) + "-chirp" : "chirp";
  }

  assert(chirp(3) == "chirp-chirp-chirp",
      "Calling the named function comes naturally.");

</script>
```

❶ Declares a recursive chirping function that calls itself by name until it determines that it's done.

❷ Asserts that a ninja can chirp as planned.

In this listing, we declare a function named chirp() that employs recursion by calling itself by name ❶, just as we did in the palindrome example. Our test verifies that the function works as intended ❷.

> **About recursion**
>
> The function in listing 4.2 satisfies two criteria for recursion: a reference to self, and convergence towards termination.
>
> The function clearly calls itself, so the first criterion is satisfied. And because the value of parameter n decreases with each iteration, it will sooner or later reach a value of one or less and stop the recursion, satisfying the second criterion.
>
> Note that a "recursive" function that doesn't converge toward termination is better known as an infinite loop!

It's pretty clear how all this works with a named function, but what if we were to use anonymous functions?

4.2.2 Recursion with methods

In the previous section, we said that we were going to give our ninja the ability to chirp, but we really didn't. What we created was a standalone function for chirping.

Let's fix that by declaring the recursive function as a method of a ninja object. This complicates things a bit, because the recursive function becomes an anonymous function assigned to an object's property, as you can see in the next listing.

Listing 4.3 Method recursion within an object

```javascript
<script type="text/javascript">

  var ninja = {
    chirp: function(n) {
```

❶ Declares a recursive chirp function as a property of the ninja object. We now need to call the method from within itself using the reference to the object's method.

```
      return n > 1 ? ninja.chirp(n - 1) + "-chirp" : "chirp";
    }
  };
  assert(ninja.chirp(3) == "chirp-chirp-chirp",
         "An object property isn't too confusing, either.");
</script>
```

In this test, we defined our recursive function as an anonymous function referenced by the chirp property of the ninja object ❶. Within the function, we invoke the function recursively via a reference to the object's property: ninja.chirp(). We can't reference it directly by its name as we did in listing 4.2, because it doesn't have one.

The relationship is shown in figure 4.2.

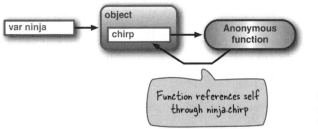

Function references self
through ninja.chirp

Figure 4.2   Our function, now a method, references itself through the object's chirp property.

That's all fine as it stands, but because we're relying upon an *indirect* reference to the function—namely, the chirp property of ninja—we could be standing on thin ice. And that's not a wise move for a ninja of any standing. Let's look at why we're heading for a fall.

4.2.3   *The pilfered reference problem*

The example in listing 4.3 relied on the fact that we had a reference to the function to be called recursively in the property of an object. But unlike a function's actual name, such references may be transient, and relying upon them can trip us up in confounding ways.

Let's modify the previous example by adding a new object, let's say samurai, that also references the anonymous recursive function in the ninja object. Consider the next listing.

Listing 4.4   Recursion using a missing function reference

```
<script type="text/javascript">
  var ninja = {
    chirp: function(n) {
      return n > 1 ? ninja.chirp(n - 1) + "-chirp" : "chirp";
    }
  };

  var samurai = { chirp: ninja.chirp };
```

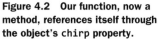

Creates a chirp() method on samurai by referencing the existing method of same name on ninja. Why write the code twice when we already have an implementation?

```
ninja = {};

try {
  assert(samurai.chirp(3) == "chirp-chirp-chirp",
         "Is this going to work?");
}
catch(e){
  assert(false,
         "Uh, this isn't good! Where'd ninja.chirp go?");
}
```

2 Redefines ninja such that it has no properties. This means that its chirp property goes away!

3 Tests if things still work. Hint: they don't!

```
</script>
```

We can see how things can quickly break down in this scenario. We copied a reference to the chirping function into the samurai object **1**, so now both ninja.chirp and samurai.chirp reference the same anonymous function. A diagram of the relationships created is shown in figure 4.3. Part A (which you'll recognize from figure 4.2) shows the constructs after the ninja object is created, and part B shows them after the samurai object is created.

At that point, there really isn't any problem—it's not at all uncommon for functions to be referenced from multiple places. The potential booby trap is that the function is recursive and uses the ninja.chirp reference to call itself, regardless of whether the function is invoked as a method of ninja or of samurai.

So what would happen if ninja were to go away, leaving samurai holding the bag? To test this, we redefine ninja with an empty object **2**, depicted in part C of figure 4.3. The anonymous function still exists and can be referenced through the samurai.chirp property, but the ninja.chirp property no longer exists. And because the function recursively calls itself through that now-defunct reference, things go badly awry **3** when the function is invoked.

We can rectify this problem by fixing the initially sloppy definition of the recursive function. Rather than explicitly referencing ninja in the anonymous function, we should have used the function context (this) as follows:

```
var ninja = {
  chirp: function(n) {
    return n > 1 ? this.chirp(n - 1) + "-chirp" : "chirp";
  }
};
```

Remember that when a function is invoked as a method, the function context refers to the object through which the method was invoked. When invoked as ninja .chirp(), this refers to ninja, but when invoked by samurai.chirp(), this refers to samurai and all is well.

Using the function context (this) makes our chirp() method much more robust, and it's the way that the method should have been declared in the first place. So, problem solved.

But...

```
var ninja = {
  chirp: function(n) {
    return n > 1 ? ninja.chirp(n - 1) + "-chirp" : "chirp";
  }
};
```

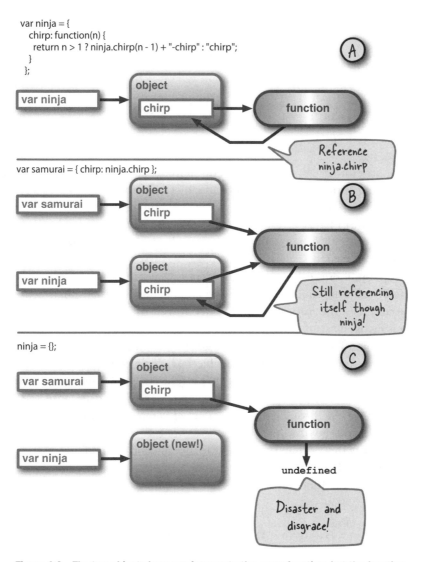

```
var samurai = { chirp: ninja.chirp };
```

```
ninja = {};
```

Figure 4.3   The two objects have a reference to the same function, but the function refers to itself through only one of the objects. Thin ice!

4.2.4   Inline named functions

The solution we came up with in the previous section works perfectly well when functions are used as methods of an object. In fact, the technique of using the function context, regardless of whether the method is recursive or not, to reference the "owning object" of the method is one that's very common and accepted. We'll be seeing a lot more about that in chapter 6.

But now we have another problem. The solution relied upon the fact that the function would be a method named chirp() of any object within which the method is defined. What if the properties don't have the same name? Or what if one of the references to the function isn't even an object property? Our solution only works in the specific case where the function is used as a method, and where the property name of the method is identical in all its uses. Can we develop a more general technique?

Let's consider another approach: what if we give the anonymous function a *name*?

At first, this may seem completely crazy; if we're going to use a function as a method, why would we also give it its own name? Well, remember that when declaring a function literal, the name of the function is optional, and we've been leaving it off for all but top-level functions. But as it turns out, there's nothing wrong with giving *any* function literal a name, even those that are declared as callbacks or methods.

No longer *anonymous*, these functions are better called *inline functions*, rather than "anonymous named functions" to avoid the oxymoron.

Observe the use of this technique in the following listing.

Listing 4.5 Using an inline function in a recursive fashion

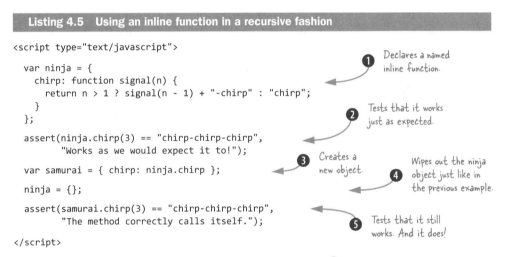

```
<script type="text/javascript">

  var ninja = {
    chirp: function signal(n) {
      return n > 1 ? signal(n - 1) + "-chirp" : "chirp";
    }
  };
  assert(ninja.chirp(3) == "chirp-chirp-chirp",
       "Works as we would expect it to!");

  var samurai = { chirp: ninja.chirp };

  ninja = {};

  assert(samurai.chirp(3) == "chirp-chirp-chirp",
       "The method correctly calls itself.");

</script>
```

❶ Declares a named inline function.

❷ Tests that it works just as expected.

❸ Creates a new object.

❹ Wipes out the ninja object just like in the previous example.

❺ Tests that it still works. And it does!

Here we assign the name signal to the inline function ❶ and use that name for the recursive reference within the function body, and then we test that calling as a method of ninja still works ❷. As before, we copy the reference to the function to samurai .chirp ❸ and wipe out the original ninja object ❹.

Upon testing calling the function as a method of samurai ❺, we find that everything still works, because wiping out the chirp property of ninja had no effect on the name we gave to the inline function and used to perform the recursive call.

This ability to name an inline function extends even further. It can even be used within normal variable assignments, with some seemingly bizarre results, as shown in the following listing.

Listing 4.6 Verifying the identity of an inline function

```
<script type="text/javascript">

  var ninja = function myNinja(){
```

❶ Declares a named inline function and assigns it to variable.

```
    assert(ninja == myNinja,
        "This function is named two things at once!");
};

ninja();

assert(typeof myNinja == "undefined",
        "But myNinja isn't defined outside of the function.");

</script>
```

2 Tests that two names are equivalent inside the inline function.

3 Invokes the function to perform the internal test.

4 Tests that the inline function's name isn't available outside the inline function.

This listing brings up the most important point regarding inline functions: even though inline functions can be named, those names are *only* visible within the functions themselves. Remember the scoping rules we talked about back in chapter 3? Inline function names act somewhat like variable names, and their scope is limited to the function within which they're declared.

> **NOTE**   This is why top-level functions are created as methods on window. Without the window properties, we'd have no way to reference the functions.

We declare an inline function with the name myNinja **1** and internally test to be sure that the name, and the reference to which the function is assigned, refer to the same thing **2**. Calling the function invokes this test **3**.

Then, we test that the function name isn't externally visible **4**. And, as expected, when we run the code, the test passes.

So while giving inline functions a name may provide a means to clearly allow recursive references within those functions (arguably, this approach provides more clarity than using this), it has limited utility elsewhere.

Are there other techniques we can employ?

4.2.5   *The callee property*

Let's look at still another way to approach recursion that introduces yet another concept concerning functions: the callee property of the arguments parameter.

> **WARNING**   The callee property is on the chopping block for an upcoming version of JavaScript, and the ECMAScript 5 standard forbids its use in "strict" mode. It's OK to use this property in current browsers, but its use isn't future-proof, and we'd likely not want to use callee in new code. Nevertheless, we present it here as you may come across it in existing code.

Consider the following code.

> **Listing 4.7   Using arguments.callee to reference the calling function**

```
<script type="text/javascript">
    var ninja = {
        chirp: function(n) {
            return n > 1 ? arguments.callee(n - 1) + "-chirp" : "chirp";
```

References arguments.callee property.

```
     }
   };
   assert(ninja.chirp(3) == "chirp-chirp-chirp",
        "arguments.callee is the function itself.");
</script>
```

Tests that we can chirp as much as we'd like!

As we discovered in section 3.3, the `arguments` parameter is implicitly passed to every function, and `arguments` has a property named `callee` that refers to the currently executing function. This property can serve as a reliable way to always access the function itself. Later on in this chapter, as well as in the following chapter (chapter 5, on closures), we'll take a closer look at what can be done with this particular property.

All together, these different techniques for referencing functions will be of great benefit to us as we start to scale in complexity, providing us with various means to reference functions without resorting to hardcoded and fragile dependencies like variable and property names.

The next step in our functional journey is to understand how the object-oriented nature of functions in JavaScript can help take our code to the next level.

4.3 Fun with function as objects

As we've consistently harped on throughout this chapter, functions in JavaScript aren't like functions in many other languages. JavaScript gives functions many capabilities, not the least of which is their treatment as first-class objects.

We've seen that functions can have properties, can have methods, can be assigned to variables and properties, and generally enjoy all the abilities of plain vanilla objects, but with an amazing superpower: they're callable.

In this section, we'll examine some ways that we can exploit the similarities that functions share with other object types. But to start with, let's recap a few key concepts that we're going to take advantage of.

Let's start with assigning functions to variables:

```
var obj = {};
var fn = function(){};
assert(obj && fn, "Both the object and function exist.");
```

Just as we can assign an object to a variable, we can do so with a function. This also applies to assigning functions to object properties in order to create methods.

> **NOTE** One thing that's important to remember is the semicolon after `function(){}` definitions. It's a good practice to have semicolons at the end of all statements, and especially after variable assignments. Doing so with anonymous functions is no exception. When compressing code, properly placed semicolons will allow for greater flexibility in compression techniques.

Another capability that may have surprised you is that, just as with any other object, we can attach properties to a function:

```
var obj = {};
var fn = function(){};
obj.prop = "hitsuke (distraction)";
fn.prop = "tanuki (climbing)";
```

This aspect of functions can be used in a number of different ways throughout a library or general on-page code, and this is especially true when it comes to topics like event callback management. Let's look at a couple of the more interesting things that can be done with this capability; first we'll look at storing functions in collections and then at a technique known as "memoizing."

4.3.1   Storing functions

There are times when we may want to store a collection of related but unique functions, event callback management being the most obvious example (and one that we'll be examining in excruciating detail in chapter 13). When adding functions to such a collection, a challenge we can face is determining which functions are actually new to the collection and should be added, and which are already resident and shouldn't be added.

An obvious, but naïve, technique would be to store all the functions in an array and loop through the array checking for duplicate functions. Unfortunately, this performs poorly, and as ninjas we want to make things work *well*, not merely work.

We can make use of function properties to achieve this with an appropriate level of sophistication, as shown in in the next listing.

Listing 4.8   Storing a collection of unique functions

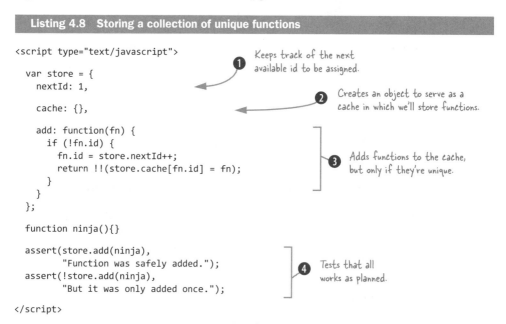

```
<script type="text/javascript">

  var store = {
    nextId: 1,                            ❶ Keeps track of the next
                                            available id to be assigned.

    cache: {},                            ❷ Creates an object to serve as a
                                            cache in which we'll store functions.

    add: function(fn) {
      if (!fn.id) {
        fn.id = store.nextId++;           ❸ Adds functions to the cache,
        return !!(store.cache[fn.id] = fn);  but only if they're unique.
      }
    }
  };

  function ninja(){}

  assert(store.add(ninja),
         "Function was safely added.");   ❹ Tests that all
  assert(!store.add(ninja),                 works as planned.
         "But it was only added once.");

</script>
```

In this listing, we create an object assigned to variable store (we used a noun in this case), in which we'll store a unique set of functions. This object has two data properties: one that stores a next available id value ❶, and one within which we'll cache the stored functions ❷. Functions are added to this cache via the add() method ❸.

Within add(), we first check to see if an id property has been added to the function, and if so, we assume that the function has already been processed and we ignore it. Otherwise, we assign an id property to the function (incrementing the nextId property along the way) and add the function as a property of the cache, using the id value as the property name.

We then return the value true, which we compute the hard way by converting the function to its Boolean equivalent, so that we can tell when the function was added after a call to add().

> **TIP** The !! construct is a simple way of turning any JavaScript expression into its Boolean equivalent. For example: !!"he shot me down" === true and !!0 === false. In listing 4.8 we end up converting a function into its Boolean equivalent, which will always be true. (Sure we could have hardcoded true, but then we wouldn't have had a chance to introduce !!).

Running the page in the browser shows that when our tests try to add the ninja() function twice ❹, the function is only added once, as shown in figure 4.4.

Another useful trick that we can pull out of our sleeves using function properties is giving a function the ability to modify itself. This technique could be used to remember previously computed values, saving time during future computations.

4.3.2 *Self-memoizing functions*

Memoization (no, that's not a typo) is the process of building a function that's capable of remembering its previously computed values. This can markedly increase performance by avoiding needless complex computations that have already been performed.

We'll take a look at this technique in the context of storing the answer to expensive computations, and then we'll look at a more real-world example of storing a list of DOM elements that we've looked up.

MEMOIZING EXPENSIVE COMPUTATIONS

As a basic example, let's look at a simplistic (and certainly not particularly efficient) algorithm for computing prime numbers. This is just a simple example of a complex

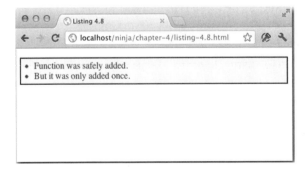

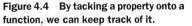
Figure 4.4 By tacking a property onto a function, we can keep track of it.

calculation, but this technique is readily applicable to other expensive computations, such as deriving the MD5 hash for a string, that are too complex to present as examples here.

From the outside, the function will appear to be just like any normal function, but we'll surreptitiously build in an "answer cache" in which the function will save the answers to the computations it performs. Look over the following code.

Listing 4.9   Memoizing previously computed values

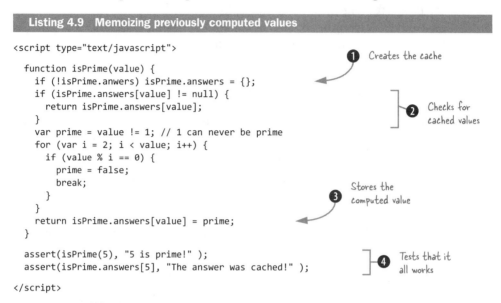

```
<script type="text/javascript">

  function isPrime(value) {
    if (!isPrime.anwers) isPrime.answers = {};          ❶ Creates the cache
    if (isPrime.answers[value] != null) {
      return isPrime.answers[value];                    ❷ Checks for
    }                                                       cached values
    var prime = value != 1; // 1 can never be prime
    for (var i = 2; i < value; i++) {
      if (value % i == 0) {
        prime = false;
        break;                                          ❸ Stores the
      }                                                    computed value
    }
    return isPrime.answers[value] = prime;
  }

  assert(isPrime(5), "5 is prime!" );                   ❹ Tests that it
  assert(isPrime.answers[5], "The answer was cached!" );   all works

</script>
```

Within the isPrime() function, we start by checking to see if the answers property that we'll use as a cache has been created, and if not, we create it ❶. The creation of this initially empty object will only occur on the first call to the function; after that, the cache will exist.

Then we check to see if the answer for the passed value has already been cached in answers ❷. Within this cache, we'll store the computed answer (true or false) using the value as the property key. If we find a cached answer, we simply return it.

If no cached value is found, we go ahead and perform the calculations needed to determine whether the value is prime (which can be an expensive operation for larger values) and store the result in the cache as we return it ❸.

Some simple tests ❹ show that the memoization is working!

This approach has two major advantages:

- The end user enjoys performance benefits for function calls asking for a previously computed value.
- It happens completely seamlessly and behind the scenes; neither the end user nor the page author need to perform any special requests or do any extra initialization in order to make it all work.

But it's not all roses and violins; there are disadvantages that may need to be weighed against the advantages:

- Any sort of caching will certainly sacrifice memory in favor of performance.
- Purists may consider that caching is a concern that should not be mixed with the business logic; a function or method should do one thing and do it well.
- It's difficult to load-test or measure the performance of an algorithm such as this one.

Let's take a look at another kindred example.

Memoizing DOM elements

Querying for a set of DOM elements by tag name is a fairly common operation, and one that may not be particularly performant. We can take advantage of our newfound function memoization superpowers by building a cache within which we can store the matched element sets. Consider this example:

```
function getElements(name) {
  if (!getElements.cache) getElements.cache = {};
  return getElements.cache[name] =
    getElements.cache[name] ||
    document.getElementsByTagName(name);
}
```

The memoization (caching) code is quite simple and doesn't add that much extra complexity to the overall querying process. But if we do some performance analysis upon the function, we'll find that this simple layer of caching yields us a 5x performance increase, as shown in table 4.1. Not a bad superpower to have.

Table 4.1 All times are in ms for 100,000 iterations in a copy of Chrome 17

Code version	Average	Minimum	Maximum	Runs
Noncached version	16.7	18	19	10
Cached version	3.2	3	4	10

Even these simple examples demonstrate the usefulness of function properties: we can store state and cache information in a single and encapsulated location, gaining not only organizational advantages but performance benefits without external storage or caching objects polluting the scope. We'll be revisiting this concept in upcoming chapters, as the utility of this technique is broadly applicable.

The ability to possess properties, just like the other objects in JavaScript, isn't the only superpower that functions have. Much of a function's power is related to its context, and we'll explore an example of that next.

4.3.3 *Faking array methods*

There are times that we may want to create an object that contains a collection of data. If the collection was all that we were worried about, we could just use an array. But in certain cases, there may be more state to store than just the collection itself—perhaps we need to store some sort of metadata regarding the collected items.

One option might be to create a new array every time you wish to create a new version of such an object, and add the metadata properties and methods to it—remember, we can add properties and methods to an object as we please, including arrays. Generally, however, this can be quite slow, not to mention tedious.

Let's examine the possibility of using a normal object and just *giving* it the functionality that we desire. Methods that know how to deal with collections already exist on the Array object (a constructor function); can we trick them into working on our own objects?

Turns out that we can, as shown in the next listing.

Listing 4.10 Simulating array-like methods

```html
<body>

  <input id="first"/>
  <input id="second"/>

  <script type="text/javascript">

    var elems = {

      length: 0,

      add: function(elem){
        Array.prototype.push.call(this, elem);
      },

      gather: function(id){
        this.add(document.getElementById(id));
      }
    };

    elems.gather("first");
    assert(elems.length == 1 && elems[0].nodeType,
           "Verify that we have an element in our stash");

    elems.gather("second");
    assert(elems.length == 2 && elems[1].nodeType,
           "Verify the other insertion");

  </script>
</body>
```

① Stores the count of elements. If we're going to pretend we're an array, we're going to need someplace to store the number of items that we're storing.

② Implements the method to add elements to our collection. The prototype for Array already has a method to do this, so why not use it instead of reinventing the wheel?

③ Implements a method named gather() to find elements by their id values and add them to our collection.

④ Tests the gather() and add() methods.

In this example, we're creating a "normal" object and instrumenting it to mimic some of the behaviors of an array. First, we define a length property to record the number of element that are stored ①, just like an array. Then we define a method to add an element to the end of our simulated array, calling this method simply add() ②. Rather than write our own code, we've decided to leverage a native method of JavaScript arrays: `Array.prototype.push`. (Don't worry about the `prototype` part of that reference—we'll be looking at that in chapter 6. For now, just think of it as a property where constructors stash their methods.)

Normally, the `Array.prototype.push()` method would operate on its own array via its function context. But here, we're tricking the method to use *our* object as its context by using the `call()` method and forcing our object to be the context of the `push()` method. The `push()` method, which increments the `length` property (thinking that it's the `length` property of an array), adds a numbered property to the object referencing the passed element. In a way, this behavior is almost subversive (how fitting for ninjas!), but it exemplifies what we're capable of doing with mutable object contexts.

Our `add()` method expects an element reference to be passed for storage. While there may be times that we have such a reference around, more often than not we won't, so we also define a convenience method, `gather()`, that looks up the element by its `id` value and adds it to storage ❸.

Finally, we run two tests that each add an item to the object via `gather()`, check that the `length` was correctly adjusted, and check that elements were added at the appropriate points ❹.

The borderline nefarious behavior we demonstrated in this section not only reveals the power that malleable function contexts gives us, but also serves as an excellent segue into discussing the complexities of dealing with function arguments.

4.4   *Variable-length argument lists*

JavaScript, as a whole, is very flexible in what it can do, and much of that flexibility defines the language as we know it today. One of these flexible and powerful features is the ability for functions to accept an arbitrary number of arguments. This flexibility offers developers great control over how their functions, and therefore their applications, can be written.

Let's take a look at a few prime examples of how we can use flexible argument lists to our advantage. We'll see

- How to supply multiple arguments to functions that can accept any number of them
- How to use variable-length argument lists to implement function overloading
- How to understand and use the `length` property of argument lists

Because JavaScript has no function overloading (a capability of object-oriented languages to which you may be accustomed), the flexibility of the argument list is key to gaining similar advantages that overloading gives us in other languages.

Let's start with using `apply()` to hand off a variable number of arguments.

4.4.1   *Using apply() to supply variable arguments*

With any language, there are often things we need to do that seem to have been mysteriously overlooked by the developers of the language, and JavaScript is no exception.

One of these odd vacuums involves finding the smallest or the largest values contained within an array. It seems like that would be done often enough to warrant inclusion in JavaScript, but if we poke around, the closest thing we'll find is a set of methods on the Math object named min() and max().

At first we might think that these methods are the answer to our problem, but on examination, we'll see that each of these methods expects a variable-length argument list, and not an array. How silly not to have provided both.

That means calls to Math.max(), for example, could look like this:

```
var biggest = Math.max(1,2);
var biggest = Math.max(1,2,3);
var biggest = Math.max(1,2,3,4);
var biggest = Math.max(1,2,3,4,5,6,7,8,9,10,2058);
```

When it comes to arrays, we can't very well resort to something like this:

```
var biggest = Math.max(list[0],list[1],list[2]);
```

Unless we know exactly how big the array is, how would we know how many arguments to pass? And even if we did know the array size, that's far from a satisfactory solution.

Before abandoning Math.max() and resorting to looping through the contents ourselves to find the minimum and maximum values, let's pull on our ninja hoods and ponder whether there's an easy and supported way to use an array as a variable-length argument list.

Eureka! The apply() method!

You may recall, the call() and apply() methods exist as methods of *all* functions—even of the built-in JavaScript functions (we saw this with our "fake array" example). Let's see how we can use that ability to our advantage in defining our array-inspecting functions, as shown in the next listing.

Listing 4.11   Generic min() and max() functions for arrays

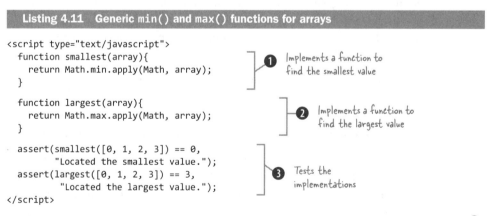

```
<script type="text/javascript">
  function smallest(array){
    return Math.min.apply(Math, array);
  }

  function largest(array){
    return Math.max.apply(Math, array);
  }

  assert(smallest([0, 1, 2, 3]) == 0,
         "Located the smallest value.");
  assert(largest([0, 1, 2, 3]) == 3,
         "Located the largest value.");
</script>
```

❶ Implements a function to find the smallest value

❷ Implements a function to find the largest value

❸ Tests the implementations

In this code we define two functions: one to find the smallest value within an array ❶, and one to find the largest value ❷. Notice how both functions use the apply() method to supply the value in the passed arrays as variable-length argument lists to the Math functions.

A call to smallest(), passing the array [0,1,2,3] (as we did in our tests ❸), results in a call to Math.min() that's functionally equivalent to

```
Math.min(0,1,2,3);
```

Also note that we specify the context as being the Math object. This isn't necessary (the min() and max() methods will continue to work regardless of what's passed in as the context), but there's no reason not to be tidy in this situation.

Now that we know how to *use* variable-length argument lists when calling functions, let's take a look at how we can declare our own functions to accept them.

4.4.2   *Function overloading*

Back in section 3.3, we introduced the built-in arguments parameter that's implicitly passed to all functions. We're now ready to take a closer look at that parameter.

All functions are implicitly passed this important parameter, which gives our functions the power to handle any number of passed arguments. Even if we only define a certain number of parameters, we'll always be able to access *all* passed arguments through the arguments parameter.

Let's take a quick look at an example of using this power to implement effective function overloading.

DETECTING AND TRAVERSING ARGUMENTS

In other, more pure, object-oriented languages, method overloading is usually effected by declaring distinct implementations of methods of the same name but with differing parameter lists. That's not how it's done in JavaScript. In JavaScript, we "overload" functions with a single implementation that modifies its behavior by inspecting the number and nature of the passed arguments. Let's see how that can be done.

In the following code, we're going to merge the properties of multiple objects into a single root object. This can be an essential utility for effecting inheritance (which we'll discuss more when we talk about object prototypes in chapter 6).

Listing 4.12   Traversing variable-length argument lists

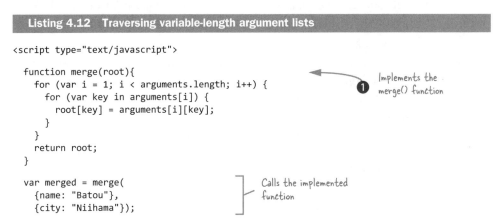

```
<script type="text/javascript">
  function merge(root){                              Implements the
    for (var i = 1; i < arguments.length; i++) {  ❶  merge() function
      for (var key in arguments[i]) {
        root[key] = arguments[i][key];
      }
    }
    return root;
  }

  var merged = merge(                    Calls the implemented
    {name: "Batou"},                     function
    {city: "Niihama"});
```

```
    assert(merged.name == "Batou",
           "The original name is intact.");
    assert(merged.city == "Niihama",
           "And the city has been copied over.");
</script>
```

Tests that it did
the right things

The first thing that you'll notice about the implementation of the merge() function ❶ is that its signature only declares a single parameter: root. This doesn't mean that we're limited to calling the function with a single parameter. Far from it! We can, in fact, call merge() with any number of parameters, including none.

There's no proscription in JavaScript that enforces passing the same number of arguments to a function as there are declared parameters in the function declaration. Whether the function can successfully deal with those arguments (or lack of arguments) is entirely up to the definition of the function itself, but JavaScript imposes no rules in this regard. The fact that we declared the function with a single parameter, root, means that only one of the possible passed arguments can be referenced by name—the first one.

> **TIP**   To check whether an argument that corresponds to a named parameter
> was passed, we can use the expression paramname === undefined, which will eval-
> uate to true if there's no corresponding argument.

So we can get at the first passed argument via root, but how do we access the rest of any arguments that may have been passed? Why, with the arguments parameter, of course, which references a collection of all of the passed arguments.

Remember that what we're trying to do is to merge the properties of any object passed as the second through *n*th arguments into the object passed as root (the first argument). So we iterate through the arguments in the list, starting at index 1 in order to skip the first argument.

During each iteration, in which the iteration item is an object passed to the function, we loop through the properties of that passed object and copy any located properties to the root object.

> **TIP**   If you haven't seen a for-in statement before, it simply iterates through all
> the properties of an object, setting the property name (key) as the iteration item.

As should be evident by now, the ability to access and traverse the arguments collection is a powerful mechanism for creating complex and intelligent methods. We can use it to inspect the arguments passed to any function in order to allow our function to flexibly operate on the arguments, even when we don't know in advance exactly what is going to be passed.

Libraries such as jQuery UI use function overloading extensively. Consider a method to create and manage a UI widget such as a floating dialog box. The same method, dialog(), is used to both create and to perform operations on the dialog box. To create the dialog box, a call such as the following is made:

```
$("#myDialog").dialog({ caption: "This is a dialog" });
```

The exact same method is used to perform operations, such as opening the dialog box:

```
$("#myDialog").dialog("open");
```

What the `dialog()` method actually does is determined by an inspection of exactly what is being passed to it.

Let's take a look at another example where the use of the `arguments` parameter isn't as clear-cut as in the example of listing 4.12.

SLICING AND DICING AN ARGUMENTS LIST

For our next example, we'll build a function that multiplies the first argument with the largest of the remaining arguments. This probably isn't something that's particularly applicable in our applications, but it is an example of yet more techniques for dealing with arguments within a function.

This might seem simple enough—we'll grab the first argument and multiply it by the result of using the `Math.max()` function (which we've already become familiar with) on the remainder of the argument values. Because we only want to pass the array that starts with the second element in the arguments list to `Math.max()`, we'll use the `slice()` method of arrays to create an array that omits the first element.

So, we go ahead and write up the code shown in the following listing.

Listing 4.13 Slicing the arguments list

```
<script type="text/javascript">
  function multiMax(multi){
    return multi * Math.max.apply(Math, arguments.slice(1));
  }

  assert(multiMax(3, 1, 2, 3) == 9, "3*3=9 (First arg, by largest.)");
</script>
```

But when we execute this script, we get a surprise, as shown in figure 4.5. What's up with that? Apparently it wasn't as simple as we first thought.

As we pointed out earlier in the chapter, the `arguments` parameter doesn't reference a true array. Even though it looks and feels a lot like one—we can iterate over it with a `for` loop, for example—it lacks all of the basic array methods, including the very handy `slice()`.

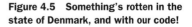

Figure 4.5 Something's rotten in the state of Denmark, and with our code!

We could create our own sets of array slice-and-dice methods—a hand-built *Argu-matic* utensil, if you will. Or we could create our own array by copying the values into a *true* array. But either of these approaches seems ham-handed and redundant when we know that Array already has the functionality we seek.

Before we resort to copying the data or creating the *Argu-matic*, recall the lesson of listing 4.10, in which we fooled an Array function into treating a non-array as an array. Let's use that knowledge and rewrite the code as shown in the next listing.

> **Listing 4.14   Slicing the arguments list—successfully this time**

```
<script type="text/javascript">

  function multiMax(multi){
    return multi * Math.max.apply(Math,
      Array.prototype.slice.call(arguments, 1));
  }
  assert(multiMax(3, 1, 2, 3) == 9,
         "3*3=9 (First arg, by largest.)");

</script>
```

Fools the slice() method into working on the arguments list, which you may recall isn't an instance of Array.

We use the same technique that we applied in listing 4.10 to coerce the Array's slice() method into treating the arguments "array" as a true array, even if it isn't one.

Now that we've learned a bit regarding how to deal with the arguments parameter, let's look at some techniques for overloading functions based upon what we find there.

FUNCTION OVERLOADING APPROACHES

When it comes to function overloading—the technique of defining a function that does different things based upon what's passed to it—it's easy to imagine that such a function could be easily implemented by using the mechanisms we've learned so far to inspect the argument list, and to perform different actions in if-then and else-if clauses. Often, that approach will serve us well, especially if the actions to be taken are on the simpler side.

But once things start getting a bit more complicated, lengthy functions using many such clauses can quickly become unwieldy. In the remainder of this section, we're going to explore a technique by which we can create multiple functions—seemingly with the same name, but each differentiated from the others by the number of arguments they expect—that can be written as distinct and separate anonymous functions rather than as a monolithic if-then-else-if block.

All of this hinges on a little-known property of functions that we need to learn about first.

THE FUNCTION'S LENGTH PROPERTY

There's an interesting property on all functions that isn't very well known, but that gives us an insight into how the function was declared: the length property. This property, not to be confused with the length property of the arguments parameter, equates to the number of named parameters with which the function was declared.

Thus, if we declare a function with a single formal parameter, its `length` property will have a value of 1. Examine the following code:

```
function makeNinja(name){}
function makeSamurai(name, rank){}
assert(makeNinja.length == 1, "Only expecting a single argument");
assert(makeSamurai.length == 2, "Two arguments expected");
```

As a result, within a function, we can determine two things about its arguments:

- How many named parameters it was declared with, via the `length` property
- How many arguments were passed on the invocation, via `arguments.length`

Let's see how this property can be used to build a function that we can use to create overloaded functions, differentiated by argument count.

OVERLOADING FUNCTIONS BY ARGUMENT COUNT

There are any number of ways that we can decide to overload what a function does based upon its arguments. One common approach is to perform different operations based upon the type of the passed arguments. Another could be switching based upon whether certain parameters are present or absent. Still another is based upon the *count* of the passed arguments. We'll be looking at this approach in this section.

Suppose we want to have a method on an object that performs different operations based upon argument count. If we want to have long, monolithic functions, we could do something like the following:

```
var ninja = {
  whatever: function() {
      switch (arguments.length) {
        case 0:
          /* do something */
          break;
        case 1:
          /* do something else */
          break;
        case 2:
          /* do yet something else */
          break;
      //and so on ...
      }
    }
}
```

In this approach, each case would perform a different operation based upon the argument count, obtaining the actual arguments through the `arguments` parameter. But that's not very tidy, and certainly not very ninja, is it?

Let's posit another approach. What if we wanted to add the overloaded method using syntax along the following lines:

```
var ninja = {};
addMethod(ninja,'whatever',function(){ /* do something */ });
addMethod(ninja,'whatever',function(a){ /* do something else */ });
addMethod(ninja,'whatever',function(a,b){ /* yet something else */ });
```

Here we create the object and then add methods to it using the same name (whatever), but with separate functions for each overload. Note how each overload has a different number of parameters specified. This way, we actually create a separate anonymous function for each overload. Nice and tidy!

But the addMethod() function doesn't exist, so we'll need to create it ourselves. Keep your arms in the cart at all times, as this one's going to be a bit of a short but wild ride.

Take a look at the following listing.

Listing 4.15   A method-overloading function

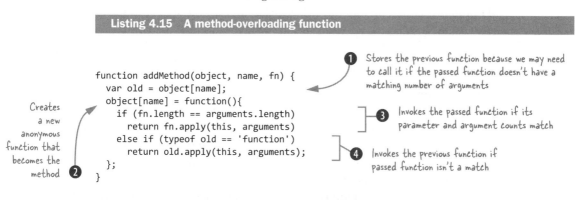

Creates a new anonymous function that becomes the method ❷

```
function addMethod(object, name, fn) {
  var old = object[name];
  object[name] = function(){
    if (fn.length == arguments.length)
      return fn.apply(this, arguments)
    else if (typeof old == 'function')
      return old.apply(this, arguments);
  };
}
```

❶ Stores the previous function because we may need to call it if the passed function doesn't have a matching number of arguments

❸ Invokes the passed function if its parameter and argument counts match

❹ Invokes the previous function if passed function isn't a match

Our addMethod() function accepts three arguments:

- An object upon which a method is to be bound
- The name of the property to which the method will be bound
- The declaration of the method to be bound

Look again at our usage example:

```
var ninja = {};
addMethod(ninja,'whatever',function(){ /* do something */ });
addMethod(ninja,'whatever',function(a){ /* do something else */ });
addMethod(ninja,'whatever',function(a,b){ /* yet something else */ });
```

The first call to addMethod() will create a new anonymous function that, when called with a zero-length argument list, will call the passed fn function. Because ninja is a new object at this point, there's no previously established method to worry about.

On the *next* call to addMethod(), we store a reference to the anonymous function that we created in the previous invocation in the variable old ❶, and we proceed to create another anonymous function that becomes the method ❷. This newer method will check to see if the number of passed arguments is 1, and if so, will invoke the function passed as fn ❸. Failing that, it will call the function stored in old ❹, which as you'll recall, will check for zero parameters and call the version of fn with zero parameters.

On the third call to addMethod(), we pass an fn that takes two parameters, and we go through the process again: creating yet another anonymous function that becomes the method, and calling the two-parameter fn when two arguments are passed, and deferring to the previously created one-argument function.

It's almost as if we're winding the functions around each other like the layers of an onion, each layer checking for a matching number of arguments and deferring to a previously created layer if no match is found.

There's a bit of sleight of hand going on here with regard to how the inner anonymous function accesses old and fn, and it involves a concept called *closures*, which we'll take a close look at in the next chapter. For now, just accept that when it executes, the inner function has access to the current values of old and fn.

Let's test our new function in the next listing.

Listing 4.16   Testing the addMethod() function

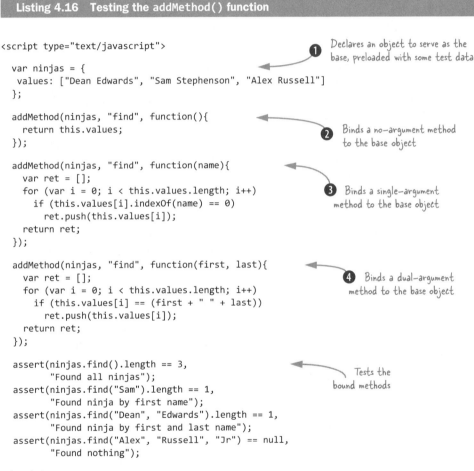

```javascript
<script type="text/javascript">

  var ninjas = {
    values: ["Dean Edwards", "Sam Stephenson", "Alex Russell"]
  };

  addMethod(ninjas, "find", function(){
    return this.values;
  });

  addMethod(ninjas, "find", function(name){
    var ret = [];
    for (var i = 0; i < this.values.length; i++)
      if (this.values[i].indexOf(name) == 0)
        ret.push(this.values[i]);
    return ret;
  });

  addMethod(ninjas, "find", function(first, last){
    var ret = [];
    for (var i = 0; i < this.values.length; i++)
      if (this.values[i] == (first + " " + last))
        ret.push(this.values[i]);
    return ret;
  });

  assert(ninjas.find().length == 3,
         "Found all ninjas");
  assert(ninjas.find("Sam").length == 1,
         "Found ninja by first name");
  assert(ninjas.find("Dean", "Edwards").length == 1,
         "Found ninja by first and last name");
  assert(ninjas.find("Alex", "Russell", "Jr") == null,
         "Found nothing");

</script>
```

Annotations for the listing:
- ❶ Declares an object to serve as the base, preloaded with some test data
- ❷ Binds a no-argument method to the base object
- ❸ Binds a single-argument method to the base object
- ❹ Binds a dual-argument method to the base object
- Tests the bound methods

Loading this page to run the tests shows that they all succeed, as shown in figure 4.6.

To test our method-overloading function, we define a base object containing some test data consisting of well-known JavaScript ninjas ❶, to which we'll bind three methods, all with the name find. The purpose of all these methods will be to find a ninja based upon criteria passed to the methods.

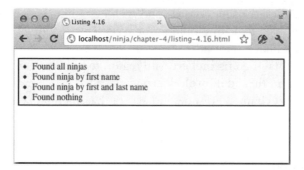

Figure 4.6   Ninjas found, all using the same overloaded method name `find()`

We declare and bind three versions of a `find()` method:

- One expecting no arguments that returns all ninjas ❷
- One that expects a single argument and that returns any ninjas whose name starts with the passed text ❸
- One that expects two arguments and that returns any ninjas whose first and last names match the passed strings ❹

This technique is especially nifty because these bound functions aren't actually stored in any typical data structure. Rather, they're all saved as references within closures. Again, we'll talk much more about closures in the next chapter.

It should be noted that there are some caveats to be aware of when using this particular technique:

- The overloading only works for different numbers of arguments; it doesn't differentiate based on type, argument name, or anything else. Which is frequently exactly what we'll want to do.
- Such overloaded methods will have some function call overhead. We'll want to take that into consideration in high-performance situations.

Nonetheless, this function provides a good example of some functional techniques, as well as an opportunity to introduce the `length` property of functions.

So far in this chapter, we've seen how functions are treated as first-class objects by JavaScript. Now let's look at one more thing we might do to functions as objects: checking to see if an object is a function.

4.5   *Checking for functions*

To close out our look at functions in JavaScript, let's take a look at how we can detect when a particular object is an instance of a function, and therefore something that can be called. It's a seemingly simple task, but it's not without its cross-browser issues.

Typically the `typeof` statement is more than sufficient to get the job done, such as in the following code:

```
function ninja(){}

assert(typeof ninja == "function",
       "Functions have a type of function");
```

This should be the typical way that we check if a value is a function, and this will always work if what we're testing is indeed a function. But there are a few cases where this test may yield some false-positives that we need to be aware of:

- *Firefox*—Doing a typeof on the HTML <object> element yields an inaccurate "function" result, instead of "object" as we might expect.
- *Internet Explorer*—When attempting to find the type of a function that was part of another window (such as an iframe) that no longer exists, its type will be reported as "unknown."
- *Safari*—Safari considers a DOM NodeList to be a function. So typeof document.body.childNodes == "function".

For situations in which these specific cases cause our code to trip up, we need a solution that will work in all of our target browsers, allowing us to detect if those particular functions (and non-functions) report themselves correctly.

There are a lot of possible avenues for exploration here; unfortunately almost all of the techniques end up in a dead-end. For example, we know that functions have apply() and call() methods, but those methods don't exist on Internet Explorer's problematic functions. One technique that *does* work fairly well is to convert the function to a string and determine its type based upon its serialized value, as in the following code:

```
function isFunction(fn) {
  return Object.prototype.toString.call(fn) === "[object Function]";
}
```

Even this test isn't perfect, but in situations like the preceding ones, it'll pass all the cases that we listed, giving us a correct value to work with.

> **NOTE** We'll be covering exactly what a function's prototype property is for and how it operates quite extensively in chapter 6. For now, just be aware that it's an important part of a constructor function that dictates what properties and methods will be part of a constructed object.

There is one notable exception, however. (Isn't there always?) Internet Explorer reports methods of DOM elements with a type of "object," like so: typeof domNode.getAttribute == "object" and typeof inputElem.focus == "object". So this particular technique doesn't cover this case.

The implementation of isFunction() requires a little bit of magic in order to make it work correctly: we access the internal toString() method of the Object.prototype. This particular method, by default, is designed to return a string that represents the internal representation of an object (such as a Function or String). Using this method, we can then call it against any object to access its true type. (This technique expands beyond just determining whether something is a function and also works for Strings, RegExp, Date, and other objects.)

The reason why we don't just directly call fn.toString() to try and get this result is twofold:

- Individual objects are likely to have their own toString() implementations.
- Most types in JavaScript already have a predefined toString() method that overrides the method provided by Object.prototype.

By accessing the Object.prototype method directly, we ensure that we're not getting an overridden version of toString(), and we end up with the exact information that we need.

This is just a quick taste of the strange world of cross-browser scripting. Writing code that works seamlessly in multiple browsers can be quite challenging, but it's a necessary skill for anyone who wants to write code that's robust and workable on the web. We'll explore lots more cross-browser strategies as we go along, and they'll be the entire focus of chapter 11.

4.6   Summary

In this chapter, we took the knowledge that we gained in chapter 3 and wielded it to solve a number of problems that we're likely to find in applications.

In particular

- Anonymous functions let us create smaller units of execution rather than large functions full of imperative statements.
- Looking at recursive functions, we learned how functions can be referenced in various ways, including:
  - By name
  - As a method (via an object property name)
  - By an inline name
  - Through the callee property of arguments
- Functions can have properties and those properties can be used to store any information we might wish to use, including
  - Storing functions in function properties for later reference and invocation.
  - Using function properties to create a cache (memoization).
- By controlling what function context is passed to a function invocation, we can "fool" methods into operating on objects that aren't the object that they're methods for. This can be useful for leveraging already existing methods on objects like Array and Math to operate on our own data.
- Functions can perform different operations based upon the arguments that are passed to it (function overloading). We can inspect the arguments list to determine what it is we'd like to do given the type or number of the passed arguments.
- An object can be checked to see if it's an instance of a function by testing if the result of the typeof operator is "function". This isn't without its cross-browser issues.

One of our examples, listing 4.15 to be precise, made heavy use of a concept known as a *closure*, which controls what data values are available to a function while it's executing. Let's spend a chapter taking a closer look at this essential concept.

Closing in on closures 5

In this chapter we discuss

- What closures are and how they work
- Using closures to simplify development
- Improving performance using closures
- Solving common scoping issues with closures

Closely tied to the functions that we learned all about in the previous chapters, closures are a defining feature of JavaScript. While scores of page authors get along writing on-page script without understanding the benefits of closures, the use of closures can not only help us reduce the amount and complexity of the script necessary to add advanced features to our pages, they allow us to do things that would simply not be possible, or would simply be too complex to be feasible, without them. The landscape of the language, and how we write our code using it, is forever shaped by the inclusion of closures.

Traditionally, closures have been a feature of purely functional programming languages. Having them cross over into mainstream development has been particularly encouraging, and it's not uncommon to find closures permeating JavaScript libraries, along with other advanced code bases, due to their ability to drastically simplify complex operations.

In this chapter, we'll explore what closures are all about and look at how we can use them to elevate our on-page script to world-class levels.

5.1 How closures work

Succinctly put, a *closure* is the scope created when a function is declared that allows the function to access and manipulate variables that are external to that function. Put another way, closures allow a function to access all the variables, as well as other functions, that are in scope when the function itself is declared.

That may seem rather intuitive until you remember that a declared function can be called at any later time, even *after* the scope in which it was declared has gone away.

This concept is probably best explained through code, so let's start small with the following listing.

Listing 5.1 A simple closure

```
<script type="text/javascript">

  var outerValue = 'ninja';          ❶ Defines a value in
                                          global scope

  function outerFunction() {         ❷ Declares a
    assert(outerValue == "ninja","I can see the ninja.");   function in
  }                                      global scope

  outerFunction();                   ❸ Executes the
                                          function
</script>
```

In this code example, we declare a variable ❶ and a function ❷ in the same scope—in this case, the global scope. Afterwards, we cause the function to execute ❸.

As can be seen in figure 5.1, the function is able to "see" and access the outerValue variable. You've likely written code such as this hundreds of times without realizing that you were creating a closure!

Not impressed? I guess that's not surprising. Because both the outer value and the outer function are declared in global scope, that scope (which is actually a closure) never goes away (as long as the page is loaded), and it's not surprising that the function can access the variable because it's still in scope and viable. Even though the closure exists, its benefits aren't yet clear.

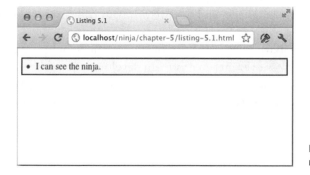

Figure 5.1 Our function has found the ninja, who was hiding in plain sight.

Let's spice it up a little in the next listing.

Listing 5.2   A not-so-simple closure

```
<script type="text/javascript">

  var outerValue = 'ninja';

  var later;

  function outerFunction() {
    var innerValue = 'samurai';

    function innerFunction() {
      assert(outerValue,"I can see the ninja.");
      assert(innerValue,"I can see the samurai.");
    }

    later = innerFunction;
  }

  outerFunction();

  later();

</script>
```

Declares an empty variable that we'll use later. See how proper naming helps us understand what something is used for?

Declares a value inside the function. This variable's scope is limited to the function and cannot be accessed from outside the function.

Declares an inner function within the outer function. Note that innerValue is in scope when we declare this function.

Stores a reference to the inner function in the later variable. Because later is in the global scope, it will allow us to call the function later.

Invokes the outer function, which causes the inner function to be declared and its reference assigned to later.

Invokes the inner function through later. We can't invoke it directly because its scope (along with innerValue) is limited to within outerFunction().

Let's over-analyze the code in innerFunction() and see if we predict what might happen.

The first assert is certain to pass: outerValue is in the global scope and is visible to everything. But what about the second?

We're executing the inner function *after* the outer function has been executed via the trick of copying a reference to the function to a global reference (later). When the inner function executes, the scope inside the outer function is long gone and not visible at the point at which we're invoking the function through later.

So we could very well expect the assert to fail, as innerValue is sure to be undefined. Right?

But when we run the test, we see the display shown in figure 5.2.

How can that be? What magic allows the innerValue variable to still be "alive" when we execute the inner function, long after the scope in which it was created has gone away? The answer, of course, is closures.

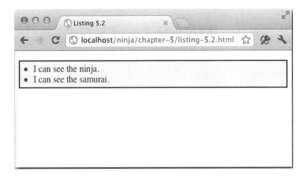

Figure 5.2   Despite trying to hide inside a function, the samurai has been spied!

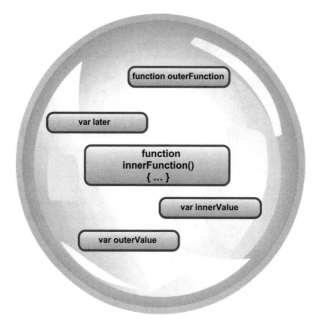

Figure 5.3   **Like a protective bubble, the closure for** `innerFunction()` **keeps the variables in the function's scope from being garbage-collected as long as the function exists.**

When we declared `innerFunction()` inside the outer function, not only was the function declaration defined, but a closure was also created that encompasses not only the function declaration, but also all variables that are in scope *at the point of the declaration*.

When `innerFunction()` eventually executes, even if it's executed *after* the scope in which it was declared goes away, it has access to the original scope in which it was declared through its closure, as shown in Figure 5.3.

That's what closures are all about. They create a "safety bubble," if you will, of the function and the variables that are in scope at the point of the function's declaration, so that the function has all it will need to execute.

This "bubble," containing the function and its variables, stays around as long as the function itself does.

Let's augment that example with a few additions to observe a few more core principles of closures. Take a look at the following listing, in which the additions are highlighted in bold.

Listing 5.3   What else closures can see

```
<script type="text/javascript">

  var outerValue = 'ninja';
  var later;

  function outerFunction() {
    var innerValue = 'samurai';

    function innerFunction(paramValue) {
      assert(outerValue,"Inner can see the ninja.");
```

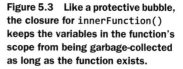

❶ Added a parameter to inner function.

Looks for a
later value in
the same
scope. Will **3**
this fail as
asserted? Or
pass?

```
        assert(innerValue,"Inner can see the samurai.");
        assert(paramValue,"Inner can see the wakizashi.");
        assert(tooLate,"Inner can see the ronin.");
    }

    later = innerFunction;
}
assert(!tooLate,"Outer can't see the ronin.");

var tooLate = 'ronin';

outerFunction();
later('wakizashi');

</script>
```

Tests if we can see the
parameter (duh!), and also
2 tests to see if the closure
includes variables that are
declared after the function is
declared. What do you think
will happen?

4 Declares a value after the
inner function declaration.

5 Calls the inner function to run its contained
tests. Can you predict the results?

Enough suspense ... here's what happens. To our previous code we've made a number
of interesting additions. We added a parameter ❶ to the inner function, and we pass
a value to the function when it's invoked through later ❺. We also added a variable
that's declared after the outer function declaration ❹.

When the tests inside ❷ and outside ❸ the inner function execute, we can see the
display in figure 5.4.

This shows three more interesting concepts regarding closures:

- Function parameters are included in the closure of that function. (Seems obvious, but now we've said it for sure.)
- All variables in an outer scope, even those declared *after* the function declaration, are included.
- Within the same scope, variables not yet defined cannot be forward-referenced.

The second and third points explain why the inner closure can see variable tooLate,
but the outer closure cannot.

It's important to note that while all of this structure isn't readily visible anywhere
(there's no "closure" object holding all of this information that you can inspect),
there's a direct cost to storing and referencing information in this manner. It's important to remember that each function that accesses information via a closure has a "ball
and chain," if you will, attached to it carrying this information around. So while closures

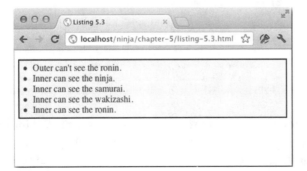

**Figure 5.4 Turns out that inner can see
farther than outer!**

are incredibly useful, they certainly aren't free of overhead. All that information needs to be held in memory until it's absolutely clear to the JavaScript engine that it will no longer be needed (and is safe to garbage-collect), or until the page unloads.

5.2   *Putting closures to work*

Now that we understand what closures are and how they work (at least at a high level), let's see how we can put them to work on our pages.

5.2.1   *Private variables*

A common use of closures is to encapsulate some information as a "private variable" of sorts—in other words, to limit the scope of such variables. Object-oriented code written in JavaScript is unable to use traditional private variables: properties of the object that are hidden from outside parties. But by using the concept of a closure, we can achieve an acceptable approximation, as demonstrated by the following code.

Listing 5.4   Using closures to approximate private variables

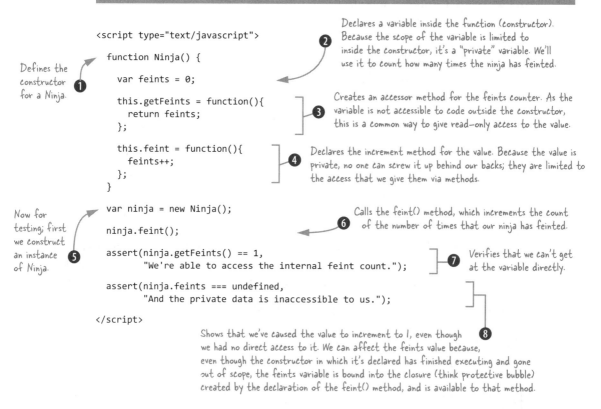

Defines the constructor for a Ninja. ❶

Declares a variable inside the function (constructor). Because the scope of the variable is limited to inside the constructor, it's a "private" variable. We'll use it to count how many times the ninja has feinted. ❷

Creates an accessor method for the feints counter. As the variable is not accessible to code outside the constructor, this is a common way to give read-only access to the value. ❸

Declares the increment method for the value. Because the value is private, no one can screw it up behind our backs; they are limited to the access that we give them via methods. ❹

Now for testing; first we construct an instance of Ninja. ❺

Calls the feint() method, which increments the count of the number of times that our ninja has feinted. ❻

Verifies that we can't get at the variable directly. ❼

```
<script type="text/javascript">

  function Ninja() {

    var feints = 0;

    this.getFeints = function(){
      return feints;
    };

    this.feint = function(){
      feints++;
    };
  }

var ninja = new Ninja();

ninja.feint();

assert(ninja.getFeints() == 1,
        "We're able to access the internal feint count.");

assert(ninja.feints === undefined,
        "And the private data is inaccessible to us.");

</script>
```

Shows that we've caused the value to increment to 1, even though we had no direct access to it. We can affect the feints value because, even though the constructor in which it's declared has finished executing and gone out of scope, the feints variable is bound into the closure (think protective bubble) created by the declaration of the feint() method, and is available to that method. ❽

In listing 5.4, we create a function that is to serve as a constructor ❶. We introduced the concept of using a function as a constructor in the previous chapter, and we'll be taking an in-depth look at it again in chapter 6. For now, just recall that when using the new keyword on a function ❺, a new object instance is created and the function is called, with that new object as its context, to serve as a constructor to that object. So this within the function is a newly instantiated object.

Within the constructor, we define a variable to hold state, feints ❷. The JavaScript scoping rules for this variable limit its accessibility to *within* the constructor. To give access to the value of the variable from code that's outside the scope, we define an *accessor* method ❸, getFeints(), which can be used to read, but not write to, the private variable. (Accessor methods are frequently called "getters.")

An implementation method, feint(), is then created to give us control over the value of the variable in a controlled fashion ❹. In a real-world application, this might be some business method; in this example, it merely increments the value of feints.

After the constructor has been established, we invoke it with the new operator ❺ and then call the feint() method ❻.

Our tests ❼ ❽ show that we can use the accessor method to obtain the value of the private variable, but that we cannot access it directly. This effectively prevents us from being able to make uncontrolled changes to the value of the variable, just as if it were a private variable in a fully object-oriented language.

This situation is depicted in figure 5.5.

This allows the state of the ninja to be maintained within a method, without letting it be directly accessed by a user of the method, because the variable is available to the inner methods via their closures, but not to code that lies outside the constructor.

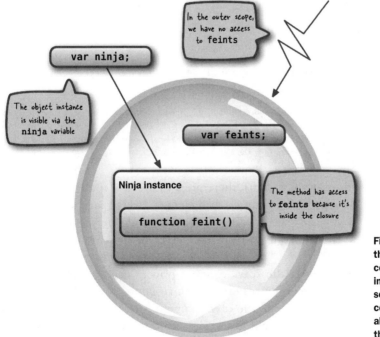

Figure 5.5 Hiding the variable inside the constructor keeps it invisible to the outer scope, but where it counts, the variable is alive and well inside the closure.

This is a glimpse into the world of object-oriented JavaScript, which we'll explore in much greater depth in the upcoming chapter.

For now, let's focus on another common use of closures.

5.2.2   Callbacks and timers

Another one of the most common areas in which we can use closures is when dealing with callbacks or timers. In both cases, a function is being asynchronously called at an unspecified later time, and within such functions we frequently need to access outside data.

Closures act as an intuitive way of accessing that data, especially when we wish to avoid creating extra top-level variables just to store that information. Let's look at a simple example of an Ajax request, using the jQuery JavaScript Library, as shown in the following listing.

Listing 5.5   Using closures from a callback for an Ajax request

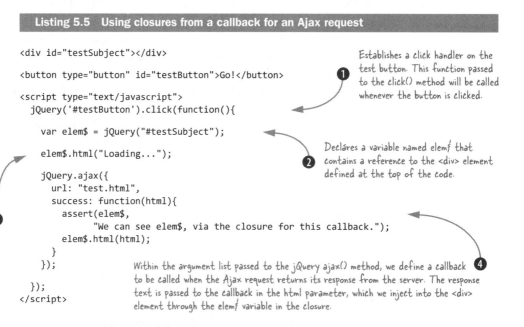

```
<div id="testSubject"></div>

<button type="button" id="testButton">Go!</button>
```
❶ Establishes a click handler on the test button. This function passed to the click() method will be called whenever the button is clicked.

```
<script type="text/javascript">
  jQuery('#testButton').click(function(){

    var elem$ = jQuery("#testSubject");
```
❷ Declares a variable named elem$ that contains a reference to the <div> element defined at the top of the code.

```
    elem$.html("Loading...");

    jQuery.ajax({
      url: "test.html",
      success: function(html){
        assert(elem$,
            "We can see elem$, via the closure for this callback.");
        elem$.html(html);
      }
    });

  });
</script>
```
❸ Preloads the <div> with some text to let the users know that something's going on.

❹ Within the argument list passed to the jQuery ajax() method, we define a callback to be called when the Ajax request returns its response from the server. The response text is passed to the callback in the html parameter, which we inject into the <div> element through the elem$ variable in the closure.

Even though this example is short, there are a number of interesting things going on in listing 5.5. We start with an empty <div> element, which on the click of a button ❶ we want to load with the text "Loading..." ❸. Meanwhile an Ajax request will be under way that will fetch new content from the server to load into that <div> when the response returns.

We need to reference the <div> element twice: once to preload it, and once to load it with the server content whenever the response comes back from the server. We *could* look up a reference to the <div> element each time, but we want to be stingy regarding performance, so we'll just look it up once and store it away in a variable named elem$ ❷.

TIP Using the $ sign as a suffix or prefix is a jQuery convention to indicate that the variable holds a jQuery object reference.

Within the arguments passed to the jQuery ajax() method, we define an anonymous function ❹ to serve as the response callback. Within this callback, we reference the elem$ variable via the closure and use it to stuff the response text into the <div>.

Even though the code was fairly short, a lot of complicated things went on in that example. Be sure you understand why the callback can access elem$ before proceeding. If you like, load the example into a browser and set a breakpoint at the callback to look around at what's in scope when you get there.

Now let's look at the slightly more complicated example that creates a simple animation in the next listing.

Listing 5.6 Using a closure in a timer interval callback

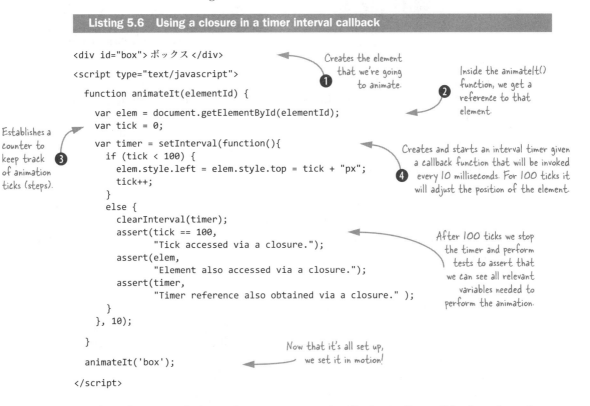

```
<div id="box"> ボックス </div>
<script type="text/javascript">
  function animateIt(elementId) {
    var elem = document.getElementById(elementId);
    var tick = 0;
    var timer = setInterval(function(){
      if (tick < 100) {
        elem.style.left = elem.style.top = tick + "px";
        tick++;
      }
      else {
        clearInterval(timer);
        assert(tick == 100,
            "Tick accessed via a closure.");
        assert(elem,
            "Element also accessed via a closure.");
        assert(timer,
            "Timer reference also obtained via a closure." );
      }
    }, 10);

  }
  animateIt('box');

</script>
```

Creates the element that we're going to animate. ❶

Inside the animateIt() function, we get a reference to that element. ❷

Establishes a counter to keep track of animation ticks (steps). ❸

Creates and starts an interval timer given a callback function that will be invoked ❹ every 10 milliseconds. For 100 ticks it will adjust the position of the element.

After 100 ticks we stop the timer and perform tests to assert that we can see all relevant variables needed to perform the animation.

Now that it's all set up, we set it in motion!

Loading the example into a browser, we see the display in figure 5.6 when the animation has completed.

What's especially important about the code in listing 5.6 is that it uses a single anonymous function ❹ to accomplish the animation of the target element ❶. That function accesses three variables, via a closure, to control the animation process.

The three variables (the reference to the DOM element ❷, the tick counter ❸, and the timer reference ❹) all must be maintained *across* the steps of the animation. And we need to keep them out of the global scope.

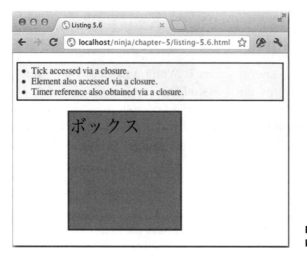

Figure 5.6 Closures can be used to keep track of the steps of an animation

But why? The example will still work fine if we move the variables out of the animateIt() function and into the global scope. So why all the arm flailing about not polluting the global scope?

Go ahead and move the variables into the global scope and verify that the example still works. Now modify the example to animate two elements: add another element with a unique ID, and call the animateIt() method with that ID right after the original call.

The problem immediately becomes obvious. If we keep the variables in the global scope, we need a set of three variables for *each* animation—otherwise they'll step all over each other trying to use the same set of variables to keep track of multiple states.

By defining the variables *inside* the function, and by relying upon the closures to make them available to the timer callback invocations, each animation gets its own private "bubble" of variables, as shown in figure 5.7.

Without closures, doing multiple things at once, whether event handling, animations, or even Ajax requests, would be incredibly difficult. If you've been waiting for a reason to care about closures, this is it!

There's another important concept that this example makes clear. Not only do we see the values that these variables had at the time the closure was created, but we can also update them within the closure while the function within the closure executes. In other words, the closure isn't simply a snapshot of the state of the scope at the time of creation, but an active encapsulation of that state that can be modified as long as the closure exists.

This example is a particularly good one for demonstrating how the concept of closures is capable of producing some surprisingly intuitive and concise code. By simply including the variables in the animateIt() function, we create an implied closure without needing any complex syntax.

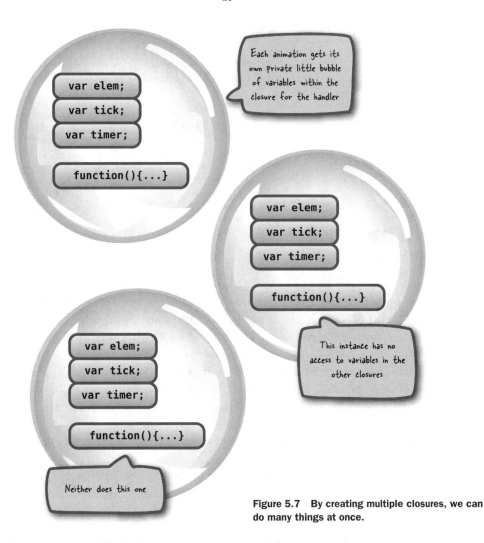

Figure 5.7 By creating multiple closures, we can do many things at once.

Now that we've seen closures used in various callbacks, let's take a look at some of the other ways in which they can be applied, starting with using them to bend function contexts to our wills.

5.3 Binding function contexts

During our discussion of function contexts in the previous chapter, we saw how the call() and apply() methods could be used to manipulate the context of a function. While this manipulation can be incredibly useful, it can also be potentially harmful to object-oriented code.

Consider the following code, in which a function that serves as an object method is bound to a DOM element as an event listener.

Listing 5.7   Binding a specific context to a function

Creates a button element to which we'll assign event handler. **❶**

```
<button id="test">Click Me!</button>

<script type="text/javascript">
  var button = {

    clicked: false,

    click: function(){
      this.clicked = true;
      assert(button.clicked,"The button has been clicked");
    }

  };

  var elem = document.getElementById("test");
  elem.addEventListener("click",button.click,false);

</script>
```

❷ Defines an object to retain state regarding our button. With it, we'll track whether the button has been clicked or not.

❸ Declares the method that we'll use as the click handler. Because it's a method of the object, we use this within the function to get a reference to the object.

❹ Within the method, we test that the button state has been correctly changed after a click.

❺ Establishes the click handler on the button.

In this example, we have a button **❶**, and we want to know whether it has ever been clicked or not. In order to retain that state information, we create a backing object named button **❷**, in which we'll store the clicked state. In that object, we'll also define a method that will serve as an event handler **❸** that will fire when the button is clicked. That method, which we establish as a click handler for the button **❺**, sets the clicked property to true and then tests **❹** that the state was properly recorded in the backing object.

When we load the example into a browser and click the button, we see by the display of figure 5.8 that something is amiss; the stricken text indicates that the test has failed.

The code in listing 5.7 fails because the context of the click function is *not* referring to the button object as we intended.

Recalling the lessons of chapter 3, if we had called the function via

```
button.click()
```

the context *would* indeed have been the button. But in our example, the event-handling system of the browser defines the context of the invocation to be the target element of the event, which causes the context to be the <button> element, not the button object. So we set our click state on the wrong object!

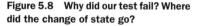

Figure 5.8   Why did our test fail? Where did the change of state go?

Setting the context to the target element when an event handler is invoked is a perfectly reasonable default, and one that we can, and *will*, count on in many situations. But in this instance, it's in our way. Luckily, closures give us a way around this.

We can force a particular function invocation to always have a desired context by using a mix of anonymous functions, apply(), and closures. Take a look at the following code, which updates the code of listing 5.7 with additions (in bold) to bend the function context to our wills.

Listing 5.8 Binding a specific context to an event handler

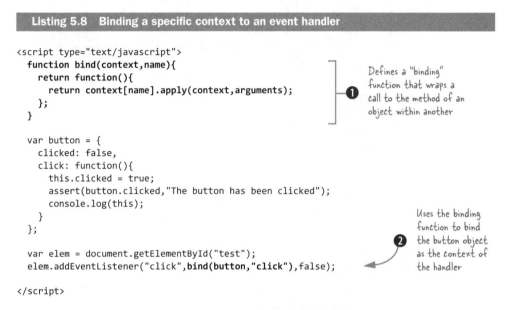

```
<script type="text/javascript">
  function bind(context,name){
    return function(){
      return context[name].apply(context,arguments);
    };
  }

  var button = {
    clicked: false,
    click: function(){
      this.clicked = true;
      assert(button.clicked,"The button has been clicked");
      console.log(this);
    }
  };

  var elem = document.getElementById("test");
  elem.addEventListener("click",bind(button,"click"),false);

</script>
```

❶ Defines a "binding" function that wraps a call to the method of an object within another

❷ Uses the binding function to bind the button object as the context of the handler

The secret sauce that we've added here is the bind() method ❶. This method is designed to create and return a new anonymous function that calls the original function, using apply(), so that we can force the context to be whatever object we want. In this case, it's whatever object we pass to bind() as its first argument. This context, along with the name of the method to call as the end function, is remembered through the anonymous function's closure, which includes the parameters passed to bind().

Later, when we establish the event handler, we use the bind() method to specify the event handler rather than using button.click directly ❷. This causes the wrapping anonymous function to become the event handler. And when the button is clicked, that anonymous function will be invoked, which will in turn call the click method, forcing the context to be the button object.

The relationships created are depicted in figure 5.9.

This particular implementation of a binding function makes the assumption that we're going to be using an existing method of an object (a function attached as a property), and that we want that object to be the context. With that assumption,

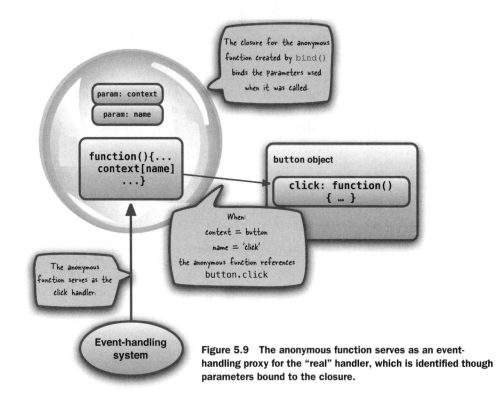

Figure 5.9 The anonymous function serves as an event-handling proxy for the "real" handler, which is identified though parameters bound to the closure.

bind() only needs two pieces of information: a reference to the object containing the method, and the name of the method.

This bind() function is a simplified version of a function popularized by the Prototype JavaScript library, which promotes writing code in a clean and classical object-oriented manner.

The original Prototype version of the method looks something like the following code.

Listing 5.9 An example of the function-binding code used in the Prototype library

```
Function.prototype.bind = function(){
  var fn = this, args = Array.prototype.slice.call(arguments),
    object = args.shift();

  return function(){
    return fn.apply(object,
      args.concat(Array.prototype.slice.call(arguments)));
  };
};

var myObject = {};
function myFunction(){
  return this == myObject;
}
```

❶ Adds the bind() method to all functions via its prototype. That's something we'll see in the next chapter.

```
assert( !myFunction(), "Context is not set yet" );

var aFunction = myFunction.bind(myObject)
assert( aFunction(), "Context is set properly" );
```

This method is quite similar to the function we implemented in listing 5.8, but with a couple of notable additions. To start, it attaches itself to all functions, rather than presenting itself as a globally accessible function ❶ by adding itself as a property of the prototype of JavaScript's Function. We'll be exploring prototypes in chapter 6, but for now just think of a prototype as the central blueprint for a JavaScript type; in this case, for all functions.

We'd use this function, bound as a method to all functions (via the prototype), like so: var boundFunction = myFunction.bind(myObject). Additionally, with this method, we're able to bind arguments to the anonymous function. This allows us to pre-specify some of the arguments, in a form of partial function application (which we'll discuss in the very next section).

It's important to realize that Prototype's bind() (or our own implementation of it) isn't meant to be a replacement for methods like apply() or call(). Remember, the underlying purpose is controlling the context for delayed execution via the anonymous function and closure. This important distinction makes apply() and call() especially useful for delayed execution callbacks for event handlers and timers.

> **NOTE** A native bind() method is defined on functions as of JavaScript 1.8.5.

Now, what about those prefilled function arguments we mentioned a moment ago?

5.4   *Partially applying functions*

"Partially applying" a function is a particularly interesting technique in which we can *prefill* arguments to a function before it's even executed. In effect, partially applying a function returns a new function with predefined arguments, which we can later call.

This sort of proxy function—one that stands in for another function and calls that function when executed—is exactly the technique we used in the previous section to "bind" specific contexts to function invocations. Here we'll put the same technique to a different use.

This technique of filling in the first few arguments of a function (and returning a new function) is typically called *currying*. As usual, this is best understood through examples. But before we look at how we'll actually implement currying, let's look at how we might want to use it.

Let's say that we wanted to split a CSV (comma-separated value) string into its component parts, ignoring extraneous whitespace. We can easily do that with the String's split() method, supplying an appropriate regular expression:

```
var elements = "val1,val2,val3".split(/,\s*/);
```

> **NOTE** If you're rusty with regular expressions, that's OK. This one just says to match a comma followed by any amount of whitespace. You'll be an old pro at regular expressions once you've worked your way through chapter 7.

But having to remember and type that regular expression all the time can be tiresome. Let's implement a csv() method to do it for us and imagine a method that does it using currying, as shown in the following listing.

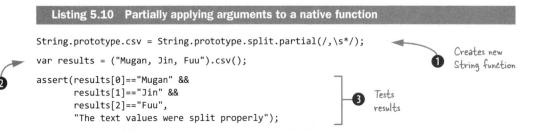

Listing 5.10   Partially applying arguments to a native function

```
String.prototype.csv = String.prototype.split.partial(/,\s*/);        ❶ Creates new
                                                                         String function
var results = ("Mugan, Jin, Fuu").csv();

assert(results[0]=="Mugan" &&
       results[1]=="Jin" &&                          ❸ Tests
       results[2]=="Fuu",                              results
       "The text values were split properly");
```

❷ Invokes curried function

In listing 5.10 we've taken the String's split() method and have imagined a partial() method (yet to be implemented, but we'll take care of that in listing 5.12) that we can use to prefill the regular expression upon which to split ❶. The result is a new function named csv() that we can call at any point to convert a list of comma-separated values ❷ into an array without having to deal with messy regular expressions.

Figure 5.10 shows the results we get when we run our test ❸ in the browser. The implementation that we're about to create works as expected. If only we had such presaging assurance in day-to-day development!

With all that in mind, let's look at how a partial/curry method is (more or less) implemented in the Prototype library, as seen in the next listing.

Listing 5.11   An example of a curry function (filling in the first specified arguments)

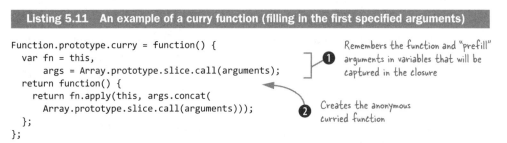

```
Function.prototype.curry = function() {
  var fn = this,
      args = Array.prototype.slice.call(arguments);        ❶ Remembers the function and "prefill"
  return function() {                                         arguments in variables that will be
    return fn.apply(this, args.concat(                        captured in the closure
    Array.prototype.slice.call(arguments)));
  };                                                        ❷ Creates the anonymous
};                                                            curried function
```

This technique is another good example of using a closure to remember state. In this case, we want to remember the function that we're augmenting (the this parameter is never included in any closure, because each function invocation has its own version of

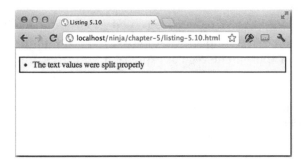

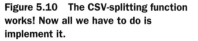

Figure 5.10   The CSV-splitting function works! Now all we have to do is implement it.

this) and the arguments to be prefilled ❶ and transfer them to the newly constructed function ❷. This new function will have the filled-in arguments and the new arguments concatenated together and passed. The result is a method that allows us to prefill arguments, giving us a new, simpler function that we can use.

While this style of partial function application is perfectly useful, we can do better. What if we wanted to fill in *any* missing argument from a given function, not just those at the beginning of the argument list?

Implementations of this style of partial function application have existed in other languages, but Oliver Steele was one of the first to demonstrate it with his Functional.js library (http://osteele.com/sources/javascript/functional/). The following listing shows a possible implementation (and this is the implementation that we used to make listing 5.10 work).

```
Function.prototype.partial = function() {
  var fn = this, args = Array.prototype.slice.call(arguments);
  return function() {
    var arg = 0;
    for (var i = 0; i < args.length && arg < arguments.length; i++) {
      if (args[i] === undefined) {
        args[i] = arguments[arg++];
      }
    }
    return fn.apply(this, args);
  };
};
```

This implementation is fundamentally similar to Prototype's curry() method, but it has a couple of important differences. Notably, the user can specify arguments anywhere in the parameter list that will be filled in later by specifying the undefined value for "missing" arguments. To accommodate this, we've increased the abilities of our argument-merging technique. Effectively, we loop through the arguments that are passed in and look for the appropriate gaps (the undefined values), filling in the missing pieces as we go along.

Thinking back to the example of constructing a string-splitting function, let's look at some other ways in which this new functionality could be used. To start, we could construct a function that has the ability to be easily delayed:

```
var delay = setTimeout.partial(undefined, 10);

delay(function(){
  assert(true,
      "A call to this function will be delayed 10 ms.");
});
```

This snippet creates a new function, named delay(), into which we can pass another function that will be called asynchronously after 10 milliseconds.

We could also create a simple function for binding events:

```
var bindClick = document.body.addEventListener
  .partial("click", undefined, false);

bindClick(function(){
  assert(true, "Click event bound via curried function.");
});
```

This technique could be used to construct simple helper methods for event-binding in a library. The result would be a simpler API where the end user wouldn't be inconvenienced by unnecessary function arguments, reducing them to a simpler function call.

Up to this point, we've used closures to reduce the complexity of our code, demonstrating some of the power that functional JavaScript programming has to offer. Now let's continue to explore using closures in code to add advanced behaviors and further simplifications.

5.5   *Overriding function behavior*

A fun side effect of having so much control over how functions work in JavaScript is that we can completely manipulate their internal behavior, unbeknownst to anyone calling the code. Specifically there are two techniques: the modification of how existing functions work (no closures needed), and the production of new self-modifying functions based upon existing static functions.

Remember memoization from chapter 4? Let's take another look.

5.5.1   *Memoization*

As we learned in chapter 4, memoization is the process of building a function that is capable of remembering its previously computed answers. As we demonstrated in that chapter, it's pretty straightforward to introduce memoization into an existing function. But we don't always have access to the functions that we'd like to optimize.

The following listing shows a method named `memoized()` that we can use to remember return values from an existing function. This implementation doesn't involve closures—we'll see that shortly.

> **Listing 5.13   A memoization method for functions**

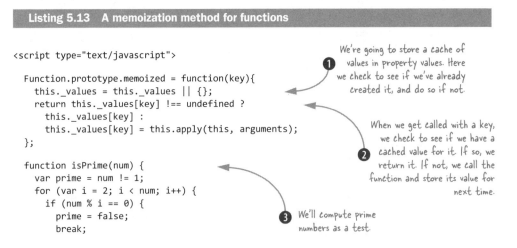

```
<script type="text/javascript">

  Function.prototype.memoized = function(key){
    this._values = this._values || {};
    return this._values[key] !== undefined ?
      this._values[key] :
      this._values[key] = this.apply(this, arguments);
  };

  function isPrime(num) {
    var prime = num != 1;
    for (var i = 2; i < num; i++) {
      if (num % i == 0) {
        prime = false;
        break;
```

1 We're going to store a cache of values in property values. Here we check to see if we've already created it, and do so if not.

2 When we get called with a key, we check to see if we have a cached value for it. If so, we return it. If not, we call the function and store its value for next time.

3 We'll compute prime numbers as a test.

```
    }
  }
  return prime;
}
assert(isPrime.memoized(5),
       "The function works; 5 is prime.");
assert(isPrime._values[5],
       "The answer has been cached.");
```

4 Tests that the function returns the right value and that the value is cached.

```
</script>
```

In this code, we use the familiar isPrime() function **3** from the previous chapter, and it's still painfully slow and awkward, making it a prime candidate for memoization.

Our ability to introspect into an existing function is limited, but we can easily add new methods to a function, or indeed to *all* functions via the prototype. We'll add a new memoized() method to all functions that gives us the ability to wrap the functions and attach properties that are associated with the function itself. This will allow us to create a data store (cache) in which all of our precomputed values can be saved. Let's look at how that works.

To start, before doing any computation or retrieval of values, we must make sure that a data store exists and that it's attached to the parent function itself. We do this via a simple short-circuiting expression **1**:

```
this._values = this._values || {};
```

If the _values property already exists, we just resave that reference to the property; otherwise we create the new data store (an initially empty object) and store its reference in the _values property.

When we call a function through this method, we look into the data store **2** to see if the stored value already exists, and if so, return that value. Otherwise we compute the value and store it in the cache for any subsequent calls.

What's interesting about the preceding code is that we do the computation and the save in a single step. The value is computed with the apply() call to the function, and it's saved directly into the data store. But this statement is within the return statement, meaning that the resulting value is *also* returned from the parent function. So the whole chain of events—computing the value, saving the value, and returning the value—is done within a single logical unit of code.

Testing the code **4** shows that we can compute values, and that the value is cached.

The problem with this approach is that a caller of the isPrime() function must remember to call it through its memoized() method in order to reap the benefits of memoization. That won't do at all.

With the memoizing method at our disposal to monitor the values coming in and out of an existing function, let's explore how we can use closures to produce a new function that's capable of having all of its function calls be memoized automatically without the caller having to do anything weird like remember to call memoized(). The result is shown in the following listing.

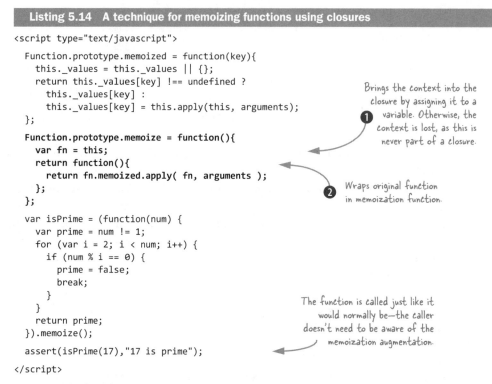

Listing 5.14   A technique for memoizing functions using closures

```
<script type="text/javascript">

  Function.prototype.memoized = function(key){
    this._values = this._values || {};
    return this._values[key] !== undefined ?
      this._values[key] :
      this._values[key] = this.apply(this, arguments);
  };

  Function.prototype.memoize = function(){
    var fn = this;
    return function(){
      return fn.memoized.apply( fn, arguments );
    };
  };

  var isPrime = (function(num) {
    var prime = num != 1;
    for (var i = 2; i < num; i++) {
      if (num % i == 0) {
        prime = false;
        break;
      }
    }
    return prime;
  }).memoize();

  assert(isPrime(17),"17 is prime");

</script>
```

Brings the context into the closure by assigning it to a ❶ *variable. Otherwise, the context is lost, as this is never part of a closure.*

❷ *Wraps original function in memoization function.*

The function is called just like it would normally be—the caller doesn't need to be aware of the memoization augmentation.

Listing 5.14 builds upon our previous example, in which we created the `memoized()` method, adding yet another new method, `memoize()`. This method returns a function that wraps the original function with the `memoized()` method applied, such that it will always return the memoized version of the original function ❷. This eliminates the need for the caller to apply `memoized()` themselves.

Note that within the `memoize()` method we construct a closure remembering the original function (obtained via the context) that we want to memoize ❶ by copying the context into a variable. This is a common technique: each function has its own context, so contexts are never part of a closure. But context values can become part of a closure by establishing a variable reference to the value. By remembering the original function, we can return a new function that will always call our `memoized()` method, giving us direct access to the memoized instance of the function.

In listing 5.14 we also show a comparatively strange means of defining a new function when we define `isPrime()`. Because we want `isPrime()` to always be memoized, we need to construct a temporary function whose results won't be memoized. We take this anonymous, prime-figuring function and memoize it immediately, giving us a new function, which is assigned to the `isPrime` variable. We'll discuss this construct in depth in section 5.6. Note that, in this case, it's impossible to compute whether a number is prime in a non-memoized fashion. Only a single `isPrime()` function exists, and it completely encapsulates the original function, hidden within a closure.

Listing 5.14 is a good demonstration of obscuring original functionality via a closure. This can be particularly useful from a development perspective, but it can also be crippling: if we obscure too much of our code, it becomes unextendable, something that is clearly undesirable. But hooks for later modification often counteract this. We'll discuss this matter in depth later in the book.

5.5.2 *Function wrapping*

Function wrapping is a technique for encapsulating the logic of a function while overwriting it with new or extended functionality in a single step. It's best used when we wish to override some previous behavior of a function, while still allowing certain use cases to execute.

A common use is when implementing pieces of cross-browser code in situations where a deficiency in a browser must be accounted for. Consider, for example, working around a bug in Opera's implementation of accessing title attributes. In the Prototype library, the function-wrapping technique is employed to work around this bug.

As opposed to having a large `if-else` block within its `readAttribute()` function (a technique that's debatably messy and not a particularly good separation of concerns), Prototype instead opted to completely override the old method by using function wrapping and deferring the rest of the functionality to the original function.

Let's take a look at that. First, we create a wrapping function used to, well, wrap functions, and then we use that function to create a wrapper for Prototype's `read-Attribute()` method.

Listing 5.15 Wrapping an old function with a new piece of functionality

① Defines generic wrapping function, taking as parameters an object whose method is to be wrapped, name of object method to be wrapped, and function to be executed in place of original method.

```
function wrap(object, method, wrapper) {

    var fn = object[method];

    return object[method] = function() {
        return wrapper.apply(this, [fn.bind(this)].concat(
            Array.prototype.slice.call(arguments)));
    };
}

if (Prototype.Browser.Opera) {

    wrap(Element.Methods, "readAttribute",
        function(original, elem, attr) {
        return attr == "title" ?
            elem.title :
            original(elem, attr);
    });

}
```

② Remembers original function so that we can later reference it via a closure should we desire.

③ "Wraps" original function by creating new function that calls function passed as wrapper. Within new function, wrapper function is called with apply(), forcing function context to object and passing as arguments the original method (using bind() to force its function context to object) and original arguments.

Uses Prototype mechanism for browser detection—remember, this code is from Prototype so it's eating its own dog food—to determine if the function needs to be wrapped.

Uses wrap() function to substitute new functionality if attr argument is "title" and uses original function if not.

Let's dig in to how the wrap() function works. It's passed a base object, the name of the method within that object to wrap, and the new wrapper function. To start, we save a reference to the original method in fn ❶; we'll access it later via the closure of an anonymous function that we're about to create.

We then proceed to overwrite the method with a new anonymous function ❷. This new function executes the passed wrapper function (brought to us via the closure), passing it an augmented arguments list. We want the first argument to be the original function that we're overriding, so we create an array containing a reference to the original function (whose context is bound, using the bind() method from listing 5.8, to be the same as the wrapper's), and add the original arguments to this array. The apply() method, as we know from chapter 3, uses this array as the argument list.

Prototype uses the wrap() function to override an existing method (in this case readAttribute()), replacing it with a new function ❸. But this new function still has access to the original functionality (in the form of the original argument) provided by the method. This means that a function can be safely overridden while still retaining access to the original functionality.

The use of the closure created by the anonymous wrapping function is depicted in figure 5.11.

The result of all this is a reusable wrap() function that we can use to override the existing functionality of object methods in an unobtrusive manner, making efficient use of closures.

Now let's look at an often-used syntax that looks deucedly odd if you've never seen it before, but that's an important part of functional programming.

Figure 5.11   The anonymous wrapping function has access to the original function, as well as the passed wrapper function, via the closure.

5.6   *Immediate functions*

An important construct used in advanced functional JavaScript, and which relies upon making good use of closures, is as follows:

```
(function(){})()
```

This single pattern of code is incredibly versatile and ends up giving the JavaScript language a ton of unforeseen power. But as its syntax, with all those braces and parentheses, may seem a little strange, let's deconstruct what's going on within it step by step.

First, let's ignore the contents of the first set of parentheses, and examine the construct:

```
(...)()
```

We know that we can call any function using the `functionName()` syntax, but in place of the function name we can use *any* expression that references a function instance. That's why we can call a function referenced by a variable that refers to the function using the variable name, like this:

```
var someFunction = function(){ ... };
result = someFunction();
```

As with other expressions, if we want an operator—in this case, the function call operator ()—to be applied to an entire expression, we'd enclose that expression in a set of parentheses. Consider how the expressions (3 + 4) * 5 and 3 + (4 * 5) differ from each other.

That means that in (...)(), the first set of parentheses is merely a set of delimiters enclosing an expression, whereas the second set is an operator. It'd be perfectly legal to change our example to the following, in which the expression that references the function is enclosed in parentheses:

```
var someFunction = function(){ ... };
result = (someFunction)();
```

It's just a bit confusing that each set of parentheses has a very different meaning. If the function call operator were something like || rather than (), the expression (...)|| would likely be less confusing.

In the end, whatever is within the first set of parentheses will be expected to be a reference to a function to be executed. Although the first set of parentheses is not *needed* in our latest example, the syntax is perfectly valid.

Now, rather than the variable name, if we directly provided the anonymous function (omitting any function body for the moment for brevity) within the first set of parentheses, we'd end up with this syntax:

```
(function(){...})();
```

If we go ahead and provide a body for the function, the syntax expands to the following:

```
(function(){
  statement-1;
  statement-2;
```

```
  ...
  statement-n;
})();
```

The result of this code is an expression that does all of the following in a single statement:

- Creates a function instance
- Executes the function
- Discards the function (as there are no longer any references to it after the statement has ended)

Additionally, because we're dealing with a function that can have a closure just like any other, we also have access to all the outside variables and parameters that are in the same scope as the statement, during the brief life of the function. As it turns out, this simple construct, called an *immediate function*, ends up being immensely useful, as we're about to see.

Let's start by looking at how scope interacts with immediate functions.

5.6.1 *Temporary scope and private variables*

Using immediate functions, we can start to build up interesting enclosures for our work. Because the function is executed immediately, and, as with all functions, all the variables inside of it are confined to its inner scope, we can use it to create a temporary scope, within which our state can be contained.

> **NOTE** Keep in mind that variables in JavaScript are scoped to the function within which they're defined. By creating a temporary function, we can use this to our advantage and create a temporary scope for our variables to live in.

Let's see how such temporary and self-contained scopes work.

CREATING A SELF-CONTAINED SCOPE
Consider the following snippet:

```
(function(){
  var numClicks = 0;
  document.addEventListener("click", function(){
    alert( ++numClicks );
  }, false);
})();
```

Because the immediate function is executed immediately (hence its name), the click handler is also bound right away. The important thing to note is that a closure is created for the handler that includes numClicks, allowing the numClicks variable to persist along with the handler, and be referenceable by the handler *but nowhere else.*

This is one of the most common ways in which immediate functions are used: as simple, self-contained wrappers for functionality. The variables needed for the unit of functionality are trapped in the closure, but they aren't visible anywhere else. How's that for modularity?

But it's important to remember that because immediate functions *are* functions, they can be used in interesting ways, like this:

```
document.addEventListener("click", (function(){
  var numClicks = 0;
  return function(){
    alert( ++numClicks );
  };
})(), false);
```

This is an alternative, and debatably more confusing, version of our previous snippet.

In this case, we're again creating an immediate function, but this time we return a value from it: a function to serve as the event handler. Because this is just like any other expression, the returned value is passed to the addEventListener() method. But the inner function that we created still gets the necessary numClicks variable via its closure.

This technique involves a very different way of looking at scope. In many languages, you can scope things based upon the block they're in. In JavaScript, variables are scoped based upon the *closure* they're in.

Moreover, using this simple construct (immediate functions), we can now scope variables to block, and sub-block, levels. The ability to scope some code to a unit as small as an argument within a function call is incredibly powerful, and it truly shows the flexibility of the language.

ENFORCING NAMES IN A SCOPE VIA PARAMETERS

Up until now, we've used immediate functions that don't get passed any parameters. But as they're functions like any other, we can also use the immediate function call to pass arguments to the immediate function that, like any other function, references those arguments via the parameter names.

Here's an example:

```
(function(what){ alert(what); })('Hi there!');
```

A more practical example of using this construct is on pages that mix jQuery with another library, such as Prototype.

jQuery introduces the name jQuery into the global scope as the name of its primary function. It also introduces the name $ as an alias to that function. The name $, however, is rather popular with JavaScript libraries, and Prototype uses it too. Recognizing this, jQuery has a supported way to revert the use of $ to any other library that wants to use it (jQuery.noConflict() if you're curious). On such pages, we must use jQuery to reference jQuery, while $ references Prototype. Or do we?

We're used to using $ for jQuery, and we'd like to be able to do so without worrying about what's going on in the rest of the page. This is especially true for reusable code that could end up on many pages, of whose makeup and nature we are unaware.

With immediate functions, we can assign the $ *back* to jQuery within the "bubble" created by an immediate function. Observe the following code.

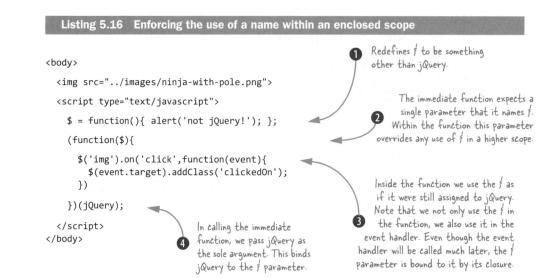

Listing 5.16   Enforcing the use of a name within an enclosed scope

```
<body>
  <img src="../images/ninja-with-pole.png">
  <script type="text/javascript">
    $ = function(){ alert('not jQuery!'); };
    (function($){
      $('img').on('click',function(event){
        $(event.target).addClass('clickedOn');
      })
    })(jQuery);
  </script>
</body>
```

❶ Redefines $ to be something other than jQuery.

❷ The immediate function expects a single parameter that it names $. Within the function this parameter overrides any use of $ in a higher scope.

❸ Inside the function we use the $ as if it were still assigned to jQuery. Note that we not only use the $ in the function, we also use it in the event handler. Even though the event handler will be called much later, the $ parameter is bound to it by its closure.

❹ In calling the immediate function, we pass jQuery as the sole argument. This binds jQuery to the $ parameter.

In this example, we first redefine $ to mean something other than jQuery ❶. This could also happen as a result of including Prototype on the page, or any other library or code that usurps the $ name.

But because we want to use the $ to refer to jQuery in a fragment of code, we define an immediate function that defines a single parameter named $ ❷. Within the function body, the parameter $ will take precedence over the global variable $. Whatever we pass to the function will become whatever $ refers to *within* the function. By passing jQuery to the immediate function ❹, the value of $ within the function is jQuery.

Note that the $ parameter becomes part of the closure of any functions created within the function body ❸, including the event handler that we pass to jQuery's on() method. So even though the event handler is likely to execute long after the immediate function has executed and been discarded, the handler can use the $ to refer to jQuery.

This is a technique employed by many jQuery plugin authors whose code will be included in pages that they didn't write. It's unsafe to assume that $ refers to jQuery, so they can include the plugin code inside an immediate function that lets them safely use $ to refer to jQuery.

Before we move on, let's look at another example from Prototype.

KEEPING CODE READABLE WITH SHORTER NAMES

Often, we'll have a fragment of code that makes frequent references to an object. If the reference is long and involved, all those repeated references to the long name can make the code difficult to read. And hard-to-read code isn't good for anybody.

A naïve approach might be to assign the reference to a variable with a short name as follows:

```
var short = Some.long.reference.to.something;
```

But while that achieves the goal of being able to use the name short in place of Some.long.reference.to.something in the code that follows, it needlessly introduces a new name into the current scope, and that's something we're learning to avoid.

Rather, the sophisticated functional programmer can use an immediate function to introduce the short name into a *limited* scope. Here's a quick example of doing just that from the Prototype JavaScript library:

```javascript
(function(v) {
  Object.extend(v, {
    href:       v._getAttr,
    src:        v._getAttr,
    type:       v._getAttr,
    action:     v._getAttrNode,
    disabled:   v._flag,
    checked:    v._flag,
    readonly:   v._flag,
    multiple:   v._flag,
    onload:     v._getEv,
    onunload:   v._getEv,
    onclick:    v._getEv,
    ...
  });
})(Element.attributeTranslations.read.values);
```

In this case, Prototype is extending an object with a number of new properties and methods. In the code, a temporary variable could have been created for Element.attributeTranslations.read.values, but instead Prototype passes it as the first argument to an immediate function. This means that the parameter v is a reference to this data structure referenced by this long name, and is contained within the scope of the immediate function.

It's easy to see how the code is made more readable by using v, as opposed to having every reference to v in that code be replaced with Element.attributeTranslations.read.values.

This ability to create temporary variables within a scope is especially useful once we start to examine looping, which we'll do without further delay.

5.6.2 Loops

Another useful application of immediate functions is the ability to solve a nasty issue with loops and closures. Consider this common piece of problematic code:

Listing 5.17 Code in which the iterator in the closure doesn't do what you want

```html
<body>

  <div>DIV 0</div>
  <div>DIV 1</div>

  <script type="text/javascript">
    var divs = document.getElementsByTagName("div");

    for (var i = 0; i < divs.length; i++) {
      divs[i].addEventListener("click", function() {
```

Gathers up a list of all <div> elements on the page; two in this case.

```
        alert("divs #" + i + " was clicked.");
      }, false);
    }
  </script>
</body>
```

We expect each handler to report the DIV number; but see below, it's not so!

Our intention is that clicking each <div> element will show its ordinal value. But when we load the page and click on "DIV 0", we see the display in figure 5.12.

In listing 5.17 we encounter a common issue with closures and looping; namely that the variable that's being closured (i in this case) is being updated *after* the function is bound. This means that every bound function handler will always alert the last value stored in i; in this case, 2.

This is due to a fact that we discussed in section 5.2.2: closures remember *references* to included variables—*not* just their values at the time at which they're created. This is an important distinction to understand, and one that trips up a lot of people.

Not to fear, though. We can combat this closure craziness with another closure (fighting fire with fire, so to speak) and immediate functions, as shown in the next listing (changes noted in bold).

Listing 5.18   Using an immediate function to handle the iterator properly

```
<div>DIV 0</div>
<div>DIV 1</div>

<script type="text/javascript">
  var div = document.getElementsByTagName("div");

  for (var i = 0; i < div.length; i++) (function(n){
    div[n].addEventListener("click", function(){
      alert("div #" + n + " was clicked.");
    }, false);
  })(i);
</script>
```

By using an immediate function as the body of the for loop (replacing the previous block), we enforce the correct ordinal value for the handlers by passing that value into the immediate function (and hence, the closure of the inner function). This means that within the scope of each step of the for loop, the i variable is defined anew, giving the closure of the click handler the value we expect.

Figure 5.12   Where did we go wrong? Why does DIV 0 think it's 2?

Figure 5.13 That's more like it! Each element now knows its own ordinal.

Running the updated page shows the expected display in figure 5.13.

This example clearly points out how we can control the scope of variables and values using immediate functions and closures. Let's see how that can help us be good on-page citizens.

5.6.3 Library wrapping

Another important use of the fine-grained control over scoping that closures and immediate functions give us is an important one to JavaScript library development. When developing a library, it's incredibly important that we don't pollute the global namespace with unnecessary variables, especially ones that are only temporarily used.

To this end, the concept of closures and immediate functions is especially useful, helping us to keep as much of the libraries as private as possible, and to only selectively introduce variables into the global namespace. The jQuery library takes great care to heed this principle, completely enclosing all of its functionality and only introducing the variables it needs, like jQuery, as shown here:

```
(function(){
  var jQuery = window.jQuery = function(){
    // Initialize
  };

  // ...
})();
```

Note that there's a double assignment performed, completely intentionally. First, the jQuery constructor (as an anonymous function) is assigned to window.jQuery, which introduces it as a global variable.

But that doesn't guarantee that it will stay that way; it's completely within the realms of possibility that code outside our control may change or remove the variable. To avoid that problem, we assign it to a local variable, jQuery, to enforce it as such with the scope of the immediate function.

This means that we can use the name jQuery throughout our library code, while externally anything could have happened to the global variable. We won't care; within the world we created via the outer immediate function, the name jQuery means only what we want it to mean. Because all of the functions and variables that are required by the library are nicely encapsulated, it ends up giving the end user a lot of flexibility in how they wish to use it.

But that isn't the only way in which that type of definition could be implemented; another is shown here:

```
var jQuery = (function(){
  function jQuery(){
    // Initialize
  }

  // ...

  return jQuery;
})();
```

This code has the same effect as that shown previously, just structured in a different manner. Here we define a jQuery function within our anonymous scope, use it freely within that scope, then return it such that it's assigned to a global variable, also named jQuery. Oftentimes this particular technique is preferred if you're only exporting a single variable, as the intention of the assignment is somewhat clearer.

In the end, the exact formats and structures used are left to developer preference, which is good, considering that the JavaScript language gives you all the power you'll need to structure any particular application to your own predilections.

5.7   *Summary*

In this chapter we dove into how closures, a key concept of functional programming, work in JavaScript:

- We started with the basics, looking at how closures are implemented, and then at how to use them within an application. We looked at a number of cases where closures were particularly useful, including in the definition of private variables and in the use of callbacks.
- We then explored a number of advanced concepts in which closures helped to sculpt the JavaScript language, including forcing function context, partially applying functions, and overriding function behavior. We then did an in-depth exploration of immediate functions, which, as we learned, have the power to let us exhibit fine-grained control over variable scoping.
- In total, understanding closures will be an invaluable asset when developing complex JavaScript applications and will aid in solving a number of common problems that we'll inevitably encounter.

In this chapter's example code, we lightly introduced the concept of *prototypes*. Now it's time to dig into prototypes in earnest. After at least a short break to let your mind absorb what we've covered so far, read on!

Object-orientation
with prototypes

Now that we've learned how functions are first-class objects in JavaScript, and how closures make them incredibly versatile and useful, we're ready to tackle another important aspect of functions: *function prototypes*.

Those already somewhat familiar with JavaScript prototypes might think of them as being closely related to objects, but once again it's all about functions. Prototypes are a convenient way to *define* types of objects, but they're actually a feature of functions.

Prototypes are used throughout JavaScript as a convenient means of defining properties and functionality that will be automatically applied to instances of objects. Once defined, the prototype's properties become properties of instantiated objects, serving as a blueprint of sorts for the creation of complex objects.

In other words, they serve a similar purpose to that of *classes* in classical object-oriented languages. Indeed, the predominant use of prototypes in JavaScript is in producing a classical style of object-oriented code and inheritance.

Let's start exploring how.

6.1   *Instantiation and prototypes*

All functions have a `prototype` property that initially references an empty object. This property doesn't serve much purpose until the function is used as a *constructor*. We saw in chapter 3 that using the `new` keyword to invoke a function calls the function as a constructor with a newly instantiated and empty object as its context.

As object instantiation is a large part of what makes constructors useful, let's take a little time to make sure we truly understand it.

6.1.1   *Object instantiation*

The simplest way to create a new object is with a statement like this:

```
var o = {};
```

This creates a new and empty object, which we can then populate with properties via assignment statements:

```
var o = {};
o.name = 'Saito';
o.occupation = 'marksman';
o.cyberizationLevel = 20;
```

But those coming from an object-oriented background might miss the encapsulation and structuring that comes with the concept of a class constructor: a function that serves to initialize the object to a known initial state. After all, if we're going to create multiple instances of the same type of object, assigning the properties individually is not only tedious but also highly error-prone. We'd like to have a means to consolidate the set of properties and methods for a class of objects in one place.

JavaScript provides such a mechanism, though in a very different form than most other languages. Like object-oriented languages such as Java and C++, JavaScript employs the `new` operator to instantiate new objects via constructors, but there's no class definition in JavaScript. Rather, the `new` operator, applied to a constructor function (as we observed in chapters 3 and 4), triggers the creation of a newly allocated object.

What we didn't learn in the previous chapters was that the prototype is used as a sort of blueprint. Let's see how that works.

PROTOTYPES AS OBJECT BLUEPRINTS

Let's examine a simple case of using a function, both with and without the `new` operator, and see how the `prototype` property provides properties for the new instance. Consider the following code.

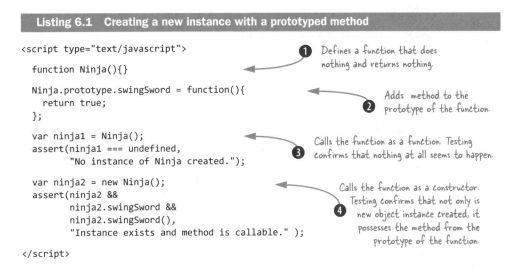

Listing 6.1 Creating a new instance with a prototyped method

```
<script type="text/javascript">

  function Ninja(){}

  Ninja.prototype.swingSword = function(){
    return true;
  };

  var ninja1 = Ninja();
  assert(ninja1 === undefined,
         "No instance of Ninja created.");

  var ninja2 = new Ninja();
  assert(ninja2 &&
         ninja2.swingSword &&
         ninja2.swingSword(),
         "Instance exists and method is callable." );

</script>
```

① Defines a function that does nothing and returns nothing.

② Adds method to the prototype of the function.

③ Calls the function as a function. Testing confirms that nothing at all seems to happen.

④ Calls the function as a constructor. Testing confirms that not only is new object instance created, it possesses the method from the prototype of the function.

In this code, we define a seemingly do-nothing function named Ninja() ① that we'll invoke in two ways: as a "normal" function ③, and as a constructor ④. After the function is created, we add a method, swingSword(), to its prototype ②. Then we put the function through its paces.

First, we call the function normally ③ and store its result in variable ninja1. Looking at the function body ①, we see that it returns no value, so we'd expect ninja1 to test as undefined, which we assert to be true. As a simple function, Ninja() doesn't appear to be all that useful.

Then we call the function via the new operator, invoking it as a *constructor*, and something completely different happens. The function is once again called, but this time a newly allocated object has been created and set as the context of the function. The result returned from the new operator is a reference to this new object. We test for two things: that ninja2 has a reference to the newly created object, and that that object has a swingSword() method that we can call.

This shows that the function's prototype serves as a sort of blueprint for the new object when the function is used as a constructor. The results of the tests are shown in figure 6.1.

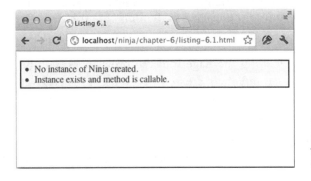

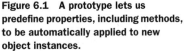

Figure 6.1 A prototype lets us predefine properties, including methods, to be automatically applied to new object instances.

Note that we didn't do anything overt in the constructor to make this happen. The swingSword() method is attached to the new object simply by adding it to the constructor's prototype property.

Also note that we said *attached* rather than *added*. Let's find out why.

INSTANCE PROPERTIES

When the function is called as a constructor via the new operator, its context is defined as the new object instance. This means that in addition to attaching properties via the prototype, we can initialize values within the constructor function via the this parameter. Let's examine the creation of such instance properties in the next listing.

Listing 6.2   Observing the precedence of initialization activities

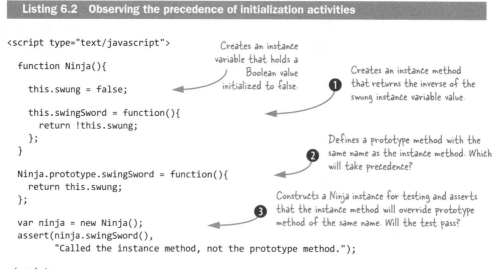

```
<script type="text/javascript">

  function Ninja(){

    this.swung = false;

    this.swingSword = function(){
      return !this.swung;
    };
  }

Ninja.prototype.swingSword = function(){
  return this.swung;
};

var ninja = new Ninja();
assert(ninja.swingSword(),
       "Called the instance method, not the prototype method.");

</script>
```

Annotations in figure:
- Creates an instance variable that holds a Boolean value initialized to false.
- ① Creates an instance method that returns the inverse of the swung instance variable value.
- ② Defines a prototype method with the same name as the instance method. Which will take precedence?
- ③ Constructs a Ninja instance for testing and asserts that the instance method will override prototype method of the same name. Will the test pass?

Listing 6.2 is very similar to the previous example in that we define a method by adding it to the prototype property ❷ of the constructor. But we also add an identically named method within the constructor function itself ❶. The two methods are defined to return opposing results so we can tell which will be called.

> **NOTE**   This isn't anything we'd actually advise doing in real-world code; quite the opposite. We're doing it here just to demonstrate the precedence of initializers.

When we run the test ❸ by loading the page into the browser, we see that the test passes! This shows that instance members created inside a constructor will occlude properties of the same name defined in the prototype.

The precedence of the initialization operations is important and goes as follows:

1 Properties are bound to the object instance from the prototype.
2 Properties are added to the object instance within the constructor function.

Binding operations within the constructor always take precedence over those in the prototype. Because the this context within the constructor refers to the instance itself, we can perform initialization actions in the constructor to our heart's content.

Let's find out more about how instance properties and prototypes relate to each other by learning how JavaScript reconciles object property references.

RECONCILING REFERENCES

A vitally important concept to understand about prototypes is how JavaScript goes about reconciling references and how the prototype property comes into play during this process.

The previous examples may have led you to believe that when a new object is created and passed to a constructor, the properties of the constructor's prototype are copied to the object. That would certainly account for the fact that a property assigned within the constructor body overrides the prototype value. But as it turns out, there are some behaviors that wouldn't make sense if this was really what was going on.

If we were to assume that the prototype values are simply copied to the object, then any change to the prototype made *after* the object was constructed would not be reflected in the object, right? Let's rearrange the code a bit in the following listing and see what happens.

Listing 6.3 Observing the behavior of changes to the prototype

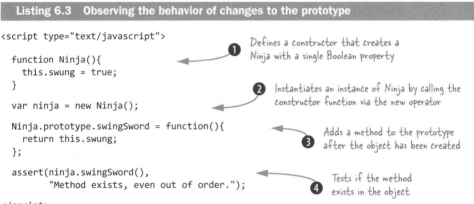

```
<script type="text/javascript">

  function Ninja(){
    this.swung = true;
  }
  var ninja = new Ninja();

  Ninja.prototype.swingSword = function(){
    return this.swung;
  };

  assert(ninja.swingSword(),
      "Method exists, even out of order.");

</script>
```

❶ Defines a constructor that creates a Ninja with a single Boolean property

❷ Instantiates an instance of Ninja by calling the constructor function via the new operator

❸ Adds a method to the prototype after the object has been created

❹ Tests if the method exists in the object

In this example, we define a constructor ❶ and proceed to use it to create an object instance ❷. *After* the instance has been created, we add a method to the prototype ❸. Then we run a test to see if the change we made to the prototype after the object was constructed takes effect.

Our test ❹ succeeds, showing that the assertion is true as shown in figure 6.2. Clearly there's more to all this than a simple copying of properties when the object is created.

What's really going on is that properties in the prototype aren't copied anywhere, but rather, the prototype is attached to the constructed object and consulted during the reconciling of property references made to the object.

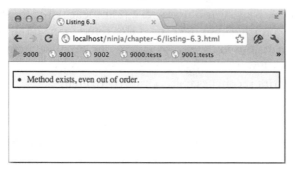

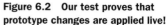

• Method exists, even out of order.

Figure 6.2 Our test proves that prototype changes are applied live!

A simplified overview of the process is as follows:

1 When a property reference to an object is made, the object itself is checked to see if the property exists. If it does, the value is taken. If not ...

2 The prototype associated with the object is located, and *it* is checked for the property. If it exists, the value is taken. If not ...

3 The value is undefined.

We'll see later on in the chapter that things get a little more complicated than this, but this is a good enough understanding for now.

How does all this work? Look at the diagram in figure 6.3.

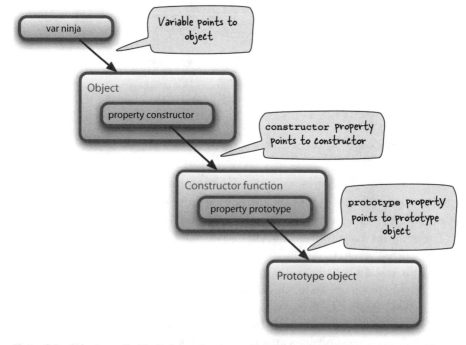

Figure 6.3 Objects are tied to their constructors, which are in turn tied to prototypes for objects created by the constructor.

Figure 6.4 Inspecting the structure of an object reveals the path to its prototype.

Each object in JavaScript has an implicit property named `constructor` that references the constructor that was used to create the object. And because the prototype is a property of the constructor, each object has a way to find its prototype.

Take a look at figure 6.4, which shows a capture of the JavaScript console (in Chrome) when the code from listing 6.3 is loaded into the browser.

When we type the reference `ninja.constructor` into the console, we see that it references the `Ninja()` function, as we'd expect, because the object was created by using that function as a constructor. A deeper reference to `ninja.constructor` `.prototype.swingSword` shows how we can access prototype properties from the object instance.

This explains why changes to the prototype made after the object has been constructed take effect. The prototype is actively attached to the object, and any references made to object properties are reconciled, using the prototype if necessary, *at the time of reference.*

These seamless "live updates" give us an incredible amount of power and extensibility, to a degree that isn't typically found in other languages. Allowing for these live updates makes it possible for us to create a functional framework that users can extend with further functionality, even well after objects have been instantiated.

The relationships are shown in figure 6.5.

In the figure, an object reference by variable `ninja` has properties `member1` and `member2`. A reference to either of these is resolved by those properties. If a property not present in the object, in this case `member3`, is referenced, it's looked for in the constructor's prototype. A reference to `member4` would result in `undefined`, as it doesn't exist anywhere.

Before we move on, let's try one more variation on this theme to drive the point home, as shown in the following listing.

Listing 6.4 Further observing the behavior of changes to the prototype

```
<script type="text/javascript">

  function Ninja(){
    this.swung = true;
    this.swingSword = function(){
```

1 Defines an instance method with same name as a prototype method

```
    return !this.swung;
  };
}

var ninja = new Ninja();

Ninja.prototype.swingSword = function(){
  return this.swung;
};

assert(ninja.swingSword(),
      "Called the instance method, not the prototype method.");
```

</script>

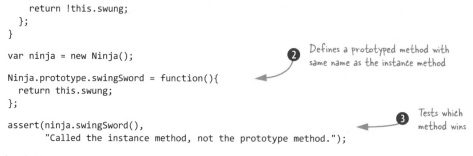

2 Defines a prototyped method with same name as the instance method

3 Tests which method wins

In this example, we re-introduce an instance method ❶ with the same name as the prototyped method ❷, as we did back in listing 6.2. In that example, the instance

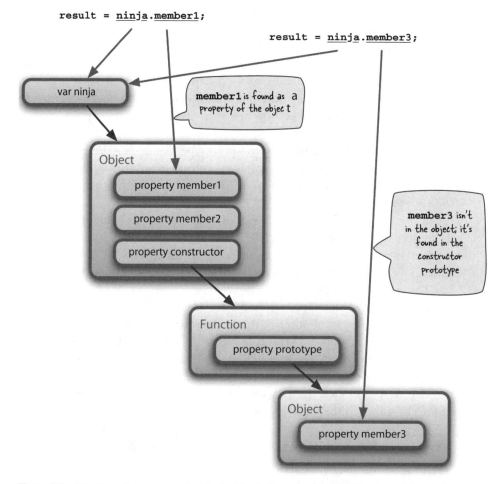

Figure 6.5 Property references are first looked for in the object itself; if they're not found, the constructor's prototype is inspected.

method took precedence over the prototyped method. This time, however, the prototyped method is added after the constructor has been executed. Which method will reign supreme in this case?

Our test ❸ shows that, even when the prototyped method is added *after* the instance method has been added, the instance method takes precedence. This makes perfect sense. The prototype is only consulted when a property reference on the object itself fails. Because the object directly possesses a `swingSword` property, the prototyped version doesn't come into play, even though it was the most recent "version" of the method created.

The point is that property references are resolved in the object *first*, defaulting to inspecting the prototype only if that fails.

Now that we know how to instantiate objects via function constructors, let's learn a bit more about the nature of those objects.

6.1.2 *Object typing via constructors*

Although it's great to know how JavaScript uses the prototype during the reconciliation of property references, it's also handy for us to know which function constructed the object instance.

As we've seen, the constructor of an object is available via the `constructor` property. We can refer back to the constructor at any time, possibly even using it as a form of type checking, as shown in the next listing.

Listing 6.5 Examining the type of an instance and its constructor

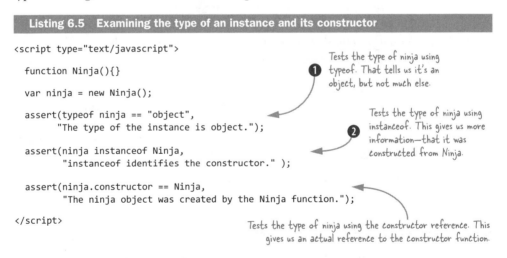

```
<script type="text/javascript">

  function Ninja(){}

  var ninja = new Ninja();

  assert(typeof ninja == "object",
      "The type of the instance is object.");

  assert(ninja instanceof Ninja,
      "instanceof identifies the constructor." );

  assert(ninja.constructor == Ninja,
      "The ninja object was created by the Ninja function.");

</script>
```

Tests the type of ninja using typeof. That tells us it's an object, but not much else.

Tests the type of ninja using instanceof. This gives us more information—that it was constructed from Ninja.

Tests the type of ninja using the constructor reference. This gives us an actual reference to the constructor function.

In listing 6.5 we define a constructor and create an object instance using it. Then we examine the type of the instance using the `typeof` operator ❶. This isn't very revealing, as all instances will be objects, thus always returning `"object"` as the result. Much more interesting is the `instanceof` operator ❷, which is really helpful in that it gives us a clear way to determine whether an instance was created by a particular function constructor.

On top of this, we can also make use of the constructor property, that we now know is added to all instances, as a reference back to the original function that created it. We can use this to verify the origin of the instance (much like how we can with the instanceof operator).

Additionally, because this is just a reference back to the original constructor, we can instantiate a new Ninja object using it, as shown in the next listing.

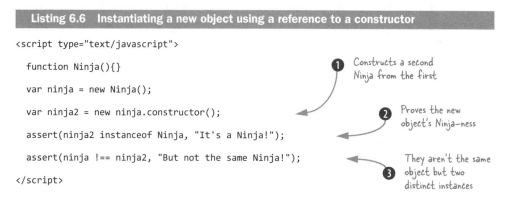

Listing 6.6   Instantiating a new object using a reference to a constructor

```
<script type="text/javascript">

  function Ninja(){}

  var ninja = new Ninja();

  var ninja2 = new ninja.constructor();

  assert(ninja2 instanceof Ninja, "It's a Ninja!");

  assert(ninja !== ninja2, "But not the same Ninja!");

</script>
```

❶ Constructs a second Ninja from the first

❷ Proves the new object's Ninja-ness

❸ They aren't the same object but two distinct instances

We define a constructor and create an instance using that constructor. Then we use the constructor property of the created instance to construct a second instance ❶. Testing ❷ shows that a second Ninja has been constructed and that the variable doesn't merely point to the same instance ❸.

What's especially interesting is that we can do this without even having access to the original function; we can use the reference completely behind the scenes, even if the original constructor is no longer in scope.

NOTE   Although the constructor property of an object can be changed, doing so doesn't have any immediate or obvious constructive purpose (though one might think of some malicious ones), as its reason for being is to inform us from where the object was constructed. If the constructor property is overwritten, the original value will simply be lost.

That's all very useful, but we've just scratched the surface of the superpowers that prototypes confer on us. Now things get really interesting.

6.1.3   *Inheritance and the prototype chain*

There's an additional feature of the instanceof operator that we can use to our advantage to utilize a form of object inheritance. But in order to make use of it, we need to understand how inheritance works in JavaScript and what role the *prototype chain* plays.

Let's consider the example in the following listing, in which we'll attempt to add inheritance to an instance.

Listing 6.7 Trying to achieve inheritance with prototypes

```
<script type="text/javascript">

  function Person(){}
  Person.prototype.dance = function(){};

  function Ninja(){}

  Ninja.prototype = { dance: Person.prototype.dance };

  var ninja = new Ninja();
  assert(ninja instanceof Ninja,
        "ninja receives functionality from the Ninja prototype" );
  assert( ninja instanceof Person, "... and the Person prototype" );
  assert( ninja instanceof Object, "... and the Object prototype" );

</script>
```

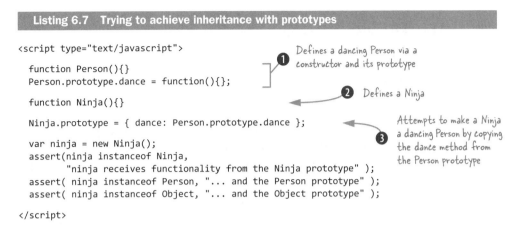

❶ Defines a dancing Person via a constructor and its prototype

❷ Defines a Ninja

❸ Attempts to make a Ninja a dancing Person by copying the dance method from the Person prototype

As the prototype of a function is just an object, there are multiple ways of copying functionality (such as properties or methods) to effect inheritance. In this code, we define a Person ❶, and then a Ninja ❷. And because a Ninja is clearly a person, we want Ninja to inherit the attributes of Person. We attempt to do so in this code by copying ❸ the dance property of the Person prototype's method to a similarly named property in the Ninja prototype.

Running our test reveals that while we may have taught the ninja to dance, we failed to make the Ninja a Person, as shown in figure 6.6. Although we've taught the Ninja to mimic the dance of a person, it hasn't *made* the Ninja a Person. That's not inheritance—it's just copying.

This approach is a big old FAIL. Not much of a loss though, because by using this approach, we'd need to copy each property of Person to the Ninja prototype individually. That's no way to do inheritance. Let's keep exploring.

NOTE It's interesting to note that even without doing anything overt, all objects are instances of Object. Execute the statement console.log({}.constructor) in a browser's debugger, and see what you get.

What we really want to achieve is a *prototype chain* so that a Ninja can *be* a Person, and a Person can be a Mammal, and a Mammal can be an Animal, and so on, all the way to Object.

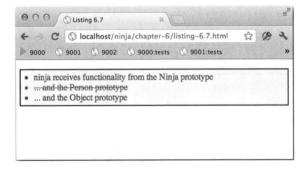

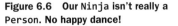

Figure 6.6 Our Ninja isn't really a Person. No happy dance!

The best technique for creating such a prototype chain is to use an instance of an object as the other object's prototype:

```
SubClass.prototype = new SuperClass();
```

For example,

```
Ninja.prototype = new Person();
```

This will preserve the prototype chain because the prototype of the SubClass instance will be an instance of the SuperClass, which has a prototype with all the properties of SuperClass, and which will in turn have a prototype pointing to an instance of *its* superclass, and on and on.

Let's change the code of listing 6.7 slightly to use this technique in the next listing.

Listing 6.8　Achieving inheritance with prototypes

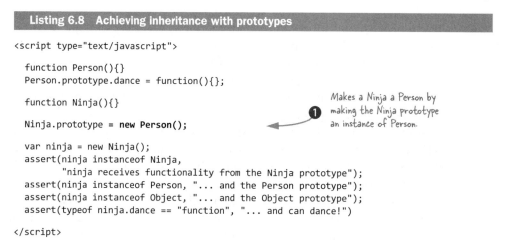

```
<script type="text/javascript">

    function Person(){}
    Person.prototype.dance = function(){};

    function Ninja(){}                                    Makes a Ninja a Person by
                                                    ❶  making the Ninja prototype
    Ninja.prototype = new Person();                      an instance of Person.

    var ninja = new Ninja();
    assert(ninja instanceof Ninja,
            "ninja receives functionality from the Ninja prototype");
    assert(ninja instanceof Person, "... and the Person prototype");
    assert(ninja instanceof Object, "... and the Object prototype");
    assert(typeof ninja.dance == "function", "... and can dance!")

</script>
```

The only change we made to the code was to use an instance of Person as the prototype for Ninja ❶. Running the tests shows that we've succeeded, as shown in figure 6.7.

The very important implications of this are that when we perform an instanceof operation, we can determine whether the function inherits the functionality of any object in its prototype chain.

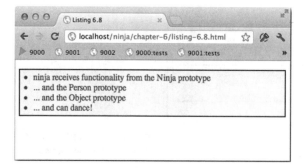

Figure 6.7　Our Ninja is a Person! Let the victory dance begin.

NOTE Another technique that may have occurred to you, and that we advise strongly against, is to use the Person prototype object directly as the Ninja prototype, like this: `Ninja.prototype = Person.prototype;`. By doing this, any changes to the Ninja prototype will also change the Person prototype because they're the same object, and that's bound to have undesirable side effects.

An additional happy side effect of doing prototype inheritance in this manner is that all inherited function prototypes will continue to live-update. The manner in which the prototype chain is applied for our example is shown in figure 6.8.

It's important to note that our object also has properties that are inherited from the Object prototype.

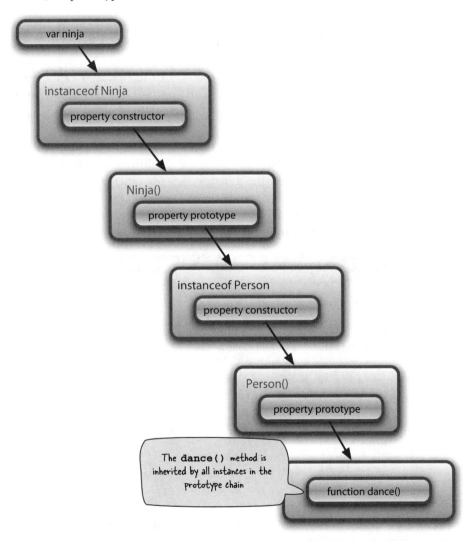

Figure 6.8 The prototype chain through which properties are reconciled for the dancing ninja

All native JavaScript object constructors (such as `Object`, `Array`, `String`, `Number`, `RegExp`, and `Function`) have prototype properties that can be manipulated and extended, which makes sense, as each of those object constructors is itself a function. This proves to be an incredibly powerful feature of the language. Using it, we can extend the functionality of the language *itself*, introducing new or missing pieces of the language.

> **NOTE**   As with most advanced techniques, this can be a double-edged sword that needs to be wielded with care. A good summary is available on the *Perfection Kills* blog (http://perfectionkills.com/extending-built-in-native-objects-evil-or-not/).

One such case where this would be quite useful is in anticipating some of the features of future versions of JavaScript. For example, JavaScript 1.6 introduced a couple of useful helper methods, including some for arrays.

One such method is `forEach()`, which allows us to iterate over the entries in an array, calling a function for every entry. This can be especially handy for situations where we want to plug in different pieces of functionality without changing the overall looping structure.

Although this method has made its appearance in most modern browsers, it doesn't exist in all browsers that currently have significant use and that we may need to support. We can implement this functionality for older browsers, eliminating the need to worry about it in the rest of our code.

The following listing shows a possible implementation of `forEach()` that we could use to fill the gap in older browsers.

Listing 6.9   A future-proof JavaScript 1.6 `forEach()` method implementation

```
<script type="text/javascript">

  if (!Array.prototype.forEach) {

    Array.prototype.forEach = function(callback, context) {
      for (var i = 0; i < this.length; i++) {
        callback.call(context || null, this[i], i, this);
      }
    };
  }

  ["a", "b", "c"].forEach(function(value, index, array) {
    assert(value,
      "Is in position " + index + " out of " +
      (array.length - 1));
  });

</script>
```

① Tests for the pre-existence of the method. We don't want to redefine it in browsers that provide it for us.

② Adds the method to the Array prototype. After this, it's a method of all arrays.

③ Calls the callback function for each array entry.

Puts our implementation through its paces.

Before we stomp on an implementation that might already be there, we check to make sure that `Array` doesn't already have a `forEach()` method defined ①, and we skip the whole thing if it does. This makes the code future-compatible, because when it executes in an environment where the method is defined, it will defer to the native method.

If we determine that the method doesn't exist, we go ahead and add it to the `Array` prototype ❷, simply looping through the array using a traditional `for` loop and calling the callback method for each entry ❸. The values passed to the callback are the entry, the index, and the original array. Note that the expression `context || null` prevents us from passing a possible `undefined` value to `call()`.

Because all the built-in objects, like `Array`, include prototypes, we have all the power necessary to extend the language to our desires. But an important point to remember when implementing properties or methods on native objects is that introducing them is every bit as dangerous as introducing new variables into the global scope. Because there's only ever one instance of a native object prototype, there's a significant possibility that naming collisions will occur.

Also, when implementing features on native prototypes that are forward-looking (such as our `forEach()` implementation) there's a danger that our anticipated implementation may not exactly match the final implementation, causing issues to occur when a browser finally does implement the method. We should always take great care when treading in these waters.

We've seen that we can use prototypes to augment the native JavaScript objects; now let's turn our attention to the DOM.

6.1.4 *HTML DOM prototypes*

A fun feature in modern browsers, including Internet Explorer 8+, Firefox, Safari, and Opera, is that all DOM elements inherit from an `HTMLElement` constructor. By making the `HTMLElement` prototype accessible, the browsers provide us with the ability to extend any HTML node of our choosing.

Let's explore that in the next listing.

Listing 6.10   Adding a new method to all HTML elements via the `HTMLElement` prototype

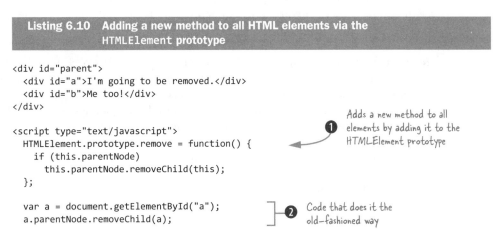

```
<div id="parent">
  <div id="a">I'm going to be removed.</div>
  <div id="b">Me too!</div>
</div>

<script type="text/javascript">
  HTMLElement.prototype.remove = function() {
    if (this.parentNode)
      this.parentNode.removeChild(this);
  };

  var a = document.getElementById("a");
  a.parentNode.removeChild(a);
```

❶ Adds a new method to all elements by adding it to the HTMLElement prototype

❷ Code that does it the old-fashioned way

```
document.getElementById("b").remove();

assert(!document.getElementById("a"),"a is gone.");
assert(!document.getElementById("b"),"b is gone too.");
</script>
```

❸ Code that uses the new method, which is both shorter and clearer

In this code, we add a new `remove()` method to all DOM elements by augmenting the prototype of the base `HTMLElement` constructor ❶. Then we remove element a using the native means ❷ for comparison, and then we remove b using our new method ❸. In both cases, we assert that the elements are removed from the DOM.

> **TIP** More information about this particular feature can be found in the HTML5 specification at www.whatwg.org/specs/web-apps/current-work/multipage/section-elements.html.

One JavaScript library that makes very heavy use of this feature is the Prototype library, which adds much functionality to existing DOM elements, including the ability to inject HTML and manipulate CSS.

The most important thing to realize, when working with these `HTMLElement` prototypes, is that they don't exist in versions of Internet Explorer prior to IE 8. If older versions of IE aren't a target platform for you, then these features could serve you well.

Another point that we need to be aware of is whether HTML elements can be instantiated directly from their constructor function. We might consider doing something like this:

```
var elem = new HTMLElement();
```

But that doesn't work at all. Even though browsers expose the root constructor and prototype, they selectively disable the ability to actually call the constructor (presumably to limit element-creation for internal use).

Save for the gotcha that this feature presents with regards to platform compatibility with older browsers, if you want to attach methods to DOM elements, this feature's benefits with respect to clean code can be quite dramatic.

> **NOTE** This technique isn't without its detractors. They, with good reason, feel that modifying the actual DOM elements is too intrusive and can introduce instability into a page, as other components being used on the page may be unaware of the changes and might be tripped up by any changes made to the elements. It's best to tread lightly if you choose to employ this technique. Adding methods is usually fairly benign, but changing the way that existing code acts should be considered very carefully.

And speaking of gotchas...

6.2 The gotchas!

As with most things in life, JavaScript has several gotchas associated with prototypes, instantiation, and inheritance. Some of them can be worked around, but a number of them will require a dampening of our excitement.

Let's take a look at some of them.

6.2.1 Extending Object

Perhaps the most egregious mistake that we can make with prototypes is to extend the native `Object.prototype`. The difficulty is that when we extend this prototype, *all* objects receive those additional properties. This can be especially problematic when we iterate over the properties of the object and these new properties appear, potentially causing all sorts of unexpected behavior. Let's illustrate that with an example in Listing 6.11.

Let's say that we wanted to do something seemingly innocuous, such as adding a `keys()` method to `Object` that would return an array of all the names (keys) of the properties in the object.

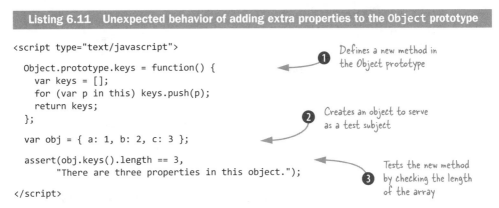

Listing 6.11 Unexpected behavior of adding extra properties to the `Object` prototype

```
<script type="text/javascript">

  Object.prototype.keys = function() {            ① Defines a new method in
    var keys = [];                                   the Object prototype
    for (var p in this) keys.push(p);
    return keys;
  };                                              ② Creates an object to serve
                                                     as a test subject
  var obj = { a: 1, b: 2, c: 3 };

  assert(obj.keys().length == 3,                     Tests the new method
      "There are three properties in this object."); ③ by checking the length
                                                        of the array
</script>
```

First we define the new method ①, which simply iterates over the properties and collects the keys into an array, which we return. We then define a test subject with three properties ②, and then test that we get a three-element array as a result ③.

But the test fails, as shown in figure 6.9.

What went wrong, of course, is that in adding the `keys()` method to `Object`, we introduced *another* property that will appear on all objects and that is included in the count. This affects all objects and will force any code to have to account for the extra property. This could break code that's based upon perfectly reasonable assumptions made by page authors. This is obviously unacceptable. Don't do it!

There still exists the problem that someone *else* might do this and trip up our code. What can we do about that? As it turns out, there *is* a workaround that we can use to protect ourselves from these well-meaning but misguided coders.

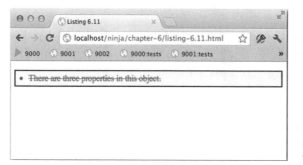

Figure 6.9   Whoa! We screwed up a
fundamental assumption of objects.

JavaScript provides a method called hasOwnProperty(), which can be used to determine
whether properties are actually defined on an object instance versus imported from
a prototype.

Let's observe its use in the next listing by modifying the code from listing 6.11.

Listing 6.12   Using the hasOwnProperty() method to tame Object prototype extensions

```
<script type="text/javascript">
  Object.prototype.keys = function() {
    var keys = [];
    for (var i in this)
      if (this.hasOwnProperty(i)) keys.push(i);
    return keys;
  };

  var obj = { a: 1, b: 2, c: 3 };

  assert(obj.keys().length == 3,
         "There are three properties in this object.");

</script>
```

Ignores prototyped properties
by using hasOwnProperty() to
❶ skip over properties from the
prototype

Tests the method by
❷ counting entries

Our redefined method ignores non-instance properties **❶** so that this time the
test **❷** succeeds.

But just because it's possible for us to work around this issue doesn't mean that it
should be abused and become a burden for the users of our code. Looping over the
properties of an object is an incredibly common behavior, but it's uncommon for people to use hasOwnProperty() within their own code—many page authors probably don't
even know of its existence. Generally, we should use such workarounds to protect ourselves from transgressing code, but we should never expect other authors to have to
protect themselves from ours.

Now we'll take a look at another pitfall that could trap us.

6.2.2   *Extending Number*

Except for Object, as we examined in the previous section, it's generally safe to extend
most native prototypes. But one other problematic native is Number.

Due to how numbers, and properties of numbers, are parsed by the JavaScript engine, some results can be rather confusing, as in the following listing.

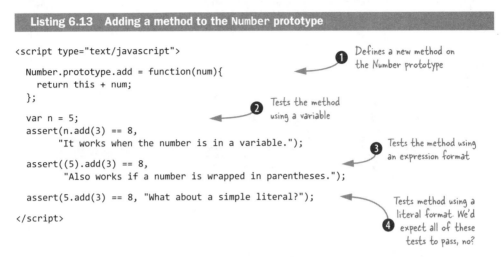

Listing 6.13 Adding a method to the Number prototype

```javascript
<script type="text/javascript">

  Number.prototype.add = function(num){
    return this + num;
  };

  var n = 5;
  assert(n.add(3) == 8,
      "It works when the number is in a variable.");

  assert((5).add(3) == 8,
        "Also works if a number is wrapped in parentheses.");

  assert(5.add(3) == 8, "What about a simple literal?");

</script>
```

❶ Defines a new method on the Number prototype

❷ Tests the method using a variable

❸ Tests the method using an expression format

❹ Tests method using a literal format. We'd expect all of these tests to pass, no?

Here we define a new add() method on Number ❶ that will take its argument, add it to the number's value, and return the result. Then we test the new method using various number formats:

- With the number in a variable ❷
- With the number as an expression ❸
- Directly, with the number as a numeric literal ❹

But when we try to load the page into a browser, the page won't even load, as shown in figure 6.10. It turns out that the syntax parser can't handle the literal case.

This can be a frustrating issue to deal with, as the logic behind it can be rather obtuse. There have been libraries that have continued to include Number prototype functionality, regardless of these issues, simply stipulating how they should be used (Prototype being one of them). That's certainly an option, albeit one that requires the library to explain the issues with good documentation and clear tutorials. In general, it's best to avoid mucking around with the Number prototype unless you really need to.

Now let's look at some issues we can encounter when we subclass, rather than augment, native objects.

6.2.3 *Subclassing native objects*

Another tricky point that we might stumble across concerns the subclassing of native objects. The one object that's quite simple to subclass is Object (as it's the root of all prototype chains to begin with).

But once we start wanting to subclass other native objects, the situation becomes less clear-cut. For example, with Array, everything might *seem* to work as we expect it to, but let's take a look at the following code.

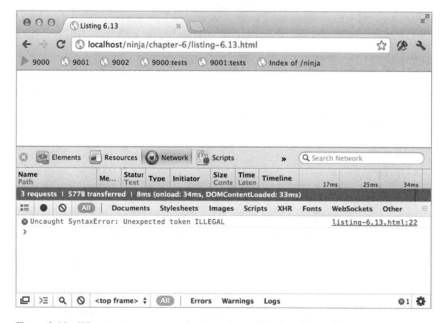

Figure 6.10   When tests won't even load, we know there's a big problem.

Listing 6.14   Subclassing the Array object

```
<script type="text/javascript">

  function MyArray() {}

  MyArray.prototype = new Array();

  var mine = new MyArray();
  mine.push(1, 2, 3);

  assert(mine.length == 3,
        "All the items are in our sub-classed array.");
  assert(mine instanceof Array,
        "Verify that we implement Array functionality.");

</script>
```

We subclass `Array` with a new constructor of our own, `MyArray()`, and it all works fine and dandy, unless, that is, you try to load this into Internet Explorer. The `length` property is rather special and has a close relationship to the numeric indices of the `Array` object; IE's implementation doesn't react well to us mucking around with `length`.

> **NOTE**   More info on all of this with relation to ECMAScript 5 can be found on the *Perfection Kills* blog at perfectionkills.com/how-ecmascript-5-still-does-not-allow-to-subclass-an-array/.

When faced with such situations, it's a better strategy to implement individual pieces of functionality from native objects, rather than attempt to subclass them completely. Let's take a look at this approach in the next listing.

Listing 6.15 Simulating Array functionality but without the true subclassing

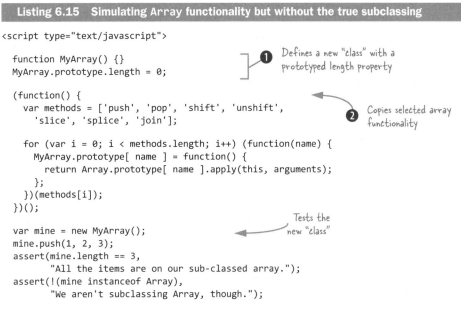

```
<script type="text/javascript">

  function MyArray() {}
  MyArray.prototype.length = 0;

  (function() {
    var methods = ['push', 'pop', 'shift', 'unshift',
      'slice', 'splice', 'join'];

    for (var i = 0; i < methods.length; i++) (function(name) {
      MyArray.prototype[ name ] = function() {
        return Array.prototype[ name ].apply(this, arguments);
      };
    })(methods[i]);
  })();

  var mine = new MyArray();
  mine.push(1, 2, 3);
  assert(mine.length == 3,
         "All the items are on our sub-classed array.");
  assert(!(mine instanceof Array),
         "We aren't subclassing Array, though.");

</script>
```

❶ Defines a new "class" with a prototyped length property

❷ Copies selected array functionality

Tests the new "class"

In listing 6.15 we define a new constructor for a "class" named MyArray and give it its own length property ❶. Then, rather than trying to subclass Array, which we've already learned won't work across all browsers, we use an immediate function ❷ to add selected methods from Array to our class using the apply() trick that we learned back in chapter 4. Note the use of the array of method names to keep things tidy and easy to extend.

The only property that we had to implement ourselves is the length property because that's the one property that must remain mutable—the feature that Internet Explorer doesn't provide.

Now let's see what we can do about a common problem that people trying to use our code might run into.

6.2.4 Instantiation issues

We've already noted that functions can serve a dual purpose, as "normal" functions and as constructors. Because of this, it may not always be clear to the users of our code which is which.

Let's start by looking at a simple case of what happens when someone gets it wrong, as shown in the following listing.

Listing 6.16 The result of leaving off the new operator from a function call

```
<script type="text/javascript">

  function User(first, last){
```

❶ Defines a User class with a name property

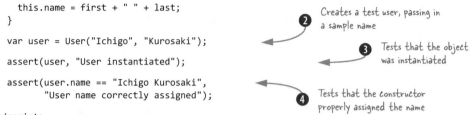

```
    this.name = first + " " + last;
  }

  var user = User("Ichigo", "Kurosaki");

  assert(user, "User instantiated");

  assert(user.name == "Ichigo Kurosaki",
         "User name correctly assigned");
```

② Creates a test user, passing in a sample name

③ Tests that the object was instantiated

④ Tests that the constructor properly assigned the name

`</script>`

In the code, we define a User class ❶ (yeah, we know it's not really a "class" as defined by other object-oriented languages, but that's what people tend to call it, so we'll go with the flow) whose constructor accepts a first and last name and concatenates them to form a full name, which gets stored in the name property.

We then create an instance of the class in the user variable ❷ and test that the object was instantiated ❸ and that the constructor performed correctly ❹.

But things go horribly awry when we try it out, as shown in figure 6.11.

The test reveals that the first test fails, indicating that the object wasn't even instantiated, which causes the second test to throw an error.

On a quick inspection of the code, it may not have been immediately obvious that the User() function is actually something that's meant to be called with the new operator, or maybe we just slipped up and forgot. In either case, the absence of the new operator caused the function to be called in a normal fashion, not as a constructor, and without the instantiation of a new object. A novice user might easily fall into this trap, trying to call the function without the operator, causing bafflingly unexpected results (for example, user would be undefined).

NOTE You may have noticed that since the beginning of this book, we've used a naming convention in which some functions start with a lowercase letter and others start with an uppercase character. As noted in the previous chapters, this is a common convention in which functions serving as constructors use

```
○ ○ ○      Listing 6.16           ×

← → C    localhost/ninja/chapter-6/listing-6.16.html          ☆  ◆  ⚙

▶ 9000    9001    9002    9000:tests    9001:tests    Index of /ninja

• User instantiated

⊗   Elements    Resources    Network    Scripts    »    Q Search Console

⊗ ▶ Uncaught TypeError: Cannot read property 'name' of undefined        listing-6.16.html:18
>

▢ ≽ Q ⊘  <top frame> ↕  All  │  Errors  Warnings  Logs          ⊗1 ⚙
```

Figure 6.11 Our object didn't even get instantiated.

an uppercase opening character, and non-constructor functions don't. Moreover, constructors tend to be nouns that identify the "class" that they're constructing: Ninja, Samurai, Tachikoma and so on, whereas normal functions are named as verbs, or verb/object pairs, that describe what they do: throwShuriken, swingSword, hideBehindAPlant.

More than merely causing unexpected errors, when a function meant to be called as a constructor isn't, it can have subtle side effects such as polluting the current scope (frequently the global namespace), causing even more unexpected results. For example, inspect this code.

Listing 6.17 Accidentally introducing a variable into the global namespace

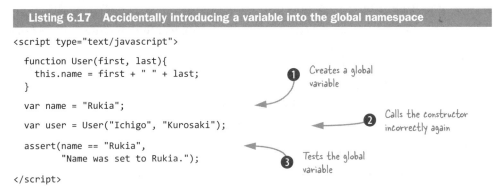

```
<script type="text/javascript">

  function User(first, last){
    this.name = first + " " + last;
  }

  var name = "Rukia";

  var user = User("Ichigo", "Kurosaki");

  assert(name == "Rukia",
         "Name was set to Rukia.");

</script>
```

① Creates a global variable
② Calls the constructor incorrectly again
③ Tests the global variable

This code is similar to that of the previous example, except that this time there happens to be a global variable named name in the global namespace ①. It makes the same mistake ② as the previous example: forgetting to use new.

But *this* time we don't have a test that catches that mistake. Rather, the test we have shows that the value of the global name variable has been overwritten ③, as it fails when executed. Doh!

To find out why, look at the code of the constructor. When called *as* a constructor, the context of the function invocation is the newly allocated object. But what is the context when called as a normal function? Recall from chapter 3 that it's the global scope, which means that the reference this.name refers not to the name property of a newly allocated object, but to the name variable of the global scope.

This can result in a debugging nightmare. The developer may try to interact with the name variable again (being unaware of the error that occurred from misusing the User function) and be forced to dance down the horrible nondeterministic wormhole that's presented to them (why is the value of their variable being pulled out from underneath their feet?).

As JavaScript ninjas, we may want to be sensitive to the needs of our user base, so let's ponder what we can do about the situation.

In order to do anything about it, we need a way to determine when the situation comes up in the first place. Is there a way that we can determine whether a function that we intend to be used as a constructor is being incorrectly called? Consider the next code listing.

Listing 6.18 Determining whether we're called as a constructor

```
<script type="text/javascript">

  function Test() {
    return this instanceof arguments.callee;
  }

  assert(!Test(), "We didn't instantiate, so it returns false.");
  assert(new Test(), "We did instantiate, returning true.");

</script>
```

Recall a few important concepts:

- We can get a reference to the currently executing function via `arguments.callee` (we learned this in chapter 4).
- The context of a "regular" function is the global scope (unless someone did something to make it not so).
- The `instanceof` operator for a constructed object tests for its constructor.

Using these facts, we can see that the expression,

```
this instanceof arguments.callee
```

will evaluate to `true` when executed within a constructor, but `false` when executed within a regular function.

This means that, within a function that we intend to be called as a constructor, we can test to see if someone called us without the `new` operator. Neat! But what do we do about it?

If we weren't ninjas, we might just throw an error telling the user to do it right next time. But we're better than that. Let's see if we can fix the problem for them. Consider the changes to the `User` constructor shown in the next listing.

Listing 6.19 Fixing things on the caller's behalf

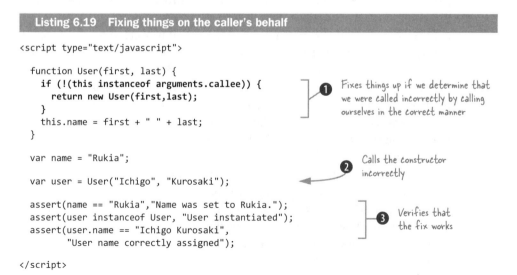

```
<script type="text/javascript">

  function User(first, last) {
    if (!(this instanceof arguments.callee)) {
      return new User(first,last);
    }
    this.name = first + " " + last;
  }

  var name = "Rukia";

  var user = User("Ichigo", "Kurosaki");

  assert(name == "Rukia","Name was set to Rukia.");
  assert(user instanceof User, "User instantiated");
  assert(user.name == "Ichigo Kurosaki",
        "User name correctly assigned");

</script>
```

1 Fixes things up if we determine that we were called incorrectly by calling ourselves in the correct manner

2 Calls the constructor incorrectly

3 Verifies that the fix works

By using the expression we developed in listing 6.18 to determine whether the user has called us incorrectly, we instantiate a User ourselves ❶ and return it as the result of the function. The outcome is that, regardless of whether the caller invokes us as a normal function ❷ or not, they end up with a User instance, which our tests ❸ verify. Now *that's* user-friendly! Who says ninjas are mean?

But before we pat ourselves on the back too hard, we need to stop and wonder if this is the right thing to do. Here are some things we should ponder:

- We learned in chapter 4 that the callee property is deprecated in future versions of JavaScript and prohibited in strict mode. This workaround is only possible in environments where strict mode isn't intended to ever be used. And going forward, why would we not want to use strict mode?
- Is this really a good coding practice? It's a neat technique, but its "goodness" could be debatable.
- Can we ascertain with 100% certainty that we know the user's intentions? Are we acting with hubris?

Ninjas need to think of such matters. Remember, just because we can figure out a clever way to do something doesn't always mean that we *should*.

OK, enough of the problems. Let's take a look at how we can use these newfound powers to write more class-like code.

6.3   *Writing class-like code*

While it's great that JavaScript lets us use a form of inheritance via prototypes, a common desire for many developers, especially those from a classical object-oriented background, is a simplification or abstraction of JavaScript's inheritance system into one that they're more familiar with.

This inevitably leads us toward the realm of classes; that is, what a typical object-oriented developer would expect, even though JavaScript doesn't support classical inheritance natively.

Generally there is a handful of features that such developers crave:

- A system that trivializes the syntax of building new constructor functions and prototypes
- An easy way to perform prototype inheritance
- A way of accessing methods overridden by the function's prototype

There are a number of existing JavaScript libraries that simulate classical inheritance, but two of them stand above the others: the implementations within base2 and Prototype. Although they each contain a number of advanced features, their object-oriented core is an important part of these libraries. We'll distill what they offer and come up with a proposed syntax that will make things a tad more natural for classically trained, object-oriented developers.

The following listing shows an example of a syntax that could achieve the preceding goals.

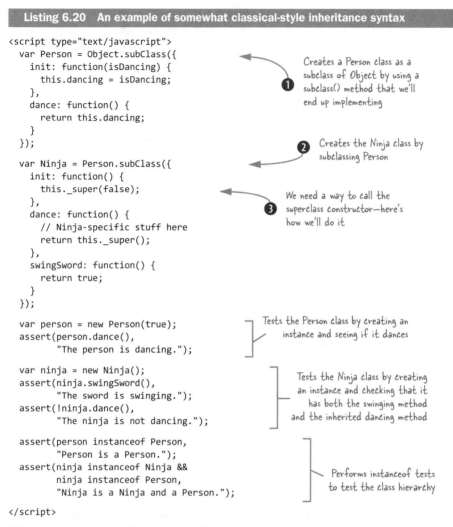

Listing 6.20   An example of somewhat classical-style inheritance syntax

```
<script type="text/javascript">
  var Person = Object.subClass({
    init: function(isDancing) {
      this.dancing = isDancing;
    },
    dance: function() {
      return this.dancing;
    }
  });

  var Ninja = Person.subClass({
    init: function() {
      this._super(false);
    },
    dance: function() {
      // Ninja-specific stuff here
      return this._super();
    },
    swingSword: function() {
      return true;
    }
  });

  var person = new Person(true);
  assert(person.dance(),
        "The person is dancing.");

  var ninja = new Ninja();
  assert(ninja.swingSword(),
        "The sword is swinging.");
  assert(!ninja.dance(),
        "The ninja is not dancing.");

  assert(person instanceof Person,
        "Person is a Person.");
  assert(ninja instanceof Ninja &&
         ninja instanceof Person,
        "Ninja is a Ninja and a Person.");

</script>
```

❶ Creates a Person class as a subclass of Object by using a subclass() method that we'll end up implementing

❷ Creates the Ninja class by subclassing Person

❸ We need a way to call the superclass constructor—here's how we'll do it

Tests the Person class by creating an instance and seeing if it dances

Tests the Ninja class by creating an instance and checking that it has both the swinging method and the inherited dancing method

Performs instanceof tests to test the class hierarchy

There are a number of important things to note about this example:

- Creating a new "class" is accomplished by calling a subClass() method of the existing constructor function for the superclass, as we did here by creating a Person class from Object ❶ and creating a Ninja class from Person ❷.
- We wanted the creation of a constructor to be simple. In our proposed syntax, we simply provide an init() method for each class, as we did for Person and for Ninja.
- All our "classes" eventually inherit from a single ancestor: Object. Therefore, if we want to create a brand new class, it must be a subclass of Object or a class that inherits from Object in its class hierarchy (completely mimicking the current prototype system).

- The most challenging aspect of this syntax is enabling access to overridden methods with their context properly set. We can see this with the use of this._super(), calling the original init() ❸ and dance() methods of the Person superclass.

Proposing a syntax that we'd like to use to accomplish an inheritance scheme was the easy part. Now we need to implement it.

The code in listing 6.21 enables the notion of "classes" as a structure, maintains simple inheritance, and allows for the supermethod calling. Be warned that this is pretty involved code—but we're all here to become ninjas, and this is Master Ninja territory. So don't feel bad if it takes a while for you to grok it.

In fact, to make it a bit easier to digest, we're going to present the code in complete form in the next listing so that we can see how all the parts fit together. Then we'll dissect it piece by piece in the subsections that follow.

Listing 6.21 A subclassing method

```
(function() {
  var initializing = false,
      superPattern =
        /xyz/.test(function() { xyz; }) ? /\b_super\b/ : /.*/;

  Object.subClass = function(properties) {
    var _super = this.prototype;

    initializing = true;
    var proto = new this();
    initializing = false;

    for (var name in properties) {

      proto[name] = typeof properties[name] == "function" &&
              typeof _super[name] == "function" &&
              superPattern.test(properties[name]) ?
        (function(name, fn) {
          return function() {
            var tmp = this._super;

            this._super = _super[name];

            var ret = fn.apply(this, arguments);
            this._super = tmp;

            return ret;
          };
        })(name, properties[name]) :
        properties[name];
    }

    function Class() {
      // All construction is actually done in the init method
      if (!initializing && this.init)
```

This gnarly regular expression determines if functions can be serialized. Read on to see ❶ what all that means.

❷ Adds a subClass() method to Object.

❸ Instantiates the superclass.

❹ Copies properties into the prototype.

❺ Defines an overriding function.

Creates a dummy class constructor.

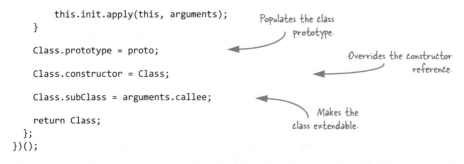

```
        this.init.apply(this, arguments);
    }
    Class.prototype = proto;

    Class.constructor = Class;

    Class.subClass = arguments.callee;

    return Class;
  };
})();
```

Populates the class prototype.

Overrides the constructor reference.

Makes the class extendable.

The two most important parts of this implementation are the initialization and super-method portions. Having a good understanding of what's being achieved in these areas will help with understanding the full implementation. But as it'd be confusing to jump right into the middle of this rather complex code, we'll start at the top and work our way through it from top to bottom.

Let's start with something you might not ever have seen before.

6.3.1 *Checking for function serializability*

Unfortunately, the code that starts out our implementation is something that's rather esoteric, and it could be confusing to most. Later on in the code, we're going to need to know if the browser supports function serialization. But the test for that is one with rather complex syntax, so we're going to get it out of the way now, and store the result so that we don't have to complicate the later code, which will already be complicated enough in its own right.

Function serialization is simply the act of taking a function and getting its text source back. We'll need this approach later to check if a function has a specific reference within it that we're interested in.

In most modern browsers, the function's toString() method will do the trick. Generally, a function is serialized by using it in a context that expects a string, causing its toString() method to be invoked. And so it is with our code to test if function serialization works.

After we set a variable named initializing to false (we'll see why in just a bit), we test if function serialization works with this expression ❶:

```
/xyz/.test(function() { xyz; })
```

This expression creates a function that contains the text "xyz" and passes it to the test() method of a regular expression that tests for the string "xyz". If the function is correctly serialized (the test() method expects a string, which triggers the function's toString() method), the result will be true.

Using this text expression, we set up a regular expression to be used later in the code as follows:

```
superPattern =  /xyz/.test(function() { xyz; }) ? /\b_super\b/ : /.*/;
```

This establishes a variable named superPattern that we'll use later to check if a function contains the string "_super". We can only do that if function serialization is supported, so in the browsers that don't allow us to serialize functions, we substitute a pattern that matches anything.

We'll be using this result later on, but by doing the check now, we don't have to embed this expression, with its rather complicated syntax, in the later code.

NOTE We'll be investigating regular expressions at length in the next chapter.

Now let's move on to the actual implementation of the subclassing method.

6.3.2 *Initialization of subclasses*

At this point, we're ready to declare the method that will subclass a superclass ❷, which we accomplish with the following code:

```
Object.subClass = function(properties) {
  var _super = this.prototype;
```

This adds a subClass() method to Object that accepts a single parameter that we'll expect to be a hash of the properties to be added to the subclass.

In order to simulate inheritance with a function prototype, we use the previously discussed technique of creating an instance of the superclass and assigning it to the prototype. *Without* using our preceding implementation, it could look something like this code:

```
function Person(){}
function Ninja(){}
Ninja.prototype = new Person();
assert((new Ninja()) instanceof Person,
       "Ninjas are people too!");
```

What's challenging about this snippet is that all we *really* want are the benefits of instanceof, but not the whole cost of instantiating a Person object and running its constructor. To counteract this, we have a variable in our code, initializing, that's set to true whenever we want to instantiate a class with the sole purpose of using it for a prototype.

Thus, when it comes time to construct an instance, we can make sure that we're not in an initialization mode and run or skip the init() method accordingly:

```
if (!initializing && this.init)
  this.init.apply(this, arguments);
```

What's especially important about this is that the init() method could be running all sorts of costly startup code (connecting to a server, creating DOM elements, who knows), so we circumvent any unnecessary and expensive startup code when we're simply creating an instance to serve as a prototype.

What we need to do next is copy any subclass-specific properties that were passed to the method to the prototype instance. But that's not quite as easy as it sounds.

6.3.3   *Preserving super-methods*

In most languages supporting inheritance, when a method is overridden, we retain the ability to access the overridden method. This is useful, because sometimes we want to completely replace a method's functionality, but sometimes we just want to augment it. In our particular implementation, we create a new temporary method named _super, which is only accessible from within a subclassed method and which references the original method in the superclass.

For example, recall from listing 6.20, when we wanted to call a superclass's constructor, we did that with the following code (parts omitted for brevity):

```
var Person = Object.subClass({
  init: function(isDancing){
    this.dancing = isDancing;
  }
});

var Ninja = Person.subclass({
  init: function(){
    this._super(false);
  }
});
```

Within the constructor for Ninja, we call the constructor for Person, passing an appropriate value. This prevents us from having to copy code—we can leverage the code within the superclass that already does what we need it to do.

Implementing this functionality (in the code of listing 6.21) is a multistep process. In order to augment our subclass with the object hash that's passed into the subClass() method, we simply need to merge the superclass properties and the passed properties.

To start, we create an instance of the superclass to use as a prototype ❸ with the following code:

```
initializing = true;
var proto = new this();
initializing = false;
```

Note how we "protect" the initialization code, as we discussed in the previous section, with the value of the initializing variable.

Now we're ready to merge the passed properties into this proto object (a prototype of a prototype, if you will) ❹. If we were unconcerned with superclass functions that would be an almost trivial task:

```
for (var name in properties) proto[name] = properties[name];
```

But we *are* concerned with superclass functions, so the preceding code will work for all properties except functions that want to call their superclass equivalent. When we're overriding a function with one that will be calling it via _super, we'll need to wrap the subclass function with one that defines a reference to the superclass function via a property named _super.

But before we can do that, we need to detect the condition under which we need to wrap the subclass function. We can do that with the following conditional expression:

```
typeof properties[name] == "function" &&
typeof _super[name] == "function" &&
superPattern.test(properties[name])
```

This expression contains clauses that check three things:

- Is the subclass property a function?
- Is the superclass property a function?
- Does the subclass function contain a reference to _super()?

Only if all three clauses are `true` do we need to do anything other than copy the property value. Note that we use the regular expression pattern that we set up in section 6.3.1, along with function serialization, to test whether the function calls its superclass equivalent.

If the conditional expression indicates that we must wrap the function, we do so by assigning the result of the following immediate function ❺ to the subclass property:

```
(function(name, fn) {
  return function() {
    var tmp = this._super;

    this._super = _super[name];

    var ret = fn.apply(this, arguments);
    this._super = tmp;

    return ret;
  };
})(name, properties[name])
```

This immediate function creates and returns a new function that wraps and executes the subclass function while making the superclass function available via the _super property. To start, we need to be good citizens and save a reference to the old `this._super` (regardless of whether it already exists) and restore it after we're done. This will help in the case where a variable with the same name already exists (we don't want to accidentally blow it away).

Next we create the new _super method, which is just a reference to the method that exists in the superclass prototype. Thankfully, we don't have to make any additional changes or do any rescoping here; the context of the function will be set automatically when it's a property of our object (`this` will refer to our instance as opposed to that of the superclass).

Finally we call our original method, which does its work (possibly making use of _super as well), and then we restore _super to its original state and return from the function.

There are any number of ways in which similar results could be achieved (there are implementations that have bound the _super method to the method itself, accessible from `arguments.callee`), but this particular technique provides a good mix of usability and simplicity.

6.4   *Summary*

Adding object-orientation to JavaScript via function prototypes and prototypal inheritance can provide an incredible amount of wealth to developers who prefer an object-oriented slant to their code. By allowing for the greater degree of control and structure that object-orientation can bring to the code, JavaScript applications can improve in clarity and quality.

In this chapter, we looked at how using the `prototype` property of functions allows us to bring object orientation to JavaScript code:

- We started by examining exactly what `prototype` is, and what role it plays when a function is paired with the `new` operator to become a constructor. We observed how functions behave when used as constructors, and how this differs from direct invocation of the function.

- Then we saw how to determine the type of an object, and how to discover which constructor resulted in its coming into being.

- We then dug into the object-oriented concept of inheritance and learned how to use the prototype chain to effect inheritance in JavaScript code.

- In order to avoid common pitfalls, we looked at some common "gotchas" that could trap the unwary, with regards to extending `Object` and other native objects. We also saw how to guard against instantiation issues caused by the improper use of our constructors.

- We wrapped up the chapter by proposing a syntax that could be used to enable the subclassing of objects in JavaScript, and we then created a method that implements that syntax. (Not for the faint of heart, that example!)

- Due to the inherit extensibility that prototypes provide, they afford a versatile platform for future development.

In the final example of this chapter, we caught a glimpse of the use of regular expressions. In the next chapter, we'll take an in-depth look at this frequently overlooked, but very powerful, feature of the JavaScript language.

Wrangling
regular expressions

7

This chapter covers

- A refresher on regular expressions
- Compiling regular expressions
- Capturing with regular expressions
- Frequently encountered idioms

Regular expressions are a necessity of modern development. There, we said it.

While many a web developer could go through life happily ignoring regular expressions, there are some problems that need to be solved in JavaScript code that can't be addressed elegantly without regular expressions.

Sure, there may be other ways to solve the same problems. But frequently, something that might take a half-screen of code can be distilled down to a single statement with the proper use of regular expressions. Every JavaScript ninja will have the regular expression as an essential part of his or her toolkit.

Regular expressions trivialize the process of tearing apart strings and looking for information. Everywhere you look in mainstream JavaScript libraries, you'll see the prevalent use of regular expressions for various spot tasks:

- Manipulating strings of HTML nodes
- Locating partial selectors within a CSS selector expression

- Determining if an element has a specific class name
- Extracting the opacity from Internet Explorer's `filter` property
- And more...

Let's start by looking at an example.

> **TIP** Getting fluent with regular expressions requires a lot of practice. You might find a site such as *JS Bin* (jsbin.com) handy for playing around with examples quickly. Another useful site expressly dedicated to regular expression testing is the *Regular Expression Test Page for JavaScript* (www.regexplanet .com/advanced/javascript/index.html).

7.1 *Why regular expressions rock*

Let's say that we wanted to validate that a string, perhaps entered into a form by a website user, follows the format for a nine-digit U.S. postal code. We all know that the U.S. Postal Service has little sense of humor, and they insist that a U.S. postal code (also known as a ZIP code) follow a specific format,

99999-9999

where each 9 represents a decimal digit. The format is five decimal digits, followed by a hyphen, followed by four decimal digits. If you use any other format, your package or letter gets diverted into the black hole of the hand-sorting department, and good luck predicting how long it will take to emerge again from the event horizon.

Let's create a function that, given a string, will verify that the U.S. Postal Service will stay happy. We could resort to simply performing a comparison on each character, but we're ninjas and that's too inelegant a solution, resulting in a lot of needless repetition. Rather, consider the following solution.

Listing 7.1 Testing for a specific pattern in a string

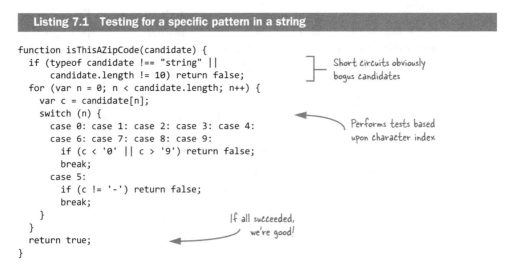

```
function isThisAZipCode(candidate) {
  if (typeof candidate !== "string" ||
      candidate.length != 10) return false;        Short circuits obviously
  for (var n = 0; n < candidate.length; n++) {     bogus candidates
    var c = candidate[n];
    switch (n) {
      case 0: case 1: case 2: case 3: case 4:      Performs tests based
      case 6: case 7: case 8: case 9:              upon character index
        if (c < '0' || c > '9') return false;
        break;
      case 5:
        if (c != '-') return false;
        break;
    }
  }                              If all succeeded,
  return true;                   we're good!
}
```

This code takes advantage of the fact that we only have two different checks to make depending upon the position of the character within the string. We still need to perform up to nine comparisons at runtime, but we only have to write each comparison once.

Even so, would anyone consider this solution *elegant?* It's more elegant than the brute-force, non-iterative approach would be, but it still seems like an awful lot of code for such a simple check.

Now consider this approach:

```
function isThisAZipCode(candidate) {
  return /^\d{5}-\d{4}$/.test(candidate);
}
```

Except for some rather esoteric syntax in the body of the function, that's a lot more succinct and elegant, no?

That's the power of regular expressions, and it's just the tip of the iceberg. Don't worry if that syntax looks like someone's pet iguana walked across the keyboard; we're about to recap regular expressions before we dive into seeing how to use them in ninja-like fashion on our pages.

7.2   A regular expression refresher

Much as we'd like to, we can't offer you an exhaustive tutorial on regular expressions in the space we have. After all, entire books have been dedicated to regular expressions. But we'll do our best to hit all the important points.

For more detail than we can offer in this chapter, the books *Mastering Regular Expressions* by Jeffrey E.F. Friedl, *Introducing Regular Expressions* by Michael Fitzgerald, and *Regular Expressions Cookbook* by Jan Goyvaerts and Steven Levithan, all from O'Reilly, are popular choices.

Let's dig in.

7.2.1   Regular expressions explained

The term *regular expression* stems from mid-century mathematics when a mathematician named Stephen Kleene described models of computational automata as "regular sets." But that won't help us understand anything about regular expressions, so let's simplify things and say that a regular expression is simply a way to express a *pattern* for matching strings of text. The expression itself consists of terms and operators that allow us to define these patterns. We'll see what those terms and operators consist of very shortly.

In JavaScript, as with most other object types, we have two ways to create a regular expression: via a regular expression literal, and by constructing an instance of a RegExp object.

For example, if we wanted to create a rather mundane regular expression (or *regex*, for short) that matches the string "test" exactly, we could do so with a regex literal:

```
var pattern = /test/;
```

That might look a bit strange with those forward slashes, but regex literals are delimited using forward slashes in the same way that string literals are delimited with quote characters.

Alternatively, we could construct a RegExp instance, passing the regex as a string:

```
var pattern = new RegExp("test");
```

Both of these formats result in the same regex being created in the variable pattern.

The literal syntax is preferred when the regex is known at development time, and the constructor approach used when the regex is constructed at runtime by building it up dynamically in a string.

One of the reasons that the literal syntax is preferred over expressing regexes in a string is that (as we shall soon see) the backslash character plays an important part in regular expressions. But the backslash character is *also* the escape character for string literals, so to express a backslash within a string literal, we need to use \\ (double backslash). This can make regular expressions, which already possess a rather cryptic syntax, even more odd-looking when expressed within strings.

In addition to the expression itself, there are three flags that can be associated with a regex:

- i—Makes the regex case-insensitive, so /test/i matches not only "test", but also "Test", "TEST", "tEsT", and so on.
- g—Matches all instances of the pattern, as opposed to the default of "local," which matches only the first occurrence. More on this later.
- m—Allows matches across multiple lines, as might be obtained from the value of a textarea element.

These flags are appended to the end of the literal (for example, /test/ig) or passed in a string as the second parameter to the RegExp constructor (new RegExp("test", "ig")).

Simply matching the exact string "test" (even in a case-insensitive manner) isn't very interesting—after all, we can do that particular check with a simple string comparison. So let's take a look at the terms and operators that give regular expressions their immense power to match more compelling patterns.

7.2.2 Terms and operators

Regular expressions, like most other expressions we're familiar with, are made up of terms and operators that qualify those terms. In the sections that follow, we'll take a look at these terms and operators and see how they can be used to express patterns.

EXACT MATCHING

Any character that's not a special character or operator (which we'll be introducing as we go along) represents a character that must appear literally in the expression. For example, in our /test/ regex, there are four terms that represent characters that must appear literally in a string for it to match the expressed pattern.

Placing such characters one after the other implicitly denotes an operation that means "followed by." So /test/ means "t" followed by "e" followed by "s" followed by "t".

MATCHING FROM A CLASS OF CHARACTERS

Many times, we won't want to match a specific literal character, but a character from a finite set of characters. We can specify this with the set operator (also called the *character class* operator) by placing the set of characters that we wish to match in square brackets: [abc].

The preceding example would signify that we want to match any of the characters "a", "b", or "c". Note that even though this expression spans five characters, it matches only a single character in the candidate string.

Other times, we want to match anything *but* a finite set of characters. We can specify this by placing a caret character (^) right after the opening bracket of the set operator:

[^abc]

This changes the meaning to any character *but* "a", "b", or "c".

There's one more invaluable variation to the set operation: the ability to specify a range of values. For example, if we wanted to match any one of the lowercase characters between "a" and "m", we could write [abcdefghijklm]. But we can express that much more succinctly as follows:

[a-m]

The dash indicates that all characters from "a" though "m" inclusive (and lexicographically) are included in the set.

ESCAPING

Not all characters represent their literal equivalent. Certainly all of the alphabetic and decimal digit characters represent themselves, but as we'll shortly see, special characters such as $ and the period (.) character either represent matches to something other than themselves, or operators that qualify the preceding term. In fact, we've already seen how the [,], -, and ^ characters are used to represent something other than their literal selves.

How do we specify that we want to match a literal [or $ or ^ or other special character? Within a regex, the backslash character escapes whatever character follows it, making it a literal match term. So \[specifies a literal match to the [character, rather than the opening of a character class expression. A double backslash (\\) matches a single backslash.

BEGINS AND ENDS

Frequently we may wish to ensure that a pattern matches at the beginning of a string, or perhaps at the end of a string. The caret character, when used as the first character of the regex, anchors the match at the beginning of the string, such that /^test/ only matches if the substring "test" appears at the beginning of the string being matched. (Note that this is an overloading of the ^ character, because it's also used to negate a character class set.)

Similarly, the dollar sign ($) signifies that the pattern must appear at the end of the string: /test$/.

Using both the ^ and the $ indicates that the specified pattern must encompass the entire candidate string:

/^test$/

REPEATED OCCURRENCES

If we wanted to match a series of four "a" characters, we might express that with /aaaa/, but what if we wanted to match *any* number of the same character?

Regular expressions give us the means to specify a number of different repetition options:

- We can specify that a character is optional (in other words, can appear either once or not at all) by following it with ?. For example, /t?est/ matches both "test" and "est".

- If we want a character to appear one or many times, we use +, as in /t+est/, which matches "test", "ttest", and "tttest", but not "est".

- If we want the character to appear *zero* or many times, * is used, as in /t*est/, which matches "test", "ttest", "tttest", *and* "est".

- We can specify a fixed number of repetitions with the number of allowed repetitions between braces. For example, /a{4}/ indicates a match on four consecutive "a" characters.

- We can also specify a range for the repetition count by specifying the range with a comma separator. For example, /a{4,10}/ matches any string of four through ten consecutive "a" characters.

- The second value in a range can be omitted (but leaving the comma) to indicate an open-ended range. The regex /a{4,}/ matches any string of four or more consecutive "a" characters.

Any of these repetition operators can be *greedy* or *nongreedy*. By default, they're greedy: they will consume all the possible characters that comprise a match. Annotating the operator with a ? character (an overload of the ? operator), as in a+?, makes the operation nongreedy: it will consume *only* enough characters to make a match.

For example, if we were matching against the string "aaa", the regular expression /a+/ would match all three a characters, whereas the nongreedy expression /a+?/ would match only one a character, because a single a character is all that's needed to satisfy the a+ term.

PREDEFINED CHARACTER CLASSES

There are some characters that we'd like to match that are impossible to specify with literal characters (such as control characters like a carriage return), and there are also character classes that we might often want to match, such as the set of decimal digits, or the set of whitespace characters. The regular expression syntax gives us a number of predefined terms that represent these characters or commonly used classes so that we can use control-character matching in our regular expressions, and so that we don't need to resort to the character class operator for commonly used sets of characters.

Table 7.1 lists these terms and what character or set of characters they represent.

Table 7.1   Predefined character class and character terms

Predefined term	Matches
\t	Horizontal tab
\b	Backspace
\v	Vertical tab
\f	Form feed
\r	Carriage return
\n	Newline
\cA : \cZ	Control characters
\x0000 : \xFFFF	Unicode hexadecimal
\x00 : \xFF	ASCII hexadecimal
.	Any character, except for newline (\n)
\d	Any decimal digit; equivalent to [0-9]
\D	Any character but a decimal digit; equivalent to [^0-9]
\w	Any alphanumeric character including underscore; equivalent to [A-Za-z0-9_]
\W	Any character but alphanumeric and underscore characters; equivalent to [^A-Za-z0-9_]
\s	Any whitespace character (space, tab, form feed, and so on)
\S	Any character but a whitespace character
\b	A word boundary
\B	Not a word boundary (inside a word)

These predefined sets help us to keep our regular expressions from looking excessively cryptic.

GROUPING

So far we've seen that operators (such as + and *) only affect the preceding term. If we want to apply the operator to a group of terms, we can use parentheses for groups just as in a mathematical expression. For example, /(ab)+/ matches one or more consecutive occurrences of the substring "ab".

When a part of a regex is grouped with parentheses, it serves double duty, also creating what's known as a *capture*. There's a lot to captures, and we'll be discussing them in more depth in section 7.4.

ALTERNATION (OR)

Alternatives can be expressed using the | (pipe) character. For example: /a|b/ matches either the "a" or "b" character, and /(ab)+|(cd)+/ matches one or more occurrences of either "ab" or "cd".

BACKREFERENCES

The most complex of terms we can express in regular expressions are backreferences to *captures* defined in the regex. We'll be addressing captures at length in section 7.4, but for now just think of them as the portions of a candidate string that are successfully matched against terms in the regular expression.

The notation for such a term is the backslash followed by the number of the capture to be referenced, beginning with 1, such as \1, \2, and so on.

An example could be /^([dtn])a\1/, which matches a string that starts with any of the "d", "t", or "n" characters, followed by an "a", followed by whatever character matched the first capture. This latter point is important! This isn't the same as /[dtn] a[dtn]/. The character following the "a" can't be any of "d", or "t", or "n", but must be whichever one of those triggered the match for the first character. As such, which character the \1 will match can't be known until evaluation time.

A good example of where this might be useful is in matching XML-type markup elements. Consider the following regex:

```
/<(\w+)>(.+)<\/\1>/
```

This allows us to match simple elements such as "whatever". Without the ability to specify a backreference, this would not be possible, because we'd have no way to know what closing tag would match the opening tag ahead of time.

> **TIP**   That was kind of a whirlwind crash course on regular expressions. If they're still making you pull your hair out and you find yourself bogged down in the material that follows, we strongly recommend using one of the resources we mentioned earlier in this chapter.

Now that we have a handle on what regular expressions are, let's look at how we can use them wisely in our code.

7.3   *Compiling regular expressions*

Regular expressions go through multiple phases of processing, and understanding what happens during each of these phases can help us optimize JavaScript code that utilizes regular expressions. The two prominent phases are compilation and execution.

Compilation occurs when the regular expression is first created. Execution is when we use the compiled regular expression to match patterns in a string.

During compilation, the expression is parsed by the JavaScript engine and converted into its internal representation (whatever that may be). This phase of parsing and conversion must occur every time a regular expression is created (discounting any internal optimizations performed by the browser).

Frequently browsers *are* smart enough to determine when identical regular expressions are being used, and to cache the compilation results for that particular expression. But we can't count on this being the case in all browsers. For complex expressions, in particular, we can begin to get some noticeable speed improvements by predefining (and thus precompiling) our regular expressions for later use.

As we learned in our regular expression overview in the previous section, there are two ways of creating a compiled regular expression in JavaScript: via a literal and via a constructor. Let's look at an example in the next listing.

Listing 7.2 Two ways to create a compiled regular expression

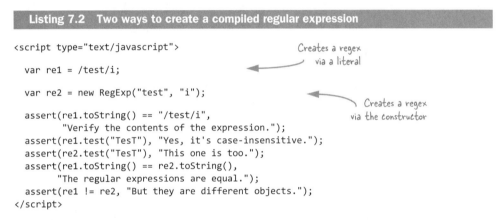

```
<script type="text/javascript">

  var re1 = /test/i;                              Creates a regex
                                                    via a literal

  var re2 = new RegExp("test", "i");
                                                          Creates a regex
  assert(re1.toString() == "/test/i",                   via the constructor
        "Verify the contents of the expression.");
  assert(re1.test("TesT"), "Yes, it's case-insensitive.");
  assert(re2.test("TesT"), "This one is too.");
  assert(re1.toString() == re2.toString(),
        "The regular expressions are equal.");
  assert(re1 != re2, "But they are different objects.");
</script>
```

In this example, both regular expressions are in their compiled state after creation. If we were to replace every reference to re1 with the literal /test/i, it's possible that the same regex would be compiled time and time again, so compiling a regex *once* and storing it in a variable for later reference can be an important optimization.

Note that each regex has a unique object representation: every time a regular expression is created (and thus compiled), a new regular expression object is created. This is unlike other primitive types (like string, number, and so on) because the result will always be unique.

Of particular importance is the use of the constructor (new RegExp(...)) to create a regular expression. This technique allows us to build and compile an expression from a string that we can dynamically create at runtime. This can be immensely useful for constructing complex expressions that will be heavily reused.

For example, let's say that we wanted to determine which elements within a document have a particular class name, whose value we won't know until runtime. As elements are capable of having multiple class names associated with them (inconveniently stored in a space-delimited string), this serves as an interesting example of runtime, regular-expression compilation (see the following listing).

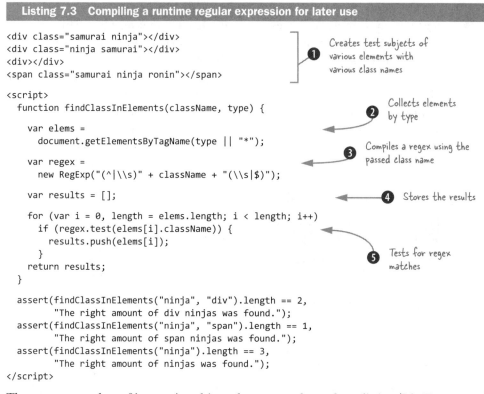

Listing 7.3   Compiling a runtime regular expression for later use

```
<div class="samurai ninja"></div>
<div class="ninja samurai"></div>
<div></div>
<span class="samurai ninja ronin"></span>

<script>
  function findClassInElements(className, type) {

    var elems =
      document.getElementsByTagName(type || "*");

    var regex =
      new RegExp("(^|\\s)" + className + "(\\s|$)");

    var results = [];

    for (var i = 0, length = elems.length; i < length; i++)
      if (regex.test(elems[i].className)) {
        results.push(elems[i]);
      }
    return results;
  }

  assert(findClassInElements("ninja", "div").length == 2,
      "The right amount of div ninjas was found.");
  assert(findClassInElements("ninja", "span").length == 1,
      "The right amount of span ninjas was found.");
  assert(findClassInElements("ninja").length == 3,
      "The right amount of ninjas was found.");
</script>
```

Annotations:
- ❶ Creates test subjects of various elements with various class names
- ❷ Collects elements by type
- ❸ Compiles a regex using the passed class name
- ❹ Stores the results
- ❺ Tests for regex matches

There are a number of interesting things that we can learn from listing 7.3. To start, we set up a number of test-subject <div> and <span> elements with various combinations of class names ❶. Then we define our class-name checking function, which accepts as parameters the class name for which we'll check and the element type to check within.

Then we collect all the elements of the specified type ❷ and set up our regular expression ❸. Note the use of the new RegExp() constructor to compile a regular expression based upon the class name passed to the function. This is an instance where we're unable to use a regex literal, as the class name for which we'll search isn't known in advance.

We construct (and hence, compile) this expression once in order to avoid frequent and unnecessary recompilation. Because the contents of the expression are dynamic (based upon the incoming className argument) we can realize major performance savings by handling the expression in this manner.

The regex itself matches either the beginning of the string or a whitespace character, followed by our target class name, followed by either a whitespace character or the end of the string. Something to notice is the use of a double-escape (\\) within the new regex: \\s. When creating literal regular expressions with terms including the backslash, we only have to provide the backslash once. But because we're writing these backslashes within a string, we must double-escape them. This is a nuisance, to be sure, but one that we must be aware of when constructing regular expressions in strings rather than literals.

Once the regex is compiled, using it to collect ❹ the matching elements is a snap via the `test()` method ❺.

Preconstructing and precompiling regular expressions so that they can be reused (executed) time and time again is a recommended technique that affords us performance gains that can't be ignored. Virtually all complex regular expression situations can benefit from the use of this technique.

Back in the introductory section of this chapter, we mentioned that the use of parentheses in regular expressions served not only to group terms for operator application, but also created what are known as *captures*. Let's find out more about that.

7.4   *Capturing matching segments*

The height of usefulness with respect to regular expressions is realized when we *capture* the results that are found so that we can do something with them. Simply determining if a string matches a pattern is an obvious first step and often all that we need, but determining *what* was matched is also useful in many situations.

7.4.1   *Performing simple captures*

Take a situation in which we want to extract a value that's embedded in a complex string. A good example of such a string might be the manner in which opacity values are specified for legacy Internet Explorer.

Rather than the conventional `opacity` rule with a numerical value employed by the other browsers, IE 8 and earlier versions use a rule like this:

```
filter:alpha(opacity=50);
```

In the following listing, we extract the opacity value out of this filter string.

Listing 7.4   A simple function for capturing an embedded value

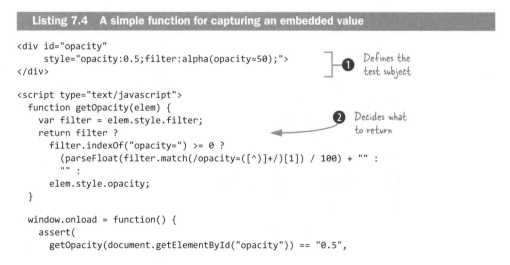

```
<div id="opacity"
     style="opacity:0.5;filter:alpha(opacity=50);">       ❶ Defines the
</div>                                                        test subject

<script type="text/javascript">
  function getOpacity(elem) {
    var filter = elem.style.filter;                       ❷ Decides what
    return filter ?                                           to return
      filter.indexOf("opacity=") >= 0 ?
        (parseFloat(filter.match(/opacity=([^)]+)/)[1]) / 100) + "" :
        "" :
      elem.style.opacity;
  }

  window.onload = function() {
    assert(
      getOpacity(document.getElementById("opacity")) == "0.5",
```

```
    "The opacity of the element has been obtained.");
  };
</script>
```

We define an element that specifies both styles for opacity (one for standards-compliant browsers, and one for legacy IE) that we'll use as a test subject ❶. Then we create a function that will return the opacity value as the standards-defined value from 0.0 to 1.0, regardless of how it was defined.

The opacity parsing code may seem a little bit confusing at first ❷, but it's not too bad once we break it down. To start with, we need to determine if a `filter` property even exists for us to parse. If not, we try to access the `opacity` style property instead. If the `filter` property is resident, we need to verify that it will contain the opacity string that we're looking for. We do that with the `indexOf()` call.

At this point, we can get down to the actual opacity value extraction. The `match()` method of a regular expression returns an array of captured values if a match is found, or `null` if no match is found. In this case, we can be confident that there *will* be a match, as we already determined that with the `indexOf()` call.

The array returned by `match` always includes the entire match in the first index, and then each subsequent capture following.

So the zeroth entry would be the entire matched string of `filter:alpha(opacity=50)`, while the entry at the next position would be `50`.

Remember that the captures are defined by parentheses in the regular expression. Thus, when we match the opacity value, the value is contained in the `[1]` position of the array, because the only capture we specified in our regex was created by the parentheses that we embedded after the `opacity=` portion of the regex.

This example used a local regular expression and the `match()` method. Things change a bit when we use global expressions. Let's see how.

7.4.2 *Matching using global expressions*

As we saw in the previous section, using a local regular expression (one without the global flag) with the `String` object's `match()` methods returns an array containing the entire matched string, along with any matched captures in the operation.

But when we supply a global regular expression (one with the g flag included), `match()` returns something rather different. It's still an array of results, but in the case of a global regular expression, which matches all possibilities in the candidate string rather than just the first match, the array returned contains the global matches; captures *within* each match aren't returned in this case.

We can see this in action in the following code and tests.

> **Listing 7.5 Differences between a global and local search with match()**

```
<script type="text/javascript">

  var html = "<div class='test'><b>Hello</b> <i>world!</i></div>";

  var results = html.match(/<(\/?)(\w+)([^>]*?)>/);
```
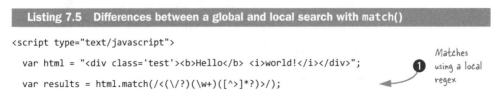

Matches using a local regex ❶

```
assert(results[0] == "<div class='test'>", "The entire match.");
assert(results[1] == "", "The (missing) slash.");
assert(results[2] == "div", "The tag name.");
assert(results[3] == " class='test'", "The attributes.");

var all = html.match(/<(\/?)(\w+)([^>]*?)>/g);

assert(all[0] == "<div class='test'>", "Opening div tag.");
assert(all[1] == "<b>", "Opening b tag.");
assert(all[2] == "</b>", "Closing b tag.");
assert(all[3] == "<i>", "Opening i tag.");
assert(all[4] == "</i>", "Closing i tag.");
assert(all[5] == "</div>", "Closing div tag.");
```
❷ *Matches using a global regex*

```
</script>
```

We can see that when we do a local match ❶, a single instance is matched and the captures within that match are also returned, but when we use a global match ❷, what's returned is the list of matches.

If captures are important to us, we can regain this functionality while still performing a global search by using the regular expression's exec() method. This method can be repeatedly called against a regular expression, causing it to return the next matched set of information every time it's called. A typical pattern for how it can be used is shown in the following listing.

Listing 7.6 Using the exec() method to do both capturing and a global search

```
<script type="text/javascript">

  var html = "<div class='test'><b>Hello</b> <i>world!</i></div>";
  var tag = /<(\/?)(\w+)([^>]*?)>/g, match;
  var num = 0;

  while ((match = tag.exec(html)) !== null) {
    assert(match.length == 4,
           "Every match finds each tag and 3 captures.");
    num++;
  }

  assert(num == 6, "3 opening and 3 closing tags found.");

</script>
```
❶ *Repeatedly calls exec()*

In this example, we repeatedly call the exec() method ❶, which retains state from its previous invocation so that each subsequent call progresses to the next global match. Each call returns the next match *and* its captures.

By using either match() or exec(), we can always find the exact matches (and captures) that we're looking for. But we'll need to dig further if we want to refer back to the captures themselves within the regex.

7.4.3 Referencing captures

There are two ways in which we can refer back to portions of a match that we've captured: one within the match itself, and one within a replacement string (where applicable).

For example, let's revisit the match in listing 7.6 (in which we match an opening or closing HTML tag) and modify it in the following listing to also match the inner contents of the tag itself.

Listing 7.7   Using backreferences to match the contents of an HTML tag

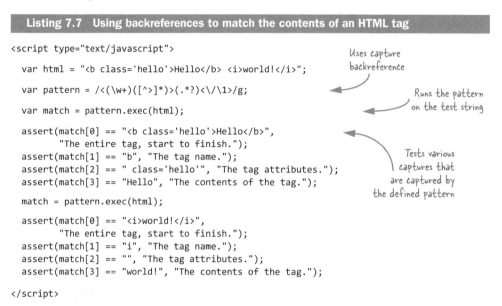

```
<script type="text/javascript">

  var html = "<b class='hello'>Hello</b> <i>world!</i>";

  var pattern = /<(\w+)([^>]*)>(.*?)<\/\1>/g;

  var match = pattern.exec(html);

  assert(match[0] == "<b class='hello'>Hello</b>",
       "The entire tag, start to finish.");
  assert(match[1] == "b", "The tag name.");
  assert(match[2] == " class='hello'", "The tag attributes.");
  assert(match[3] == "Hello", "The contents of the tag.");

  match = pattern.exec(html);

  assert(match[0] == "<i>world!</i>",
       "The entire tag, start to finish.");
  assert(match[1] == "i", "The tag name.");
  assert(match[2] == "", "The tag attributes.");
  assert(match[3] == "world!", "The contents of the tag.");

</script>
```

Uses capture backreference

Runs the pattern on the test string

Tests various captures that are captured by the defined pattern

In listing 7.7, we use \1 to refer back to the first capture within the expression, which in this case is the name of the tag. Using this information, we can match the appropriate closing tag, referring back to whatever the capture matched. (This all assumes, of course, that there aren't any embedded tags of the same name within the current tag, so this is hardly an exhaustive example of tag matching.)

Additionally, there's a way to get capture references within the replace string of a call to the replace() method. Instead of using the backreference codes, as in the example of listing 7.7, we use the syntax of $1, $2, $3, up through each capture number. Here's an example of such usage:

```
assert("fontFamily".replace(/([A-Z])/g, "-$1").toLowerCase() ==
      "font-family", "Convert the camelCase into dashed notation.");
```

In this code, the value of the first capture (in this case, the capital letter F) is referenced in the *replace string* (via $1). This allows us to specify a replace string without even knowing what its value will be until matching time. That's a pretty powerful ninja-esque weapon to wield.

The ability to reference regular-expression captures helps to make a lot of code that would otherwise be rather difficult, quite easy. The expressive nature that it provides ends up allowing for some terse statements that could otherwise be rather obtuse, convoluted, and lengthy.

As both captures and expression grouping are specified using parentheses, there's no way for the regular-expression processor to know which sets of parentheses we added to the regex for grouping and which were intended to indicate captures. It treats all sets of parentheses as both groups and captures, which can result in the capture of more information than we really intended, because we needed to specify some grouping in the regex. What can we do in such cases?

7.4.4 Non-capturing groups

As we noted, parentheses serve a double duty: they not only group terms for operations, they also specify captures. This is usually not an issue, but in regular expressions in which lots of grouping is going on, it could cause lots of needless capturing to go on, which may make sorting through the resulting captures tedious.

Consider the following regex:

```
var pattern = /((ninja-)+)sword/;
```

Here, our intent is to create a regex that allows the prefix "ninja-" to appear one or more times before the word "sword", and we want to capture the entire prefix. This regex requires two sets of parentheses:

- The parentheses that define the capture (everything before the string `sword`)
- The parentheses that group the text `ninja-` for the + operator

This all works fine, but it results in more than the single intended capture due to the inner set of grouping parentheses.

To allow us to indicate that a set of parentheses should not result in a capture, the regular expression syntax lets us put the notation `?:` immediately after the opening parenthesis. This is known as a *passive subexpression*.

Changing our regular expression to

```
var pattern = /((?:ninja-)+)sword/;
```

causes only the outer set of parentheses to create a capture. The inner parentheses have been converted to a passive subexpression.

To test this, take a look at the following code.

Listing 7.8 Grouping without capturing

```
<script type="text/javascript">

  var pattern = /((?:ninja-)+)sword/;

  var ninjas = "ninja-ninja-sword".match(pattern);

  assert(ninjas.length == 2,"Only one capture was returned.");
  assert(ninjas[1] == "ninja-ninja-",
       "Matched both words, without any extra capture.");

</script>
```

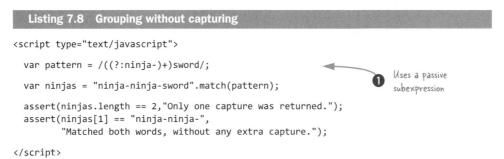 ❶ Uses a passive subexpression

Running these tests, we can see that the passive subexpression ❶ prevents unnecessary captures.

Wherever possible in our regular expressions, we should strive to use non-capturing (passive) groups in place of capturing when the capture is unnecessary, so that the expression engine will have much less work to do in remembering and returning the captures. If we don't need captured results, there's no need to ask for them! The price that we pay is that it can make what are likely already-complex regular expressions a tad more cryptic.

Now let's turn our attention to another way that regular expressions give us ninja powers: using functions with the String's replace() method.

7.5   *Replacing using functions*

The replace() method of the String object is a powerful and versatile method, which we saw used briefly in our discussion of captures. When a regular expression is provided as the first parameter to replace(), it will cause a replacement on a match (or *matches* if the regex is global) to the pattern rather than on a fixed string.

For example, let's say that we wanted to replace all uppercase characters in a string with "X". We could write the following:

```
"ABCDEfg".replace(/[A-Z]/g,"X")
```

This results in a value of "XXXXXfg". Nice.

But perhaps the most powerful feature presented by replace() is the ability to provide a function as the replacement value rather than a fixed string.

When the replacement value (the second argument) is a function, it's invoked for each match found (remember that a global search will match all instances of the pattern in the source string) with a variable list of parameters:

- The full text of the match
- The captures of the match, one parameter for each
- The index of the match within the original string
- The source string

The value returned from the function serves as the replacement value.

This gives us a tremendous amount of leeway to determine what the replacement string should be at runtime, with lots of information regarding the nature of the match at our fingertips.

For example, in the following listing we use the function to provide a dynamic replacement value to convert a string with words separated by dashes to its camel-cased equivalent.

Listing 7.9   Converting a dashed string to camel case

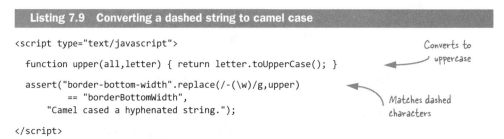

```
<script type="text/javascript">

  function upper(all,letter) { return letter.toUpperCase(); }                    Converts to
                                                                                 uppercase
  assert("border-bottom-width".replace(/-(\w)/g,upper)
         == "borderBottomWidth",                                        Matches dashed
      "Camel cased a hyphenated string.");                              characters

</script>
```

Here, we provided a regex that matches any character preceded by a dash character. A capture in the global regex identifies the character that was matched (without the dash). Each time the function is called (twice in this example), it's passed the full match string as the first argument, and the capture (only one for this regex) as the second argument. We aren't interested in the rest of the arguments, so we didn't specify them.

The first time the function is called it's passed "-b" and "b", and the second time it's called it's passed "-w" and "w". In each case, the captured letter is uppercased and returned as the replacement string. We end up with "-b" replaced by "B" and with "-w" replaced by "W".

Because a global regex will cause such a replace function to be executed for every match in a source string, this technique can even be extended beyond doing rote replacements and can be used as a means of string traversal, instead of doing the exec()-in-a-while-loop technique that we saw earlier in this chapter.

For example, let's say that we were looking to take a query string and convert it to an alternative format that suits our purposes. We'd turn a query string such as

```
foo=1&foo=2&blah=a&blah=b&foo=3
```

into one that looks like this:

```
foo=1,2,3&blah=a,b"
```

A solution using regular expressions and `replace()` could result in some especially terse code, as shown in the next listing.

Listing 7.10   A technique for compressing a query string

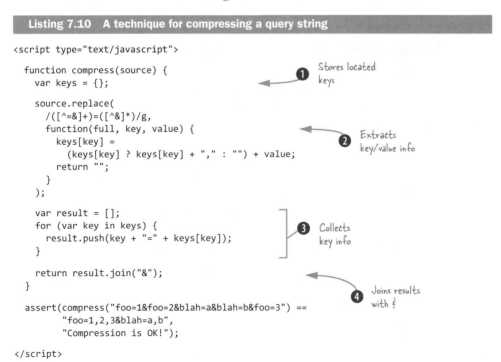

```
<script type="text/javascript">
  function compress(source) {
    var keys = {};                                         ❶ Stores located
                                                              keys
    source.replace(
      /([^=&]+)=([^&]*)/g,
      function(full, key, value) {                         ❷ Extracts
        keys[key] =                                           key/value info
          (keys[key] ? keys[key] + "," : "") + value;
        return "";
      }
    );

    var result = [];
    for (var key in keys) {                                ❸ Collects
      result.push(key + "=" + keys[key]);                     key info
    }

    return result.join("&");                               ❹ Joins results
  }                                                            with &

  assert(compress("foo=1&foo=2&blah=a&blah=b&foo=3") ==
         "foo=1,2,3&blah=a,b",
         "Compression is OK!");
</script>
```

The most interesting aspect of listing 7.10 is how it uses the string `replace()` method as a means of traversing a string for values, rather than as an actual search-and-replace mechanism. The trick is twofold: passing in a function as the replacement value argument, and instead of returning a value, simply utilizing it as a means of searching.

The example code first declares a hash in which we store the keys and values that we find in the source query string ❶. Then we call the `replace()` method ❷ on the source string, passing a regex that will match the key-value pairs, and capture the key and the value. We also pass a function that will be passed the full match, the key capture, and the value capture. These captured values get stored in the hash for later reference.

Note how we simply return the empty string because we really don't care what substitutions happen to the source string—we're just using the side effects rather than the actual result.

Once `replace()` returns, we declare an array in which we'll aggregate the results and iterate through the keys that we found, adding each to the array ❸. Finally, we join each of the results we stored in the array using & as the delimiter, and we return the result ❹.

Using this technique, we can co-opt the `String` object's `replace()` method as our very own string-searching mechanism. The result isn't only fast but also simple and effective. The level of power that this technique provides, especially in light of the small amount of code necessary, should not be underestimated.

In fact, all of these regular expression techniques can have a huge impact on how we write script on our pages. Let's see how we can apply what we've learned to solve some common problems we might encounter.

7.6 Solving common problems with regular expressions

In JavaScript, a few idioms tend to occur again and again, but their solutions aren't always obvious. Our knowledge of regular expressions can definitely come to our rescue, and in this section we'll look at a few common problems that we can solve with a regex or two.

7.6.1 Trimming a string

Removing extra whitespace from the beginning and end of a string is a common need, but one that was (until recently) omitted from the `String` object. Almost every JavaScript library provides and uses an implementation of string trimming for older browsers that don't have the `String.trim()` method.

The most commonly used approach looks something like the following code.

Listing 7.11   A common solution to stripping whitespace from a string

```
<script type="text/javascript">
  function trim(str) {
    return (str || "").replace(/^\s+|\s+$/g, "");
  }
```

Trims a string without looping

```
assert(trim(" #id div.class ") == "#id div.class",
    "Extra whitespace trimmed from a selector string.");

</script>
```

"Look, Ma! No looping!"

Rather than iterating over characters to determine which ones need to be trimmed, a single call to the replace() method with a regex that matches whitespace at the beginning or end of a string does the job.

Steven Levithan, one of the authors of the *Regular Expressions Cookbook* (O'Reilly, 2009), has done a lot of research into this subject, producing a number of alternative solutions, which he details in his *Flagrant Badassery* blog: http://blog.stevenlevithan .com/archives/faster-trim-javascript. It's important to note, however, that in his test cases he works against an incredibly large document, which is certainly a fringe case for most applications.

Of those solutions, two are of particular interest. The first is accomplished using regular expressions, but with no \s+ and no | operator, as shown in the next listing.

Listing 7.12 An alternative double-replacement trim implementation

```
<script type="text/javascript">

  function trim(str) {
    return str.replace(/^\s\s*/, '')            ⎤── Trims using two
            .replace(/\s\s*$/, '');             ⎦   replacements
  }

  assert(trim(" #id div.class ") == "#id div.class",
      "Extra whitespace trimmed from a selector string.");

</script>
```

This implementation performs two replacements: one for the leading whitespace, and one for trailing whitespace.

Dave's second technique completely discards any attempt at stripping whitespace from the end of the string using a regular expression and does it manually, as the following listing shows.

Listing 7.13 A trim method that slices at the end of the string

```
<script type="text/javascript">

  function trim(str) {
    var str = str.replace(/^\s\s*/, ''),        ← Trims using
        ws = /\s/,                                 regex and slicing
        i = str.length;
    while (ws.test(str.charAt(--i)));
    return str.slice(0, i + 1);
  }

  assert(trim(" #id div.class ") == "#id div.class",
      "Extra whitespace trimmed from a selector string.");

</script>
```

This implementation uses a regex to trim at the leading edge and a slice operation at the trailing edge.

If you compare the performance of these implementations for short strings and document-length strings, the difference becomes quite noticeable. Table 7.2 shows the time in milliseconds to perform 1000 iterations of the trim() method.

Table 7.2   Performance comparison of three `trim()` implementations

Trim implementation	Short string	Document
Listing 7.11	8.7 ms	2,075.8 ms
Listing 7.12	8.5 ms	3,706.7 ms
Listing 7.13	13.8 ms	169.4 ms

This comparison makes it easy to see which implementation is the most scalable. While the implementation of listing 7.13 fared poorly against the other implementations for short strings, it left the others in the dust for much longer (document-length) strings.

Ultimately, which will fare better depends on the situation in which you're going to perform the trimming. Most libraries use the first solution, and it's likely that we'll be using it on smaller strings, so that seems to be the safest bet for legacy browsers.

Let's move on to another common need.

7.6.2   *Matching newlines*

When performing a search, it's sometimes desirable for the . (period) term, which matches any character except for newline, to also include newline characters. Regular expression implementations in other languages frequently include a flag for making this possible, but JavaScript's implementation doesn't.

Let's look at a couple of ways of getting around this omission in JavaScript, as shown in the next listing.

Listing 7.14   Matching *all* characters, including newlines

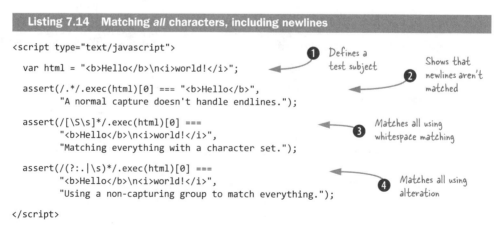

```
<script type="text/javascript">

    var html = "<b>Hello</b>\n<i>world!</i>";                    ❶ Defines a test subject

    assert(/.*/.exec(html)[0] === "<b>Hello</b>",                ❷ Shows that newlines aren't matched
        "A normal capture doesn't handle endlines.");

    assert(/[\S\s]*/.exec(html)[0] ===                           ❸ Matches all using whitespace matching
        "<b>Hello</b>\n<i>world!</i>",
        "Matching everything with a character set.");

    assert(/(?:.|\s)*/.exec(html)[0] ===                         ❹ Matches all using alteration
        "<b>Hello</b>\n<i>world!</i>",
        "Using a non-capturing group to match everything.");

</script>
```

In this example, we define a test subject string ❶ containing a newline. Then we try a number of ways of matching all of the characters in the string.

In the first test ❷, we verify that newlines aren't matched by the . operator.

Ninjas won't be denied, so in the next test ❸ we get our way with an alternative regex, /[\S\s]*/, in which we define a character class that matches anything that's *not* a whitespace character and anything that *is* a whitespace character. This union is the set of all characters.

Another approach is taken in the next test ❹, where we use an alternation regex, /(?:.|\s)*/, in which we match everything matched by ., which is everything but newline, and everything considered whitespace, which includes newline. The resulting union is the set of all characters including newline. Note the use of a passive subexpression to prevent any unintended captures.

Due to its simplicity (and implicit speed benefits), the solution provided by /[\S\s]*/ is generally considered optimal.

Next, let's take a step to widen our view to a worldwide scope.

7.6.3 *Unicode*

Frequently in the use of regular expressions, we want to match alphanumeric characters, such as an ID selector in a CSS selector engine implementation. But assuming that the alphabetic characters will only be from the set of English characters is rather shortsighted.

Expanding the set to include Unicode characters is sometimes desirable, explicitly supporting multiple languages not covered by the traditional alphanumeric character set (see the next listing).

Listing 7.15 Matching Unicode characters

```
<script type="text/javascript">

  var text ="\u5FCD\u8005\u30D1\u30EF\u30FC";

  var matchAll =
    /[\w\u0080-\uFFFF_-]+/;                    Matches all
                                               including Unicode
  assert((text).match(matchAll),
         "Our regexp matches unicode!");

</script>
```

Listing 7.15 includes the entire range of Unicode characters in the match by creating a character class that includes the \w term, to match all the "normal" word characters, plus a range that spans the entire set of Unicode characters above character code 128 (hex 0x80). Starting at 128 gives us some high ASCII characters along with all Unicode characters.

The astute among you might note that by adding the entire range of Unicode characters above \u0080, we match not only alphabetic characters, but also all Unicode punctuation and other special characters (arrows, for example). But that's OK, because the point of the example is to show how to match Unicode characters in general. If you have a specific range of characters that you want to match, you can use the lesson of this example to add whatever range you wish to the character class.

Before we move on from our examination of regular expressions, let's tackle one more common issue.

7.6.4   Escaped characters

It's common for page authors to use names that conform to program identifiers when assigning id values to page elements, but that's just a convention; id values can contain characters other than "word" characters, including punctuation. For example, a web developer might use the id value form:update for an element.

A library developer, when writing an implementation for, say, a CSS selector engine, would like to support this via escaped characters. This allows the user to specify complex names that don't conform to typical naming conventions. So let's develop a regex that will allow us to match escaped characters. Consider the following code.

Listing 7.16   Matching escaped characters in a CSS selector

```
<script type="text/javascript">

  var pattern = /^((\w+)|(\\.))+$/;

  var tests = [
    "formUpdate",
    "form\\.update\\.whatever",
    "form\\:update",
    "\\f\\o\\r\\m\\u\\p\\d\\a\\t\\e",
    "form:update"
  ];

  for (var n = 0; n < tests.length; n++) {
    assert(pattern.test(tests[n]),
           tests[n] + " is a valid identifier" );
  }

</script>
```

This regular expression allows any sequence composed of a sequence of word characters, a backslash followed by any character (even a backslash), or both.

Sets up various test subjects. All should pass but the last, which fails to escape its non-word character (:).

Runs through all the test subjects.

This particular expression works by allowing for a match of either a word character sequence or a sequence of a backslash followed by any character.

7.7   Summary

Let's recap what we've learned about regular expressions:

- Regular expressions are a powerful tool that permeates modern JavaScript development, with virtually every aspect of any sort of matching depending upon their use. With a good understanding of the advanced regex concepts that have been covered in this chapter, any developer should feel comfortable in tackling a challenging piece of code that could benefit from regular expressions.

- We saw what the various terms and operators that go into a regex mean, and how to combine them to form pattern-matching regular expressions.

- We learned how to precompile regular expressions, and how doing so can give us an enormous performance gain over letting a regex be recompiled every time it's needed.

- We learned how to use regular expression to test a string for a match against the pattern that the expression represents, and even more importantly, we learned how to capture the segments of the source string that were matched.

- We learned how to use useful methods like the exec() method of regular expressions, as well as regex-oriented methods of String such as match() and replace(). And we did so while learning the difference between local and global regular expressions.

- We saw how the segments that we captured could be used as backreferences and replacement strings, and how to avoid unnecessary captures with passive subexpressions.

- We examined the utility of providing a function to dynamically determine a replacement string. Then we rounded out the chapter with solutions to some common idioms, such as string trimming and matching such characters as newlines and Unicode.

All told, that's quite an arsenal of powerful tools to stuff into our ninja backpacks.

Back at the beginning of chapter 3, we talked about the event loop and stated that JavaScript executed all event callbacks in a single thread, each in its own turn. In the next chapter, we're going to examine JavaScript threading in detail and discuss its effects upon timers and intervals.

Taming threads and timers

8

This chapter covers

- How JavaScript handles threading
- An examination of timer execution
- Processing large tasks using timers
- Managing animations with timers
- Better testing with timers

Timers are an often misused and poorly understood feature available to us in JavaScript, but they can provide great benefit to the developer in complex applications when used properly.

Note that we referred to timers as a feature that's *available* in JavaScript, but we didn't call them a feature of JavaScript itself—they're not. Rather, timers are provided as part of the objects and methods that the web browser makes available. This means that if we choose to use JavaScript in a non-browser environment, it's very likely that timers may not exist, and we'd have to implement our own version of them using implementation-specific features (such as threads in Rhino).

Timers provide the ability to asynchronously delay the execution of a piece of code by a number of milliseconds. Because JavaScript is, by nature, single-threaded (only one piece of JavaScript code can execute at a time), timers provide a way to dance around this restriction, resulting in a rather oblique way of executing code.

> **NOTE**   HTML5 web workers will change a lot of this, but modern browsers aren't quite there yet, so it's still important to understand how browsers are currently working.

This chapter will take a look at how this all works.

8.1   *How timers and threading work*

Due to their sheer usefulness, it's important to understand how timers work at a fundamental level. They may seem to behave non-intuitively at times because of the single thread within which they execute; many programmers will most probably be accustomed to how timers work in a multi-threaded environment.

We'll examine the ramifications of JavaScript's single-threaded restrictions in a moment, but let's start by examining the functions we can use to construct and manipulate timers.

8.1.1   *Setting and clearing timers*

JavaScript provides us with two methods to create timers and two corresponding methods to clear (remove) them. All are methods of the window (global context) object.

They're described in table 8.1.

Table 8.1   JavaScript's timer manipulation methods (all methods of `window`)

Method	Format	Description
setTimeout	id = setTimeout(fn,delay)	Initiates a timer that will execute the passed callback exactly once after the delay has elapsed. A value that uniquely identifies the timer is returned.
clearTimeout	clearTimeout(id)	Cancels (clears) the timer identified by the passed value if the timer has not yet fired.
setInterval	id = setInterval(fn,delay)	Initiates a timer that will continually execute the passed callback at the specified delay interval, until canceled. A value that uniquely identifies the timer is returned.
clearInterval	clearInterval(id)	Cancels (clears) the interval timer identified by the passed value.

These methods allow us to set and clear timers that either fire a single time, or that fire periodically at a specified interval. In practice, most browsers allow you to use either clearTimeout() or clearInterval() to cancel either timer, but it's recommended that the methods be used in matched pairs if for nothing other than clarity.

An important concept that needs to be understood with regard to JavaScript timers is that the timer delay isn't guaranteed. The reason for this has a great deal to do with the nature of JavaScript threading.

Let's explore that concept.

8.1.2 *Timer execution within the execution thread*

Until web workers come into the picture, all JavaScript code in a browser executes in a single thread. One. Just one.

The unavoidable result of this fact is that the handlers for asynchronous events, such as interface events and timers, are only executed when there's nothing else already executing. This means that handlers must queue up to execute when a slot is available, and that no handler will ever interrupt the execution of another.

This is best demonstrated with a timing diagram, as shown in figure 8.1.

There's a lot of information to digest in figure 8.1, but understanding it completely gives us a better understanding of how asynchronous JavaScript execution works. This diagram is one-dimensional, with time (in milliseconds) running from left to right along the *x* axis. The boxes represent portions of JavaScript code under execution, extending for the amount of time they're running. For example, the first block of mainline JavaScript code executes for approximately 18 ms, the mouse-click block for approximately 10 ms, and so on.

Because JavaScript can only execute one block of code at a time due to its single-threaded nature, each of these units of execution is blocking the progress of other asynchronous events. This means that when an asynchronous event occurs (like a

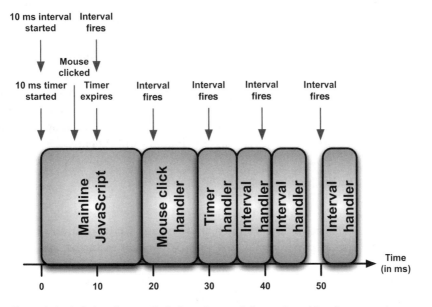

Figure 8.1 A timing diagram that shows how mainline code and handlers execute within a single thread

mouse click, a timer firing, or even the completion of an XMLHttpRequest), it gets queued up to be executed when the thread next frees up. How this queuing actually occurs varies from browser to browser, so consider this to be a simplification, but one that's close enough for us to understand the concepts.

Starting out at time 0, during the execution of the first block of JavaScript, which will take 18 ms to complete, a number of important events occur:

- At 0 ms a timeout timer is initiated with a 10 ms delay, and an interval timer is also initiated with a 10 ms delay.
- At 6 ms the mouse is clicked.
- At 10 ms the timeout timer expires and the first interval expires.

Under normal circumstances, if there were no code currently under execution, we'd expect the mouse-click handler to be executed immediately at 6 ms and the timer handlers to execute when they expire at 10 ms. Note, however, that none of these handlers can execute at those times because the initial block of code is still executing. Due to the single-threaded nature of JavaScript, the handlers are queued up in order to be executed at the next available moment.

When the initial block of code ends execution at 18 ms, there are three code blocks queued up for execution: the click handler, the timeout handler, and the first invocation of the interval handler. We'll assume that the browser is going to use a FIFO technique (first in, first out), but remember, the browser may choose a more complicated algorithm if it so chooses. That means the waiting click handler (which we'll assume takes 10 ms to execute) begins execution.

While the timeout handler is executing, the second interval expires at 20 ms. Again, because the thread is occupied executing the timeout handler, the interval handler can't execute. But this time, because an instance of an interval callback is already queued and awaiting execution, this invocation is dropped. The browser will not queue up more than one instance of a specific interval handler.

The click handler completes at 28 ms, and the waiting timeout handler, which we expected to run at the 10 ms mark, actually ends up starting at the 28 ms mark. That's what was meant earlier by there being no guarantee that the delay that's specified can be counted on to determine exactly when the handler will execute.

At 30 ms, the interval fires again, but once more, no additional instance is queued because there's already a queued instance for this interval timer.

At 34 ms, the timeout handler finishes, and the queued interval handler begins to execute. But that handler takes 6 ms to execute, so while it's executing, another interval expires at the 40 ms mark, causing the invocation of the interval handler to be queued. When the first invocation finishes at 42 ms, this queued handler executes.

This time, the handler finishes (at 47 ms) before the next interval expires at 50 ms. So the fifth firing of the interval doesn't have its handler queued but executes as soon as the interval expires.

The important concept to take away from all of this is that, because JavaScript is single-threaded, only one unit of execution can ever be running at a given time, and that we can never be certain that timer handlers will execute exactly when we expect.

This is especially true of interval handlers. We saw in this example that even though we scheduled an interval that we expected to fire at the 10, 20, 30, 40, and 50 ms marks, only three of those instances executed at all, and at the 35, 42, and 50 ms marks.

As we can see, intervals have some special considerations that don't apply to timeouts. Let's look at those a tad more closely.

8.1.3 *Differences between timeouts and intervals*

At first glance, an interval may look like a timeout that periodically repeats itself. But the differences are a little deeper than that. Let's take a look at an example to better illustrate the differences between `setTimeout()` and `setInterval()`, as shown in the following listing.

> **Listing 8.1   Two ways to create repeating timers**

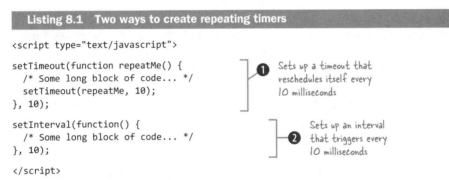

```
<script type="text/javascript">

setTimeout(function repeatMe() {
  /* Some long block of code... */
  setTimeout(repeatMe, 10);
}, 10);

setInterval(function() {
  /* Some long block of code... */
}, 10);

</script>
```

❶ Sets up a timeout that reschedules itself every 10 milliseconds

❷ Sets up an interval that triggers every 10 milliseconds

The two pieces of code in listing 8.1 may *appear* to be functionally equivalent, but they aren't. Notably, the `setTimeout()` variant of the code ❶ will always have at least a 10 ms delay after the previous callback execution (it may end up being more, but never less), whereas `setInterval()` ❷ will attempt to execute a callback every 10 ms regardless of when the last callback was executed.

Recall from the example of the previous section how the timeout callback is never guaranteed to execute exactly when it's fired. Rather than being fired every 10 ms, as the interval is, it will reschedule itself for 10 ms after it gets around to executing.

Let's recap:

- JavaScript engines execute only a single thread at a time, forcing asynchronous events to queue up awaiting execution.
- If a timer is blocked from immediately executing, it will be delayed until the next available time of execution (which may be longer, but never shorter, than the specified delay).
- Intervals may end up executing back to back with no delay if they get backed up enough, and multiple instances of the same interval handler will never be queued up.

- setTimeout() and setInterval() are fundamentally different in how their firing frequencies are determined.

All of this is incredibly important knowledge. Knowing how a JavaScript engine handles asynchronous code, especially with the large number of asynchronous events that typically occur in the average scripted page, makes for a great foundation for building advanced pieces of application code.

In this section we used delay values that are fairly small; 10 ms showed up a lot, for example. We'd like to find out whether or not those values are overly optimistic, so let's turn our attention to examining the granularity with which we can specify those delays.

8.2   *Minimum timer delay and reliability*

While it's pretty obvious that we can specify timer delays of seconds, minutes, hours—or whatever interval values we desire—what isn't obvious is what the smallest practical timer delay that we can choose might be.

At a certain point, a browser is simply incapable of providing fine enough resolution on the timers in order to handle them accurately, because they themselves are limited by the timing restrictions of the operating system.

Up until just a few years ago, specifying delays as short as 10 ms was rather laughably overoptimistic. But there's been a lot of recent focus on improving the performance of JavaScript in the browsers, so we put it to the test. We set off an interval timer, specifying a delay of 1 ms, and for the first 100 "ticks" of the timer, measured the actual delay between interval invocations.

The results are displayed in figures 8.2 and 8.3.

These charts plot the number of times, out of the 100 tick run, that each interval value was achieved.

Under OS X, for Firefox we found that the average value was around 4 ms, almost always with some much longer outlying results, such as the single interval that took 22 ms. Chrome was much more consistent and also averaged around 4 or 5 ms, while Safari was rather slower, averaging out at 10 ms. Opera 11 proved to be the fastest browser with a whopping 56 intervals out of 100 taking the prescribed 1 ms delay.

The Windows results showed Firefox once again being the most sporadic, with results all over the board and no clear peak. Chrome fared well with an average of 4 ms, whereas IE 9 clocked in with a rather miserable peak at 21 ms. Opera once again took the commanding lead delivering all but one interval in the specified 1 ms.

> **NOTE** These tests were conducted on a MacBook Pro with a 2.5 GHz Intel Core 2 Duo processor, and 4 GB of RAM running OS X 10.6.7, and a Windows 7 laptop with an Intel Quad Q9550 2.83 GHz processor and 4 GB of RAM.

We can draw the conclusion that modern browsers are generally not yet able to realistically and sustainably achieve interval delays to the granularity level of 1 ms, but some of them are getting really, really close.

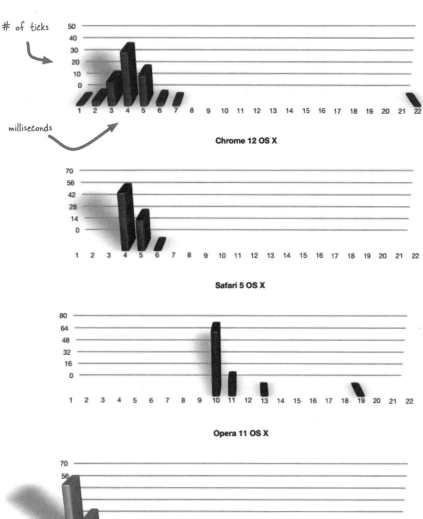

Figure 8.2   Interval timer performance measured on OS X browsers shows that some browsers get pretty close to 1 ms granularity; others aren't so close.

In our tests, we specified a delay of 1 ms, but you can also specify a value of 0 to get the smallest possible delay. There's one catch, though: Internet Explorer fumbles when we provide a 0 ms delay to setInterval(); whenever a 0 ms delay is specified for setInterval(), the interval executes the callback only once, just as if we had used setTimeout() instead.

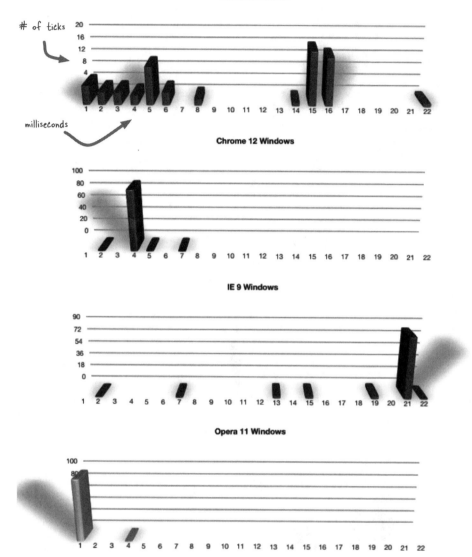

Figure 8.3   Interval timer performance as measured on Windows browsers is equally all over the place.

There are a few other things that we can learn from these charts. The most important is simply a reinforcement of what we learned previously: browsers don't guarantee the exact delay interval that we specify. Although specific delay values can be asked for, the exact accuracy isn't always guaranteed, especially with smaller values.

This needs to be taken into account in our applications when using timers. If the difference between 10 ms and 15 ms is problematic, or if you require finer granularity than the browsers are capable of delivering, you might have to rethink your approach, as the browsers just aren't capable of delivering that accurate a level of timing.

> **NOTE** In most situations, closures are used to "pass" data into timer and interval callbacks. But modern WebKit, Mozilla, and Opera browsers (but not any version of IE from IE 9 and earlier) also allow us to pass extra arguments on the setup call. For example, setTimeout(callback,interval,arg`1, arg2,arg3) would cause arguments arg1, arg2, and arg3 to be passed to the timeout callback.

With all that under our belts, let's take a look at how our understanding of timers can help us avoid some performance pitfalls.

8.3   *Dealing with computationally expensive processing*

The single-threaded nature of JavaScript is probably the largest "gotcha" in complex JavaScript application development. While JavaScript is busy executing, user interaction in the browser can become, at best, sluggish and, at worst, unresponsive. This can cause the browser to stutter or seem to hang, because all updates to the rendering of a page are suspended while JavaScript is executing.

Because of this, reducing all complex operations that take any more than a few hundred milliseconds into manageable portions becomes a necessity if we want to keep the interface responsive. Additionally, some browsers (such as Firefox and Opera) will produce a dialog box warning the user that a script has become "unresponsive" if it has run nonstop for at least five seconds. Other browsers, such as that on the iPhone, will silently kill any script running for more than five seconds.

You may have been to a family reunion where a garrulous uncle won't stop talking and insists on telling the same stories over and over again. If no one else gets a chance to break in and get a word in edgewise, the conversation's not going to be very pleasant for anyone (except for Uncle Bruce, of course). Likewise, code that hogs all the processing time results in an outcome that's less than desirable; producing an unresponsive user interface is never good. But there will almost certainly arise situations in which we'll need to process a significant amount of data; situations such as manipulating a couple of thousand DOM elements, for example.

These are occasions when timers can come to the rescue and become especially useful. As timers are capable of effectively suspending the execution of a piece of JavaScript until a later time, they can also break up the individual pieces of code into fragments that aren't long enough to cause the browser to hang.

Taking this into account, we can convert intensive loops and operations into non-blocking operations.

Let's look at the following example, in which a task is likely to take a long time.

Listing 8.2 A long-running task

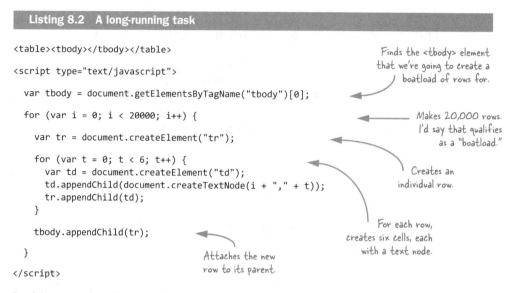

```
<table><tbody></tbody></table>

<script type="text/javascript">

  var tbody = document.getElementsByTagName("tbody")[0];

  for (var i = 0; i < 20000; i++) {

    var tr = document.createElement("tr");

    for (var t = 0; t < 6; t++) {
      var td = document.createElement("td");
      td.appendChild(document.createTextNode(i + "," + t));
      tr.appendChild(td);
    }

    tbody.appendChild(tr);

  }

</script>
```

Finds the <tbody> element that we're going to create a boatload of rows for.

Makes 20,000 rows. I'd say that qualifies as a "boatload."

Creates an individual row.

For each row, creates six cells, each with a text node.

Attaches the new row to its parent.

In this example we're creating a total of 240,000 DOM nodes, populating a table with a large number of cells. This is incredibly expensive and will likely hang the browser for a noticeable period while executing, preventing the user from performing normal interactions. Much in the same way that Uncle Bruce dominates the conversation at the family get-together.

What we need to do is shut Uncle Bruce up at regular intervals so that other people can get a chance to join the conversation. In our code, we can introduce timers into this situation to create just such "breaks in the conversation," as shown in the next listing.

Listing 8.3 Using a timer to break up a long-running task

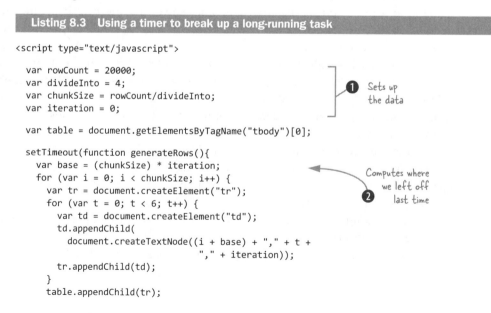

```
<script type="text/javascript">

  var rowCount = 20000;
  var divideInto = 4;
  var chunkSize = rowCount/divideInto;
  var iteration = 0;

  var table = document.getElementsByTagName("tbody")[0];

  setTimeout(function generateRows(){
    var base = (chunkSize) * iteration;
    for (var i = 0; i < chunkSize; i++) {
      var tr = document.createElement("tr");
      for (var t = 0; t < 6; t++) {
        var td = document.createElement("td");
        td.appendChild(
          document.createTextNode((i + base) + "," + t +
                                  "," + iteration));
        tr.appendChild(td);
      }
      table.appendChild(tr);
```

❶ Sets up the data

Computes where we left off last time ❷

```
    }
    iteration++;
    if (iteration < divideInto)
      setTimeout(generateRows,0);
  },0);
```

 ❸ Schedules the next phase

```
</script>
```

In this modification to our example, we've broken up our lengthy operation into four smaller operations, each creating its own share of DOM nodes. These smaller operations are much less likely to interrupt the flow of the browser.

Note how we've set it up so that the data values controlling the operation are collected into easily tweakable variables ❶, should we find that we need to break the operations up into, let's say, ten parts instead of four.

Also important to note is the little bit of math that we needed to do to keep track of where we left off in the previous iteration ❷, and how we automatically schedule the next iterations until we determine that we're done ❸.

What's rather impressive is just how little our code had to change in order to accommodate this new, asynchronous approach. We have to do a *little* more work to keep track of what's going on, to ensure that the operation is correctly conducted, and to schedule the execution parts. But beyond that, the core of the code looks very similar to what we started off with.

The most perceptible change resulting from this technique, from the user's perspective, is that a long browser hang is now replaced with four (or however many we choose) visual updates of the page. Although the browser will attempt to execute our code segments as quickly as possible, it will also render the DOM changes after each step of the timer. In the original version of the code, it needed to wait for one large bulk update.

Much of the time, these types of updates are imperceptible to the user, but it's important to remember that they do occur, and we should strive to make sure that any code we introduce into the page doesn't perceptibly interrupt the normal operation of the browser.

One situation in which this technique has served one of your authors particularly well was in an application constructed to compute schedule permutations for college students. Originally, the application was a typical CGI (communicating from the client to the server, where the schedules were computed and sent back), but it was converted to move all schedule computation to the client side. A view of the schedule computation screen can be seen in figure 8.4.

These operations were quite expensive (running through thousands of permutations in order to find the correct results). The resulting performance problems were solved by breaking up clumps of schedule computations into tangible bites, updating the user interface with a percentage of completion as it went along. In the end, the user was presented with a usable interface that was fast, responsive, and highly usable.

It's often surprising just how useful this technique can be. You'll frequently find it being used in long-running processes such as test suites, which we'll be discussing at

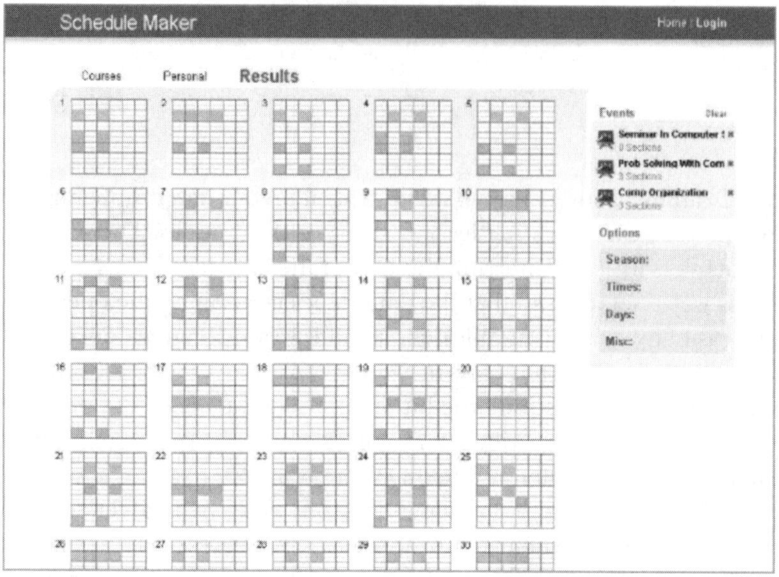

Figure 8.4   **A web-based schedule-generation application with client-side computation**

the end of this chapter. Most importantly, though, this technique shows us just how easy it is to work around the restrictions of the single-threaded browser environment using timers, while still providing a useful experience to the user.

But all is not completely rosy; handling large numbers of timers can get unwieldy. Let's see what we can do about that.

8.4   Central timer control

A problem that can arise in the use of timers is managing a large number of them. This is especially critical when dealing with animations, because we'll likely be attempting to manipulate a large number of properties simultaneously, and we'll need a way to manage that.

Managing multiple timers is problematic for a number of reasons. There's not only the issue of needing to retain references to lots of interval timers that, sooner or later, must be cancelled (though we know how to help tame that kind of mess with closures), but also of interfering with the normal operation of the browser. We saw previously that, by making sure that no one timer-handler invocation performs excessively lengthy operations, we can prevent our code from blocking other operations, but there are other browser considerations. One of these is garbage collection.

Firing off a large number of simultaneous timers will increase the chances of a garbage-collection task occurring in the browser. Garbage collection, roughly speaking, is when the browser goes through its allocated memory and tries to tie up any loose ends by removing unused objects. Timers are a particular problem, because they're generally managed outside of the flow of the normal single-threaded JavaScript engine (through other browser threads).

While some browsers are more capable of handling this situation, others can exhibit long garbage-collection cycles. You might have noticed this when you see a nice, smooth animation in one browser, but view it in another and see it stutter its way to completion. Reducing the number of simultaneous timers being used will drastically help with this situation, and this is why all modern animation engines utilize a technique called a *central timer control.*

Having a central control for our timers gives us a lot of power and flexibility:

- We only need one timer running per page at a time.
- We can pause and resume the timers at will.
- The process for removing callback functions is trivialized.

Let's take a look at an example that uses this technique for managing multiple functions that are animating separate properties. First, we'll create a facility for managing multiple handler functions with a single timer, as shown in the next listing.

Listing 8.4 A central timer control to manage multiple handlers

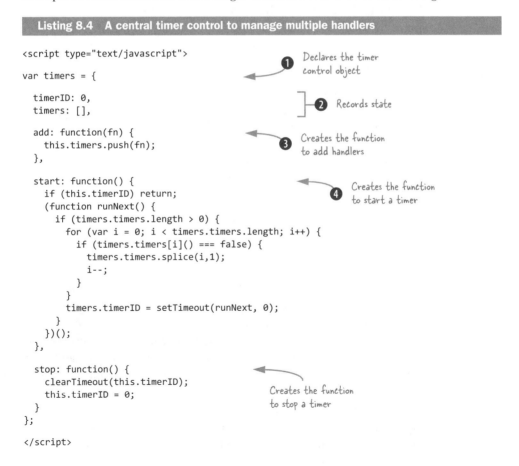

```
<script type="text/javascript">

var timers = {                                    ❶ Declares the timer
                                                     control object
  timerID: 0,
  timers: [],                                     ❷ Records state

  add: function(fn) {                             ❸ Creates the function
    this.timers.push(fn);                            to add handlers
  },

  start: function() {                             ❹ Creates the function
    if (this.timerID) return;                        to start a timer
    (function runNext() {
      if (timers.timers.length > 0) {
        for (var i = 0; i < timers.timers.length; i++) {
          if (timers.timers[i]() === false) {
            timers.timers.splice(i,1);
            i--;
          }
        }
        timers.timerID = setTimeout(runNext, 0);
      }
    })();
  },

  stop: function() {                              Creates the function
    clearTimeout(this.timerID);                   to stop a timer
    this.timerID = 0;
  }
};

</script>
```

In listing 8.4 we've created a central control structure ❶, to which we can add any number of timer callback functions, and through which we can start and stop their execution. Additionally, we'll allow the callback functions to remove themselves at any time by returning false, which is much more convenient than the typical clear-Timeout() call.

Let's step through the code to see how it works.

To start, all of the callback functions are stored in an array named timers, along with the ID of any current timer ❷. These variables constitute the only state that our timer construct needs to maintain.

The add() method accepts a callback handler ❸ and simply adds it to the timers array.

The real meat comes in with the start() method ❹. In this method, we first verify that there isn't already a timer running (by checking if the timerID member has a value), and if we're in the clear, we execute an immediate function to start our central timer.

Within the immediate function, if there are any registered handlers, we run though a loop and execute each handler. If a handler returns false, we remove it from the array of handlers and schedule the next "tick" of the animation.

Putting this construct to use, we create an element to animate:

```
<div id="box">Hello!</div>
```

Then we start the animation with this code:

```
var box = document.getElementById("box"), x = 0, y = 20;

timers.add(function() {
  box.style.left = x + "px";
  if (++x > 50) return false;
});

timers.add(function() {
  box.style.top = y + "px";
  y += 2;
  if (y > 120) return false;
});

timers.start();
```

We get a reference to the element, add a handler that moves the element horizontally and another handler that moves it vertically, and start the whole shebang.

The result, after the animation completes, is shown in figure 8.5.

It's important to note that organizing timers in this manner ensures that the callback functions will always execute in the order in which they're added. That isn't always guaranteed with normal timers, where the browser could choose to execute one before another.

This manner of timer organization is critical for large applications or any form of JavaScript animations. Having a solution in place will certainly help in any future application development and especially when creating animations.

Figure 8.5 After running multiple animation handlers, the element has moved down and across the page.

In addition to animations, central timer control can help us on the testing front. Let's see how.

8.5 *Asynchronous testing*

Another situation in which a centralized timer control comes in mighty handy is when we wish to perform asynchronous testing. The issue here is that when we want to perform testing on actions that may not complete immediately (such as handlers for a timer, or even an XMLHttpRequest) we need to break our test suite out so that it works completely asynchronously.

As we saw in test examples in the previous chapters, we can easily run the tests as we come to them, and most of the time this is fine. But when we need to do asynchronous testing, we need to break all of those tests out and handle them separately, as in the following listing. You shouldn't be surprised to find that this code looks somewhat familiar.

Listing 8.5   A simple asynchronous test suite

```
<script type="text/javascript">

  (function() {

    var queue = [], paused = false;          Retains state

    this.test = function(fn) {               Defines the test
      queue.push(fn);                        registration function
      runTest();
    };

    this.pause = function() {                Defines the function
      paused = true;                         to pause testing
    };

    this.resume = function() {               Defines the
      paused = false;                        resume function
      setTimeout(runTest, 1);
    };

    function runTest() {                     Runs the tests
      if (!paused && queue.length) {
        queue.shift()();
        if (!paused) resume();
```

```
      }
    }
  })();
</script>
```

The single most important aspect in listing 8.5 is that each function passed to `test()` will contain, at most, one asynchronous test. Its asynchronicity is defined by the use of the `pause()` and `resume()` functions, to be called before and after the asynchronous event. Really, this code is nothing more than a means of keeping asynchronous behavior-containing functions executing in a specific order (it doesn't have to be used exclusively for test cases, but that's where it's especially useful).

Let's look at the code necessary to make this behavior possible, which is very similar to the code we introduced with listing 8.4. The bulk of the functionality is contained within the `resume()` and `runTest()` functions. It behaves very similarly to the `start()` method in the previous example but handles a queue of data instead. Its sole purpose is to dequeue a function and execute it if there is one waiting. Otherwise, it completely stops the interval from running.

The important point here is that because the queue-handling code is completely asynchronous (being contained within an interval), it's guaranteed to attempt execution after we've already called our `pause()` function.

This brief piece of code forces the test suite to behave in a purely asynchronous manner while still maintaining the order of test execution (which can be very critical in some test suites, if their results are destructive and could affect other tests). Thankfully, we can see that it doesn't require very much overhead at all to add reliable asynchronous testing to an existing test suite with the effective use of timers.

8.6   Summary

Learning about how JavaScript timers function has been illuminating! Let's review what we've discovered:

- Seemingly simple features, timers are actually quite complex in their implementation. Taking all their intricacies into account, however, gives us great insight into how we can best exploit them for our gain.
- It has become apparent that timers end up being especially useful in complex applications, including
  - Computationally intensive code
  - Animations
  - Asynchronous test suites
- Due to their ease of use (especially with the addition of closures), they tend to make even the most complex situations easy to manage.

So far, we've discussed a number of features and techniques that we can use to create sophisticated code while keeping its complexity in check. In the next chapter, we'll take a look at how JavaScript performs runtime evaluations and how we can harness that power to our own ends.

Part 3

Ninja training

Now that you've snatched the pebble and graduated from your apprenticeship, this part of the book takes the fundamentals you've learned and teaches you how to survive in the often-hostile environment of the browser. Techniques for dealing with the difficult situations that the browsers put us into are presented, based on the knowledge garnered from the minds of the greatest ninjas.

In chapter 9, we'll charge right into the advanced topic of code evaluation—a technique usually reserved for the mightiest of JavaScript warriors, and one that will be added to your arsenal.

Chapter 10 will cover the with statement, a controversial language construct that, although contraindicated for new code, is liable to exist in any legacy code you need to deal with.

In chapter 11, you'll learn how to deal with cross-browser issues and survive the ordeal.

Your ninja training completes with chapter 12, which explores the realm of attributes, object properties, and related subjects such as styles and CSS.

After chapter 12, if you're thirsting for more, a fourth part of this book—Master Training—continues with the dark arts of JavaScript mastery.

Ninja alchemy: runtime code evaluation

This chapter covers

- How runtime code evaluation works
- Different techniques for evaluating code
- Using evaluation in applications
- Decompiling functions
- Namespacing
- Compressing and obfuscating

One of the many powerful abilities that distinguish JavaScript from many other languages is its ability to dynamically interpret and execute pieces of code at runtime. Code evaluation is simultaneously a powerful, as well as a frequently misused, feature of JavaScript. Understanding the situations in which it can and *should* be used, along with the best techniques for using it, can give us a marked advantage when creating advanced application code.

In this chapter, we'll explore the various ways of interpreting code at runtime and the situations in which this powerful ability can lift our code into the big leagues. We'll learn about the various mechanisms that JavaScript provides to cause code to be evaluated at runtime, and we'll see how runtime evaluation can be applied to various interesting scenarios that we're likely to run into when creating web applications.

To start, let's find out just how we can cause code to be evaluated at runtime.

9.1 Code evaluation mechanisms

Within JavaScript there are a number of different mechanisms for evaluating code. Each has its own advantages and disadvantages, and which one we use should be chosen carefully based upon the context in which it's being employed.

These various means include

- The eval() function
- Function constructors
- Timers
- The <script> element

While we examine each of these mechanisms, we'll discuss evaluation scope and then learn safe practices to keep in mind when evaluating code at runtime.

Let's start by examining the most common way that page authors trigger code evaluation.

9.1.1 Evaluation with the eval() method

The eval() method is likely the most commonly used means of evaluating code at runtime. Defined as a function in global scope, the eval() method executes the code passed into it in string form, within the current context. The result returned from the method is the result of the last evaluated expression.

BASIC FUNCTIONALITY

Let's look at the basic functionality of eval() in action. We expect two fundamental things from eval():

- It will evaluate the code passed to it as a string.
- It will execute that code in the scope within which eval() is called.

Take a look at the following code, which attempts to prove these assertions.

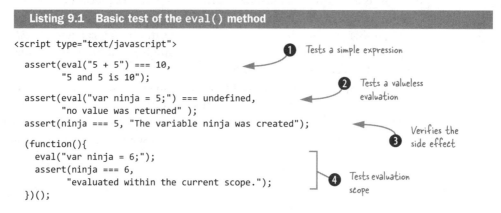

Listing 9.1   Basic test of the eval() method

```
<script type="text/javascript">
  assert(eval("5 + 5") === 10,                    ❶ Tests a simple expression
      "5 and 5 is 10");
  assert(eval("var ninja = 5;") === undefined,    ❷ Tests a valueless
      "no value was returned" );                     evaluation
  assert(ninja === 5, "The variable ninja was created");
                                                  ❸ Verifies the
  (function(){                                       side effect
    eval("var ninja = 6;");
    assert(ninja === 6,                           ❹ Tests evaluation
        "evaluated within the current scope.");      scope
  })();
```

```
assert(window.ninja === 5,
    "the global scope was unaffected");
assert(ninja === 5,
    "the global scope was unaffected");
```

⑤ Tests for scope "leakage"

```
</script>
```

In this listing, we test a number of basic assumptions about eval(). The results of these tests are shown in figure 9.1.

First, we send a string containing a simple expression into the eval() method **❶** and verify that it produces the expected result.

Then we try a statement that produces no value, the assignment ninja=5, and verify that the expected value (none) is returned **❷**. But wait, that's not enough of a test. We expected no result, but was that because the expression was evaluated and produced no result or because nothing happened at all? A further test is needed.

We expect the code to be evaluated in the current scope, in this case the global scope, so we'd expect a side effect of the evaluation to be the creation of a globally scoped variable named ninja. And indeed, another simple test **❸** bears that out.

Next, we want to test that an evaluation in a nonglobal scope works as expected. We create an immediate function and evaluate the phrase varninja=6; within it **❹**. A test that the variable exists with the expected value is conducted. But once again, that's not quite enough. Is ninja evaluating to 6 because we created a new variable in the local scope, or did we modify the global ninja variable?

One further test **❺** proves that the global scope was untouched.

EVALUATION RESULTS

The eval() method will return the result of the last expression in the passed code string. For example, if we were to call

```
eval('3+4;5+6')
```

the result would be 11.

It should be noted that anything that isn't a simple variable, primitive, or assignment will need to be wrapped in parentheses in order for the correct value to be returned. For example, if we wanted to create a simple object using eval(), we might be tempted to write this:

```
var o = eval('{ninja: 1}');
```

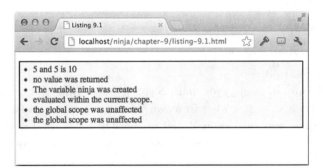

- 5 and 5 is 10
- no value was returned
- The variable ninja was created
- evaluated within the current scope.
- the global scope was unaffected
- the global scope was unaffected

Figure 9.1 Proving that eval() can evaluate various expressions and is confined to the local scope

But that wouldn't do what we want. Rather, we'd need to surround the object literal with parentheses as follows:

```
var o = eval('({ninja: 1})');
```

Let's run some more tests, as shown in the next listing.

Listing 9.2   Testing returned values from `eval()`

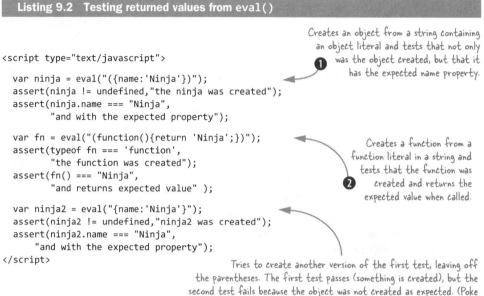

```
<script type="text/javascript">
  var ninja = eval("({name:'Ninja'})");
  assert(ninja != undefined,"the ninja was created");
  assert(ninja.name === "Ninja",
         "and with the expected property");

  var fn = eval("(function(){return 'Ninja';})");
  assert(typeof fn === 'function',
         "the function was created");
  assert(fn() === "Ninja",
         "and returns expected value" );

  var ninja2 = eval("{name:'Ninja'}");
  assert(ninja2 != undefined,"ninja2 was created");
  assert(ninja2.name === "Ninja",
      "and with the expected property");
</script>
```

❶ Creates an object from a string containing an object literal and tests that not only was the object created, but that it has the expected name property.

❷ Creates a function from a function literal in a string and tests that the function was created and returns the expected value when called.

Tries to create another version of the first test, leaving off the parentheses. The first test passes (something is created), but the second test fails because the object was not created as expected. (Poke around in a JavaScript debugger to see what was created.)

Here we create an object ❶ and a function ❷ on the fly using `eval()`. Note how in both cases, the phrases needed to be enclosed in parentheses. As an exercise, make a copy of listing-9.2.html, remove the parentheses, and load the file. See how far you get!

If you ran this test under Internet Explorer 8 or earlier, you may have gotten a nasty surprise. Versions of IE prior to IE 9 have a problem executing that particular syntax. We're forced to use some Boolean-expression trickery to get the call to `eval()` to execute correctly. The following technique from jQuery creates a function using `eval()` in broken versions of IE:

```
var fn = eval("false||function(){return true;}");
assert(fn() === true,
       "The function was created correctly.");
```

This particular issue is fixed in IE 9.

You might be wondering why we'd ever want to create a function in this manner. Well, we usually wouldn't. If we know what function we want to create, we'd usually define it using one of the means that we explored in chapter 3. But what if we don't know in advance what the syntax of the function is? We might want to generate the code at runtime, or perhaps obtain the code from someone else. (If that latter possibility sets off your alarms, fear not; we'll explore security considerations in just a bit.)

Just as when we create a function in a particular scope using "normal" means, functions created with eval() inherit the closure of that scope—a ramification of the fact that eval() executes within the local scope.

It turns out that if we don't need that additional closure, there's another alternative that we can make use of.

9.1.2 Evaluation via the Function constructor

All functions in JavaScript are an instance of Function; we learned that back in chapter 3. There we saw how we could create named functions using syntax such as functionname(...){...}, or omit the name to create anonymous functions.

But we can also instantiate functions directly using the Function constructor, as shown in the following code:

```
var add = new Function("a", "b", "return a + b;");
assert(add(3,4) === 7, "Function created and working!");
```

The *last* argument of a variable argument list to the Function constructor is always the code that will become the body of the function. Any preceding arguments represent the names of the parameters for the function.

So our previous example is equivalent to the following:

```
var add = function(a,b) { return a + b; }
```

While these are functionally equivalent, a glaring difference is that in the Function constructor approach, the function body is provided by a runtime string.

Another difference that's vitally important to realize is that no closures are created when functions are created via the Function constructor. This can be a good thing when we don't want to incur any of the overhead associated with unneeded closures.

9.1.3 Evaluation with timers

Another way that we can cause strings of code to be evaluated, and in this case asynchronously, is through the user of timers.

Normally, as we saw in chapter 8, we'd pass an inline function or a function reference to a timer. This is the recommended use of the setTimeout() and setInterval() methods, but these methods *also* accept strings that will be evaluated when the timers fire.

Consider this example:

```
var tick = window.setTimeout('alert("Hi!")',100);
```

It's rather rare that we'd need to use this behavior (it's roughly equivalent to using the newFunction() approach), and its use is discouraged except in the cases where the code to be evaluated must be a runtime string.

9.1.4 Evaluation in the global scope

We stressed, when discussing the eval() method, that the evaluation executes in the scope within which eval() is called, and we proved it with the test in listing 9.1. But frequently, we may want to evaluate strings of code in the global scope despite the fact that it may not be the current execution scope.

For example, within some functions we may want to execute code in the global scope, as follows:

```
(function(){
  eval("var test = 5;");
})();

assert(test === 5,                              Fails!
       "Variable created in global scope");
```

If we expected the variable test to be created in the global scope as a result of the execution of the immediate function, our test results would be discouraging—the test fails. Because the execution scope of the evaluation is within the immediate function, so is the variable scope.

The situation is depicted in figure 9.2.

A naïve solution would be to change the code to be evaluated as follows:

```
eval("window.test = 5;");
```

Although this *would* cause the variable to be defined in the global scope, it doesn't change the scope in which the evaluation takes place, and any other expectations we have about scope will still be local rather than global. In this example, we're simply assigning a number literal, but it becomes important if we start pointing to variables from the local scope.

But there's a tactic that we can use in modern browsers to achieve our goal: injecting a dynamic <script> tag into the document with the script contents that we want to execute.

Andrea Giammarchi (a self-professed JavaScript Jedi and PHP ninja) developed a technique for making this work properly across multiple platforms.

> **NOTE** We won't even attempt to distinguish between what constitutes a Jedi versus a ninja. We'll just acknowledge that both exhibit a mastery of their chosen craft.

His original work can be found on his *Web Reflection* blog at http://webreflection .blogspot.com/2007/08/global-scope-evaluation-and-dom.html. An adaptation can be found in the following listing.

Listing 9.3 Evaluating code in the global scope

```
<script type="text/javascript">

  function globalEval(data) {                        ❶  Defines the global
    data = data.replace(/^\s*|\s*$/g, "");               eval function
```

```
    if (data) {
      var head = document.getElementsByTagName("head")[0] ||
                 document.documentElement,
        script = document.createElement("script");

      script.type = "text/javascript";
      script.text = data;

      head.appendChild(script);
      head.removeChild(script);
    }
  }
  window.onload = function() {
    (function() {
      globalEval("var test = 5;");
    })();

    assert(test === 5, "The code was evaluated globally.");
  };

</script>
```

② Creates a script node

③ Attaches it to the DOM

④ Blows it away

The code for this is surprisingly simple. In place of eval(), we define a function named globalEval() ❶ that we can call whenever we want an evaluation to take place in the global scope.

This function strips any leading and trailing whitespace from the passed string (review chapter 7 on regular expressions if that statement doesn't make sense to you), and then, locating either the <head> element of the DOM or the document itself, we create a detached <script> element ❷.

We set the type of the script element, and then load its body with the passed string to be evaluated.

Attaching the script element to the DOM as a child of the head element ❸ causes the script to be evaluated in the global scope. Then, having done its duty, the script element is unceremoniously discarded ❹. The results of the test are shown in figure 9.3.

A common use case for this code is when we're dynamically executing code returned from a server. It's almost always a requirement that code of that nature be executed within the global scope, making the use of our new function a necessity.

But can we trust that server?

9.1.5 Safe code evaluation

One question that frequently arises with respect to code evaluation concerns the safe execution of JavaScript code. In other words, is it possible to safely execute untrusted JavaScript on our pages without compromising the integrity of the site? After all, if we didn't provide the code to be evaluated, goodness knows what it could contain!

Some naïve coder might supply us with a string of code that executes an infinite loop, or removes necessary DOM elements, or tromps all over vital data. Or, even worse, a malicious hooligan could purposefully inject code that compromises the security of the site.

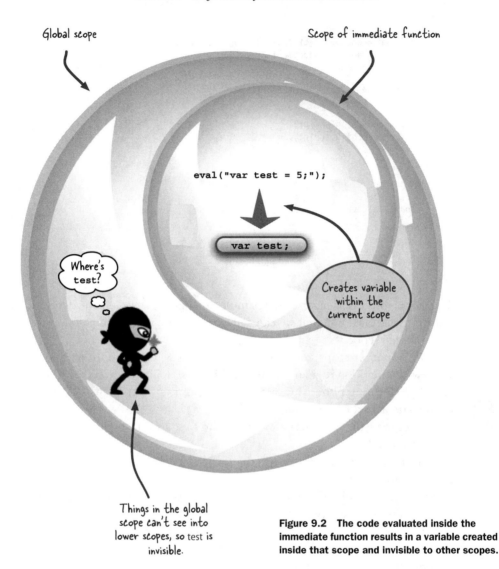

Figure 9.2   **The code evaluated inside the immediate function results in a variable created inside that scope and invisible to other scopes.**

Generally, the answer to the question is "no." There are simply too many ways that arbitrary code can skirt around any barriers put forth and can result in code getting access to information that it's not supposed to view, or cause other problems for us.

There is hope, however. A Google project named *Caja* attempts to create a translator for JavaScript that converts JavaScript into a safer form that's immune to malicious attacks. You can find more information on Caja at http://code.google.com/p/google-caja/.

As an example, look at the following code:

```
var test = true;
(function(){ var foo = 5; })();
Function.prototype.toString = function(){};
```

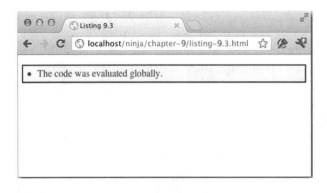

Figure 9.3 We can execute evaluated code in the global context using a bit of DOM manipulation trickery

Caja will cajole that code into the following:

```
___.loadModule(function (___, IMPORTS___) {
{
  var Function = ___.readImport(IMPORTS___, 'Function');
  var x0___;
  var x1___;
  var x2___;
  var test = true;
  ___.asSimpleFunc(___.primFreeze(___.simpleFunc(function () {
    var foo = 5;
  })))();
  IMPORTS___[ 'yield' ] ((x0___ = (x2___ = Function,
    x2___.prototype_canRead___?
  x2___.prototype: ___.readPub(x2___, 'prototype')),
  x1___ = ___.primFreeze(___.simpleFunc(function () {})),
  x0___.toString_canSet___? (x0___.toString = x1___):
  ___.setPub(x0___, 'toString', x1___)));
}
});
}
```

Note the extensive use of built-in methods and properties to verify the integrity of the data, most of which is verified at runtime. Also note that all those gnarly names with the multiple underscores are an attempt to not accidentally collide with other names that might be in use on the page.

The desire for securely executing random JavaScript code frequently stems from wanting to create mashups and safe advertisement embedding without worrying about security becoming compromised. We're certainly going to see a lot of work in this realm, and Google Caja may lead the way.

OK, we now know a number of ways to take a string and get it converted to code that's immediately evaluated. What about going in the opposite direction?

9.2 Function "decompilation"

Most JavaScript implementations also provide a means to "decompile" already-evaluated JavaScript code.

Back in chapter 6, we called this process *serialization*, but the term *decompile* is also used. But we're certainly using the term *decompile* here quite liberally. In most contexts, *to decompile* would mean to reconstitute source code from assembly or byte code, which clearly isn't the case with JavaScript. But aside from serialization (which also has its semantic issues) there really isn't any readily appropriate term, and "de-evaluate" doesn't roll off the tongue easily, so we'll use "decompile" in this section while acknowledging that it may not be the most accurate term in this context.

As complicated as decompiling may sound, it's actually quite simple, and it's performed by the `toString()` method of functions. Let's test this in the next listing.

Listing 9.4   Decompiling a function into a string

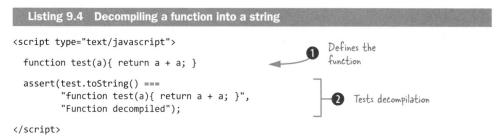

```
<script type="text/javascript">

  function test(a){ return a + a; }                    ➊ Defines the
                                                           function
  assert(test.toString() ===
         "function test(a){ return a + a; }",          ➋ Tests decompilation
         "Function decompiled");

</script>
```

In this test, we create a simple function named `test` ➊ and then assert that the function's `toString()` method returns the original text of the function ➋.

There's one thing to be aware of: the value returned by `toString()` will contain all the whitespace of the original declaration, *including* line terminators. For testing purposes, we punted in listing 9.4, defining a simple function on a single line. If you make a copy of the file and fool around with the formatting of the function declaration, you'll find that the test fails until you change the test string to match the exact formatting of the declaration. So be aware that the whitespace and formatting of a function body need to be taken into account when using function decompilation.

The act of decompilation has a number of potential uses, especially in the area of macros and code rewriting. One of the more interesting uses is one presented in the Prototype JavaScript library, where the code decompiles a function in order to read out its arguments, resulting in an array of named arguments. This is frequently used to introspect into functions to determine what sort of values they're expecting to receive.

The following listing shows a simplification of the code in Prototype to infer function parameter names.

Listing 9.5   A function for finding the argument names of a function

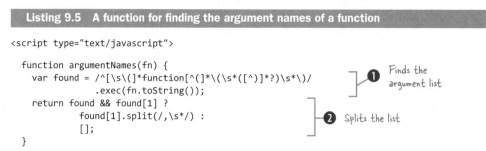

```
<script type="text/javascript">

  function argumentNames(fn) {
    var found = /^[\s\(]*function[^(]*\(\s*([^)]*?)\s*\)/     ➊ Finds the
               .exec(fn.toString());                             argument list
    return found && found[1] ?
           found[1].split(/,\s*/) :                          ➋ Splits the list
           [];
  }
```

```
assert(argumentNames(function(){}).length === 0,
       "Works on zero-arg functions.");

assert(argumentNames(function(x){})[0] === "x",
       "Single argument working.");

var results = argumentNames(function(a,b,c,d,e){});
assert(results[0] == 'a' &&
       results[1] == 'b' &&
       results[2] == 'c' &&
       results[3] == 'd' &&
       results[4] == 'e',
       "Multiple arguments working!");
```

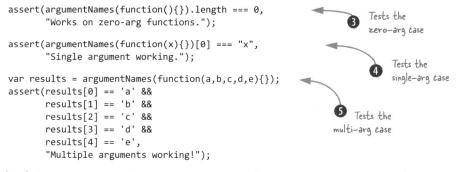

❸ Tests the zero-arg case

❹ Tests the single-arg case

❺ Tests the multi-arg case

```
</script>
```

The function comprises just a few lines of code but uses a lot of advanced JavaScript features in those few statements. First, the function decompiles the passed function and uses a regular expression to extract the comma-delimited argument list ❶. (We covered regular expressions in chapter 7, if you need a refresher.)

Note that because the exec() method *expects* a string, we could have left the toString() off the function argument, and it would have been implicitly called. But we included it here explicitly for clarity.

Then, the result of that extraction is split into its component values, performing checks to make sure that cases such as zero-argument lists are accounted for ❷.

Finally, we test that zero-argument ❸, single-argument ❹, and multi-argument ❺ cases work as expected, as shown in figure 9.4.

There's an important point to take into consideration when working with functions in this manner: it's possible that a browser may not support decompilation. While there aren't many that don't, one such browser is Opera Mini. If that's on your list of supported browsers, you'll need to take that into consideration in code that uses function decompilation.

As emphasized previously in this book (and particularly in upcoming chapters), we certainly don't want to resort to browser detection to determine whether function decompilation is supported. Rather, we'll use feature simulation (which we'll discuss at length in chapter 11) to test whether a browser supports decompilation. One means could be as follows:

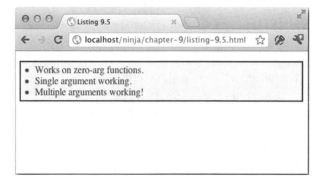

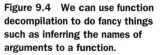

Figure 9.4 We can use function decompilation to do fancy things such as inferring the names of arguments to a function.

```
var FUNCTION_DECOMPILATION = /abc(.|\n)*xyz/.test(function(abc){xyz;});
assert(FUNCTION_DECOMPILATION,
     "Function decompilation works in this browser");
```

Again, using regular expressions (which are a sadly underused workhorse in Java-Script), we pass a function to the `test()` method (here letting the invocation of `toString()` happen implicitly because the method expects a string) and store the result in a variable for later use (or for testing, as shown here).

At this point, we've covered the various means of performing runtime code evaluation; now let's put that knowledge into action.

9.3   *Code evaluation in action*

We saw in section 9.1 that there are a number of ways in which code evaluation can be performed. We can use this ability for both interesting and practical purposes throughout our code. Let's examine some examples of evaluation in order to get a better understanding of when and where we can or should use it in our code.

9.3.1   *Converting JSON*

Probably the most widespread use of runtime evaluation is in converting JSON strings into their JavaScript object representations. As JSON data is simply a subset of the JavaScript language, it's perfectly capable of being evaluated as JavaScript code.

Most modern browsers support the native JSON object with its `parse()` and `stringify()` methods, but a number of earlier browsers that don't provide this object are still in the wild. For these browsers, it's still important to know how to deal with JSON without `window.JSON`.

But as frequently happens to the best of plans, there *is* one minor gotcha that we have to take into consideration. We need to wrap the text representing our constructs in parentheses in order for it to evaluate correctly. That's quite simple to do (see the next listing); we just need to remember to do it.

Listing 9.6   Converting a JSON string into a JavaScript object

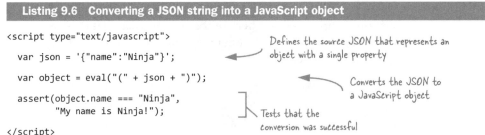

```
<script type="text/javascript">

  var json = '{"name":"Ninja"}';          Defines the source JSON that represents an
                                           object with a single property
  var object = eval("(" + json + ")");
                                           Converts the JSON to
  assert(object.name === "Ninja",         a JavaScript object
       "My name is Ninja!");
                                        Tests that the
</script>                               conversion was successful
```

Pretty simple stuff—and it performs well in most JavaScript engines.

But there's a major caveat to using `eval()` for JSON parsing: often, JSON data is coming from a remote server, and, as pointed out earlier, blindly executing untrusted code from a remote server is rarely a good thing.

The most popular JSON converter script is written by Douglas Crockford, the original creator of the JSON markup. In it, he does some initial parsing of the JSON string in an attempt to prevent any malicious information from passing through. The full code can be found on GitHub at https://github.com/douglascrockford/JSON-js.

Douglas Crockford's function performs some important preprocessing prior to the actual evaluation:

- Guards against certain Unicode characters that can cause problems in some browsers
- Guards against non-JSON patterns that could indicate malicious intent, including the assignment operator and the `new` operator
- Makes sure that only JSON-legal characters are included

If the JSON that's to be evaluated comes from our own code and servers, or from some other trusted source, we usually don't need to worry about malicious code injection (although a healthy dose of paranoia is never a bad thing in this respect). But when we have no reason to trust the JSON that we're going to evaluate, using safeguards such as those provided by Douglas Crockford is just prudent.

The subject of dealing with untrusted code is explored in far greater depth in the following Manning books:

- *Single Page Web Applications* by Michael S. Mikowski and Josh C. Powell (http://www.manning.com/mikowski/)
- *Third-Party JavaScript* by Ben Vinegar and Anton Kovalyov (http://manning.com/vinegar/)

Now let's look at another common use of runtime evaluation.

9.3.2 *Importing namespaced code*

In chapter 3, we talked about namespacing code to keep from polluting the current context—usually the global context. And that's a good thing. But what about when we want to take code that's been namespaced and bring it into the current context deliberately?

This can be a challenging problem, considering that there's no simple or supported way to do it in the JavaScript language. Most of the time, we have to resort to actions similar to the following:

```
var DOM = base2.DOM;
var JSON = base2.JSON;
// etc.
```

The base2 library provides a very interesting solution to the problem of importing namespaces into the current context. Because there's no way to automate this problem, we can make use of runtime evaluation to make the preceding easier to implement.

Whenever a new class or module is added to a base2 package, a string of executable code is constructed that can be evaluated to introduce the functions into the current context, as shown in the following listing (which assumes that base2 has been loaded).

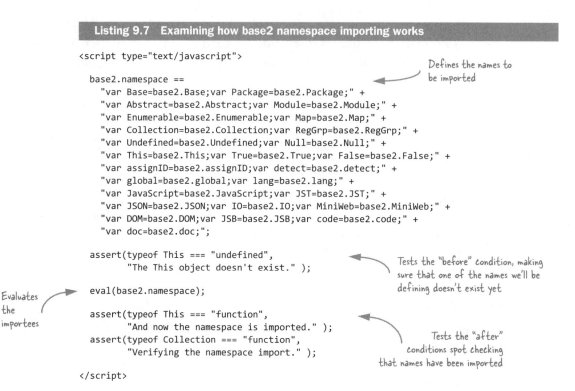

Listing 9.7   Examining how base2 namespace importing works

```
<script type="text/javascript">

  base2.namespace ==
    "var Base=base2.Base;var Package=base2.Package;" +
    "var Abstract=base2.Abstract;var Module=base2.Module;" +
    "var Enumerable=base2.Enumerable;var Map=base2.Map;" +
    "var Collection=base2.Collection;var RegGrp=base2.RegGrp;" +
    "var Undefined=base2.Undefined;var Null=base2.Null;" +
    "var This=base2.This;var True=base2.True;var False=base2.False;" +
    "var assignID=base2.assignID;var detect=base2.detect;" +
    "var global=base2.global;var lang=base2.lang;" +
    "var JavaScript=base2.JavaScript;var JST=base2.JST;" +
    "var JSON=base2.JSON;var IO=base2.IO;var MiniWeb=base2.MiniWeb;" +
    "var DOM=base2.DOM;var JSB=base2.JSB;var code=base2.code;" +
    "var doc=base2.doc;";

  assert(typeof This === "undefined",
         "The This object doesn't exist." );

  eval(base2.namespace);

  assert(typeof This === "function",
         "And now the namespace is imported." );
  assert(typeof Collection === "function",
         "Verifying the namespace import." );

</script>
```

Defines the names to be imported

Tests the "before" condition, making sure that one of the names we'll be defining doesn't exist yet

Evaluates the importees

Tests the "after" conditions spot checking that names have been imported

This is a very ingenious way of tackling a complex problem. It may not be done in the most graceful manner, but until future versions of JavaScript exist that support this, we'll have to make do with what we have.

And speaking of ingenious, another use of evaluation is the packing of JavaScript code. Let's learn about that.

9.3.3   *JavaScript compression and obfuscation*

One of the realities of client-side code is that it needs to somehow actually *get* to the client side. As such, keeping the transmission footprint as small as possible is a worthy goal. We could try to write our code in as few characters as possible, but that leads to crappy and unreadable code. Rather, it's best to write our code with as much clarity as possible, and then to compress it for transmission.

A popular piece of JavaScript software that helps with the second part is Dean Edwards's Packer. This clever script compresses JavaScript code, providing a JavaScript file that's significantly smaller than the original, while still being capable of executing and self-extracting itself to run again. Dean Edwards's Packer can be found at http://dean.edwards.name/packer/.

The result of using this tool is an encoded string that's converted into a string of JavaScript code and executed using the eval() function. The result typically looks something like this:

```
eval(function(p,a,c,k,e,r){e=function(c){return(c<a?'':e(
    parseInt(c/a)))+((c=c%a)>35?String.fromCharCode(c+29):
    c.toString(36))};if(!''.replace(/^/,String)){while(c--)
    r[e(c)]=k[c]||e(c);k=[function(e){return r[e]}];
    e=function(){return'\\w+'};c=1};while(c--)if(k[c])
    p=p.replace(new RegExp('\\b'+e(c)+'\\b','g'),k[c]);
    return p}(' // ... long string ...
```

While this technique is clever and quite interesting, it has some fundamental flaws, the most debilitating being that the overhead of uncompressing the script every time it loads is quite costly.

When distributing a piece of JavaScript code, it's normal to think that the smallest code (bytewise) will download and load the fastest. But this isn't always true—smaller code may download faster, but doesn't always *evaluate* faster. And when all is said and done, it's the combination of downloading *and* evaluating that's important to the performance of your pages. It breaks down to a simple formula:

```
load time = download time + evaluation time
```

Let's take a look at the speed of loading jQuery in three forms:

- Normal (uncompressed)
- Minimized, using Yahoo!'s YUI Compressor, which removes whitespace and performs a few other simple tricks
- Packed using Dean Edwards's Packer, with massive rewriting and decompression using eval()

By order of file size, packed is the smallest, then minimized, followed by uncompressed, and we'd rightly expect their download times to be proportional to the file size. But the packed version has significant overhead: it must be uncompressed and evaluated on the client side. This unpacking has a tangible cost in load time, and means, in the end, that using a minimized version of the code is much faster than the packed version, even though its file size is quite a bit larger.

The results of the study (more information on which can be found at http://ejohn.org/blog/library-loading-speed/) are shown in table 9.1.

Table 9.1   A comparison of load speeds for various formats of the jQuery JavaScript library

Compression scheme	Average time (ms)	Number of samples
Normal	645.4818	12,589
Minimized	519.7214	12,611
Packed	591.6636	12,606

This isn't to say that using code from Packer is worthless—far from it. But if your goals are limited to performance, it may not be your best choice.

But performance may not always be your number one focus. Even with the additional overhead, the Packer can be a valuable tool if *obfuscation* is what you're after. Unlike server-side code, which in a reasonably secured web application is completely inaccessible from the client, JavaScript code must be sent to the client for execution. After all, the browser can't execute any code that it doesn't receive.

Back when the most complicated scripts on web pages were for trivial activities such as image rollovers, no one much cared that the code was shipped off to the client and was available for viewing by anyone on the receiving end. But these days, in the era of highly functional Ajax pages and so-called single-page applications, the amount and complexity of code can be high, and some organizations can be leery of exposing that code to the public.

The obfuscation provided by scripts such as Packer, while not an undefeatable solution, may be part of the answer such organizations are looking for.

If nothing else, Packer serves as a good example of using eval() to effect runtime evaluation.

> **TIP** If you're interested in compressors, you can check out the YUI Compressor at http://developer.yahoo.com/yui/compressor/, and Google's Closure Compiler at https://developers.google.com/closure/compiler/. Yahoo! also provides some other interesting performance information at http://developer.yahoo.com/performance/rules.html.

Let's move on to another activity that we might use runtime code evaluation for: rewriting code.

9.3.4 *Dynamic code rewriting*

Because we have the ability to decompile existing JavaScript functions using a function's toString() method, as described in section 9.2, we can create new functions from existing ones by extracting and massaging the old function's contents.

One case where this has been done is in the unit-testing library Screw.Unit (https://github.com/nkallen/screw-unit).

Screw.Unit takes existing test functions and dynamically rewrites their contents to use the functions provided by the library. For example, a typical Screw.Unit test looks like this:

```
describe("Matchers", function() {
  it("invokes the provided matcher on a call to expect", function() {
    expect(true).to(equal, true);
    expect(true).to_not(equal, false);
  });
});
```

Note the methods: describe(), it(), and expect(). None of these exist in the global scope. To make this code possible, Screw.Unit *rewrites* this code on the fly to wrap all the functions with multiple with(){} statements (which we'll talk about in chapter 10), injecting the function internals with the functions that it needs in order to execute. Here's an example:

```
var contents = fn.toString().match(/^[^{]*{((.*\n*)*)}/m)[1];
var fn = new Function("matchers", "specifications",
  "with (specifications) { with (matchers) { " + contents + " } }"
);

fn.call(this, Screw.Matchers, Screw.Specifications);
```

This is a case of using code evaluation to provide a simpler user experience for test writers without having to introduce a bunch of variables into the global scope.

Next, the term AOP has been bandied about for the past few years in the world of server-side code. Why should they have all the fun?

9.3.5 *Aspect-oriented script tags*

AOP, or aspect-oriented programming, is defined by Wikipedia as "a programming paradigm which aims to increase modularity by allowing the separation of cross-cutting concerns." Yeah, that made our heads hurt too.

Stripped down to its bare bones, AOP is a technique by which code is injected and executed at runtime to handle "cross-cutting" things like logging, caching, security, and so on. Rather than weighing down code with a bunch of logging statements, an AOP engine will add the logging code at runtime, keeping it out of the programmer's face during development.

> **TIP** For more information on AOP, see the Wikipedia article at http://en.wikipedia.org/wiki/Aspect-oriented_programming. And if you're interested in using AOP in Java, take a gander at *AspectJ in Action* by Ramnivas Laddad (www.manning.com/laddad2/).

The injection and evaluation of code at runtime sounds right up our alley in this chapter, doesn't it? Let's see how we might use the ideas of AOP to our advantage.

> **NOTE** Remember the memoization example of section 5.5? That was actually a good example of applying AOP in JavaScript. You've already done it without even knowing it!

We've previously discussed using script tags that have invalid type attributes as a means of including new pieces of data in the page that you don't want the browser to touch. We can take that concept one step further and use it to enhance existing JavaScript.

Let's say that, for whatever reason, we create a new script type called "onload".

What? A new script *type*? How can we do that?

As it turns out, defining custom script types is easy because the browsers will ignore any script type that it doesn't understand. We can force the browser to completely ignore a script block (and use it for whatever nefarious purposes we want) by using a type value that's not standard.

If we want to create new type called "onload", we could do so easily by specifying a script block as follows:

```
<script type="x/onload">  ... custom script here ... </script>
```

Note that we're following the convention of using "x" to mean "custom." We'll intend such blocks to contain normal JavaScript code that will be executed whenever the page is loaded, as opposed to being normally executed inline.

Examine the following code listing.

Listing 9.8   Creating a script tag type that executes only after the page has loaded

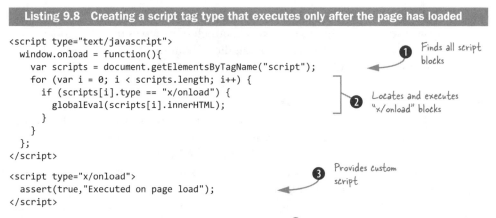

```
<script type="text/javascript">
  window.onload = function(){
    var scripts = document.getElementsByTagName("script");
    for (var i = 0; i < scripts.length; i++) {
      if (scripts[i].type == "x/onload") {
        globalEval(scripts[i].innerHTML);
      }
    }
  };
</script>

<script type="x/onload">
  assert(true,"Executed on page load");
</script>
```

❶ Finds all script blocks

❷ Locates and executes "x/onload" blocks

❸ Provides custom script

In this example, we provide a custom script block ❸ that's ignored by the browser. In the onload handler for the page, we search for all script blocks ❶, and upon finding any that are of our custom type, we use the globalEval() function that we developed earlier in this chapter to cause the script to be evaluated in the global context ❷.

This is a simple example, but this technique could be used for more complex and meaningful purposes. For example, custom script blocks are used with the jQuery .tmpl() method to provide runtime templates. We could use this to execute scripts on user interaction, or when the DOM is ready to be manipulated, or even relatively based upon adjacent elements. The application of this technique is limited only by the imagination of the page author.

Now let's see another advanced use of runtime evaluation.

9.3.6   Metalanguages and DSLs

One of the most important examples of the power of runtime code evaluation can be seen in the implementation of other programming languages on top of the Java-Script language; *metalanguages*, if you will, that can be dynamically converted into JavaScript source and evaluated. Frequently, such custom languages are very specific to the developer's business needs, and the term *domain-specific language* (DSL) has been coined to name such creations.

There are two such DSLs that have been especially interesting.

PROCESSING.JS

Processing.js is a port of the Processing visualization language (see http://processing .org/), which is typically implemented using Java. The port to JavaScript, running on the HTML 5 Canvas element, was created by John Resig.

This port is a full programming language that can be used to manipulate the visual display of a drawing area. Arguably, Processing.js is particularly well suited to this task, making it an effective port.

An example of Processing.js code, utilizing a script block with a type of "application/ processing", follows:

```
<script type="application/processing">
class SpinSpots extends Spin {
  float dim;
  SpinSpots(float x, float y, float s, float d) {
    super(x, y, s);
    dim = d;
  }
  void display() {
    noStroke();
    pushMatrix();
    translate(x, y);
    angle += speed;
    rotate(angle);
    ellipse(-dim/2, 0, dim, dim);
    ellipse(dim/2, 0, dim, dim);
    popMatrix();
  }
}
</script>
```

The preceding Processing.js code is converted into JavaScript code and executed using a call to eval(). This is the resulting JavaScript:

```
function SpinSpots() {with(this){
  var __self=this;function superMethod(){
  extendClass(__self,arguments,Spin);
  this.dim = 0;
  extendClass(this, Spin);
  addMethod(this, 'display', function() {
    noStroke();
    pushMatrix();
    translate(x, y);
    angle += speed;
    rotate(angle);
    ellipse(-dim/2, 0, dim, dim);
    ellipse(dim/2, 0, dim, dim);
    popMatrix();
  });
  if ( arguments.length == 4 ) {
    var x = arguments[0];
    var y = arguments[1];
    var s = arguments[2];
    var d = arguments[3];
    superMethod(x, y, s);
    dim = d;
  }
}}
```

The details of the translation from a metalanguage to JavaScript would require a chapter of its own (or maybe even a whole book) and is beyond the scope of this discussion. So if it blew by you, don't worry about it too much. It's pretty esoteric stuff.

But why use a meta-language at all? By using the Processing.js language, we gain a few immediate benefits over using JavaScript:

- We get the benefits of Processing's advanced language features (such as classes and inheritance)
- We get Processing's simple but powerful drawing API
- We get all of the existing documentation and demos on Processing

More information can be found at http://ejohn.org/blog/processingjs/.

The important point to take away from this is that all of this advanced processing is made possible through the code-evaluation capabilities of the JavaScript language.

Let's look at another such project.

OBJECTIVE-J

A second major project using these capabilities is Objective-J, a port of the Objective-C programming language to JavaScript by the company 280 North. Objective-J was used for the product 280 Slides (an online slideshow builder).

The 280 North team had extensive experience developing applications for OS X, which are primarily written in Objective-C, so in order to create a more productive environment to work within, they ported the Objective-C language to JavaScript. In addition to providing a thin layer over the JavaScript language, Objective-J allows JavaScript code to be mixed in with the Objective-C code. An example is shown here:

```
// DocumentController.j
// Editor
//
// Created by Francisco Tolmasky.
// Copyright 2005 - 2008, 280 North, Inc. All rights reserved.

import <AppKit/CPDocumentController.j>
import "OpenPanel.j"
import "Themes.j"
import "ThemePanel.j"
import "WelcomePanel.j"

@implementation DocumentController : CPDocumentController
{
    BOOL    _applicationHasFinishedLaunching;
}

- (void)applicationDidFinishLaunching:(CPNotification)aNotification
{
    [CPApp runModalForWindow:[[WelcomePanel alloc] init]];
    _applicationHasFinishedLaunching = YES;
}

- (void)newDocument:(id)aSender
{
    if (!_applicationHasFinishedLaunching)
        return [super newDocument:aSender];
```

```
[[ThemePanel sharedThemePanel]
    beginWithInitialSelectedSlideMaster:SaganThemeSlideMaster
      modalDelegate:self
        didEndSelector:@selector(themePanel:didEndWithReturnCode:)
          contextInfo:YES];
}

- (void)themePanel:(ThemePanel)aThemePanel
  didEndWithReturnCode:(unsigned)aReturnCode
{
    if (aReturnCode == CPCancelButton)
        return;

    var documents = [self documents],
        count = [documents count];

    while (count--)
        [self removeDocument:documents[0]];

    [super newDocument:self];
}
```

In the Objective-J parsing application, which is written in JavaScript and converts the Objective-J code on the fly at runtime, they use light expressions to match and handle the Objective-C syntax without disrupting the existing JavaScript. The result is a string of JavaScript code that's evaluated using runtime evaluation.

While this implementation has less far-reaching benefits (it's a specific hybrid language that can only be used within this context), its potential benefits to users who are already familiar with Objective-C, but who wish to explore web programming, will be self-evident.

9.4 Summary

In this chapter we've learned the fundamentals of runtime code evaluation in JavaScript.

- There are a number of mechanisms that JavaScript provides for evaluating strings of JavaScript code at runtime:
  - The eval() method
  - Function constructors
  - Timers
  - Dynamic <script> blocks
- JavaScript also provides a means to go in the opposite direction—obtaining a string for the code of a function via a function's toString() method. This process is known as *function decompilation.*
- We also explored a variety of use cases for runtime evaluation, including such activities as:
  - JSON conversion
  - moving definitions between namespaces
  - minimization and obfuscation of JavaScript code

- dynamic code rewriting and injection
- and even creating metalanguages

While the potential for misuse of this powerful feature is possible, the incredible power that comes with harnessing code evaluation makes it an excellent tool to wield in our quest for JavaScript ninja-hood.

With statements

10

This chapter covers

- Why the with statement is controversial
- How with statements work
- Code simplification with with
- Tricky with gotchas
- Templating with with

The with statement is a powerful, frequently misunderstood, and controversial feature of JavaScript. A with statement allows us to put all the properties of an object within the current scope, allowing us to reference and assign to them *without* having to prefix them with a reference to their owning object.

It's important to know that this statement's continued existence within JavaScript is fleeting. The ECMAScript 5 specification prohibits its use in strict mode, to the extent of considering it a syntax error.

Moreover, the with statement, even prior to ECMAScript 5, was not without its detractors. One of these high-profile skeptics is none less than Douglas Crockford (JavaScript Ninja Extraordinaire, inventor of JSON, and author of *JavaScript: The Good Parts*), who, in 2006, published a famous blog post titled "with Statement Considered Harmful," in which he states:

> If you can't read a program and be confident that you know what it is going to do, you can't have confidence that it is going to work correctly. For this reason, the with statement should be avoided.
>
> Douglas Crockford, April 2006 (http://yuiblog.com/blog/
> 2006/04/11/with-statement-considered-harmful/)

Mr. Crockford was not alone. Many JavaScript editors and IDEs (integrated development environments) have flagged uses of with with warnings, advising against their use. So why are we even talking about it?

Well, there's a lot of existing code that utilizes with, and you're likely to run up against the with statement in code that's out in the wild, so it's something you should be familiar with even if you shouldn't plan to use it in new code.

With that said (pun absolutely intended), let's learn about the with statement.

10.1 What's with "with"?

A with statement creates a scope within which the properties of a specified object can be referenced without a prefix.

As we'll explore in this chapter, there are a number of use cases in which this might be handy:

- Shortening references to an object in a deep hierarchy
- Simplifying test code
- Exposing properties as top-level references to a template
- And more

But first, let's see how it all works.

10.1.1 Referencing properties within a with scope

To start off, let's jump right into looking at the basics of how the with statement works, as shown in the following listing.

Listing 10.1   Creating a with scope using an object

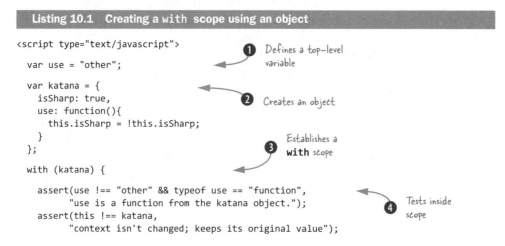

```
<script type="text/javascript">
  var use = "other";                                    Defines a top-level
                                                   ❶   variable

  var katana = {
    isSharp: true,                              ❷  Creates an object
    use: function(){
      this.isSharp = !this.isSharp;
    }
  };                                                     Establishes a
                                                   ❸   with scope
  with (katana) {

    assert(use !== "other" && typeof use == "function",
        "use is a function from the katana object.");        Tests inside
    assert(this !== katana,                          ❹   scope
        "context isn't changed; keeps its original value");
```

```
    }
    assert(use === "other",
            "outside the with use is unaffected.");
    assert(typeof isSharp === "undefined",
            "outside the with the properties don't exist.");
```

⑤ Tests outside scope

```
</script>
```

In the preceding code, we can see how the properties of the katana object are introduced into the scope created by the with statement. Within the scope, we can reference the properties directly without the katana prefix as if they were top-level variables and methods.

To verify this, we start by defining a top-level variable with the name use **❶**. Then we create an inline object that has a property with that same name, use, along with another named isSharp **❷**. This object is referenced by a variable named katana.

Things get interesting when we establish a with scope using katana **❸**. Within this scope, the properties of katana can be referenced directly without the katana prefix. We test this **❹** by verifying that a reference to use doesn't have the value of the top-level variable named use, and that it's a function, as we'd expect if the reference to use pointed to the katana.use() method.

Figure 10.1 shows that the assertions pass.

Our testing continues outside the scope of the with statement **❺**, verifying that references to use refer to the top-level variable, and that the isSharp property is no longer available.

Note that within the scope of the with statement, the object's properties take absolute precedence over variables of the same name defined in higher-level scopes. This is one of the primary reasons that with is derided; code within a with scope can be ambiguous as to its meaning.

We have also proven that the function context (this) is unaffected by the statement.

OK, that covers reading the values of properties. What about writing to them?

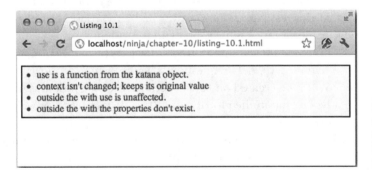

Figure 10.1 With a with statement, we can cause simple references to resolve to an object's properties

10.1.2 *Assignments within a with scope*

Let's take a look at assignments within a with scope, as shown in the next listing.

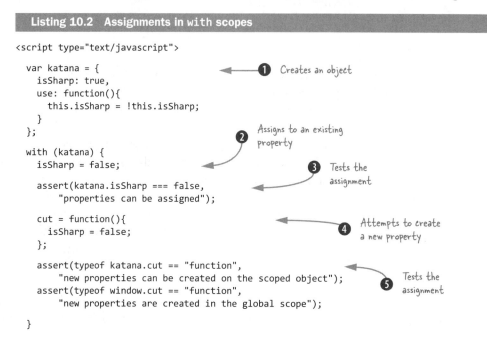

Listing 10.2 Assignments in with scopes

```
<script type="text/javascript">

  var katana = {                        ① Creates an object
    isSharp: true,
    use: function(){
      this.isSharp = !this.isSharp;
    }
  };
                                        ② Assigns to an existing
  with (katana) {                          property
    isSharp = false;
                                        ③ Tests the
    assert(katana.isSharp === false,       assignment
       "properties can be assigned");

    cut = function(){                   ④ Attempts to create
      isSharp = false;                     a new property
    };

    assert(typeof katana.cut == "function",
       "new properties can be created on the scoped object");
    assert(typeof window.cut == "function",    ⑤ Tests the
       "new properties are created in the global scope");   assignment

  }

</script>
```

In this code, we create the same katana object as in our previous test, with use and
isSharp properties ①, and we once again create a with scope using that object. But
instead of referencing the properties, we're going to try some assignments.

First, we assign a value of false to the isSharp property ②. If isSharp resolves to the
katana property, we'd expect that the value of the property would be flipped from its
initial value of true to false. We explicitly test the property ③ and, peeking ahead to
figure 10.2, we see that this test passes. This proves that we can use unprefixed references to the object's properties for both reading and for assignments.

Then we try something a little less straightforward: we create a function and assign
it to a new reference named cut ④. The question is, within which scope will this new
property be created? Will it be created on katana because the assignment is within the
with scope? Or will it be created in the global scope (the window object) as we'd expect
outside of any with scope?

To find out which of these situations transpires, we write two tests ⑤, only one of
which can succeed. The first test asserts that the property will be created within katana,
and the second test asserts that the property will be created in the global scope.

Figure 10.2 clearly shows that, because the second test is the one that passes, unref-
erenced assignments that are not to an existing property on the with scope's object are
made to the global context.

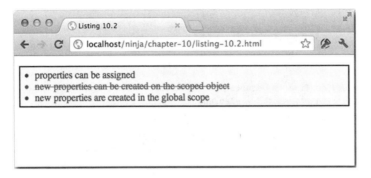

Figure 10.2 Test results show that unprefixed references can't be used to create new properties.

If we wanted to create the new property on katana, we'd need to use the object reference prefix, even though we are within a with scope, as follows:

```
katana.cut = function(){
  isSharp = false;
};
```

OK, that's easy enough; that's what we'd need to do without a with scope in any case, but it rather defeats the purpose of with scopes in the first place. Nevertheless, this *does* point out that care needs to be taken within with scopes, because a simple typo in a property name can lead to strange and unexpected results; namely that a new global variable will be introduced rather than modifying the intended existing property on the with scope's object. Of course, this is something we need to generally be aware of, so we'll need to carefully test our code, as always.

What other considerations should we be aware of?

10.1.3 *Performance considerations*

There's another major factor that we must be aware of when using with: it slows down the execution performance of any JavaScript that it encompasses. And that's not just limited to objects that it interacts with. Let's look at a timing test in the next listing.

Listing 10.3 Performance testing the with statement

```
<script type="text/javascript">
  var ninja = { foo: "bar" },
      value,
      maxCount = 1000000,
      n,
      start,
      elapsed;

  start = new Date().getTime();
  for (n = 0; n < maxCount; n++) {
    value = ninja.foo;
  }
  elapsed = new Date().getTime() - start;
  assert(true,"Without with: " + elapsed);
```

❶ Sets up some variables

❷ Tests without with

```
start = new Date().getTime();
with(ninja){
  for (n = 0; n < maxCount; n++) {
    value = foo;
  }
}
elapsed = new Date().getTime() - start;
assert(true,"With (with access): " + elapsed);

start = new Date().getTime();
with(ninja){
  for (n = 0; n < maxCount; n++) {
    foo = n;
  }
}
elapsed = new Date().getTime() - start;
assert(true,"With (with assignment): " + elapsed);

start = new Date().getTime();
with(ninja){
  for (n = 0; n < maxCount; n++) {
    value = "no test";
  }
}
elapsed = new Date().getTime() - start;
assert(true,"With (without access): " + elapsed);
```

❸ Tests referencing

❹ Tests assignments

❺ Tests with no access

```
</script>
```

For these performance tests, we set up a number of variables, including one (ninja) that will be the target of the with scope ❶. Then we run four performance tests, each performing an action a million times and displaying its results:

- The first test assigns the value of the ninja.foo property to the variable value without declaring any with scope ❷.
- The second test performs the same assignment as the first test, except that the assignment takes place within a with scope and doesn't prefix the reference to property foo ❸.
- The third test assigns a value (the loop counter) to the foo property within a with scope, and without prefixing the property reference ❹.
- The final test performs an assignment to the variable value within a with scope, but without any access to the ninja object at all ❺.

The results of running these tests are shown in table 10.1. All tests were run on the listed browsers executing on a MacBook Pro running OS X Lion 10.7.3 with a 2.8 GHz Core i7 processor and 8 GB of RAM. The IE test was executed on a Windows 7 instance running in a Parallels virtual machine. All times are in milliseconds.

The results are dramatic and could be rather surprising. Not only are there wildly varying times across the browsers (it's clear who's been focusing on JavaScript performance), but across the tests.

Regardless of which browser the tests were executed within, the code executed within with scopes was dramatically slower. This might not be too surprising for the

Table 10.1 Results of running the performance tests of listing 10.3, in milliseconds

Browser	Without with scope	with scope and reference	with scope and assignment	with scope but no access
Chrome 21	87	1456	1395	1282
Safari 5.1	6	264	308	279
Firefox 14	256	717	825	648
Opera 11	13	677	679	623
IE 9	13	173	157	139

tests in which the with scope's object was referenced or assigned, but look at the times in the rightmost column whose test performed no access to the object at all. The mere fact that the code was inside a with scope dramatically slowed it down, by as much as a factor of 41, even though there was no access to the scoped object at all!

We must be sure that we are comfortable with this level of extra overhead when we decide that we want to enjoy any convenience that the with statement brings to the party. And, obviously, the with statement is completely out of the picture for code in which performance is a major consideration.

10.2 *Real-world examples*

Inarguably, the most common reason for using with is the convenience of not having to duplicate variable references for property access. JavaScript libraries frequently use this as a means of simplifying statements that would otherwise be visually complex.

Here are a few examples from a couple of the major libraries, starting with one from Prototype:

```
Object.extend(String.prototype.escapeHTML, {
  div:  document.createElement('div'),
  text: document.createTextNode('')
});

with (String.prototype.escapeHTML) div.appendChild(text);
```

Here, Prototype uses with to avoid having to prefix references to the div and text properties of String.prototype.escapeHTML, which we must admit is a mouthful of a prefix.

But is with really necessary for this purpose? Can you think of something that we've already discussed that could achieve the same goal, without resorting to a with scope? Consider the following:

```
(function(s){
  s.div.appendChild(s.text);
})(String.prototype.escapeHTML);
```

It's our old friend, the immediate function!

Within the scope of the immediate function, the long reference String.prototype.escapeHTML can be referenced as simply s via the parameter of the function. Although this isn't exactly the same as a with scope—the prefix is not eliminated, it's replaced with a shorter reference—many ninja developers would assert that aliasing a complex reference to a simpler one is far superior to the passive-aggressive complete elimination of the prefix. And because with is on the endangered species list, using immediate functions gives us a way to alias complex references with language constructs that are well understood and will continue to be supported.

Here's another with example from the base2 JavaScript library:

```
with (document.body.style) {
  backgroundRepeat = "no-repeat";
  backgroundImage =
    "url(http://ie7-js.googlecode.com/svn/trunk/lib/blank.gif)";
  backgroundAttachment = "fixed";
}
```

In this snippet, base2 uses with as a simple means of not having to repeat a lengthy prefix, in this case document.body.style, again and again. This allows for some super-simple modification of a DOM element's style object.

Another example from base2 follows:

```
var Rect = Base.extend({
  constructor: function(left, top, width, height) {
    this.left = left;
    this.top = top;
    this.width = width;
    this.height = height;
    this.right = left + width;
    this.bottom = top + height;
  },

  contains: function(x, y) {
    with (this)
      return x >= left && x <= right && y >= top && y <= bottom;
  },

  toString: function() {
    with (this) return [left, top, width, height].join(",");
  }
});
```

This second example from base2 uses with as a means of simply accessing instance properties. Normally this code would be much longer, but the terseness that with is able to provide adds some much-needed clarity.

The final example is from the Firebug developer extension for Firefox:

```
const evalScriptPre = "with(__scope__.vars){ with(__scope__.api){" +
  " with(__scope__.userVars){ with(window){";
const evalScriptPost = "}}}}";
```

These lines from Firebug are especially complex—quite possibly the most complex uses of with in a publicly accessible piece of code. These statements are being used within the debugger portion of the extension, allowing the user to access local variables, the firebug API, and the global object, all within the JavaScript console. Operations like this are generally outside the scope of most applications, but it helps to show the power of with and how it can simplify complex pieces of code.

One especially interesting takeaway from the Firebug example is the dual use of with, bringing precedence to the window object over other objects.

Back in listing 10.1, we saw that normally when there is a name collision, the object of the with scope takes precedence over the global values. Structuring code as follows,

```
with ( x ) { with ( window ) { ... } }
```

allows us to have the x object's properties be introduced by with, while still allowing global variables to take precedence in the event of a name collision.

Now let's see another use to which the with statement has been put.

10.3   *Importing namespaced code*

As previously shown, one of the most common uses for the with statement is to simplify statements that have numerous references to object properties. We can see this frequently in namespaced code in which objects are defined within objects to provide an organized structure and naming for the code.

A side effect of this technique is that it can sometimes become rather tedious to retype the object namespace names again and again.

Observe the two statements in the following snippet, which both perform the same operation using the YUI JavaScript library. The first statement is as we would write it without the use of with, and the second with with:

```
YAHOO.util.Event.on(
  [YAHOO.util.Dom.get('item'), YAHOO.util.Dom.get('otheritem')],
  'click', function(){
    YAHOO.util.Dom.setStyle(this,'color','#c00');
  }
);
with (YAHOO.util.Dom) {
  YAHOO.util.Event.on([get('item'), get('otheritem')], 'click',
    function(){ setStyle(this,'color','#c00'); });
}
```

The addition of the single with statement allows for a considerable increase in code simplicity.

Now let's see if the with statement has anything to say for itself when it comes to testing.

10.4   *Testing*

When testing pieces of functionality within a test suite, there are a couple things that we always have to watch out for. The primary of these is attending to the synchronization between the assertion methods and the test case currently being run. Typically this isn't much of a problem, but it can become troublesome when we begin dealing with asynchronous tests.

A common solution to this issue is to create a central tracking object for each test run. The test runner used by the Prototype and script.aculo.us libraries follows this model, providing a central object as the context to each test run. The object contains all the needed assertion methods and easily collects the results back to a central location. We can see an example of this in the following snippet:

```
new Test.Unit.Runner({
  testSliderBasics: function(){with(this){
    var slider = new Control.Slider('handle1', 'track1');
    assertInstanceOf(Control.Slider, slider);
    assertEqual('horizontal', slider.axis);
    assertEqual(false, slider.disabled);
    assertEqual(0, slider.value);
    slider.dispose();
  }},
  // ...
});
```

Note the use of `with(this)` in the preceding test run. The instance variable contains all the assertion methods (`assertInstanceOf`, `assertEqual`, and so on). The method calls could have also been written explicitly as `this.assertEqual`, but by using `with(this)` to introduce the methods that we wish to use, we can get an extra level of simplicity in our code.

Now let's look at an advanced use of `with` that you might not have thought to consider: templating.

10.5   Templating with "with"

The final, and likely most compelling, example of using `with` that we'll consider is within a simplified templating system.

The customary goals for a templating system usually include the following:

- There should be a way to run embedded code and to print out data.
- There should be a means of caching compiled templates.
- It should (perhaps, most importantly) be simple to access mapped data.

This last point is where `with` becomes especially useful.

Before we look at how `with` is used in the implementation, let's take a look at a template that uses the templating system, as shown in the next listing.

Listing 10.4   A sample template to generate an HTML page

```
<html>
<head>
  <script type="text/tmpl" id="colors">
    <p>Here's a list of <%= items.length %> items:</p>
    <ul>
      <% for (var i = 0; i < items.length; i++) { %>
        <li style='color:<%= colors[i % colors.length] %>'>
          <%= items[i] %></li>
      <% } %>
```

```
    </ul>
    and here's another...
  </script>
  <script type="text/tmpl" id="colors2">
    <p>Here's a list of <%= items.length %> items:</p>
    <ul>
      <% for (var i = 0; i < items.length; i++) {
        print("<li style='color:", colors[i % colors.length], "'>",
          items[i], "</li>");
      } %>
    </ul>
  </script>
  <script type="text/javascript" src="tmpl.js"></script>
  <script type="text/javascript">
    var colorsArray = ['red', 'green', 'blue', 'orange'];

    var items = [];
    for (var i = 0; i < 10000; i++) {
      items.push( "test" );
    }

    function replaceContent(name) {
      document.getElementById('content').innerHTML =
        tmpl(name, {colors: colorsArray, items: items});
    }
  </script>
</head>
<body>
  <input type="button" value="Run Colors"
    onclick="replaceContent('colors')">
  <input type="button" value="Run Colors2"
    onclick="replaceContent('colors2')">
  <p id="content">Replaced Content will go here</p>
</body>
</html>
```

Within this template, the special delimiters are used to differentiate embedded JavaScript code (<% and %>) and expressions to be evaluated (<%= and %>). The Java-savvy may recognize that these delimiters match those of old-style JSP 1 templating delimiters (JSP 2 replaced these with a more modern version in 2002).

Now let's look at the implementation in the next listing.

Listing 10.5   A templating solution using with

```
(function(){
  var cache = {};

    this.tmpl = function tmpl(str, data){

    var fn = !/\W/.test(str) ?
      cache[str] = cache[str] ||
        tmpl(document.getElementById(str).innerHTML) :

      new Function("obj",
        "var p=[],print=function(){p.push.apply(p,arguments);};" +
```

Figures out if we're getting a template or if we need to load the template and be sure to cache the result

Generates a reusable function that will serve as the template generator (and which will be cached)

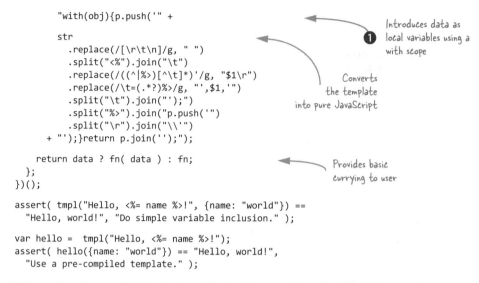

```
          "with(obj){p.push('" +

          str
            .replace(/[\r\t\n]/g, " ")
            .split("<%").join("\t")
            .replace(/((^|%>)[^\t]*)'/g, "$1\r")
            .replace(/\t=(.*?)%>/g, "',$1,'")
            .split("\t").join("');")
            .split("%>").join("p.push('")
            .split("\r").join("\\'")
        + "');}return p.join('');");

      return data ? fn( data ) : fn;
  };
})();
```

Introduces data as local variables using a with scope

Converts the template into pure JavaScript

Provides basic currying to user

```
assert( tmpl("Hello, <%= name %>!", {name: "world"}) ==
  "Hello, world!", "Do simple variable inclusion." );

var hello =  tmpl("Hello, <%= name %>!");
assert( hello({name: "world"}) == "Hello, world!",
  "Use a pre-compiled template." );
```

We aren't going to dig deeply into the implementation details of the templating system; even though it doesn't use any concepts that we haven't already covered, it's put together in a rather sophisticated manner, and you shouldn't feel bad if you don't completely grok it at this point. The important point is how a with scope is used ❶ to provide the properties of the passed data object to the template. This allows the properties of the data object to be referenced within the template as if they were top-level variables.

While complex, this templating system provides a quick-and-dirty solution to simple variable substitution. By giving the user the ability to pass in an object (containing the names and values of template variables that they want to populate) in conjunction with an easy means of accessing the variables, the result is a simple and reusable system. This is made possible largely due to the existence of the with statement, which allows the properties to be easily referenced within the templates.

The templating system works by converting the provided template strings into an array of values, eventually concatenating them together. The individual statements, like <%=name%>, are then translated into the more palatable name, folding them inline into the array construction process. The result is a template construction system that is blindingly fast and efficient.

Additionally, all of these templates are generated dynamically (out of necessity, because inline code is allowed to be executed). In order to facilitate reuse of the generated templates, we can place all of the constructed template code inside a new Function(...), which will give us a template function that we can actively plug our data into.

The full templating system is pulled together with the use of embedded templates. There's a great loophole that we've exploited already, provided by modern browsers and search engines: <script> elements that specify a type that they don't understand are completely ignored. This means that we can specify scripts that contain our templates, give them a type of "text/tmpl", along with a unique ID, and use our system to extract the templates later on.

The total result is a templating system that's easy to use, in large part, because of the abilities of the with statement.

10.6 *Summary*

Here's what we learned in this chapter:

- The most glaringly obvious point is that the primary goal of the with statement is to simplify complex code by allowing properties of an object to be referenced without the need for a reference to the object holding the properties. This can make code that contains many references to the object's properties a lot terser and more easily understandable.

- We saw how this simplification could be applied to areas such as namespacing, testing, and even building templating systems, and we looked at some examples of how with is used by some of the popular JavaScript libraries.

- As with all powerful tools, discretion should be exercised when using with; it's just as easy to obfuscate code using this feature as it is to clarify it.

- The with statement, controversial throughout its lifetime, has no future, and its use in new code should be avoided.

During the course of this chapter, we didn't run across any browser incompatibilities with respect to using with scopes, but we certainly ran into our share in the chapters leading up to this one. In the next chapter, we're going to discuss ways for coping with cross-browser madness while retaining our own sanity.

Developing
cross-browser strategies

This chapter covers

- Strategies for developing reusable, cross-browser JavaScript code
- Analyzing the issues needing to be tackled
- Tackling those issues in a smart way

Anyone who's been developing on-page JavaScript code for more than five minutes knows that there's a wide range of pain points when it comes to making sure that the code works flawlessly across a set of supported browsers. These considerations span everything from the basic development for immediate needs, to planning for future browser releases, all the way to reusing code on web pages that have yet to be created.

Coding for multiple browsers is certainly a nontrivial task, and one that must be balanced according to the development methodologies that you have in place, as well as the resources available to your project. As much as we'd love for our pages to work perfectly in every browser that ever existed or will ever exist, reality rears its ugly head and we must realize that we have finite development resources. We must plan to apply those resources appropriately and carefully, getting the biggest bang for our buck from them.

This starts with choosing our supported browsers carefully.

11.1 Choosing which browsers to support

The primary concern when deciding where to direct our limited resources is deciding which browsers we'll primarily support with our code.

As with virtually any aspect of web development, we need to carefully choose the browsers upon which we want our users to have an optimal experience. When we choose to support a browser, we're typically making the following promises:

- We'll actively test against that browser with our test suite.
- We'll fix bugs and regressions associated with that browser.
- The browser will execute our code with a reasonable level of performance.

As an example, most JavaScript libraries end up supporting about a dozen or so browsers. This set is usually the previous release, the current release, and the upcoming beta release (if available) of the *Big Five* browsers:

- Internet Explorer
- Firefox
- Safari
- Chrome
- Opera

That's an enormous browser set to support, especially when you consider that these browsers need to be tested on multiple platforms, and that for browsers such as Internet Explorer, there are many versions in simultaneous use. The mainstream JavaScript libraries (such as jQuery) have the luxury of a large staff (even if most are volunteers) that the average page author doesn't have at his or her disposal. So realistic choices must be made regarding which browsers to support.

> **NOTE** We can choose to leverage the work already done by the mainstream JavaScript libraries and automatically gain browser support, but this book doesn't make the assumption that you'll be using a library and aims to help you choose which browsers to support in your own code.

To decide upon a browser set to support, you might want to make a *browser support matrix*, as shown in table 11.1, and fill it in for your own purposes. (The selections in this table are just an example and don't reflect any judgment values on the selected browsers.) The remainder of this chapter should help you decide which boxes to check and which to "x out."

Note that you may need to further differentiate the browsers based upon platform if you don't plan to support the browsers equally across the platforms on which they exist.

Table 11.1   An example "browser support" chart—fill one in with your own decisions

	Chrome	Firefox	Safari	IE	Opera
Previous	✔	✔	✔	✔	✔
Current	✔	✔	✔	✔	✔
Beta	✔	✔	✗	✗	✗

Any piece of reusable JavaScript code, whether it's a mass-consumption JavaScript library or our own on-page code, should be developed to work in as many environments as feasible, concentrating on the browsers and platforms that are important to the end user. For mass-consumption libraries, that's a large set; for more targeted applications, perhaps the required set may be narrower.

But it's vitally important not to bite off more than can be chewed, and quality should never be sacrificed for coverage. That's important enough to repeat; in fact, we urge you to read it out loud:

> *Quality should never be sacrificed for coverage.*

In this chapter, we're going to examine the different situations that JavaScript code will find itself up against with regards to cross-browser support, and then we'll examine some of the best ways to write that code with the aim of alleviating any potential problems that those situations pose.

This should go a long way in helping you decide which of these techniques it's worth your time to adopt, and it should help you fill out your own browser-support chart.

11.2   The five major development concerns

With any piece of nontrivial code, there are myriad development concerns to worry about. But five major points pose the biggest challenges to our reusable JavaScript code, as illustrated in figure 11.1.

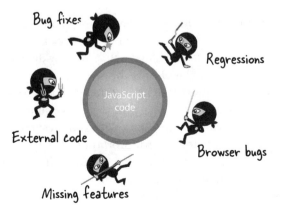

Figure 11.1   The five major points of concern for the development of reusable JavaScript

These are the five points:

- Browser bugs
- Browser bug fixes
- Missing features in the browsers
- External code
- Browser regressions

We'll want to balance how much time we spend on each point against how much benefit we get as an end result. For example, is an extra 40 hours of development time worth better support for an antiquated (and unsupported) browser such as IE 6?

Ultimately, these are questions that you'll have to answer yourself, applying them to your own situation. The answer to the previous question could be radically different for web applications destined for general internet access, versus an in-house application used by workers chained to IE 6 by a Luddite IT department!

An analysis of our intended audience, our development resources, and schedule are all factors that go into our decisions. There's one axiom that can be used when pondering these points:

- Remember the past
- Consider the future
- Test the present

When striving to develop reusable JavaScript code, we must take all of the points into consideration but pay closest attention to the most popular browsers that exist right now. Then we have to take into consideration the changes that are coming in the next versions of the browsers. And then we must try to maintain compatibility with older browser versions, supporting as many features as we can without sacrificing quality or features for the entire support set.

In the following sections, we'll break down these various concerns to get a better understanding of the challenges we're up against, and how to combat them.

11.2.1 *Browser bugs and differences*

A primary concern that we'll need to deal with when developing reusable JavaScript code is the handling of the various browser bugs and API differences associated with the set of browsers we've decided to support. Any features that we provide in our code should be completely and *verifiably* correct in all of those browsers.

The way we achieve this is quite straightforward, having already been presented in chapter 2 and used throughout this book: we need a comprehensive suite of tests to cover both the common and fringe use cases of the code. With good test coverage, we can feel safe in knowing that the code we develop will work in the supported set of browsers. And assuming there are no subsequent browser changes that break backward compatibility, we'll have a warm fuzzy feeling that our code will even work in future versions of those browsers.

We'll be looking at specific strategies for dealing with browser bugs and differences in section 11.3.

A tricky point in all of this is implementing fixes for current browser bugs in such a way that they're resistant to any fixes for those bugs that are implemented in future versions of the browser.

11.2.2 Browser bug fixes

Assuming that a browser will forever present a particular bug is rather foolhardy—most browser bugs eventually get fixed, and *counting* upon the presence of the bug is a dangerous development strategy. It's best to use the techniques that we'll discuss in section 11.3 to make sure that any bug workarounds are future-proofed as much as possible.

When writing a piece of reusable JavaScript code, we want to make sure that it's able to last for a good long time. As with writing any aspect of a website (CSS, HTML, and so on), we don't want to have to go back and fix code that's broken by a new browser release.

Making assumptions about browser bugs causes a common form of web site breakage: specific hacks put in place to work around bugs presented by a browser that break when the browser fixes the bugs in future releases. The issue can be circumvented by building pieces of feature simulation code (which we'll discuss at length in section 11.3.3) instead of making assumptions about the browser.

The problem with handling browser bugs is twofold:

- Our code is liable to break when the bug fix is eventually instituted.
- We could end up training browser vendors to *not* fix bugs for fear of causing websites to break.

An interesting example of the second situation occurred during the development of Firefox 3. A change was introduced that forced DOM nodes created within one document to be *adopted* by another DOM document if they were going to be injected into the other document (which is in accordance with the DOM specification).

The following bit of code shouldn't work:

```
var node = documentA.createElement("div");
documentB.documentElement.appendChild(node);
```

This is the proper way of doing it:

```
var node = documentA.createElement("div");
documentB.adoptNode(node);
documentB.documentElement.appendChild(node);
```

But because there was a bug in Firefox that allowed the first code snippet to work when it shouldn't have, users wrote their code in a manner that depended upon that code working. This forced Mozilla to roll back their change, for fear of breaking a number of websites. Mozilla acknowledges this issue in their "WRONG DOCUMENT ERR note": https://developer.mozilla.org/en-US/docs/DOM/WRONG_DOCUMENT_ERR_note.

This brings up another important point concerning bugs: when determining if a piece of functionality is potentially a bug, always verify it with the specification. In the preceding case, Internet Explorer was more forceful (throwing an exception if the node wasn't in the correct document—the correct behavior), but users assumed that it was an error with Internet Explorer and wrote conditional code to provide a fallback. This caused a situation in which users were following the specification for only a subset of browsers and forcefully rejecting it in others.

A browser bug is also different from an unspecified API. It's important to refer back to browser specifications, because those are the exact standards that the browsers use in order to develop and improve their code. In contrast, the implementation of an unspecified API could change at any point (especially if the implementation ever attempts to become standardized). In the case of inconsistencies in unspecified APIs, you should always test for your expected output, running additional cases of feature simulation (see section 11.3.3). Always be aware that future changes could occur in these APIs as they become solidified.

Additionally, there's a distinction between bug fixes and API changes. Whereas bug fixes are easily foreseen—a browser will eventually fix the bugs in its implementation, even if it takes a long time—API changes are much harder to spot. Standard APIs are unlikely to change (though it's not completely unheard of); changes are much more likely to occur with unspecified APIs.

Luckily, this will rarely happen in a way that will massively break most web applications. But if it does, it's effectively undetectable in advance (unless, of course, we test every single API that we ever touch—but the overhead incurred in such a process would be ludicrous). API changes of this sort should be handled like any other regression.

For our next point of concern, we know that no man is an island, and neither is our code. Let's explore the ramifications of that.

11.2.3 *Living with external code and markup*

Any reusable code must coexist with the code that surrounds it. Whether we're expecting our code to work within pages that we write ourselves, or on websites developed by others, we need to ensure that it's able to cohabit on the page with any other random code.

This is a double-edged sword: our code must not only be able to withstand living with poorly written external code, it must itself take care not to have adverse effects on the code with which it lives.

Exactly how much we need to be vigilant about this point of concern depends a great deal upon the environment in which we expect the code to be used. For example, if we're writing reusable code for a single or limited number of websites that we have some level of control over, it might be safe to worry less about effects of external code because we know where the code will operate, and we can, to some degree, fix any problems ourselves.

TIP This is an important enough concern to warrant an entire book on the subject. We highly recommend the Manning book *Third-Party JavaScript* by Ben Vinegar and Anton Kovalyov (http://manning.com/vinegar/) if this is an area into which you'd like to delve deeply.

If we're developing code that will have a broad level of applicability in unknown (and uncontrollable) environments, we'll need to make doubly sure that our code is robust.

Let's discuss some strategies to achieve that.

ENCAPSULATING OUR CODE

To keep our code from affecting other pieces of code on the pages where it's loaded, it's best to practice *encapsulation.*

One dictionary definition of encapsulation reads, "to place in or as if in a capsule"; a more domain-focused definition could be, "a language mechanism for restricting access to some of the object's components." Your Aunt Mathilda might summarize it more succinctly as, "keep your nose in your own business!"

Keeping an incredibly small global footprint when introducing our code into a page can go a long way to making Aunt Mathilda happy. In fact, keeping our global footprint to a handful of global variables, or better yet *one,* is fairly easy.

The jQuery library is a good example of this. It introduces one global variable (a function) named jQuery, and one alias for that global variable, $. It even has a supported means to give the $ alias back to whatever other on-page code or other library may want to use it.

Almost all operations in jQuery are made via the jQuery function. And any other functions that it provides (so-called *utility functions*) are defined as properties of jQuery (remember from chapter 3 how easy it is to define functions that are properties of other functions), thus using the name jQuery as a *namespace* for all its definitions.

We can use the same strategy. Let's say that we're defining a set of functions for our own use, or for the use of others, that we'll group under a namespace of our own choosing—we'll pick ninja.

We could, like jQuery, define a global function named ninja() that performs various operations based upon what we pass to the function. For example,

```
var ninja = function(){ /* implementation code goes here */ }
```

Defining our own utility functions that use this function as their namespace is easy:

```
ninja.hitsuke = function(){ /* code to distract guards with fire here */ }
```

If we didn't want or need ninja to be a function and to just serve as a namespace, we could define it as follows:

```
var ninja = {};
```

This creates an empty object in which we can define properties and functions in order to keep from adding these names to the global namespace.

Other practices that we wish to avoid, in order to keep our code encapsulated, are modifying any existing variables, function prototypes, or even DOM elements. Any aspect of the page that our code modifies, outside of itself, is a potential area for collision and confusion.

The other side of the two-way street is that even if *we* follow best practices and carefully encapsulate our code, we can't be assured that code that we haven't written ourselves is going to be as well behaved.

DEALING WITH LESS-THAN-EXEMPLARY CODE

There's an old joke that's been going around since Grace Hopper removed that moth from a relay back in the Cretaceous period: "The only code that doesn't suck is the code you write yourself." This may seem a rather cynical view, but when our code co-exists with code over which we have no control, we should assume the worst, just to be safe.

Other code, even if well-written, rather than just buggy, might *intentionally* be doing things like modifying function prototypes, object properties, and DOM element methods. This practice, well-meant or otherwise, can lay traps for us to step into.

In such circumstances, our code could be doing something innocuous, such as using JavaScript arrays, and no one could fault us for making the simple assumption that JavaScript arrays are going to act like JavaScript arrays. But if some other on-page code goes and modifies the manner in which arrays work, our code could end up not working as intended, through absolutely no fault of our own.

Unfortunately, there aren't many steadfast rules when dealing when situations of this nature, but there are some steps we can take to mitigate these types of problems. The next few sections will introduce these defensive steps.

AVOIDING IMPLANTED PROPERTIES

The first of these defensive steps is to learn how to avoid properties that other code may have introduced into objects behind our backs.

In order to detect such activity, we'll take advantage of the hasOwnProperty() function. This function is inherited from Object by all JavaScript objects, and it tests whether the object possesses a specified property. This is similar to JavaScript's in operator, with the important difference that it doesn't check up the prototype chain.

We can therefore use this function to detect the difference between properties that have been introduced by an extension to Object.prototype and those placed directly on the object.

We can observe the behavior of this function by inspecting tests shown in the following listing.

Listing 11.1 Using hasOwnProperty() to test for inherited properties

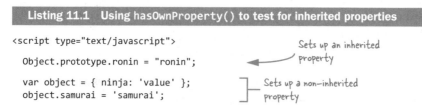

```
<script type="text/javascript">

  Object.prototype.ronin = "ronin";          Sets up an inherited
                                             property

  var object = { ninja: 'value' };           Sets up a non-inherited
  object.samurai = 'samurai';                property
```

```
  assert(object.hasOwnProperty('ronin'),"ronin is a property");
  assert(object.hasOwnProperty('ninja'),"ninja is a property");
  assert(object.hasOwnProperty('samurai'),"samurai is a property");
```

```
</script>
```

The results of running the tests are shown in figure 11.2.

The test results clearly show that the `ronin` property, added to the `Object` prototype, isn't considered an "own property" of the created objects. Thankfully, the number of scripts that use this technique is very small, but the harm that they cause can be great if the properties added to the prototype confuse our code.

This can be especially problematic when iterating through the properties of an object using a `for-in` clause. We can counter this complication by using `hasOwn-Property()` to determine if we should ignore a property or not:

```
for (var p in someObject) {
  if (someObject.hasOwnProperty(p)) {
    // do something wonderful
  }
}
```

This snippet shows how `hasOwnProperty()` can be used to ignore properties that have been added to the object's prototype.

> **TIP** The `Object.getOwnPropertyNames()` method was introduced in JavaScript 1.8.5. See https://developer.mozilla.org/en-US/docs/JavaScript/Reference/Global_Objects/Object/getOwnPropertyNames.

COPING WITH GREEDY IDS

Most browsers exhibit an *anti-feature* (we can't really call it a *bug* because the behavior is absolutely intended) that can cause our code to trip and fall unexpectedly. This feature causes element references to be added to other elements using the `id` of the original element. And when that `id` conflicts with properties that are already part of the element, bad things can happen.

Take a look at the following HTML snippet to observe what nastiness can ensue as a result of these so-called "greedy IDs":

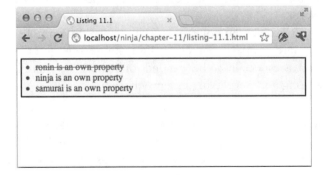

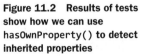

Figure 11.2 Results of tests show how we can use `hasOwnProperty()` to detect inherited properties

```
<form id="form" action="/conceal">
  <input type="text" id="action"/>
  <input type="submit" id="submit"/>
</form>
```

Now, in the browsers, let's call this:

```
var what = document.getElementById('form').action;
```

Rightly, we'd expect this to be the value of the form's action attribute. And in most cases, it would be. But if we inspect the value of variable what, we find that it's instead a reference to the input#action element! Huh?

Let's try something else:

```
document.getElementById('form').submit();
```

This statement should cause the form to be submitted, but instead, we get a script error:

```
Uncaught TypeError: Property 'submit' of object #<HTMLFormElement> is not a function
```

What's going on?

What's happened is that the browsers have added properties to the <form> element for each of the input elements within the form that reference the element. This would seem to be handy at first, until we realize that the name of the added property is taken from the id value of the input elements. And if that id value just happens to be an already-used property of the form element, such as action or submit, those original properties are replaced by the new property.

So, before the input#submit element is created, the reference form.action points to the value of the action attribute for the <form>. Afterwards, it points to the input#submit element. The same thing happens to form.submit. Eeesh!

This choice is somewhat baffling, because for this behavior to occur, the input elements must have an id, and if they have an id, they're easy to address without having to tack properties onto the form.

In any case, this particular "feature" of the browsers can cause numerous and mystifying problems in our code, and it'll have to be kept in mind when debugging in these browsers. When we encounter properties that have seemingly been inexplicably transformed into something other than what we expect them to be, greedy IDs are a cause we'll need to check for.

Luckily, we can avoid this problem in our own markup by avoiding simple id values that can conflict with standard property names, and we can encourage others to do the same. The value submit is especially to be avoided for id and name values, as it's a common source of frustrating and perplexing buggy behavior.

ORDER OF STYLESHEETS

Often we expect CSS rules to already be available by the time our code executes. One of the best ways to ensure that CSS rules provided by stylesheets are defined when our JavaScript code executes is to include the external stylesheets *prior* to including the external script files.

Not doing so can cause unexpected results, because the script attempts to access the as-yet-undefined style information. Unfortunately, this isn't an issue that can be easily rectified with pure JavaScript and should instead be handled with user documentation.

These last few sections have covered some basic examples of how externalities can affect how our code works, frequently in unintentional and confounding manners. Issues with our code will often pop up when other users try to integrate our code into *their* sites, at which point we should be able to diagnose the issue and build appropriate tests to handle them. At other times, we'll discover such problems when we integrate others' code into our pages, and hopefully the tips in these sections will help to identify what's causing the issues.

It's unfortunate that there are no better and deterministic solutions to handling these integration issues other than to take some smart first steps and to write our code defensively.

We'll now move on to the next point of concern.

11.2.4 Missing features

For browsers that aren't lucky enough to survive our support matrix, and therefore won't benefit from the testing we'll do for the "A List" browsers, there are likely to be some missing key features that our code needs in order to operate as expected.

There may even be browsers that lack needed key features but that we do need to support (perhaps for some political or business reasons).

GRACEFUL DEGRADATION

Even if we aren't going to give all browsers full support, especially those that didn't make the cut, it'll be best if we write our code defensively so that it degrades gracefully, or provides some other type of fallback for end users who choose (or are forced) to use browsers other than those we have the resources to test upon.

Our strategy at this point is to deliver the most functionality to our users, and to fail gracefully when we can't provide full functionality. This is known as *graceful degradation.*

Graceful degradation should be approached cautiously, and with due consideration. Take the case where a browser is capable of initializing and hiding a number of pieces of navigation on a page, perhaps in hopes of creating a drop-down menu, but the event-related code to power the menu doesn't work. The result is a half-functional page, which helps no one.

Be sure that any fallback provided by your code offers an alternative that *works*, even if with reduced functionality.

BACKWARD COMPATIBILITY

A better strategy would be to design our code to be as backward-compatible as possible and to actively direct known failing browsers to an alternative version of the page or a site tailored to the capabilities of the lesser browser. Yahoo! adopts this strategy with most of their websites, breaking down browsers into graded levels of support. After a certain amount of time, they "blacklist" a browser (usually when it hits an infinitesimal market share such as 0.05 percent) and direct users of that browser (based upon the detected user agent) to a pure-HTML version of the application (one with no CSS or JavaScript involved).

This means that their developers are able to provide an optimal experience for the vast majority of their users (around 99 percent), by passing off antiquated browsers to a functional equivalent (albeit with a less modern experience).

Consider the key points of this strategy:

- No assumptions are made about the user experience of old browsers. After a browser is no longer able to be tested (and has a negligible market share) it's cut off and served with a simplified page, or not supported at all (letting the chips fall where they may).

- All users of current and past browsers are guaranteed to have a page that isn't broken.

- Future and unknown browsers are assumed to work.

The primary downside of this strategy is that extra development effort (beyond the currently targeted browsers and platforms) must be expended to focus on handling older and future browsers. Despite the cost, this is a smart strategy, as it will allow your applications to stay viable longer with only minimal updates and changes.

11.2.5 Regressions

Regressions are one of the hardest problems that we'll encounter in the creation of reusable and maintainable JavaScript code. These are bugs, or non-backward-compatible API changes (mostly to unspecified APIs), that browsers have introduced and that cause our code to break in unpredictable ways.

> **NOTE**   Here we're using the term regression in its classical definition: a feature that used to work that no longer functions as expected. This is usually unintentional, but it's sometimes caused by deliberate changes that break existing code.

ANTICIPATING CHANGES

There *are* some API changes that, with some foresight, we can proactively detect and handle, as shown in listing 11.2.

For example, with Internet Explorer 9, Microsoft introduced support for DOM level 2 event handlers (bound using the addEventListener() method). For code written prior to IE 9, simple object detection was able to handle that change.

Listing 11.2   Anticipating an upcoming API change

```
function bindEvent(element, type, handle) {
  if (element.addEventListener) {
    element.addEventListener(type, handle, false);
  }
  else if (element.attachEvent) {
    element.attachEvent("on" + type, handle);
  }
}
```

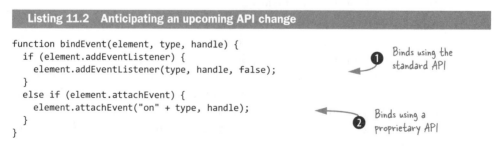

❶ Binds using the standard API

❷ Binds using a proprietary API

In this example, we future-proofed our code knowing (or hoping against hope) that someday Microsoft would bring Internet Explorer into line with DOM standards. If the browser supports the standards-compliant API, we use object detection to infer that and use the standard API ❶. If not, we check to see if the IE-proprietary method is available and use that ❷. All else failing, we do nothing.

Most future API changes, alas, aren't that easy to predict, and there's no way to predict upcoming bugs. This is but one of the very important reasons that we've stressed testing throughout this book. In the face of unpredictable changes that will affect our code, the best that we can hope for is to be diligent in monitoring our tests for each browser release, and to quickly address issues that regressions may introduce.

UNPREDICTABLE BUGS

Let's consider an example of an unpredictable bug: Internet Explorer 7 introduced a basic XMLHttpRequest wrapper around the native ActiveX request object. As a result, virtually all JavaScript libraries opted to default to using the XMLHttpRequest object to perform their Ajax requests (as they should—choosing to use a standards-based API is nearly always preferred).

But in Internet Explorer's implementation, Microsoft broke the handling of requesting local files; a site loaded from the desktop could no longer request files using the XMLHttpRequest object.

No one really caught this bug (or really could have predicted it) until it was too late, causing it to escape into the wild and break many pages in the process. The solution was to use the ActiveX implementation primarily for local file requests.

Having a good suite of tests and keeping close track of upcoming browser releases is absolutely the best way to deal with future regressions of this nature. It doesn't have to be taxing on your normal development cycle, which should already include routine testing. Running these tests on new browser releases should always be factored into the planning of any development cycle.

You can get information on upcoming browser releases from the following locations:

- Internet Explorer: http://blogs.msdn.com/ie/
- Firefox: http://ftp.mozilla.org/pub/mozilla.org/firefox/nightly/latest-trunk/
- WebKit (Safari): http://nightly.webkit.org/
- Opera: http://snapshot.opera.com/
- Chrome: http://chrome.blogspot.com/

Diligence is important. Because we can never fully predict the bugs that will be introduced by a browser, it's best to make sure that we stay on top of our code and quickly avert any crises that may arise.

Thankfully, browser vendors are doing a lot to make sure that regressions of this nature don't occur. Both Firefox and Opera have test suites from various JavaScript libraries integrated into their main browser test suite. This allows them to be sure that no future regressions will be introduced that affect those libraries directly. While this won't catch all regressions (and certainly won't in all browsers), it's a great start and shows good progress by the browser vendors toward preventing as many issues as possible.

OK, now that we know about the specific challenges we're facing and some ways to meet them, let's explore some strategies that can help us across multiple development concerns.

11.3 Implementation strategies

Knowing which issues to be aware of is only half the battle—figuring out effective strategies for dealing with them, and using them to implement robust cross-browser code, is another matter.

There are a wide a range of strategies that we can use, and while not every strategy will work in every situation, the range that we'll examine should provide a good set of tools for covering most of the concerns that we need to address within our robust code bases.

We'll start with something that's easy and almost trouble free.

11.3.1 Safe cross-browser fixes

The simplest (and safest) classes of cross-browser fixes are those that exhibit two important traits:

- They have no negative effects or side effects on other browsers.
- They use no form of browser or feature detection.

The instances in which we can apply such fixes may be rather rare, but they're a tactic that we should always strive for in our applications.

Let's look at an example. The following code snippet represents a change (plucked from jQuery) that came about when working with Internet Explorer:

```
// ignore negative width and height values
if ((key == 'width' || key == 'height') && parseFloat(value) < 0)
  value = undefined;
```

Some versions of IE throw an exception when a negative value is set on the height or width style properties. All other browsers ignore negative input. This workaround simply ignores all negative values in *all* browsers. This change prevented an exception from being thrown in Internet Explorer and had no effect on any other browser. This was a painless change that provided a unified API to the user (because throwing unexpected exceptions is never desired).

Another example of this type of fix (also from jQuery) appears in the attribute manipulation code. Consider this:

```
if (name == "type" &&
    elem.nodeName.toLowerCase() == "input" &&
    elem.parentNode)
  throw "type attribute can't be changed";
```

Internet Explorer doesn't allow us to manipulate the type attribute of input elements that are already part of the DOM—attempts to change this attribute result in a proprietary exception being thrown. jQuery came to a middle-ground solution: it disallows *all* attempts to manipulate the type attribute on injected input elements in all browsers, throwing a uniform informational exception.

This change to the jQuery code base required no browser or feature detection; it unified the API across all browsers. The action still results in an exception, but that exception is uniform across all browser types.

This particular approach could be considered quite controversial—it purposefully limits the features of the library in all browsers because of a bug that exists in only one. The jQuery team weighed this decision carefully and decided that it was better to have a unified API that worked consistently than an API that would break unexpectedly when developing cross-browser code. It's very possible that you'll come across situations like this when developing your own reusable code bases, and you'll need to consider carefully whether a limiting approach such as this is appropriate for your audience.

The important thing to remember for these types of code changes is that they provide a solution that works seamlessly across browsers without the need for browser or feature detection, effectively making them immune to changes going forward. One should always strive for solutions that work in this manner, even if the applicable instances are few and far between.

11.3.2 *Object detection*

As we've previously discussed, *object detection* is a commonly used approach when writing cross-browser code, being not only simple but also generally quite effective. It works by determining if a certain object or object property exists, and if so, assuming that it provides the implied functionality. (In the next section, we'll see what to do about cases where this assumption fails.)

Most commonly, object detection is used to choose between multiple APIs that provide duplicate pieces of functionality. For example, the code that we saw in listing 11.2, in which object detection was used to choose the appropriate event-binding APIs provided by the browser, is repeated here:

```
function bindEvent(element, type, handle) {
  if (element.addEventListener) {
    element.addEventListener(type, handle, false); }
  else if (element.attachEvent) {
    element.attachEvent("on" + type, handle); }
}
```

In this example, we checked to see if a property named addEventListener exists; if so, we assume that it's a function that we can execute and that it'll bind an event listener to that element. We then proceed to test other APIs, such as attachEvent, for existence.

Note that we tested for addEventListener, the *standard* method provided by the W3C DOM Events specification, first. This is intentional.

Whenever possible, we should default to the standard way of performing any action. As mentioned before, this will help to make our code as future-proof as possible. Moreover, pressure from mass-adoption libraries, as well as very vocal and influential voices in the Twitter-verse and other social media, can encourage browser vendors to work toward providing the standard means of performing actions.

An important use of object detection is discovering the facilities provided by the browser environment in which the code is executing. This allows us to provide features that use those facilities in our code, or to determine whether we need to provide a fallback.

The following code snippet shows a basic example of detecting the presence of a browser feature using object detection, to determine whether we should provide full application functionality or a reduced-experience fallback:

```
if (typeof document !== "undefined" &&
    (document.addEventListener || document.attachEvent) &&
    document.getElementsByTagName &&
    document.getElementById) {
  // We have enough of an API to work with to build our application
}
else {
  // Provide Fallback
}
```

Here, we test whether

- The browser has a document loaded
- The browser provides a means to bind event handlers
- The browser can find elements given a tag name
- The browser can find elements by ID

Failing any of these tests causes us to resort to a fallback position. What is done in the fallback is up to the expectations of the consumers of the code, and the requirements placed upon the code. There are a couple of options that can be considered:

- We could perform further object detection to figure out how to provide a reduced experience that still uses some JavaScript.
- We could opt to not execute any JavaScript, falling back to the unscripted HTML on the page.
- We could redirect the user to a plainer version of the site. Google does this with Gmail, for example.

Because object detection has very little overhead associated with it (it's just a simple property/object lookup) and is relatively simple in its implementation, it makes for a good way to provide basic levels of fallback, both at the API and application levels. It's a good choice for the first line of defense in your reusable code authoring.

But what if our assumption about an API working correctly just because it *exists* proves to be overly optimistic? Let's see what we can do about that.

11.3.3 *Feature simulation*

Another means that we have of dealing with regressions, and the most effective means of detecting fixes to browser bugs, is *feature simulation*. In contrast to object detection, which is simply an object/property lookup, feature simulation performs a complete run-through of a feature to make sure that it works as we'd expect it to.

While object detection is a good way to check that a feature *exists*, it doesn't guarantee that the feature will *behave* as intended. But if we know of specific bugs, we can quickly build tests to check when the feature bug is fixed as well as write code to work around the bug until that time.

As an example, Internet Explorer 8 and earlier versions will erroneously return both elements *and* comments if we execute getElementsByTagName("*"). No amount of object detection is going to determine if this will happen or not. As we hope often happens, this bug has been fixed by the Internet Explorer team in the IE 9 release of the browser.

Let's write a feature simulation to determine if the getElementsByTagName() method will work as we expect it to:

```
window.findByTagWorksAsExpected = (function(){
  var div = document.createElement("div");
  div.appendChild(document.createComment("test"));
  return div.getElementsByTagName("*").length === 0;
})();
```

In this example, we've written an immediate function that returns true if a call to getElementsByTagName("*") functions as expected, and false otherwise. The steps of this test function are fairly simple:

- Create a detached <div> element.
- Add a comment node to the <div>.
- Call the function, see how many values are returned, and return true or false depending upon the result.

Well, knowing that there's a problem is only half the battle. What can we do with this knowledge to make things better for our code? The following listing shows a use of the preceding feature-simulation snippet in a useful context: working around the bug.

Listing 11.3 Putting feature simulation into practice to work around a browser bug

```
<!DOCTYPE html>
<html>
  <head>
    <title>Listing 11.3</title>
    <script type="text/javascript" src="../scripts/assert.js"></script>
    <link href="../styles/assert.css" rel="stylesheet" type="text/css">
  </head>
  <body>
```

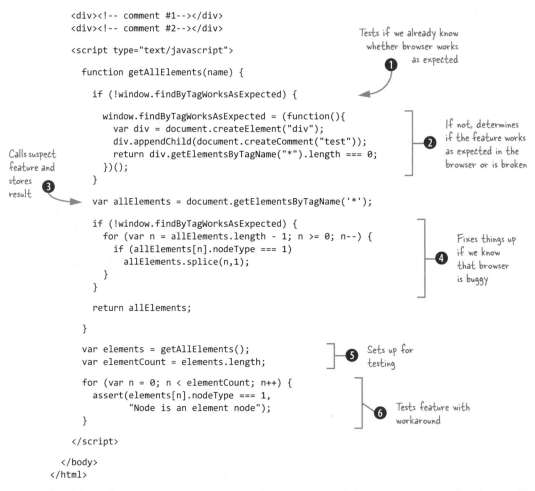

```
<div><!-- comment #1--></div>
<div><!-- comment #2--></div>

<script type="text/javascript">

  function getAllElements(name) {

    if (!window.findByTagWorksAsExpected) {

      window.findByTagWorksAsExpected = (function(){
        var div = document.createElement("div");
        div.appendChild(document.createComment("test"));
        return div.getElementsByTagName("*").length === 0;
      })();
    }

    var allElements = document.getElementsByTagName('*');

    if (!window.findByTagWorksAsExpected) {
      for (var n = allElements.length - 1; n >= 0; n--) {
        if (allElements[n].nodeType === 1)
          allElements.splice(n,1);
      }
    }

    return allElements;

  }

  var elements = getAllElements();
  var elementCount = elements.length;

  for (var n = 0; n < elementCount; n++) {
    assert(elements[n].nodeType === 1,
          "Node is an element node");
  }

</script>

</body>
</html>
```

1 Tests if we already know whether browser works as expected

2 If not, determines if the feature works as expected in the browser or is broken

3 Calls suspect feature and stores result

4 Fixes things up if we know that browser is buggy

5 Sets up for testing

6 Tests feature with workaround

In this code, we set up some <div> elements containing comment nodes that we'll later use for testing. Then we get down to business with some script.

Because using document.getElementsByTagName('*') directly is suspect, we define an alternate method, getAllElements(), to use in its place. We want this method to just factor down into a call to document.getElementsByTagName('*') on browsers that implement it correctly, but to use a fallback that produces the correct results on browsers that don't.

The first thing that our method does is to use the immediate function that we developed previously to determine if the feature works as expected **2**. Note that we store the result in a window-scoped variable so that we can refer to it later, and we check to see if it's already been set, so that we only run the (relatively expensive) feature-simulation check once **1**.

After the check, we run the call to document.getElementsByTagName('*') and store the result in a variable **3**.

At this point, we have the node list of all elements, and we know whether we're operating in a browser that has the comment node problem or not. If we had determined that the problem exists, we run through the nodes, stripping out any that aren't element nodes ❹. This process is skipped for browsers that don't have that problem.

NOTE The `nodeType` of element nodes is 1, while that of comment nodes is 8. Modern browsers (including versions 8 and 9 of IE) define a set of constants on the `Node` object, such as `Node.ELEMENT_NODE` and `Node.COMMENT_NODE`. As our fix will be triggered in older browsers, we can't assume that these constants exist, so we've used hard-coded values. You can find a complete list of node type values at https://developer.mozilla.org/en/nodeType.

Finally, we test our new method by using it ❺ and asserting that the returned node list only contains element nodes ❻.

This example demonstrates how feature simulation works in two phases.

First, a simple test is run to determine if a feature works as we expect it to. It's important to verify the integrity of a feature (making sure it works correctly) rather than explicitly testing for the presence of a bug. While that may be a semantic distinction, it's one that's important to keep in mind.

Second, the results of the test are later used in our program to speed up looping through an array of elements. Because a browser that works correctly (one that returns only elements) doesn't need to perform the element checks on every stage of the loop, we can completely skip it and not pay any performance penalties in browsers that work correctly.

That's the most common idiom used in feature simulation: making sure a feature works as expected and providing fallback code in non-working browsers.

The most important point to take into consideration when using feature simulation is that it's a trade-off. Paying the extra performance overhead of the initial simulation, along with the extra lines of code in our programs, gives us the benefit of knowing that a suspect feature will work as expected in all supported browsers and makes our code immune to breaking upon future bug fixes. This immunity can be absolutely priceless when creating reusable code bases.

Feature simulation is great when we can test whether a browser is broken or not, but what can we do about browser problems that stubbornly resist being tested?

11.3.4 *Untestable browser issues*

Unfortunately there are a number of possible problem areas in JavaScript and the DOM that are either impossible or prohibitively expensive to test for. These situations are fortunately rather rare, but when we encounter them, it always pays to spend some time investigating the matter to see if there's something we can do about it.

The following sections discuss some known issues that are impossible to test using any conventional JavaScript interactions.

EVENT HANDLER BINDINGS

One of the infuriating lapses in the browsers is the inability to determine if an event handler has been bound. The browsers don't provide any way of determining if any functions have been bound to an event listener on an element. Because of this, there's no way to remove all bound event handlers from an element unless we've maintained references to all bound handlers as we create them.

EVENT FIRING

Another aggravation is determining if an event will fire. While it's possible to determine if a browser supports a means of binding an event (as we've seen a few times earlier in this chapter), it's *not* possible to know if a browser will actually fire an event. There are a couple places where this becomes problematic.

First, if a script is loaded dynamically after the page itself has already loaded, it may try to bind a listener to wait for the window to load when, in fact, that event already happened. As there's no way to determine if the event has already occurred, the code may wind up waiting forever to execute.

The second situation occurs if a script wishes to use custom events provided by a browser as an alternative. For example, Internet Explorer provides mouseenter and mouseleave events, which simplify the process of determining when a user's mouse enters or leaves an element's boundaries. These are frequently used as alternatives to the mouseover and mouseout events, because they act slightly more intuitively than the standard events. But because there's no way of determining if these events will fire without first binding the events and waiting for some user interaction against them, it's hard to use them in reusable code.

CSS PROPERTY EFFECTS

Yet another pain point is determining whether changing certain CSS properties actually affects the presentation. A number of CSS properties only affect the visual representation of the display and nothing else; they don't change surrounding elements or affect other properties on the element. Examples are color, backgroundColor, and opacity.

Because of this, there's no way to programmatically determine if changing these style properties will generate the effects desired. The only way to verify the impact is through a visual examination of the page.

BROWSER CRASHES

Testing script that causes the browser to crash is another annoyance. Code that causes a browser to crash is especially problematic, because unlike exceptions that can be easily caught and handled, these will always cause the browser to break.

For example, in older versions of Safari, creating a regular expression that used Unicode-character ranges would always cause the browser to crash, as in the following example:

```
new RegExp("[\\w\u0128-\uFFFF*_-]+");
```

The problem with this is that it's not possible to test whether this problem exists using feature simulation, because the test itself will always produce a crash in that older browser.

Additionally, bugs that cause crashes to occur forever become embroiled in difficulty, because while it may be acceptable for JavaScript to be disabled in some segment of the population using your browser, it's never acceptable to outright crash the browser of those users.

INCONGRUOUS APIS

Back in section 11.3.1, we saw how jQuery decided to disallow the ability to change the type attribute in all browsers due to a bug in Internet Explorer. We *could* test this feature and only disable it in Internet Explorer, but that would set up an incongruity in which the API would work differently from browser to browser. In situations such as this, where a bug is so bad that it causes an API to break, the only option is to work around the affected area and provide a different solution.

In addition to impossible-to-test problems, there are issues that are *possible* to test, but that are prohibitively difficult to test effectively. Let's look at some of them.

API PERFORMANCE

Sometimes specific APIs are faster or slower in different browsers. When writing reusable and robust code, it's important to try to use the APIs that provide good performance. But it's not always obvious which API that is.

Effectively conducting performance analysis of a feature usually entails throwing a large amount of data at it, and that usually takes a relatively long time. Therefore, it's not something we can do in our code in the same way that we used feature simulation.

AJAX ISSUES

Determining if Ajax requests work correctly is another thorn in our sides. As was mentioned when we looked at regressions, Internet Explorer broke the ability to request local files via the XMLHttpRequest object in Internet Explorer 7. We could test to see if this bug has been fixed, but to do so we'd have to perform an extra request on every page load that attempted to perform a request. That's not optimal.

And not only that, but an extra file would have to be included with the library whose sole reason for being was to serve as a target for these extra requests. The overhead of both these matters is prohibitive and would certainly not be worth the extra time and resources.

Untestable features are a significant hassle that hinders our writing of reusable JavaScript, but they can frequently be worked around with a bit of effort and cleverness. By utilizing alternative techniques, or constructing our APIs in such a manner as to obviate these issues in the first place, we'll likely be able to build effective code, despite the odds stacked against us.

11.4 *Reducing assumptions*

Writing cross-browser, reusable code is a battle of assumptions, but by using clever detection and authoring, we can reduce the number of assumptions that we make in our code. When we make assumptions about the code that we write, we stand to encounter problems further down the road.

For example, assuming that an issue or a bug will always exist in a specific browser is a huge and dangerous assumption. Instead, testing for the problem (as we've done throughout this chapter) proves to be much more effective. In our coding, we should always strive to reduce the number of assumptions that we make, effectively reducing the room for error and the probability that something's going to come back and bite us in the behind.

The most common area for making assumptions in JavaScript is in user agent detection. Specifically, analyzing the user agent provided by a browser (navigator .userAgent) and using it to make an assumption about how the browser will behave—in other words, browser detection. Unfortunately, most user-agent string analysis proves to be a superb source of future-induced errors. Assuming that a bug, issue, or proprietary feature will always be linked to a specific browser is a recipe for disaster.

But reality intervenes when it comes to minimizing assumptions: it's virtually impossible to remove all of them. At some point, we'll have to assume that a browser will do what it's supposed to do. Figuring out the point at which that balance can be struck is completely up to the developer, and it's what "separates the men from the boys," as they say (with apologies to our female readers).

For example, let's re-examine the event-attaching code that we've already seen a number of times:

```
function bindEvent(element, type, handle) {
  if (element.addEventListener) {
    element.addEventListener(type, handle, false);
  }
  else if (element.attachEvent) {
    element.attachEvent("on" + type, handle);
  }
}
```

Without looking ahead, see if you can spot three assumptions that are made by this code. Go on, we'll wait.

(*Jeopardy Theme plays ...*)

How'd you do? In the preceding code, we made at least these three assumptions:

- That the properties that we're checking are, in fact, callable functions
- That they're the correct functions, performing the actions that we expect
- That these two methods are the only possible ways of binding an event

We could easily get rid of the first assumption by adding checks to see if the properties are, in fact, functions. Tackling the remaining two points is much more difficult.

In our code, we always need to decide how many assumptions are optimal for our requirements, our target audience, and for us. Frequently, reducing the number of assumptions also increases the size and complexity of the code base. It's fully possible, and rather easy, to attempt to reduce assumptions to the point of complete insanity, but at some point we'll have to stop and take stock of what we have, say "good enough," and work from there. Remember that even the least-assuming code is still prone to regressions introduced by a browser.

11.5 Summary

Let's recap what we covered in this chapter:

- Reusable cross-browser development involves juggling three factors:
  - Code size—Keeping the file size small
  - Performance overhead—Keeping the performance level above a palatable minimum
  - API quality—Making sure that the APIs provided work uniformly across browsers
- There's no magic formula for determining the correct balance of these factors.
- The development factors are something that will have to be balanced by every developer in their individual development efforts.
- Thankfully, by using smart techniques like object detection and feature simulation, it's possible to defend against the numerous directions from which reusable code will be attacked without making any undue sacrifices.

In this chapter we spent a good deal of time talking about the challenges of cross-browser differences. In the next chapter, we're going to tackle head-on the problems caused by the differing ways that the browsers handle attributes, properties, and styling.

Cutting through attributes, properties, and CSS

This chapter covers

- Understanding DOM attributes and DOM properties
- Dealing with cross-browser attributes and styles
- Handling element dimension properties
- Discovering computed styles

Excepting the previous chapter, a large percentage of this book so far has dealt with JavaScript, the language. And although there are plenty of nuances to pure Java-Script as a language, once we throw the browser DOM into the mix, things can really get confusing.

Understanding DOM concepts and how JavaScript relates to these concepts is an important part of becoming a JavaScript ninja, especially considering the baffling ways that some DOM concepts seem to defy logic. The area of DOM attributes and properties has left many JavaScript page authors quivering with confusion. Not only are there some very nuanced behaviors between attributes and properties, but there are also few other areas that are more riddled with bugs and cross-browser issues.

253

But attributes and properties are important concepts: attributes are an integral part of how the DOM gets built, and properties are the primary means by which elements hold runtime information, and by which this information can be accessed.

Let's take a look at a quick example that demonstrates the capacity for befuddlement:

```
<img src="../images/ninja-with-nunchuks.png">

<script type="text/javascript">

  var image = document.getElementsByTagName('img')[0];

  var newSrc = '../images/ninja-with-pole.png';

  image.src = newSrc;

  assert(image.src === newSrc,
          'the image source is now ' + image.src);

  assert(image.getAttribute('src') === '../images/ninja-with-nunchuks.png',
          'the image src attribute is ' + image.getAttribute('src'));

</script>
```

In this snippet, we create an image tag, get a reference to it, and change its src property to a new value. That seems pretty straightforward, but we run two tests to make sure:

- We test that the src property obtained the value we just gave it. After all, if we were to say x = 213, we'd certainly expect x's value to be 213.
- We didn't change the attribute, so it should stay the same. Right?

But when we load the code into a browser, we find that both tests fail.

We see that the src property isn't the value that we assigned, but rather something akin to

```
http://localhost/ninja/images/ninja-with-pole.png
```

We assigned a value to a property, so shouldn't we expect it to have that exact value?

Even more oddly, even though we didn't change the attribute on the element, the failing test shows that the value of the src *attribute* has changed to

```
../images/ninja-with-pole.png
```

What gives?

In this chapter, we'll examine all the conundrums that the browsers throw at us with respect to element properties and attributes, and we'll discover why the results weren't exactly what we might have expected.

The same goes for CSS and the styling of elements. Many of the difficulties that we run into when constructing a dynamic web application stem from the complications of setting and getting element styling. This book can't cover all that's known about handling element styling (that's enough to fill an entire other book), but the core essentials will be discussed.

Let's start by understanding exactly what element attributes and properties are.

12.1 DOM attributes and properties

When accessing the values of element attributes, we have two possible options: using the traditional DOM methods of `getAttribute` and `setAttribute`, or using properties of the DOM objects that correspond to the attributes.

For example, to obtain the id of an element whose reference is stored in variable e, we could use either of the following:

```
e.getAttribute('id')
e.id
```

Either way will give us the value of the id.

Let's examine the following code to better understand how attribute values and their corresponding properties behave.

Listing 12.1 Accessing attribute values via DOM methods and properties

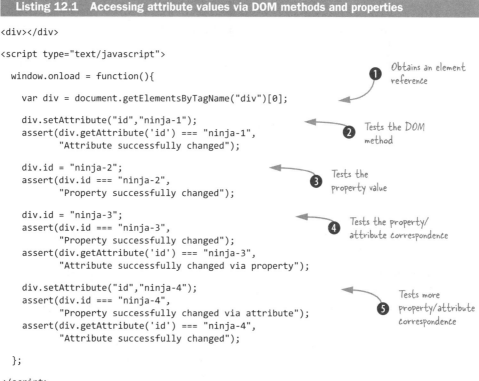

```
<div></div>

<script type="text/javascript">

  window.onload = function(){

    var div = document.getElementsByTagName("div")[0];

    div.setAttribute("id","ninja-1");
    assert(div.getAttribute('id') === "ninja-1",
         "Attribute successfully changed");

    div.id = "ninja-2";
    assert(div.id === "ninja-2",
         "Property successfully changed");

    div.id = "ninja-3";
    assert(div.id === "ninja-3",
         "Property successfully changed");
    assert(div.getAttribute('id') === "ninja-3",
         "Attribute successfully changed via property");

    div.setAttribute("id","ninja-4");
    assert(div.id === "ninja-4",
         "Property successfully changed via attribute");
    assert(div.getAttribute('id') === "ninja-4",
         "Attribute successfully changed");

  };

</script>
```

❶ Obtains an element reference

❷ Tests the DOM method

❸ Tests the property value

❹ Tests the property/attribute correspondence

❺ Tests more property/attribute correspondence

This example shows some interesting behavior with respect to element attributes and element properties. It starts by defining a simple `<div>` element that we'll use as a test subject. Within the page's load handler (to ensure that the DOM is finished being built) we obtain a reference to the lone `<div>` element ❶ and then run a few tests.

In our first test ❷, we set the id attribute to the value "ninja-1" via the set-Attribute() method. Then we assert that getAttribute() returns the same value for that attribute. It should be no surprise to find that this test works just fine when we load the page.

Similarly, in the next test **❸**, we set the id property to the value "ninja-2" and then verify that the property value was indeed changed. No problem.

The next test **❹** is when things get interesting. We again set the id property to a new value, in this case "ninja-3", and again verify that the property value was changed. But then we also assert that not only should the property value have changed, but also the value of the id *attribute*. Both assertions pass. From this we learn that the id property and the id attribute are somehow linked together. Changing the id property value also changes the id attribute value.

The next test **❺** proves that it also works the other way around: setting an attribute value also changes the corresponding property value.

But don't let this fool you into thinking that the property and attribute are sharing the same value—they aren't. We'll see later in this chapter that the attribute and corresponding property, while linked, aren't always identical. You already got a glimpse of this in the chapter introduction.

There are five important points to consider with respect to attributes and properties:

- Cross-browser naming
- Naming limitations
- HTML versus XML differences
- Custom attribute behavior
- Performance

Let's examine each of these points.

12.1.1 *Cross-browser naming*

When it comes to the naming of attributes and their corresponding properties, property names are generally more consistent from browser to browser. If we're able to access a property by a certain name in one browser, there's a good chance of the name being the same in other browsers as well. There are *some* differences, but there tend to be more differences in the naming of the attributes than the naming of properties.

For example, while the class attribute can be obtained as class in most browsers, Internet Explorer requires className. This is likely because (as we'll see in just a bit) the name of the property is className, and so within IE the name of the attribute and the property are consistent. Consistency is usually a good thing, but the naming difference across browsers can be quite frustrating.

Libraries such as jQuery help to normalize these naming discrepancies by allowing us to specify one name regardless of the platform, and it then performs any necessary translation behind the scenes. But without library assistance, we need to be aware of the differences and write our own code accordingly.

12.1.2 Naming restrictions

Attributes, being represented by strings passed to DOM methods, can be named with a rather free reign, but property names, which can be referenced as identifiers using the dot operator notation, are more restricted, as they must conform to the rules for identifiers, and there are some reserved words that are disallowed.

The ECMAScript specification (found at http://www.ecma-international.org/publications/standards/Ecma-262.htm) states that certain keywords can't be used as property names, so alternatives have been defined. For example, the `for` attribute of `<label>` elements is represented by the `htmlFor` property, because `for` is a reserved word, and the `class` attribute of all elements is represented by the `className` property, as `class` is also reserved. Additionally, attribute names that are composed of multiple words, such as `readonly` are represented by camel-case property names; `readOnly` in this case. More examples of these differences can be found in table 12.1.

Table 12.1   Cases where property names and attribute names differ

Attribute name	Property name
for	htmlFor
class	className
readonly	readOnly
maxlength	maxLength
cellspacing	cellSpacing
rowspan	rowSpan
colspan	colSpan
tabindex	tabIndex
cellpadding	cellPadding
usemap	useMap
frameborder	frameBorder
contenteditable	contentEditable

Note that HTML5 adds new elements and attributes that may need to be included in this list when the dust settles. Some are `accessKey`, `contextMenu`, `dropZone`, `spellCheck`, `hrefLang`, `dateTime`, `pubDate`, `isMap`, `srcDoc`, `mediaGroup`, `autoComplete`, `noValidate`, and `radioGroup`.

12.1.3 Differences between XML and HTML

The whole notion of properties that automatically correspond to attributes is a peculiarity of the HTML DOM. When dealing with an XML DOM, no properties are automatically created on the elements to represent attribute values. Therefore, we'll need to use the traditional DOM attribute methods to obtain attribute values. This isn't a horrible imposition, because XML documents usually don't exhibit the normal litany of naming mistakes that you see with DOM attributes in HTML documents.

> **NOTE**   If the term *XML DOM* sent you off the tracks, it's just an in-memory object structure created to represent an XML document in the same way that the HTML DOM represents an HTML document.

It's a good idea to put some form of a check in our code to determine if an element (or document) is an XML element (or document) so we can proceed appropriately. The following function shows an example of this type of check:

```
function isXML(elem) {
  return (elem.ownerDocument ||
    elem.documentElement.nodeName.toLowerCase() !== "html";
}
```

This function will return true if the element is an XML element, and false otherwise.

12.1.4 *Behavior of custom attributes*

Not all attributes are represented by element properties. While it's generally true for attributes that are natively specified by the HTML DOM, *custom attributes* that we may place on the elements in our pages don't automatically become represented by element properties. To access the value of a custom attribute, we need to use the DOM methods getAttribute() and setAttribute().

If you're not sure if a property for an attribute exists or not, you can always test for it and fall back to the DOM methods if it doesn't exist. Here's an example:

```
var value = element.someValue ? element.someValue :
                          element.getAttribute('someValue');
```

> **TIP**   In HTML5, use the prefix data- for all custom attributes to keep them valid in the eye of the HTML5 specification. It's recommended you do this even if you're still using HTML4, in order to future-proof your markup. Besides, it's a good convention that clearly separates custom attributes from native attributes.

12.1.5 *Performance considerations*

In general, property access is faster than the corresponding DOM attribute methods, especially in Internet Explorer. Let's prove that to ourselves.

Remember back in chapter 2 when we talked about performance testing? The way that we do that is to measure how long it takes to repeat an operation many times. We can't measure the performance of a single operation; the duration is far too short to capture accurately (harken back to our timer discussion in chapter 8).

If one operation is too quick to measure, what about five million of them? That's exactly what the following code measures.

Listing 12.2   Comparing the performance of DOM methods versus properties

```
<div id="testSubject"></div>

<script type="text/javascript">

  var count = 5000000;
  var n;
  var begin = new Date();
  var end;
  var testSubject = document.getElementById('testSubject');
  var value;

  for (n = 0; n < count; n++) {
    value = testSubject.getAttribute('id');
  }
  end = new Date();
  assert(true,'Time for DOM method read: ' +
      (end.getTime() - begin.getTime())));

  begin = new Date();
  for (n = 0; n < count; n++) {
    value = testSubject.id;
  }
  end = new Date();
  assert(true,'Time for property read: ' +
        (end.getTime() - begin.getTime())));

  begin = new Date();
  for (n = 0; n < count; n++) {
    testSubject.setAttribute('id','testSubject');
  }
  end = new Date();
  assert(true,'Time for DOM method write: ' +
        (end.getTime() - begin.getTime())));

  begin = new Date();
  for (n = 0; n < count; n++) {
    testSubject.id = 'testSubject';
  }
  end = new Date();
  assert(true,'Time for property write: ' +
        (end.getTime() - begin.getTime())));

</script>
```

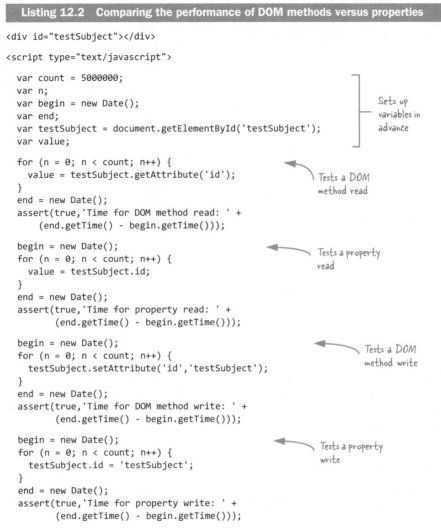

Sets up variables in advance

Tests a DOM method read

Tests a property read

Tests a DOM method write

Tests a property write

This code conducts a performance test of the DOM getAttribute() and set-Attribute() methods against similar operations for reading and writing the corresponding property.

We ran this test on multiple browsers, and the results we gathered are shown in table 12.2. All duration values are in milliseconds. As you can see, the property get and set operations are almost always faster than getAttribute() and setAttribute().

NOTE   Most of these tests were conducted on a 2011 MacBook Pro with a 2.8 GHz i7 processor and 8 GB of RAM running OS X Lion. The IE tests were conducted on a PC with the same i7 2.8GHz processor and 4 GB RAM running Windows 7 (64 bits).

Table 12.2   Performance test results pitting DOM methods versus property access

Browser	getAttribute()	Property get	setAttribute()	Property set
Internet Explorer 9	3970	940	7667	956
Firefox 14	827	434	1414	1584
Safari 5	268	142	1055	627
Chrome 21	294	159	1140	862
Opera 12	2109	1642	2370	1635

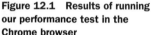

Figure 12.1   Results of running our performance test in the Chrome browser

The results of a sample run of this test are shown in figure 12.1.

While these differences in speed may not be crippling for individual operations, they can add up if performed many times—in a tight loop, for example. To improve performance, we might want to implement a method by which we can access a value by property, if the property exists, and by DOM method as a fallback when it doesn't. Consider the following code.

Listing 12.3   A function for setting and getting attribute values

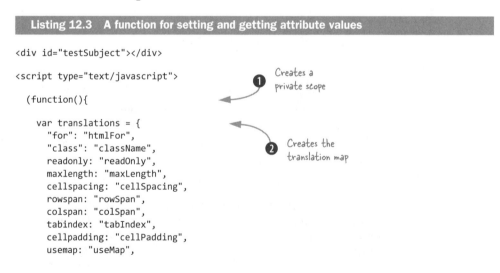

```
<div id="testSubject"></div>

<script type="text/javascript">

  (function(){

    var translations = {
      "for": "htmlFor",
      "class": "className",
      readonly: "readOnly",
      maxlength: "maxLength",
      cellspacing: "cellSpacing",
      rowspan: "rowSpan",
      colspan: "colSpan",
      tabindex: "tabIndex",
      cellpadding: "cellPadding",
      usemap: "useMap",
```

❶ Creates a private scope

❷ Creates the translation map

```
      frameborder: "frameBorder",
      contenteditable: "contentEditable"
    };
```

❸ Defines the set/get function

```
    window.attr = function(element,name,value) {
      var property = translations[name] || name,
          propertyExists = typeof element[property] !== "undefined";

      if (typeof value !== "undefined") {
        if (propertyExists) {
          element[property] = value;
        }
        else {
          element.setAttribute(name,value);
        }
      }

      return propertyExists ?
        element[property] :
        element.getAttribute(name);
    };

  })();
```

```
  var subject = document.getElementById('testSubject');
  assert(attr(subject,'id') === 'testSubject',
      "id value fetched");
```

Tests our new function

```
  assert(attr(subject,'id','other') === 'other',
      "new id value set");
  assert(attr(subject,'id') === 'other',
      "new id value fetched");

  assert(attr(subject,'data-custom','whatever') === 'whatever',
      "custom attribute set");
  assert(attr(subject,'data-custom') === 'whatever',
      "custom attribute fetched");
```

```
</script>
```

This example not only establishes a setter and getter function for attribute and property values, it also shows a number of important concepts that we can use elsewhere in our code.

In our function, we need to translate between property and attribute names, as outlined in table 12.1, so we create a translation map ❷. But we don't want to pollute the global namespace with this map; we want it to be available to the function in its local scope, but no farther than that.

We accomplish that by enclosing the map definition and function declaration within an immediate function ❶, which creates a local scope. The translation map ❷ isn't accessible outside the immediate function, but the set/get function that we also define ❸ within the immediate function has access to the map via its closure. Nifty, eh?

Another important principle is exhibited by our attr() function itself—the function can act as both a setter and a getter simply by inspecting its own argument list. If a value argument is passed to the function, the function acts as a setter, setting the passed value as the value of the attribute. If the value argument is omitted and only the first two arguments are passed, it acts as a getter, retrieving the value of the specified attribute.

In either case, the value of the attribute is returned, which makes it easy to use the function in either of its modes in a function-call chain.

It should be noted that the preceding implementation doesn't take into account many of the cross-browser issues that plague attribute access. Let's find out exactly what those issues are.

12.2   Cross-browser attribute issues

Cross-browser issues in general can be quite harrowing, and the number of cross-browser issues at play in the area of attribute values isn't trivial. Let's explore a few of the major and most commonly encountered issues, starting with DOM name expansion.

12.2.1   DOM id/name expansion

The nastiest bug to deal with is a misimplementation of the DOM code in the browsers.

As we pointed out in the previous chapter, the problem is that all of the "Big Five" browsers take the id or name values specified on form input elements and add references to the elements as properties on the parent <form> element. These generated properties actively overwrite any existing properties of the same name that might already be on the form element.

Additionally, Internet Explorer doesn't just replace the properties; it also replaces the attribute values with references to the elements.

These problems can be seen in the following listing.

Listing 12.4   Demonstrating how browsers strong-arm form elements

```
<form id="testForm" action="/">
  <input type="text" id="id"/>                    ❶ Creates a
  <input type="text" name="action"/>                test subject
</form>

<script type="text/javascript">
  window.onload = function(){

    var form = document.getElementById('testForm');
                                                    Tests if properties
    assert(form.id === 'testForm',               ❷ have been stomped
        "the id property is untouched");            upon
    assert(form.action === '/',
        "the action property is untouched");

    assert(form.getAttribute('id') === 'testForm',
        "the id attribute is untouched");           Tests if attributes
    assert(form.getAttribute('action') === '/',   ❸ have been mangled
        "the action attribute is untouched");

  };
</script>
```

This series of tests shows how this unfortunate feature can cause loss of markup data. First, we define an HTML form ❶ with two input element children. One child has an ID of id, and the other a name of action.

Out first test asserts ❷ that the form element's id and action properties should be as we set them in the HTML markup, and the second set of tests ❸ asserts that the attribute values reflect the markup.

But upon running the test in Chrome, we see the display in figure 12.2.

In all modern browsers, the id and action properties have been overwritten with references to the input elements simply because of the id and name values chosen for those elements. The original property values are gone forever! In browsers other than IE, we can obtain the original values using the DOM attribute methods, but in IE, even those values are replaced.

But we're ninjas and won't be denied. Despite the best efforts of the browsers to keep us from the values, we've got a trick up our sleeves. We can gain access to the original DOM node representing the element attribute itself. This node remains untainted by the browser tinkering. To get the value from a DOM attribute node, say the one for the action attribute, we'd use this code:

```
var actionValue = element.getAttributeNode("action").nodeValue;
```

As an exercise, see if you can use this approach to augment the attr() method that we developed in listing 12.3 to detect when a form element node's attribute has been replaced by an element reference, and fall back to getting the value from the DOM node when it has been replaced.

> **NOTE** If you're interested in the sort of problems that arise from these element expansions, we recommend checking out Juriy Zaytsev's DOMLint tool at http://kangax.github.com/domlint/, which is capable of analyzing a page for potential problems, and Garrett Smith's write-up of the issue, "Unsafe Names for HTML Form Controls," at http://jibbering.com/faq/names/.

While this issue can't be considered a bug, as it's the browsers' intended behavior, it's destructive and certainly unnecessary when element references are so easy to obtain with methods such as document.getElementById() and other similar methods.

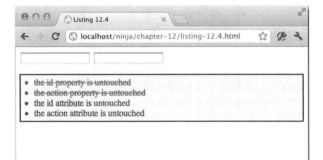

Figure 12.2 Looks as if the markup values have been stomped upon!

But this is far from the only issue with how the browsers handle attributes. Let's look at another.

12.2.2 *URL normalization*

There's a "feature" in all modern browsers that violates the principle of least surprise: when accessing a property that references a URL (such as href, src, or action) the URL value is automatically converted from its original form into a full canonical URL. (We alluded to this in the chapter introduction.)

We've already warned you about the automatic normalization, but let's write a test that demonstrates this issue in the next listing.

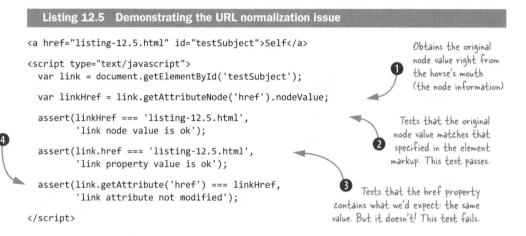

Listing 12.5   Demonstrating the URL normalization issue

```
<a href="listing-12.5.html" id="testSubject">Self</a>

<script type="text/javascript">
  var link = document.getElementById('testSubject');

  var linkHref = link.getAttributeNode('href').nodeValue;

  assert(linkHref === 'listing-12.5.html',
         'link node value is ok');

  assert(link.href === 'listing-12.5.html',
         'link property value is ok');

  assert(link.getAttribute('href') === linkHref,
         'link attribute not modified');

</script>
```

Obtains the original node value right from the horse's mouth (the node information) **1**

Tests that the original node value matches that specified in the element markup. This test passes. **2**

Tests that the href property contains what we'd expect: the same value. But it doesn't! This test fails. **3**

Tests that attribute value is what we expect, and it is! Passes. **4**

In this test, we establish an anchor tag with an href attribute that refers back to the same page. Then we obtain a reference to this element for testing.

The trick we learned in the previous section—diving down into the original nodes of the DOM to find the original value of the markup—is then employed **1**. This value is checked **2** before we blindly assume that our trick worked.

Then we test the property to see if it matches **3**. In all browsers this test fails, as the value has been normalized to a full URL.

Lastly, we test to see if the attribute value has been modified **4**. In all browsers but older versions of IE, the test passes.

Not only do these tests show the nature of the issue, they also reveal a workaround: we can use the DOM node trick to obtain such attributes when we want to be sure to obtain an unmodified value.

For older versions of IE (prior to IE 8), another workaround is a proprietary extension to the getAttribute() method in Internet Explorer. Passing the magic number 2 as a second parameter will force the result to be the unnormalized value:

```
var original = link.getAttribute('href',2);
```

We can use either workaround in modern browsers: the DOM node trick will work across all browsers, and modern browsers other than IE will ignore any second parameter passed to getAttribute(). Older versions of Opera will crash for no apparent reason when a second parameter is passed to getAttribute(), so avoid that approach if such versions of Opera are in your support matrix.

The chances that the URL normalization issue will be a problem for your code are small, unless your code absolutely needs to get at the unnormalized values.

Now let's examine an issue that may have more far-reaching consequences.

12.2.3 *The style attribute*

An important element attribute whose values are particularly challenging to set and get is the style attribute. HTML DOM elements are given a style property, which we can access to gain information about the style information of the element; for example, element.style.color. But if we want to get the original style string that was specified on the element, it becomes more challenging. For example, consider this markup:

```
<div style='color:red;'></div>
```

What if we wanted to obtain the original color:red; string?

The style property is of no help at all, as it's set to an object that contains the parsed results of the original string. And although getAttribute("style") works in most browsers, it doesn't work in Internet Explorer. Instead, IE stores a property on the style object that we can use to obtain the original style string, named cssText; for example, element.style.cssText.

While directly getting the original value of the style attribute may be a comparatively uncommon operation (as opposed to accessing the resulting style object), there's another browser problem that's likely to affect any page that creates DOM elements at runtime.

12.2.4 *The type attribute*

Another Internet Explorer gotcha, for IE 8 and earlier versions, affects the type attribute of <input> elements, and there isn't any reasonable workaround. Once an <input> element has been inserted into a document, its type attribute can no longer be changed. In fact, IE throws an exception if you attempt to change it.

For example, consider the following code in which we try to change the type of an input element after the fact.

Listing 12.6 Changing an input element's type after insertion

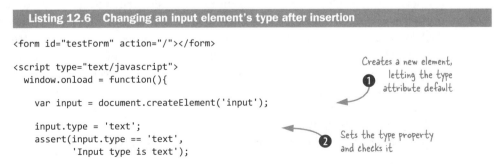

```
<form id="testForm" action="/"></form>

<script type="text/javascript">
  window.onload = function(){

    var input = document.createElement('input');

    input.type = 'text';
    assert(input.type == 'text',
           'Input type is text');
```

Creates a new element, letting the type attribute default ❶

Sets the type property and checks it ❷

```
document.getElementById('testForm')
        .appendChild(input);

input.type = 'hidden';
assert(input.type == 'hidden',
        'Input type changed to hidden');
   };
</script>
```

❸ Inserts the new input element into the DOM

❹ Changes type after insertion

In this test, we create a new `<input>` element ❶, give it a type of `text`, assert that the assignment was successful ❷, and insert the new element into the DOM ❸. *After* insertion, we change the type to `hidden` and assert that the change took place ❹.

In all modern browsers but IE, the tests pass without a problem. In IE 8 and earlier, however, an exception is thrown at the assignment attempt, and the second test never executes.

Although there's no easy workaround, there are two stopgap measures we can take:

- Rather than try to change the `type`, create a new `<input>` element, copy over all properties and attributes, and replace the original element with the newly created element. This solution seems easy enough, but it has problems. First, it's impossible to know if the element has had any event handlers established upon it using the DOM level 2 methods unless we've been tracking them ourselves. Second, any references to the original element become invalid.
- In any API you create to effect changes to properties or attributes, simply reject any attempts to change the `type` value.

Neither of these options is completely satisfying.

jQuery employs the second approach, throwing an informative exception when any attempt is made to change the `type` attribute if the element has already been inserted into the document. Obviously this is a compromise "solution," but at least the user experience is consistent across all platforms. Thankfully, this issue has been addressed in IE 9.

Let's look at yet another annoyance that the browsers bedevil us with, again within the realm of form elements.

12.2.5 *The tab index problem*

Determining the tab index of an element is another weird problem that the browsers throw at us, and it's one where there's little consensus as to how it *should* work. While it's perfectly possible to get the tab index of an element using either the `tabIndex` property or the `"tabindex"` attribute for elements that have them explicitly defined, the browser returns a value of 0 for the `tabIndex` property and null for the `"tabindex"` attribute for elements without an explicit value. This means, of course, that we have no way of knowing what tab index has been assigned to elements that we didn't explicitly set a tab index value upon.

This is a complex issue, and it's one that's especially important in the world of usability and accessibility.

The last attribute-related problem we'll consider isn't really an attribute issue at all.

12.2.6 *Node names*

While this issue isn't directly related to attributes per se, a number of workarounds we've used in this section have relied upon finding nodes, and it turns out that determining the name of a node can be slightly tricky.

Specifically, the case sensitivity of the node name changes depending upon which type of document you're examining. If it's a normal HTML document, the nodeName property will return the name of the element in all uppercase (for example, HTML or BODY). But if it's in an XML or XHTML document, the nodeName will return the name as specified by the user, which means that it could be lowercase, uppercase, or any combination of either.

The conventional solution to this hindrance is to normalize the name prior to any comparison, usually to lowercase. For example, let's say we want to perform some operation on only <div> and <ul> elements. As we don't know whether the node names that we'll be getting are "div" or "DIV" or even "dIv", we'd want to normalize the names as shown in this code:

```
var all = document.getElementsByTagName("*")[0];

for (var i = 0; i < all.length; i++) {
  var nodeName = all[i].nodeName.toLowerCase();
  if (nodeName === "div" || nodeName === "ul") {
    all[i].className = "found";
  }
}
```

When we definitively know what type of document our code will be executing within, we don't necessarily have to worry about this case sensitivity, but if we're writing reusable code that should run in any environment, it's best to be prudent and perform the normalization.

In this section, we've talked about issues with the attributes and properties of elements, and we even examined a small issue with the style property. But that was just a tiny glimpse into the heartburn that the browsers have in store for us when it comes to styling. In the next section, we'll take a look at the pain points of dealing with CSS issues in the browsers.

12.3 *Styling attribute headaches*

As with general attributes, getting and setting styling attributes can be quite the headache. Just like the attributes and properties that we examined in the previous section, we again have two approaches for handling style values: the attribute value, and the element property created from it.

The most commonly used of these is the style element property, which isn't a string but an object that holds properties corresponding to the style values specified in the element markup. In addition to this, we'll see that there's an API for accessing the computed style information of an element, where "computed style" means the actual styles that will be applied to the element after evaluating all inherited and applied style information.

This section will outline the things you should know about dealing with styles in the browsers. Let's start with a look at where style information is recorded.

12.3.1 *Where are my styles?*

The style information located on the `style` property of a DOM element is initially set from the value specified for the `style` attribute in the element markup. For example, `style="color:red;"` will result in that style information being placed into the style object. During page execution, script can set or modify values in the style object, and these changes will actively affect the display of the element.

Many script authors are disappointed to find that no values from on-page `<style>` elements or external style sheets are available in the element's `style` object. But we won't stay disappointed for long—we'll shortly see a way to obtain such information.

But for now, let's see how the `style` property gets its values. Examine the following code.

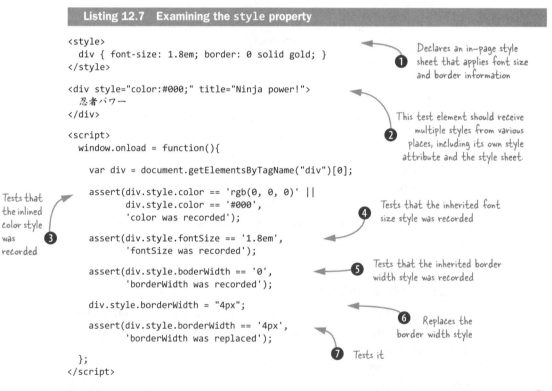

Listing 12.7 Examining the `style` property

```
<style>
  div { font-size: 1.8em; border: 0 solid gold; }
</style>

<div style="color:#000;" title="Ninja power!">
  忍者パワー
</div>

<script>
  window.onload = function(){

    var div = document.getElementsByTagName("div")[0];

    assert(div.style.color == 'rgb(0, 0, 0)' ||
           div.style.color == '#000',
           'color was recorded');

    assert(div.style.fontSize == '1.8em',
           'fontSize was recorded');

    assert(div.style.boderWidth == '0',
           'borderWidth was recorded');

    div.style.borderWidth = "4px";

    assert(div.style.borderWidth == '4px',
           'borderWidth was replaced');
  };
</script>
```

① Declares an in-page style sheet that applies font size and border information

② This test element should receive multiple styles from various places, including its own style attribute and the style sheet.

③ Tests that the inlined color style was recorded

④ Tests that the inherited font size style was recorded

⑤ Tests that the inherited border width style was recorded

⑥ Replaces the border width style

⑦ Tests it

In this example, we set up a `<style>` element to establish an internal style sheet ① whose values will be applied to the elements on the page. The style sheet specifies that all `<div>` elements will appear in a font size that's 1.8 times bigger than the default, with a solid gold border of 0 width. This means that any elements to which this is applied will possess a border; it just won't be visible because it has a width of 0.

Then we create a <div> element with an inlined style attribute that colors the text of the element black ❷.

We then begin the testing. After obtaining a reference to the <div> element, we test that the style attribute received a color property that represents the color assigned to the element ❸. Note that even though the color was specified as #000 in the inline style, it's normalized to RGB notation when set in the style property in most browsers (so we check both formats). Looking ahead to figure 12.3, we see that this test passes.

> **WARNING** The color normalization isn't always consistent across browsers or even within a specific browser. Most colors will be normalized to RGB notation, but some browsers will leave colors specified as named colors (black, for example).

Then we naively test that the font-size styling and the border width specified in the inline style sheet have been recorded in the style object ❹ ❺. But even though we can see in figure 12.3 that the font-size style has been applied to the element, the test fails. This is because the style object doesn't reflect any style information inherited from CSS style sheets.

Moving on, we use an assignment to change the value of the borderWidth property in the style object to 4 pixels wide ❻ and test that the change was applied ❼. We can see in figure 12.3 that the test passes and that the previously invisible border now has been applied to the element. This assignment causes a borderWidth property to appear in the style property of the element, as proven by the test ❼.

It should be noted that any values in an element's style property will take precedence over anything inherited by a style sheet (even if the style sheet rule uses the !important annotation).

One thing that you may have noted in listing 12.7 is that CSS specifies the font size property as font-size, but in script we referenced it as fontSize. Why is that?

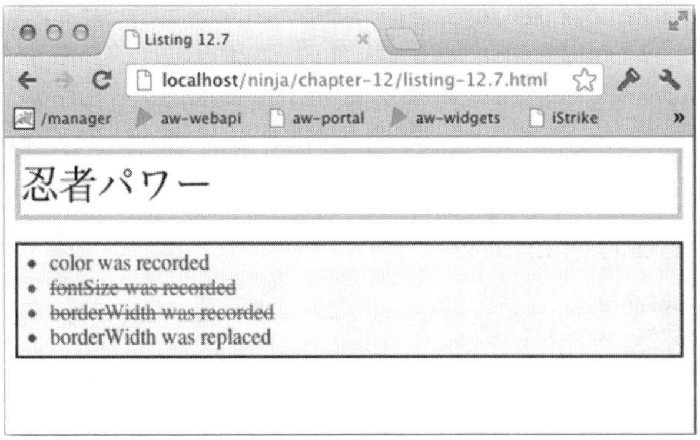

Figure 12.3 Tests show that inline and assigned styles are recorded, but inherited styles aren't.

12.3.2 *Style property naming*

With CSS attributes there are relatively few cross-browser difficulties when it comes to accessing the values provided by the browser. But differences between how CSS names styles and how we access those in script do exist, and there are some style names that differ across browsers.

CSS attributes that span more than one word separate the words with a hyphen; examples are font-weight, font-size, and background-color. You may recall that property names in JavaScript *can* contain a hyphen, but including a hyphen prevents the property from being accessed via the dot operator.

Consider this example:

```
var color = element.style['font-size'];
```

The preceding would be perfectly valid. But the following wouldn't:

```
var color = element.style.font-size;
```

The JavaScript parser would see the hyphen as a subtraction operator and nobody would be happy with the outcome. Rather than forcing page developers to always use the general form for property access, multiword CSS style names are converted to camel case when used as a property name. As a result, font-size becomes fontSize and background-color becomes backgroundColor.

We can either remember to do this, or we could write a simple API to set or get styles for us that automatically handles the camel casing, as shown in the following listing.

Listing 12.8   A simple method for accessing styles

```
<div style="color:red;font-size:10px;background-color:#eee;"></div>

<script type="text/javascript">
  function style(element,name,value){                    // Defines the style function
    name = name.replace(/-([a-z])/ig,                     // Converts name to camel case
                     function(all,letter){
                         return letter.toUpperCase();
                     });

    if (typeof value !== 'undefined') {                   // Sets value if provided
      element.style[name] = value;
    }

    return element.style[name];                           // Returns value
  }

  window.onload = function(){

    var div = document.getElementsByTagName('div')[0];

    assert(true,style(div,'color'));
    assert(true,style(div,'font-size'));
    assert(true,style(div,'background-color'));

  };
</script>
```

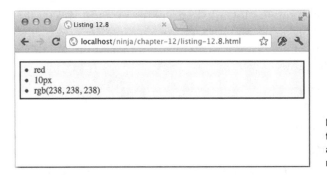

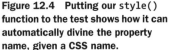

Figure 12.4 Putting our `style()` function to the test shows how it can automatically divine the property name, given a CSS name.

With the exception of the conversion of the `name` parameter to camel case, this function operates much like the `attr()` function that we developed in listing 12.3, so we won't belabor its operation.

If the regex-driven conversion operation has you scratching your head, you might want to review the material in chapter 7. Also note that despite the inclusion of a number of `assert()` calls, we haven't really performed any testing of the function—we used the assert as a lazy way of displaying the output in the page, as shown in figure 12.4.

As an exercise, write a series of asserts that thoroughly test this new function.

Earlier we mentioned that there are a number of "problem" style properties that are treated differently across browsers. Let's take a gander at one of them.

12.3.3 *The float style property*

One major naming headache in the area of style attributes is the manner in which the `float` attribute is handled. This property needs to be specially handled because the name `float` is a reserved keyword in JavaScript. The browsers need to provide an alternative name.

As has frequently happened in such cases, the standards-compliant browsers went one way, and Internet Explorer went another. Nearly all browsers chose to use the name `cssFloat` as the alternative name, whereas Internet Explorer chose `styleFloat`. Sigh.

Using the translation capability from listing 12.3 as inspiration, see if you can modify the `style()` function of listing 12.8 to accommodate this difference.

Earlier in this section, we saw how color values can be changed from one notation to another when they're added as a style property. Let's explore another such situation.

12.3.4 *Conversion of pixel values*

An important point to consider when setting style values is the assignment of numeric values that represent pixels. When specifying pixel values in deprecated attributes, such as the `height` attribute of the `<img>` tag, we're used to specifying a number and letting the browser deal with the units. When assigning pixel values to style properties, this approach can get us into a lot of trouble.

When setting a numeric value for a style property, we must specify the units in order for it to work reliably across all browsers. For example, let's say that we want to set the `height` style value of an element to 10 pixels. Either of the following is a safe way to do this across the browsers:

```
element.style.height = "10px";
element.style.height = 10 + "px";
```

The following isn't safe across browsers:

```
element.style.height = 10;
```

You might think it'd be easy to add a little logic to our `style()` function of listing 12.8 to just tack a "px" to the end of numeric value coming into the function. But not so fast! Not all numeric values represent pixels! There are a number of style properties that take numeric values that don't represent a pixel dimension:

- z-index
- font-weight
- opacity
- zoom
- line-height

For these (and any others you can think of), go ahead and extend the function of listing 12.8 to automatically handle non-pixel values.

Also, when attempting to read a pixel value out of a style attribute, the `parseFloat` method should be used to make sure that you get the intended value under all circumstances.

Now let's take a look at a set of important style properties that can be tough to handle.

12.3.5 *Measuring heights and widths*

Style properties such as `height` and `width` pose a special problem, because their values default to `auto` when not specified, so that the element sizes itself according to its contents. As a result, we can't use the `height` and `width` style properties to get accurate values unless explicit values were provided in the attribute string.

Thankfully, the `offsetHeight` and `offsetWidth` properties provide just that: a fairly reliable means to access the actual height and width of an element. But be aware that the values assigned to these two properties include the padding of the element. This information is usually exactly what we want if we're attempting to position one element over another. But sometimes we may want to obtain information about the element's dimensions with and without borders and padding.

Something to watch out for, however, is that in highly interactive sites it's likely that elements may spend some of their time in a non-displayed state (with the `display` style being set to `none`), and when an element isn't part of the display, it has no dimensions. Any attempt to fetch the `offsetWidth` or `offsetHeight` properties of a non-displayed element will result in a value of `0`.

For such hidden elements, if we wish to obtain its non-hidden dimensions, we can employ a trick and momentarily unhide the element, grab the values, and hide it again. Of course, we want to do so in such a way that there's no visible clue that this is going on behind the scenes. How can we make a hidden element not hidden without making it visible?

Employing our ninja skills, we can do it! Here's how:

1 Change the `display` property to `block`.

2 Set `visibility` to `hidden`.

3 Set `position` to `absolute`.

4 Grab the dimension values.

5 Restore the changed properties.

Changing the `display` property to `block` allows us to grab the actual values of `offsetHeight` and `offsetWidth`, but it will make the element part of the display and therefore visible. To make it invisible, we'll set the `visibility` property to `hidden`. But (there's always another "but") that will leave a big hole where the element is positioned, so we also set the `position` property to `absolute` to take the element out of the normal display flow.

All that sounds more complicated than the actual implementation, which is shown in the next listing.

Listing 12.9   Grabbing the dimensions of hidden elements

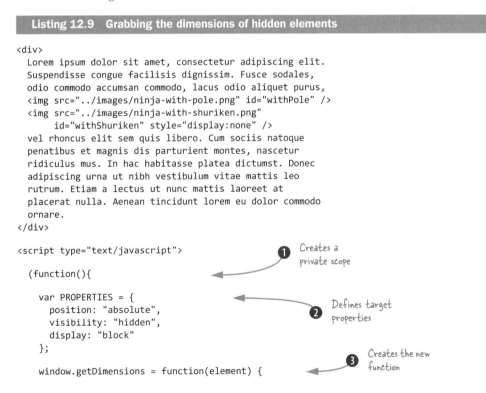

```html
<div>
  Lorem ipsum dolor sit amet, consectetur adipiscing elit.
  Suspendisse congue facilisis dignissim. Fusce sodales,
  odio commodo accumsan commodo, lacus odio aliquet purus,
  <img src="../images/ninja-with-pole.png" id="withPole" />
  <img src="../images/ninja-with-shuriken.png"
      id="withShuriken" style="display:none" />
  vel rhoncus elit sem quis libero. Cum sociis natoque
  penatibus et magnis dis parturient montes, nascetur
  ridiculus mus. In hac habitasse platea dictumst. Donec
  adipiscing urna ut nibh vestibulum vitae mattis leo
  rutrum. Etiam a lectus ut nunc mattis laoreet at
  placerat nulla. Aenean tincidunt lorem eu dolor commodo
  ornare.
</div>

<script type="text/javascript">

  (function(){                                          ❶ Creates a
                                                           private scope

    var PROPERTIES = {                                  ❷ Defines target
      position: "absolute",                                properties
      visibility: "hidden",
      display: "block"
    };
                                                        ❸ Creates the new
    window.getDimensions = function(element) {             function
```

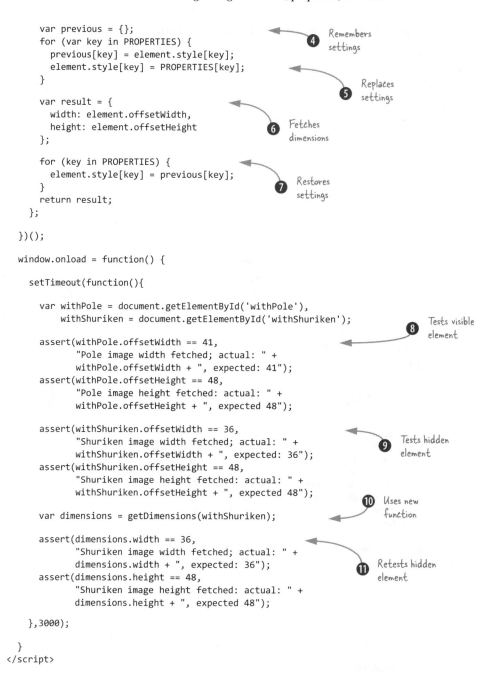

```
      var previous = {};
      for (var key in PROPERTIES) {                    ➍  Remembers
        previous[key] = element.style[key];                settings
        element.style[key] = PROPERTIES[key];
      }                                                ➎  Replaces
                                                           settings
      var result = {
        width: element.offsetWidth,                    ➏  Fetches
        height: element.offsetHeight                       dimensions
      };

      for (key in PROPERTIES) {
        element.style[key] = previous[key];            ➐  Restores
      }                                                    settings
      return result;
    };

  })();

  window.onload = function() {

    setTimeout(function(){

      var withPole = document.getElementById('withPole'),
          withShuriken = document.getElementById('withShuriken');
                                                       ➑  Tests visible
      assert(withPole.offsetWidth == 41,                  element
          "Pole image width fetched; actual: " +
          withPole.offsetWidth + ", expected: 41");
      assert(withPole.offsetHeight == 48,
          "Pole image height fetched: actual: " +
          withPole.offsetHeight + ", expected 48");

      assert(withShuriken.offsetWidth == 36,           ➒  Tests hidden
          "Shuriken image width fetched; actual: " +       element
          withShuriken.offsetWidth + ", expected: 36");
      assert(withShuriken.offsetHeight == 48,
          "Shuriken image height fetched: actual: " +
          withShuriken.offsetHeight + ", expected: 48");
                                                       ➓  Uses new
      var dimensions = getDimensions(withShuriken);        function

      assert(dimensions.width == 36,
          "Shuriken image width fetched; actual: " +
          dimensions.width + ", expected: 36");        ⓫  Retests hidden
      assert(dimensions.height == 48,                      element
          "Shuriken image height fetched: actual: " +
          dimensions.height + ", expected: 48");

    },3000);

  }
</script>
```

That's rather a long listing, but most of it is test code; the actual implementation of the new dimension-fetching function spans only a dozen or so lines of code.

Let's take a look at it piece by piece. First, we set up some elements to test: a `<div>` element containing a bunch of text with two images embedded within it, left-justified

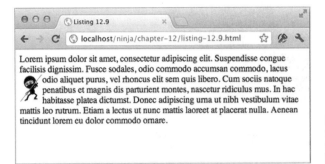

Figure 12.5 We'll use two images—one visible, one hidden—for testing the fetching of dimensions of hidden elements.

by styles in an external style sheet. These image elements will be the subjects of our tests; one is visible, and one is hidden.

Prior to running any script, the elements appear as shown in figure 12.5. If the second image were not hidden, it would appear as a second ninja just to the right of the visible one.

Then we set about defining our new function. We're going to use a hash for some important information, so we repeat the trick of listing 12.3 and enclose the local variable and the function definition in an immediate function ❶ to create a local scope and closure. The local hash to contain the properties we want to muck around with is defined ❷ and populated with the three properties and their replacement values.

Our new dimension-fetching function is then declared ❸, accepting the element that's to be measured. Within that function, we first create a hash named previous ❹ in which we'll record the previous values of the style properties that we'll be stomping on, so that we can restore them later. Looping over the replacement properties, we then record each of their previous values and replace those values with the new ones ❺.

That accomplished, we're ready to measure the element, which has now been made part of the display layout, invisible, and absolutely positioned. The dimensions are recorded in a hash assigned to local variable result ❻.

Now that we've pilfered what we came for, we erase our tracks by restoring the original values of the style properties that we modified ❼, and we return the results as a hash containing width and height properties.

All well and good, but does it work? Let's find out.

In a load handler, we perform the tests in a callback to a 3-second timer. Why, you ask? The load handler ensures we don't perform the test until we know that the DOM has been built, and the timer enables us to watch the display while the test is running, to make sure there are no display glitches while we fiddle with the properties of the hidden element. After all, if the display is disturbed in any way when we run our function, it's a bust.

In the timer callback, we first get a reference to our test subjects (the two images) and assert that we can obtain the dimensions of the visible image using the offset properties ❽. This test passes, which we can see if we peek ahead to figure 12.6.

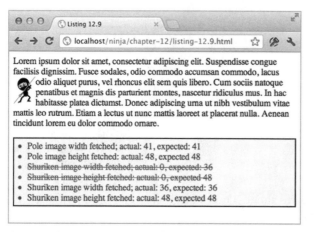

Figure 12.6 By temporarily adjusting the style properties of hidden elements, we can successfully fetch their dimensions.

Then we make the same test on the hidden element ❾, incorrectly assuming that the offset properties will work with a hidden image. Not surprisingly, because we've already acknowledged that this won't work, the test fails.

Next, we call our new function on the hidden image ❿, and then retest with those results ⓫. Success! Our test passes, as shown in figure 12.6.

If we watch the display of the page while the test is running—remember, we delay running the test until 3 seconds after the DOM is loaded—we can see that the display isn't perturbed in any way by our behind-the-scenes adjustments of the hidden element's properties.

> **TIP** Checking the `offsetWidth` and `offsetHeight` style properties for zeroes can serve as an incredibly efficient means of determining the visibility of an element.

The dimension style properties aren't the only ones that pose a challenge. Let's explore the nuances of dealing with the `opacity` property.

12.3.6 *Seeing through opacity*

The `opacity` style property is another special case that needs to be handled differently across browsers. All modern browsers, including Internet Explorer 9, natively support the `opacity` property, but versions of IE prior to IE 9 use their proprietary alpha filter notation.

Because of this, we frequently see opacity styles specified as follows in a style sheet (or directly in the `style` attribute):

```
opacity: 0.5;
filter: alpha(opacity=50);
```

The standard style uses a value from `0.0` to `1.0` to specify the opacity of an element, while the alpha filter uses an integer percentage from `0` to `100`. The preceding rules both specify an opacity value of 50 percent.

Let's say that we have an element defined with both styles as follows:

```
<div style="opacity:0.5;filter:alpha(opacity=50);">Hello</div>
```

When trying to fetch these values, the problem we're faced with is twofold:

- There are many different types of filters beyond `alpha`, such as transformations, so we have to deal with many filter types and can't just assume that a filter always specifies opacity.
- Even though IE 8 and earlier versions don't support `opacity`, the value specified for `opacity` will be returned when referencing the element's `style.opacity` property, even if it's completely ignored by the browser.

This latter point makes it hard for our code to determine if the browser has native support for `opacity` or not. But once again, we can focus our ninja powers on the problem and thumb our noses at the browsers that stubbornly try to foil us.

As it turns out, browsers that support `opacity` will always normalize an opacity value less than 1.0 with a leading 0. For example, if the opacity is specified as `opacity: .5`, a browser with native opacity support will return the value as `0.5`, whereas nonsupporting browsers will simply leave the value in its original form of `.5`.

That means we can use feature simulation (remember that from chapter 11?) to determine if a browser supports opacity natively or not. Consider the following code.

Listing 12.10   Determining if a browser supports opacity or not

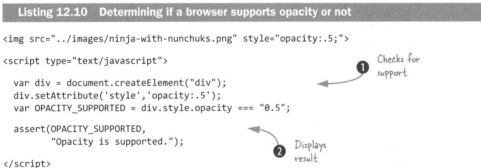

```
<img src="../images/ninja-with-nunchuks.png" style="opacity:.5;">

<script type="text/javascript">

  var div = document.createElement("div");          ❶ Checks for
  div.setAttribute('style','opacity:.5');              support
  var OPACITY_SUPPORTED = div.style.opacity === "0.5";

  assert(OPACITY_SUPPORTED,
         "Opacity is supported.");                  ❷ Displays
                                                       result
</script>
```

In this example, we define an image element with an `opacity` specified as `.5`. We won't be using this element in the code; it's just there to provide *us* with a visual indication of whether the opacity value is honored by the browser in use or not.

The meat of the test follows, where we create an unattached element ❶, which we augment with a style attribute with an `opacity` value of `.5`. We then record whether opacity is natively supported by reading the value back and checking if it's fetched as the original value (not supported), or the modified value of `0.5` (supported).

Finally, we assert the support variable, which causes the test to pass on supporting browsers and fail on nonsupporting browsers.

Figure 12.7 shows the result of loading this test ❷ into Chrome 17 (top) and Internet Explorer 7 (bottom).

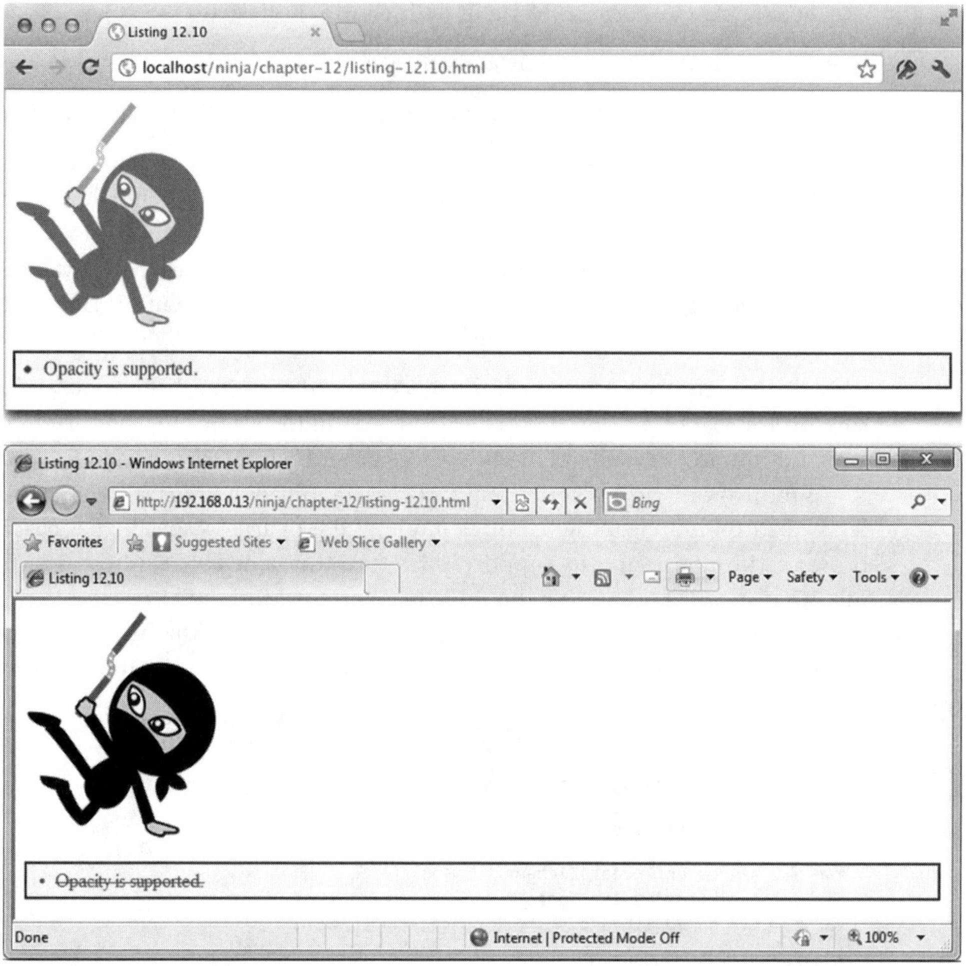

Figure 12.7   Visual clues as well as our explicit test shows that opacity is supported on Chrome but not versions of IE prior to IE 9.

Using this ninja knowledge, see if you can create a getOpacity(element) function, along the lines of the getDimensions() function of listing 12.9, that returns the opacity value for the passed element as a value between 0.0 and 1.0 regardless of the platform.

> **TIP**   In creating this function, a regular expression would be handy for finding the value of the alpha opacity filter, and the window.parseFloat() method will be your best friend. Also, return 1.0 as a failure fallback because that's the default for opacity values.

Let's now turn our eyes to yet another set of problematic style properties that cause us some pain because their values can take on many equivalent forms.

12.3.7 Riding the color wheel

We've already seen in this chapter that color values can be expressed in a variety of formats. This makes handling color values from the style property somewhat tricky. We're somewhat at the mercy of whatever formats that the page author chose, and even more so on any transformations that the browsers apply to those formats.

When we're accessing them via the different computed style methods, there's little consistency in the formats that the various browsers will return. Because of this, any attempts to gain access to the useful parts of a color—its red, blue, and green color channels, and, as we'll see, an optional alpha channel—involve a great deal of legwork.

There are numerous formats in which colors can be represented in modern browsers. They're summarized in table 12.3.

Table 12.3 CSS3 color formats

Format	Description
keyword	Any of the recognized HTML color keywords (red, green, maroon, and so on), extended SVG color keywords (bisque, chocolate, darkred, and so on), or the keyword transparent (which is equivalent to rgba(0,0,0,0)—see below).
#rgb	Short hexadecimal RGB (red, green, blue) color values, where each portion is a value from 0 to f.
#rrggbb	Long hexadecimal RGB (red, green, blue) color values, where each portion is a value from 00 to ff.
rgb(r,g,b)	RGB notation where each value is a decimal value from 0 to 255, or 0% to 100%.
rgba(r,g,b,a)	RGB notation with the addition of an alpha channel. The alpha value ranges from 0.0 (transparent) to 1.0 (fully opaque).
hsl(h,s,l)	HSL notation where the values represent hue, saturation, and lightness. The hue value ranges from 0 to 360 (the angle on the color wheel), and saturation and lightness range from 0% to 100%.
hsla(h,s,l)	HSL notation with the addition of the alpha channel.

As can be seen from the information in table 12.3, the page author has a lot of flexibility in expressing color information, which wouldn't be much of an issue for us if the browsers would transform the color values placed into style into a consistent format. But they don't, so we have a problem.

Let's write a test to see what the browsers do to torment us. Examine the following code.

Listing 12.11 Determining how a browser formats color information

```
<div style="background-color:darkslateblue"> </div>
<div style="background-color:#369"> </div>
<div style="background-color:#123456"> </div>
```

 ❶ Creates colored elements

```
<div style="background-color:rg6b(44,88,168)"> </div>
<div style="background-color:rgba(44,88,166,0.5)"> </div>
<div style="background-color:hsl(120,100%,25%)"> </div>
<div style="background-color:hsla(120,100%,25%,0.5)"> </div>

<script type="text/javascript">

  var divs = document.getElementsByTagName('div');          ❷  Collects the
                                                                elements
  for (var n = 0; n < divs.length; n++) {
    assert(true,divs[n].style.backgroundColor);          Displays
  }                                                    ❸ color info

</script>
```

We start off by creating a series of <div> elements with background color style properties expressed in seven different formats ❶. We then collect references to those elements ❷ and iterate over the collection, displaying the value stored in the style.backgroundColor property ❸.

This will show us how the browser within which the test is executed formats the color info for the different methods of specifying it. Looking at the displays in figure 12.8, we can see that the stored formats are all across the board.

Because there are so many color information differences across browsers, we're not going to take the space required to develop a getColor(element,property) method; we'll leave it for you to do so. You have all the tools you need, so it's more of a lengthy task than a difficult one.

The method should accept an element and a color property (such as color or background-color) and return a color keyword, a hash containing red, green, blue, and alpha properties, or a hash containing hue, lightness, saturation, and alpha properties. Given your knowledge of regular expressions from chapter 7, and the examples of the getDimensions() and getOpacity() methods that we developed earlier in this chapter, you should be well armed to tackle the task.

> **CHALLENGE**   If you really want a challenge, also convert any HSL values to RGB using the formula found at http://en.wikipedia.org/wiki/HSL_and_HSV# Converting_to_RGB.

Obviously, handling colors isn't a problem that hasn't already been tackled before. You may want to check out the jQuery Color plugin with code written by Blair Mitchelmore at http://plugins.jquery.com/project/color.

So far, we've covered most of the issues that we need to worry about when it comes to handling the style property of an element. But as we pointed out, that property won't include any style information that an element inherits from style sheets that are in scope for the element. There are many times that it'd be handy to know the full *computed style* that's been applied to an element, so let's see if there's a way to obtain that.

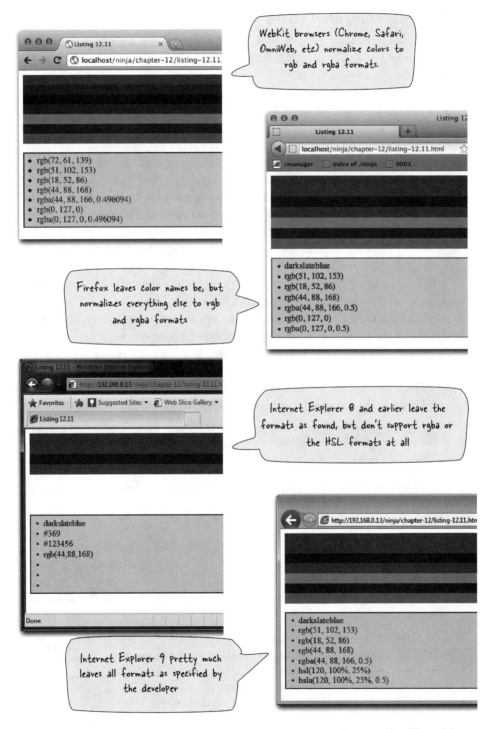

Figure 12.8 The different browser platforms deal with different color formats quite differently!

12.4   *Fetching computed styles*

At any point in time, the *computed style* of an element is a combination of all the styles applied to it via style sheets, the element's style attribute, and any manipulations of the style property by script.

The standard API specified by the W3C, implemented by all modern browsers (including Internet Explorer 9 but not earlier versions), is the window.getComputed-Style() method. This method accepts an element whose styles are to be computed and returns an interface through which property queries can be made. The returned interface provides a method named getPropertyValue() for retrieving the computed style of a specific style property.

Unlike the properties of an element's style object, the getPropertyValue() method accepts CSS property names (such as font-size and background-color) rather than camel-cased versions of those names.

Versions of Internet Explorer prior to version 9 have a proprietary technique for accessing the computed style of an element: a property named currentStyle is attached to all elements, and it behaves much like the style property except that the information provided is the live computed style information.

That gives us enough information to write a fetchComputedStyle() method that will get the computed value of any style property for an element.

Here's something to think about: why didn't we name the function getComputed-Property()?

The following listing implements our computed styles function. It uses the standard means when available and falls back to the proprietary method if not.

Listing 12.12   Fetching computed style values

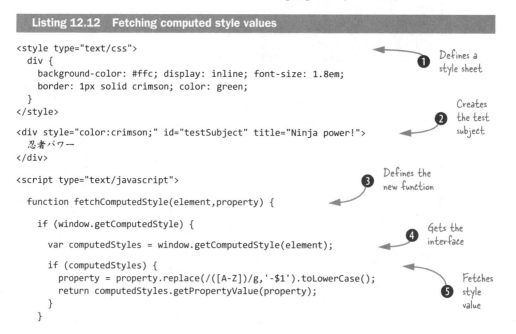

```
<style type="text/css">
  div {
    background-color: #ffc; display: inline; font-size: 1.8em;
    border: 1px solid crimson; color: green;
  }
</style>

<div style="color:crimson;" id="testSubject" title="Ninja power!">
忍者パワー
</div>

<script type="text/javascript">

  function fetchComputedStyle(element,property) {

    if (window.getComputedStyle) {

      var computedStyles = window.getComputedStyle(element);

      if (computedStyles) {
        property = property.replace(/([A-Z])/g,'-$1').toLowerCase();
        return computedStyles.getPropertyValue(property);
      }
    }
```

① Defines a style sheet

② Creates the test subject

③ Defines the new function

④ Gets the interface

⑤ Fetches style value

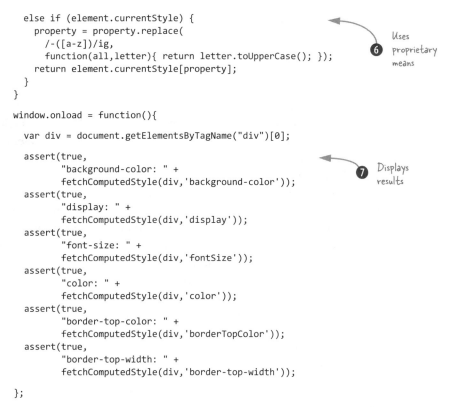

```
    else if (element.currentStyle) {
      property = property.replace(
        /-([a-z])/ig,
        function(all,letter){ return letter.toUpperCase(); });
      return element.currentStyle[property];
    }
  }

  window.onload = function(){

    var div = document.getElementsByTagName("div")[0];

    assert(true,
           "background-color: " +
           fetchComputedStyle(div,'background-color'));
    assert(true,
           "display: " +
           fetchComputedStyle(div,'display'));
    assert(true,
           "font-size: " +
           fetchComputedStyle(div,'fontSize'));
    assert(true,
           "color: " +
           fetchComputedStyle(div,'color'));
    assert(true,
           "border-top-color: " +
           fetchComputedStyle(div,'borderTopColor'));
    assert(true,
           "border-top-width: " +
           fetchComputedStyle(div,'border-top-width'));

  };

</script>
```

6 Uses proprietary means

7 Displays results

In order to test the function that we'll be creating, we set up an element that specifies style information in its markup **2** and a style sheet that provides style rules that will be applied to the element **1**. It's our expectation that the computed styles will be the result of applying both the immediate and the applied styles to the element.

We then define our new function, which accepts an element and the style property that we wish to find the computed value for **3**. And to be especially friendly (after all we're ninjas—making things easier for those using our code is part of the job), we'll allow multiword property names to be specified in either format: dashed or camel-cased. In other words, we'll accept both `backgroundColor` and `background-color`. We'll see how we can accomplish that in just a little bit.

The first thing we want to do is check if the standard means is available—which will be true in all cases but older versions of IE—and if so, proceed to obtain the computed style interface, which we store in a variable for later reference **4**. We want to do things this way because we don't know how expensive making this call may be, and it's likely best to avoid repeating it needlessly.

If that succeeds (and we can't think of any reason why it wouldn't, but it frequently pays to be cautious), we call the `getPropertyValue()` method of the interface to get the computed style value **5**. But first we adjust the name of the property to accommodate either the camel-cased or dashed version of the property name. The getPropertyValue() method expects the dashed version, so we use the String's replace() method, with a simple but clever regular expression, to insert a hyphen before every uppercase character and then lowercase the whole thing. (Bet that was easier than you thought it would be.)

If we detect that the standard method isn't available, we test to see if the IE-proprietary currentStyle property is available, and if so, we transform the property name by replacing all instances of a lowercase character preceded with a hyphen with the uppercase equivalent (to convert any dashed property names to camel case) and return the value of that property ❻.

In all cases, if anything goes awry, we simply return with no value.

To test the function, we make a number of calls to the function, passing various style names in various formats, and display the results ❼, as shown in figure 12.9.

Note that the styles are fetched regardless of whether they were explicitly declared on the element or inherited from the style sheet. Also note that the color property, specified in both the style sheet and directly on the element, returns the explicit value. Styles specified by an element's style attribute always take precedence over inherited styles, even if marked !important.

There's one more topic that we need to be aware of when dealing with style properties: *amalgam* properties. CSS allows us to use a shortcut notation for the amalgam of properties such as the border- properties. Rather than forcing us to specify colors, widths, and border styles individually and for all four borders, we can use a rule such as this:

```
border: 1px solid crimson;
```

We used this exact rule in listing 12.12. This saves us a lot of typing, but we need to be aware that when we retrieve the properties, we need to fetch the low-level individual properties. We can't fetch border, but we can fetch styles such as border-top-color and border-top-width, just as we did in our example.

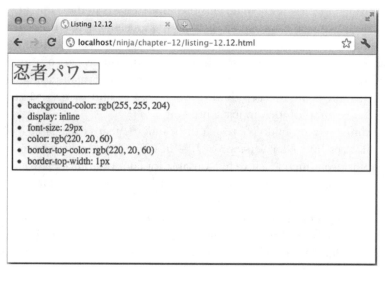

Figure 12.9
Computed styles include all styles specified on the element as well as those inherited from style sheets.

It can be a bit of a hassle, especially when all four styles are given the same values, but that's the hand we've been dealt.

12.5 Summary

When it comes to cross-browser compatibility issues, getting and setting DOM attributes, properties, and styles may not be the worst area of JavaScript development for the browsers, but it certainly has its fair share of issues. Thankfully, we've learned that these issues can be handled in ways that are cross-browser compliant without resorting to browser detection.

Here are the important points to take away from this chapter:

- Attribute *values* are set from the attributes placed on the element markup.
- When retrieved, the attribute values may represent the same values, but they may sometimes be formatted differently than specified in the original markup.
- Properties that represent the attribute values are created on the elements.
- The keys for these properties may vary from the original attribute name, as well as across browsers, and the values may be formatted differently from either the attribute value or original markup.
- When push comes to shove, we can retrieve the original markup value by diving into the original attributes nodes in the DOM and getting the value from them.
- Dealing with the properties is usually more performant than using the DOM attribute methods.
- Versions of IE prior to IE 9 don't allow the type attribute of <input> elements to be changed once the element is part of the DOM.
- The style attribute poses some unique challenges and doesn't contain the computed style for the element.
- Computed styles can be fetched from the window using a standardized API in modern browsers, and via a proprietary property on IE 8 and earlier.

In this chapter, we've mulled over the problems created by the differing implementations of how properties and attributes are handled across the browsers, and we found that there are ample headaches in this area. But perhaps no area in web development holds more cross-browser problems than the handling of events. In the next chapter, we'll tackle that head on.

Part 4

Master training

If you've survived the training up to this point, you can don your ninja garb and hold your head up high among the users of the JavaScript language.

If you want even more rigorous training, this part of the book delves deeply into JavaScript secrets. Not for the faint of heart, the chapters of this section will cover material in more depth and at a faster clip than the preceding chapters. You'll be expected to fill in the blanks and dig into areas with your newly found knowledge. Be warned: there be dragons here.

These chapters, written from the point of view of those writing the popular JavaScript libraries, will give you a glimpse into the decisions and techniques used to implement some of the knottiest areas of those libraries.

Chapter 13 focuses on cross-browser event handling, which is probably the worst of the knotty situations in which the browsers place us.

In chapter 14, we'll see how DOM manipulation techniques can be handled.

Finally, chapter 15 will cover CSS selector engines—a topic from which much knowledge can be garnered, even if writing such an engine from scratch is not on your path to enlightenment.

Strap on your weapons and make sure that your tabis are tightly fitted. This training will surely put you to the test.

Surviving events

This chapter covers
- Why events are such an issue
- Techniques for binding and unbinding events
- Triggering events
- Using custom events
- Event bubbling and delegation

The management of DOM events *should* be relatively simple, but, as you may have guessed by the fact that we're devoting an entire chapter to it, sadly it's not.

Although all browsers provide relatively stable APIs for managing events, they do so with differing approaches and implementations. And even beyond the challenges posed by browser differences, the features that *are* provided by the browsers are insufficient for most of the tasks that need to be handled by even somewhat complex applications.

Because of these shortcomings, JavaScript libraries end up needing to nearly duplicate the existing browser event-handling APIs. This book doesn't assume that you're writing your own library (it doesn't *not* assume that either), but it's useful to understand how things like event handling are being handled by any library you might choose to use, and it's helpful to know what secrets went into creating their implementations in the first place.

Everyone who's made it this far into the book is likely to be familiar with the typical use of the DOM Level 0 Event Model, in which the event handlers are established via element properties or attributes. For example, if the code is ignoring the principles of unobtrusive JavaScript, establishing an event handler for the body element might look like this:

```
<body onload="doSomething()">
```

Or, if the code keeps the behavior (event handling) out of the structural markup, it could be like the following:

```
window.onload = doSomething;
```

Both of these approaches use the DOM Level 0 Event Model.

But DOM Level 0 events have severe limitations that make them unsuitable for reusable code, or for pages with any level of complexity. The DOM Level 2 Event Model provides a more robust API, but its use is problematic as it's unavailable in IE browsers prior to IE 9. And, as already pointed out, it lacks a number of features that we really need.

We'll be dismissing the DOM Level 0 Event Model as borderline useless to us, and we'll concentrate on DOM Level 2. (In case you're wondering, there was no event model introduced with DOM Level 1.)

This chapter will help us to navigate the event-handling minefield, and explain how to survive the somewhat hostile environment in which the browsers place us.

13.1 *Binding and unbinding event handlers*

Under the DOM Level 2 Event Model, we bind and unbind event handlers with the standard addEventListener() and removeEventListener() methods for modern DOM-compliant browsers, and the attachEvent() and detachEvent() methods in legacy versions of Internet Explorer (those prior to IE 9).

For clarity, we'll simply refer to the DOM Level 2 Event Model as the *DOM Model*, and the proprietary legacy IE model as the *IE Model*. The former is available in all modern versions of the "Big Five" browsers; the latter is available in all versions of IE, but it's *all* that's available to IE versions prior to IE 9.

For the most part, the two approaches behave similarly, with one glaring exception: the IE Model doesn't provide a way to listen for the capturing stage of an event. Only the bubbling phase of the event-handling process is supported by the IE Model.

> **NOTE** For those unfamiliar with the DOM Level 2 Event Model, events propagate from the event target up to the root of the DOM during the *bubble phase*, and then they traverse down the tree back to the target during the *capture phase*.

Additionally, the IE Model's implementation doesn't properly set a context on the bound handler, resulting in this, within the handler, referring to the global context (window) instead of the target element. Moreover, the IE Model doesn't pass the event information to the handler; it tacks it onto the global context—the window object.

This means we need to use browser-specific ways to do just about anything when dealing with events:

- Binding a handler
- Unbinding a handler
- Obtaining event information
- Obtaining the event target

It'd hardly make for robust and reusable code to have to perform browser detection and do things one way or the other at each juncture in event handling, so let's see what we can do about creating a common set of APIs that'll cut through the mayhem.

Let's start by seeing how we can address the problems of multiple APIs and the fact that the context isn't set by the IE Model (see the following listing).

Listing 13.1 Providing proper context when binding event handlers

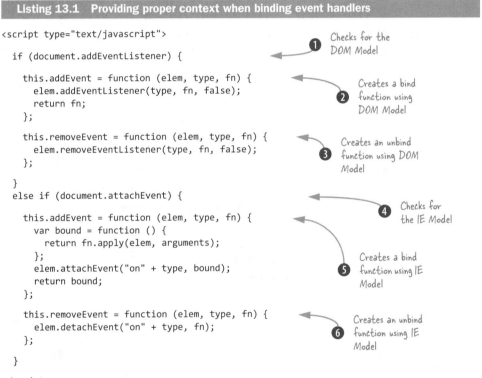

```
<script type="text/javascript">

  if (document.addEventListener) {                    ① Checks for the
                                                         DOM Model

    this.addEvent = function (elem, type, fn) {         ② Creates a bind
      elem.addEventListener(type, fn, false);              function using
      return fn;                                           DOM Model
    };

    this.removeEvent = function (elem, type, fn) {      ③ Creates an unbind
      elem.removeEventListener(type, fn, false);           function using DOM
    };                                                     Model

  }
  else if (document.attachEvent) {                    ④ Checks for
                                                         the IE Model
    this.addEvent = function (elem, type, fn) {
      var bound = function () {
        return fn.apply(elem, arguments);             ⑤ Creates a bind
      };                                                 function using IE
      elem.attachEvent("on" + type, bound);              Model
      return bound;
    };

    this.removeEvent = function (elem, type, fn) {    ⑥ Creates an unbind
      elem.detachEvent("on" + type, fn);                 function using IE
    };                                                   Model

  }

</script>
```

The preceding code adds two methods to the global context: addEvent() and removeEvent(), with implementations suited to the environment in which the script is executing. If the DOM Model is present, it's used; if not, and the IE Model is present, it's used. (No methods are created if neither model is present.)

The implementation is mostly straightforward. After checking whether the DOM Model is defined ①, we define thin wrappers around the standard DOM methods: one for binding event handlers ② and one for unbinding handlers ③.

Note that our add function returns the established handler as its value (the significance of this will be discussed in just a few moments) and passes the value false as the third parameter to the DOM event API methods. This identifies the handlers as *bubble* handlers; because they're intended for cross-browser environments, our functions don't support the capture phase.

If the DOM Model isn't present, we then check to see if the IE Model is defined ❹, and if so we define the two functions using that model.

The definition of the unbinding function is another straightforward wrapping of the model function ❻, but the binding function is another matter ❺.

Remember that one of the primary reasons for doing this at all, aside from defining a uniform API, was to fix the problem of the handler's context not being set to the event target. So, in the binding function, instead of simply passing the handler function (the fn parameter) to the model function, we first wrap it in an anonymous function that in turn calls the handler but uses the apply() method to force the context to be the target element of the event. Then we pass *that* wrapping function to the model function as the handler. That way, when the wrapped function is triggered by the event, the handler function will be called with the proper context. As with the other functions, we return the handler as the function value, though this time we return the wrapper, not the function that was passed in fn.

Returning the function is important because, in order to unbind the handler later, we need to pass a reference to the function that was established as the handler according to the model function. In this case, that's the wrapping function (stored in the bound variable).

Let's see how that works with a quick test in the next listing. The test requires user intervention, so we won't be using asserts; we'll simply interact with the page and observe the results.

Listing 13.2   Testing the event binding API

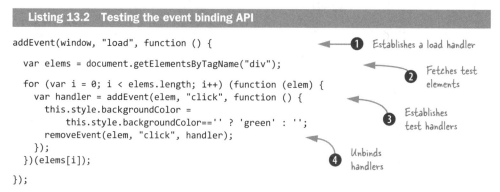

```
addEvent(window, "load", function () {                          ❶ Establishes a load handler

  var elems = document.getElementsByTagName("div");             ❷ Fetches test elements

  for (var i = 0; i < elems.length; i++) (function (elem) {
    var handler = addEvent(elem, "click", function () {
      this.style.backgroundColor =                              ❸ Establishes test handlers
          this.style.backgroundColor=='' ? 'green' : '';
      removeEvent(elem, "click", handler);
    });                                                         ❹ Unbinds handlers
  })(elems[i]);

});
```

We want to wait until the DOM is loaded before we run the test, so we use the very API that we're testing to establish the rest of the test as a load event handler ❶. If our binding function doesn't work, the test will never even get a chance to run.

Within the load handler, we fetch references to all <div> elements on the page to serve as our test subjects ❷, and we iterate over the resulting collection of elements.

For each target element, we use addEvent() to establish a click handler for it ❸, storing the returned function reference in a variable named handler. We're doing this to establish the reference in the closure for the handler, as we'll be referencing the handler function within itself. Note that we can't rely upon callee in this case because we know that when we're operating using the IE Model, the returned function won't be the same one that we passed in.

Within the click handler, we reference the target element via this (proving that the context has been correctly set), determine whether the background color of the element has been set, and if not, set it to green. If it *has* been set, we unset it. If we were to leave things at that, each subsequent click on the element would toggle the background of the element between green and nothing.

But we don't leave it at that. Before the handler exits, it uses our removeEvent() function and the handler variable bound into the closure to remove the handler ❹. Thus, once the handler has been triggered once, it should never trigger again.

If we add the following elements to our page and ensure that no background is applied to them via style sheets, we'd expect that clicking on each <div> would turn it green, and subsequent clicks would not toggle the background:

```
<div title="Click me"> 私をクリック </div>
<div title="but only once"> 一度だけ </div>
```

Loading the page into the browser and conducting this manual test verifies that our functions work as expected. The display shown in figure 13.1 depicts the state of the page when loaded into Chrome, and after the first element has been clicked on multiple times and the second element not at all.

Figure 13.2 shows the same page loaded into IE8, which doesn't support the DOM Model, after the same actions have been taken.

That's a good start, but it exhibits some weaknesses. The primary problem is that because we need to wrap the handler under legacy versions of IE, users of the API need to carefully record the reference to the handler as returned from the add-Event() function. Failing to do so will result in being unable to unbind the handler at a later point.

Another weakness is that this solution doesn't address the problem of access to the event information.

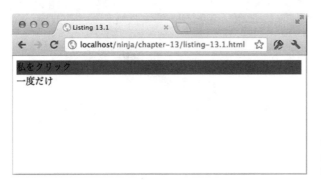

Figure 13.1 This manual test proves that a uniform API can bind and unbind events.

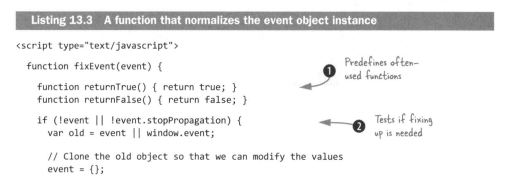

Figure 13.2   It also works in legacy versions of IE.

We've made improvements, but we're not where we want to be yet. Can we do better?

13.2 *The Event object*

As we've already pointed out, the IE Model of event handling that we're forced to deal with in legacy browsers differs from the DOM Model in a number of ways. One of these is in the manner that an instance of the Event object is made available to the handlers. In the DOM Model, it's passed to the handler as its first parameter; in the IE Model, it's fetched from a property named event placed in the global context (window.event).

To make matters even worse, the contents of the Event instance are different in the two models. What's a ninja to do?

The only reasonable way to work around this is to create a *new* object that simulates the browser's native event object, normalizing the properties within it to match the DOM Model. You might wonder why we wouldn't just modify the existing object, but that's not possible because there are many properties within it that can't be overwritten.

Another advantage to cloning the event object is that it solves a problem caused by the fact that the IE Model stores the object in the global context. Once a new event starts, any previous event object is wiped out. Transferring the event properties to a new object whose lifetime we control solves any potential issues of this nature.

Let's try our hand at a function for event normalization in the next listing.

Listing 13.3   A function that normalizes the event object instance

```
<script type="text/javascript">

  function fixEvent(event) {                              ① Predefines often-
                                                             used functions
    function returnTrue() { return true; }
    function returnFalse() { return false; }

    if (!event || !event.stopPropagation) {              ② Tests if fixing
      var old = event || window.event;                      up is needed

      // Clone the old object so that we can modify the values
      event = {};
```

```
for (var prop in old) {
  event[prop] = old[prop];
}
```

③ Clones existing properties

```
// The event occurred on this element
if (!event.target) {
  event.target = event.srcElement || document;
}

// Handle which other element the event is related to
event.relatedTarget = event.fromElement === event.target ?
    event.toElement :
    event.fromElement;

// Stop the default browser action
event.preventDefault = function () {
  event.returnValue = false;
  event.isDefaultPrevented = returnTrue;
};

event.isDefaultPrevented = returnFalse;

// Stop the event from bubbling
event.stopPropagation = function () {
  event.cancelBubble = true;
  event.isPropagationStopped = returnTrue;
};

event.isPropagationStopped = returnFalse;

// Stop the event from bubbling and executing other handlers
event.stopImmediatePropagation = function () {
  this.isImmediatePropagationStopped = returnTrue;
  this.stopPropagation();
};

event.isImmediatePropagationStopped = returnFalse;

// Handle mouse position
if (event.clientX != null) {
  var doc = document.documentElement, body = document.body;

  event.pageX = event.clientX +
      (doc && doc.scrollLeft || body && body.scrollLeft || 0) -
      (doc && doc.clientLeft || body && body.clientLeft || 0);
  event.pageY = event.clientY +
      (doc && doc.scrollTop || body && body.scrollTop || 0) -
      (doc && doc.clientTop || body && body.clientTop || 0);
}

// Handle key presses
event.which = event.charCode || event.keyCode;

// Fix button for mouse clicks:
// 0 == left; 1 == middle; 2 == right
if (event.button != null) {
  event.button = (event.button & 1 ? 0 :
      (event.button & 4 ? 1 :
          (event.button & 2 ? 2 : 0)));
```

```
        }
    }
    return event;
}
</script>
```

4 Returns fixed-
up instance

Although this is a fairly long listing, most of what it's doing is straightforward, so we aren't going to exhaustively go through it line-by-line, but we'll take the time to point out the most important aspects.

Essentially, the purpose of this function is to take an instance of Event and check to see if it conforms to the DOM model. If it doesn't, we'll do our best to make it do so. You can read about the DOM Model's Event definition on the W3C site at http://www.w3.org/TR/DOM-Level-2-Events/events.html#Events-interface.

The first thing that we do in our function is to define two functions **1**. Remember that JavaScript allows us to do this, and it limits the scope of these functions to their parent function so that we don't need to worry about polluting the global namespace. We're going to need functions that return either true or false frequently throughout our fix-up code, so rather than use redundant function literals, we predefine these two functions: one always returns true, and one always returns false.

Then we test whether we need to do anything **2**. If the instance doesn't exist (we assume that the event is defined on the global context in this case) or if it exists but the standard stopPropagation property is missing, we assume that we need to fix things up.

If we decide that fixing up is needed, we grab a copy of the existing event—either the one that was passed to us, or the one on the global context—and store it in a variable named old. Otherwise, we just fall through to the end of the function and return the existing event **4**.

If we're fixing up, we create an empty object to serve as the fixed-up event and copy all of the existing properties of the old event into this new object **3**. Then we proceed to fix things up to handle many of the common discrepancies between the W3C DOM Event object and the one provided by the IE Model.

These are a few of the important properties in the DOM Model that are "fixed" in this process:

- target—The property denoting the original source of the event. The IE Model stores this in srcElement.
- relatedTarget—Comes into use when it's used on an event that works in conjunction with another element (such as mouseover or mouseout). The toElement and fromElement properties are IE's counterparts.
- preventDefault—This property, which doesn't exist in the IE Model, prevents the default browser action from occurring. In IE, the returnValue property needs to be set to false.
- stopPropagation—This property, also absent from the IE Model, stops the event from bubbling further up the tree. For IE, setting the cancelBubble property to true will make this happen.

- pageX and pageY—These properties don't exist in the IE Model. They provide the position of the mouse relative to the whole document but can be easily duplicated using other information. clientX/Y provides the position of the mouse relative to the window, scrollTop/Left gives the scrolled position of the document, and clientTop/Left gives the offset of the document itself. Combining these three properties will give us the final pageX/Y values.
- which—This is equivalent to the key code pressed during a keyboard event. It can be duplicated by accessing the charCode and keyCode properties in the IE Model.
- button—This identifies the mouse button clicked by the user on a mouse event. The IE Model uses a bitmask (1 for left-click, 2 for right-click, 4 for middle-click) so it needs to be converted to equivalent values for the DOM Model (0, 1, and 2).

Another resource with great information on the DOM Event object and its cross-browser capabilities is the set of QuirksMode compatibility tables:

- Event object compatibility—http://www.quirksmode.org/dom/w3c_events.html
- Mouse position compatibility—http://www.quirksmode.org/dom/w3c_cssom .html#mousepos

Additionally, issues surrounding the nitty-gritty of keyboard and mouse-event object properties can be found in the excellent *JavaScript Madness* guide:

- Keyboard events—http://unixpapa.com/js/key.html
- Mouse events—http://unixpapa.com/js/mouse.html

OK, now we have a means to normalize the Event instance. Let's see what we can do about gaining a margin of control over the binding process.

13.3 Handler management

For a number of reasons, it would be advantageous to not bind event handlers directly to elements. If we use an intermediary event handler instead and store all the handlers in a separate object, we can exert a level of control over the handling process. Among other things, this will give us the ability to do the following:

- Normalize the context of handlers
- Fix up the properties of Event objects
- Handle garbage collection of bound handlers
- Trigger or remove some handlers with a filter
- Unbinding all events of a particular type
- Clone event handlers

We'll need to have access to the full list of handlers bound to an element in order to achieve all of these benefits, so it makes a lot of sense to avoid directly binding the events and to handle the binding ourselves. Let's take that on.

13.3.1 *Centrally storing associated information*

One of the best ways to manage the handlers associated with a DOM element is to give each element that we're working with a unique identifier (not to be confused with the DOM id), and then store all data associated with it in a centralized object. While it might seem more natural to store the information on each individual element, keeping the data in a central store will help us to avoid potential memory leaks in Internet Explorer, which is capable of losing memory under certain circumstances. (In IE, attaching functions to a DOM element that have a closure to a DOM node can cause memory to fail to be reclaimed after navigating away from a page.)

Let's try our hand at centrally storing information to be associated with particular DOM elements.

Listing 13.4 Implementing a central object store for DOM element information

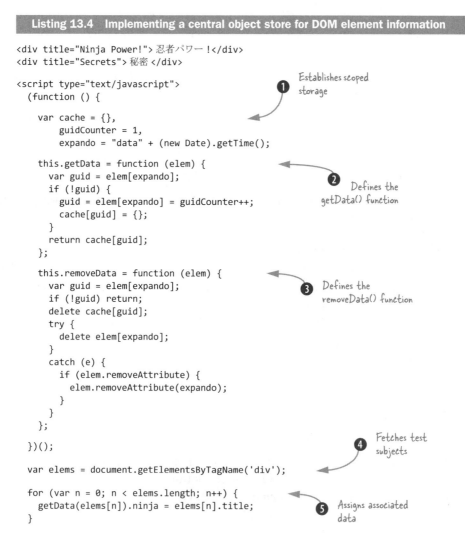

```
<div title="Ninja Power!">忍者パワー !</div>
<div title="Secrets">秘密 </div>

<script type="text/javascript">
  (function () {                                          ① Establishes scoped storage

    var cache = {},
        guidCounter = 1,
        expando = "data" + (new Date).getTime();

    this.getData = function (elem) {
      var guid = elem[expando];                           ② Defines the
      if (!guid) {                                          getData() function
        guid = elem[expando] = guidCounter++;
        cache[guid] = {};
      }
      return cache[guid];
    };

    this.removeData = function (elem) {
      var guid = elem[expando];                           ③ Defines the
      if (!guid) return;                                    removeData() function
      delete cache[guid];
      try {
        delete elem[expando];
      }
      catch (e) {
        if (elem.removeAttribute) {
          elem.removeAttribute(expando);
        }
      }
    };
  })();

  var elems = document.getElementsByTagName('div');       ④ Fetches test
                                                             subjects
  for (var n = 0; n < elems.length; n++) {
    getData(elems[n]).ninja = elems[n].title;             ⑤ Assigns associated
  }                                                          data
```

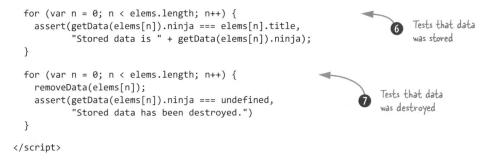

```
  for (var n = 0; n < elems.length; n++) {
    assert(getData(elems[n]).ninja === elems[n].title,
        "Stored data is " + getData(elems[n]).ninja);
  }

  for (var n = 0; n < elems.length; n++) {
    removeData(elems[n]);
    assert(getData(elems[n]).ninja === undefined,
        "Stored data has been destroyed.")
  }
```

6 Tests that data was stored

7 Tests that data was destroyed

```
</script>
```

In this example, we've set up two generic functions, `getData()` and `removeData()`, to respectively fetch the data block for a DOM element, and to remove it when it's no longer needed.

We're going to need some variables, which we don't want to contaminate the global scope with, so we do all our setup within an immediate function. This keeps any variables we declare within the scope of the immediate function, but they're still available to our functions via their closures. (We mentioned in chapter 5 that closures would play a central role in many things that we need to do.)

Within the immediate function, we set up three variables **1**:

- `cache`—The object in which we'll store the data we want to associate with elements.
- `guidCounter`—A running counter that we'll use to generate element GUIDs.
- `expando`—The property name that we'll tack onto each element to store its GUID. We form this name using the current timestamp to help prevent any potential collisions with user-defined expandos.

Then we define the `getData()` method **2**. The first thing that this function does is to try to fetch any GUID that's already been assigned to the element by a previous call to this method. If it's the first time that this method has been called on this element, the GUID won't exist, so we create a new one (bumping the counter by one each time) and assign it to the element using the property name in `expando`; we also create a new empty object associated with the GUID in the `cache`.

Regardless of whether the cache data for the element is newly created or not, it's returned as the value of the function. Callers of the function are free to add any data they would like to the cache, as follows:

```
var elemData = getData(element);
elemData.someName = 213;
elemData.someOtherName = 2058;
```

Functions are data too, so we could even indirectly associate functions with the element:

```
elemData.someFunction = function(x){ /* do something */ }
```

With the `getData()` function established, we create the `removeData()` function, with which we can wipe out all traces of the data in the event that it's no longer needed **3**.

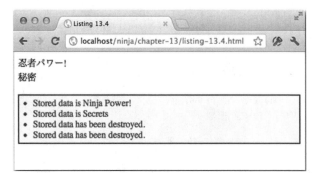

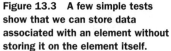

Figure 13.3 A few simple tests show that we can store data associated with an element without storing it on the element itself.

In `removeData()`, we obtain the GUID for the passed element and short-circuit the function if there isn't one; if there isn't a GUID, the element has not been instrumented by `getData()`, or it has already had the data removed.

Then we remove the associated data block from the cache, and we try to remove the expando. Under certain circumstances this may fail, in which case we catch the error and try to remove the attribute created on behalf of the expando.

This removes all traces of the instrumentation that `getData()` created: the cached data block *and* the expando placed onto the elements.

That was pretty easy; let's make sure it works. We set up two `<div>` elements to use as test subjects, each with a unique `title` attribute. We get references to those elements ❹ and then iterate over them, creating a data element, consisting of the value of the `title` attribute for the element, that we name `ninja` for each element ❺.

Then we iterate over the elements again, checking that each one has an associated data value, with the name of `ninja`, that contains the same value as its title attribute ❻.

Finally, we iterate over the set once again, calling `removeData()` on each element and verifying that the data no longer exists ❼.

Figure 13.3 shows that all these tests pass.

These functions can be quite useful beyond the scope of managing event handlers; by using these functions, we can attach any sort of data to an element. But we created these functions with the specific use case of associating event-handling information with elements in mind.

Let's now use those functions to create our own set of functions to bind and unbind event handlers to elements.

13.3.2 *Managing event handlers*

In order to exert complete control over the event-handling process, we'll need to create our own functions that wrap the binding and unbinding of events. By doing so, we can present as unified an event-handling model as possible, across all platforms.

Let's get to it. We'll start with binding event handlers.

BINDING EVENT HANDLERS

By writing a function to handle binding events, rather than just binding the handlers directly, we get the opportunity to keep track of the handlers and get our hooks into the process. We'll provide a function to establish another function as a handler (binding), and to remove a function as a handler (unbinding). We'll even throw in a few helpful utility functions.

Let's start with binding the handlers with an addEvent() function in the next listing.

Listing 13.5   A function to bind event handlers with tracking

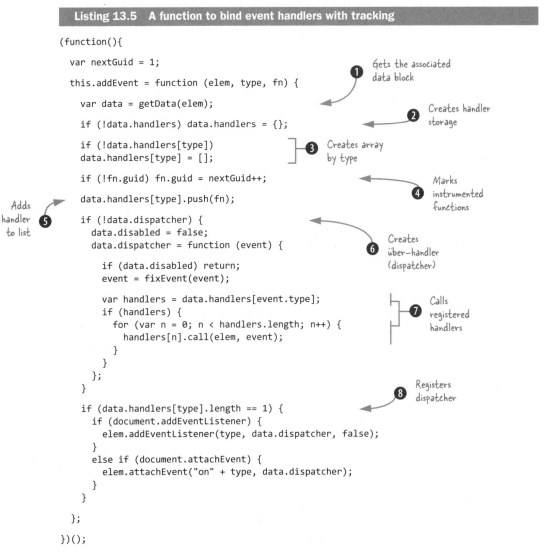

```
(function(){

  var nextGuid = 1;

  this.addEvent = function (elem, type, fn) {          ❶ Gets the associated
                                                           data block
    var data = getData(elem);
                                                         ❷ Creates handler
    if (!data.handlers) data.handlers = {};                storage

    if (!data.handlers[type])          ❸ Creates array
    data.handlers[type] = [];              by type

    if (!fn.guid) fn.guid = nextGuid++;                  ❹ Marks
                                                             instrumented
    data.handlers[type].push(fn);                            functions

    if (!data.dispatcher) {
      data.disabled = false;
      data.dispatcher = function (event) {
                                                 ❻ Creates
        if (data.disabled) return;                  über-handler
        event = fixEvent(event);                    (dispatcher)

        var handlers = data.handlers[event.type];
        if (handlers) {                            ❼ Calls
          for (var n = 0; n < handlers.length; n++) {    registered
            handlers[n].call(elem, event);               handlers
          }
        }
      };
    }
                                                     ❽ Registers
    if (data.handlers[type].length == 1) {              dispatcher
      if (document.addEventListener) {
        elem.addEventListener(type, data.dispatcher, false);
      }
      else if (document.attachEvent) {
        elem.attachEvent("on" + type, data.dispatcher);
      }
    }
  };

})();
```

Adds handler ❺ to list

Wow. That seems like there's a lot going on, but each part is straightforward, taken piece by piece.

First of all, because we're going to need some local storage (not to be confused with HTML5 storage), we use our usual trick of defining everything within an immediate function. The storage that we need is a running counter for a GUID value in the variable nextGuid. These GUID values will serve as unique markers, much like how we used them in listing 13.4. We'll see exactly how in just a moment.

Then we define the addEvent() function, which accepts an element on which the handler is to be bound, the type of event, and the handler itself.

The first thing we do, upon entering the function, is to grab the data block associated with the element ❶, using the functions that we defined in listing 13.4, and store that block in the data variable. This is done for two reasons:

- We'll be referencing it a few times, so using a variable makes later references shorter.
- There could be overhead in obtaining the data block, so we do it once.

Because we want to exert a high degree of control over the binding (and later, over the unbinding) process, rather than add the passed handler to the element directly, we're going to create our own über-handler that will serve as the actual event handler. We'll register the über-handler with the browser, and it will keep track of the bound handlers so that we can execute them ourselves when appropriate.

We'll call this über-handler the *dispatcher* to distinguish it from the bound handlers that users of our function will pass in to us. We'll be creating the dispatcher before the end of the function, but first we must create the storage needed to keep track of the bound handlers.

We'll use a lot of just-in-time creation of storage, obtaining the storage as we need it, rather than pre-allocating it all up front. After all, why create an array in which to store mouseover handlers if we never have any bound?

We're going to associate the handlers with their bound element via the element's data block (which we've conveniently obtained in the data variable), so we test to see if the data block has a property named handlers, and if it doesn't, we create it ❷. Later invocations of the function on the same element will detect that the object exists and won't try to create it subsequently.

Within this object, we'll create arrays in which we'll store references to handlers that should be executed, one for each event type. But, as we said earlier, we're going to smartly allocate them on an as-needed basis, so we test to see if the handlers object has a property named after the passed-in type, and if not, we create it ❸. This results in one array per event type, but only for the types that actually have handlers bound for them. That's a wise use of resources.

Next we want to mark the functions that we're handling on behalf of the caller of our function (for reasons we'll see when we develop the unbinding function), so we add a guid property to the passed-in function and bump the counter ❹. Note that once again we perform a check to make sure we only do this once per function, as a function can be bound as a handler multiple times if the page author wishes.

At this point, we know that we have a `handlers` object, and that it contains an array keeping track of handlers for the passed event type, so we push the passed handler onto the end of that array ❺. This is pretty much the only action within this function that's guaranteed to execute whenever this function is called.

Now we're ready to deal with the dispatcher function. The first time that this function is called, no such dispatcher will exist. But we only need *one*, so we'll check to see if it exists and create it only when it doesn't ❻.

Within the dispatcher function, which will be the function that gets triggered whenever a bound event occurs, we check to see if a `disabled` flag has been set, and we terminate if so. (We'll see in a few sections under what circumstances we might want to disable event dispatching for a time.) Then we call the `fixEvent()` function that we created in listing 13.3, and we find and iterate through the array of handlers that were recorded for the type of event identified in the `Event` instance. Each of these handlers is called, supplying the element as the function context and the `Event` object as its sole argument ❼.

Lastly, we check whether we've just created the first handler for this type, and if so, we establish the delegate as the event handler for the event type, with the browser using the means appropriate to the browser within which we're running ❽.

> **TIP** If we moved the checking clause to within the conditional creation of the event-handler array earlier in the function ❸, we could dispense with the check here. But we ordered the code as we did to make it easier to explain how it works (creating all of the data constructs prior to creating the delegate in which the constructs are used). In production code, it would be wise to move this clause and remove the need for the redundant check.

The final situation we end up with is that the functions passed to our routine are never established as actual event handlers; rather, they're stored and invoked by the delegate when an event occurs, and the real handler is the delegate. This gives us the opportunity to make sure that the following things always happen regardless of the platform:

- The `Event` instance is fixed up.
- The function context is set to the target element.
- The `Event` instance is passed to the handler as its sole argument.
- The event handlers will always be executed in the order in which they were bound.

Even Yoda would be proud of the level of control we can exert on the event-handling process using this approach.

PICKING UP AFTER OURSELVES

We have a method to bind events, so we need one to unbind them. We didn't directly bind the handlers, choosing to exert control over the process with the delegate handler, so we can't rely upon the browser-supplied unbinding functions; we need to supply our own.

In addition to unbinding the bound handlers, we want to make sure that we tidy up after ourselves carefully. We took great care *not* to use up needless allocation in the binding function; it'd be silly to be remiss about reclaiming storage that becomes unused as a result of unbinding.

As it turns out, such tidying up will need to be initiated from more than a single location, so we'll capture it in its own function, as the following listing shows.

Listing 13.6   Cleaning up the handler constructs

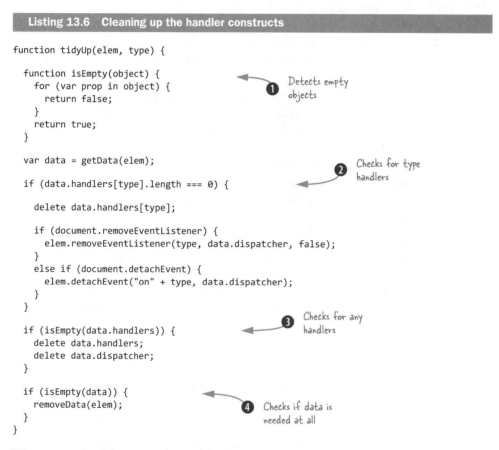

```
function tidyUp(elem, type) {

  function isEmpty(object) {
    for (var prop in object) {          Detects empty ①
      return false;                     objects
    }
    return true;
  }

  var data = getData(elem);
                                        Checks for type ②
  if (data.handlers[type].length === 0) {   handlers

    delete data.handlers[type];

    if (document.removeEventListener) {
      elem.removeEventListener(type, data.dispatcher, false);
    }
    else if (document.detachEvent) {
      elem.detachEvent("on" + type, data.dispatcher);
    }
  }
                                        Checks for any ③
  if (isEmpty(data.handlers)) {         handlers
    delete data.handlers;
    delete data.dispatcher;
  }

  if (isEmpty(data)) {
    removeData(elem);                   Checks if data is ④
  }                                     needed at all
}
```

We create a function named tidyUp() that accepts an element and an event type. The function will check to see if any handlers for this type are still around, and if not, clean up as much as possible, releasing any unneeded storage. This is a safe thing to do because, as we saw in the addEvent() function, if the storage is needed again later, that function will simply create it as needed.

We'll need to check if an object has any properties or not (if it's empty) in a number of locations. And because there's no "isempty" operator in JavaScript, we need to write our own check ①. We're only going to use this function within our tidyUp() function, so we declare the isEmpty() function within it to keep its scope as close as possible.

We're going to be cleaning up the data block associated with the element, so we fetch it and store it in the data variable for later reference. Then we start to check to see what, if anything, can be tidied away.

First, we check to see if the array of handlers associated with the passed type is empty ❷. If it is, it's no longer needed and we blow it away. Additionally, as there are no longer any handlers for this event type, we unbind the delegate that we registered with the browser, as it's no longer needed.

Now that we've removed one of the arrays of handlers for an event type, there's a possibility that it may have been the only remaining such array, and its removal could leave the handlers object empty. We test for that ❸ and remove the handlers property if it's empty and therefore useless. In such a case, the delegate is no longer needed either, so it's also removed.

Finally, we test to see if all these removals have resulted in the data block associated with the element becoming pointless ❹, and if so, we jettison it as well.

That's how we keep things spic and span.

UNBINDING EVENT HANDLERS

Now that we know we can clean up after ourselves, pleasing Mr. Clean as well as Yoda, we're ready to tackle the function to unbind handlers that were bound with our add-Event() function.

To be as flexible as possible, we're going to give the callers of our functions the following options:

- Unbinding all bound events for a particular element
- Unbinding all events of a particular type from an element
- Unbinding a particular handler from an element

We'll allow these variations simply by providing a variable-length argument list; the more information the caller provides, the more specific the remove operation.

For example, to remove all bound events from an element, we could write

```
removeEvent(element)
```

To remove all bound events of a particular type, we'd use

```
removeEvent(element, "click");
```

And to remove a particular instance of a handler, the code would be

```
removeEvent(element, "click", handler);
```

The latter assumes that we've maintained a reference to the original handler.

The unbinding function to accomplish all this is depicted in the following listing.

Listing 13.7 A function to unbind event handlers

```
this.removeEvent = function (elem, type, fn) {          ❶ Declares the function
  var data = getData(elem);                    ❷ Fetches the associated
                                                 element data
```

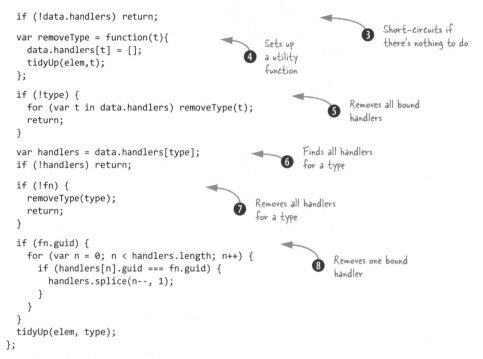

```
if (!data.handlers) return;

var removeType = function(t){
  data.handlers[t] = [];
  tidyUp(elem,t);
};

if (!type) {
  for (var t in data.handlers) removeType(t);
  return;
}

var handlers = data.handlers[type];
if (!handlers) return;

if (!fn) {
  removeType(type);
  return;
}

if (fn.guid) {
  for (var n = 0; n < handlers.length; n++) {
    if (handlers[n].guid === fn.guid) {
      handlers.splice(n--, 1);
    }
  }
}
tidyUp(elem, type);
};
```

Annotations in the figure:
- ❸ Short-circuits if there's nothing to do
- ❹ Sets up a utility function
- ❺ Removes all bound handlers
- ❻ Finds all handlers for a type
- ❼ Removes all handlers for a type
- ❽ Removes one bound handler

We start by defining our function signature with three parameters: the element, the event type, and the function ❶. Callers can omit trailing arguments as described earlier.

The next step is obtaining the data block associated with the passed element ❷.

TIP   Because we're allowing a variable-length argument list, it'd probably be a good idea to check that an element was provided—it's not optional. How would you go about doing that?

Once we've obtained the block, we check to see if there are any bound handlers and short-circuit the entire function if not ❸. Note that we didn't need to check inside the handlers object to see if it was empty, or if it contained empty lists of handlers, because of the tidying up that will happen as a result of the function that we developed in listing 13.6. That's going to help make this function a lot cleaner by eliminating empty data constructs and the need for complex checks for them.

If we make it through the previous check, we know that we're going to be removing bound handlers by event type—either all types (if the type parameter is omitted), or a specific type (identified by the type parameter). In either case, we're going to be removing by type in more than one location, so to avoid needlessly repeating code, we define a utility function ❹ that, given a type t, removes all handlers for that type by replacing the array of handlers with an empty array, and then calls the tidyUp() function on that type.

With that function in place, we check to see if the type parameter was omitted ❺, and if so, go about removing all handlers for all types on the element. In this case, we simply return because our job is finished.

NOTE We short-circuit the removeEvent() function in listing 13.7 with numerous return statements. Some developers dislike this style and prefer a single return, controlling flow with deeply nested conditionals. If you're one of those people, you could try your hand at rejigging the function to use a single return (or implied return).

If we make it to this point, we know that we've been provided with an event type for which we'll be removing either all handlers (if the fn argument is omitted), or a specific handler for that type. So, in order to reduce code clutter, we grab the list of handlers for that type and store it in a variable named handlers ❻. If there aren't any, there's nothing to do, so we return.

If the fn argument was omitted, ❼ we call our removal utility function to blow away all of the handlers for the specified event type, and return.

Failing all the previous checks that might have caused us to remove something and then return, we know that a specific handler has been passed to us for removal. But if it's not a handler that we've "touched," there's no need to bother looking for it, so we check to see if the guid property has been added to the function (which would have happened when the function was passed to the addEvent() method), and we ignore it if not.

If it's a handler that we've instrumented, we look through the list of handlers for it, removing any instances that we find (there could be more than one) ❽. And, as usual, we tidy up before we return.

SMOKE-TESTING THE FUNCTIONS

Let's look at a simple smoke test for our bind and unbind functions. As before, listing 13.8 sets up a small page that uses manual intervention to run a simple visual test.

NOTE The term "smoke-testing" means to make a cursory test of the major functions of whatever is being tested. It's far from a rigorous test and simply makes sure that the test subject seems to work on a gross basis. The term originates from the late 1800s, when smoke would be forced through pipes to find leaks. Later, in the world of electronics, the first test performed on a new circuit was to simply plug it in and see if anything burst into flames!

Listing 13.8 Smoke-testing the event functions

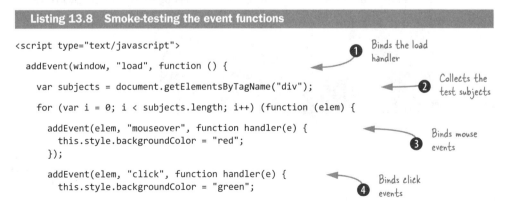

```
<script type="text/javascript">
  addEvent(window, "load", function () {                    ❶ Binds the load
                                                               handler
    var subjects = document.getElementsByTagName("div");    ❷ Collects the
                                                               test subjects
    for (var i = 0; i < subjects.length; i++) (function (elem) {
      addEvent(elem, "mouseover", function handler(e) {     ❸ Binds mouse
        this.style.backgroundColor = "red";                    events
      });
      addEvent(elem, "click", function handler(e) {         ❹ Binds click
        this.style.backgroundColor = "green";                  events
```

```
        removeEvent(elem, "click", handler);
    });

  })(subjects[i]);

  });
</script>

<div id="testSubject1" title="Click once"> 一度クリックします </div>
<div id="testSubject2" title="mouse over"> マウス </div>
<div id="testSubject3" title="many times"> 何度も </div>
```

In this simple test, we're going to bind three different types of events and unbind one of them. First, we establish a handler for the page load event ❶—our test subjects (three <div> elements) are defined after our script block, so we need to delay the execution of the rest of the script until after the DOM has been loaded.

When that event fires, our handler collects all the <div> elements ❷ and iterates over them. For each, we establish two things:

- A mouseover handler that turns the element red ❸
- A click handler that turns the element green, then unbinds itself, such that each element will react to a click exactly *once* ❹

Loading the page into a browser, we perform the following steps:

1 We mouse over the elements, observing that they all turn red when we do so. This verifies that the mouseover event was correctly bound and activated.

2 We click on an element, observing that it turns green. This verifies that the click handler was correctly bound and activated. Figure 13.4 shows the page at this stage.

3 We run the mouse over the clicked element, observe that it turns back to red (as expected because of the mouseover handler), and click on the element again.

4 If the click handlers were correctly unbound, they won't trigger (which would cause the element to turn to green again) and the element would remain red. Our observation verifies that this is the case.

This is far from a rigorous test. As an exercise, try your hand at writing a series of asserts that will automate testing of the functions, exercising all of the functions' features.

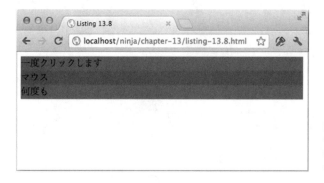

Figure 13.4 Our smoke test shows that at least some of the major features of our functions are operating correctly.

BONUS In the events.js file included in the code examples for this book, we included a handy proxy( ) function. This function can be used to cajole the function context of an event handler to be something other than the event target when triggered. This is the exact same treachery that we explored in section 4.3.

We can now exert a great deal of control over the binding and unbinding of events. Let's see what other magic wands we can wave over events.

13.4 *Triggering events*

Under normal circumstances, events are triggered when occurrences such as user actions, browser actions, or network activity take place. Sometimes, though, we might want to trigger the same response to the activity under script control. (We'll be seeing shortly that this isn't only desirable, but also necessary when working with custom events.) For example, there may be a click handler that we not only want to trigger when the user clicks the button, but when some other activity occurs that we're executing script in response to.

We could be very un-ninja-like about it and simply repeat the code, but we know better than that. One viable approach would be to factor the common code into a named function that we could call from any location. But that solution isn't without its namespace issues, and it could detract from the clarity of the code base. Besides, usually when we'd want to do this, we wouldn't want to call a function but to simulate the event. So the ability to trigger event handlers without a "real" event would be an advantage that we'd like to give ourselves.

When a triggering a handler function, we need to make sure a number of things will happen:

- Trigger the bound handler on the element that we target
- Cause the event to bubble up the DOM, triggering any other bound handlers
- Cause the default action to be triggered on the target element (when it has one)

The next listing shows a function that handles all of this, presupposing that we're utilizing the functions of the previous section to handle event binding.

> **Listing 13.9 Triggering a bubbling event on an element**

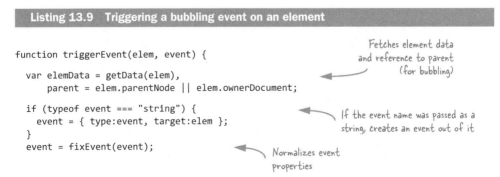

```
function triggerEvent(elem, event) {
  var elemData = getData(elem),          ← Fetches element data
      parent = elem.parentNode || elem.ownerDocument;    and reference to parent
                                                              (for bubbling)
  if (typeof event === "string") {       ← If the event name was passed as a
    event = { type:event, target:elem };    string, creates an event out of it
  }
  event = fixEvent(event);    ← Normalizes event
                                 properties
```

```
if (elemData.dispatcher) {
  elemData.dispatcher.call(elem, event);
}
if (parent && !event.isPropagationStopped()) {
  triggerEvent(parent, event);
}
else if (!parent && !event.isDefaultPrevented()) {

  var targetData = getData(event.target);

  if (event.target[event.type]) {

    targetData.disabled = true;

    event.target[event.type]();

    targetData.disabled = false;

  }

}
}
```

1 If the passed element has a dispatcher, executes the established handlers

3 If at the top of the DOM, triggers the default action unless disabled

4 Checks if the target has default action for this event

Temporarily disables event dispatching on the target because we've already executed handler **5**

6 Executes any default action

Unless explicitly stopped, recursively calls the function to bubble the event up the DOM **2**

Re-enables event dispatching

Our `triggerEvent()` function accepts two parameters:

- The element upon which the event will be triggered
- The event that's to be triggered

The latter can be either an event object or a string containing the event type.

To trigger the event, we traverse from the initial event target all the way up to the top of the DOM, executing any handlers that we find along the way **1**. When we reach the document element, the execution of bubbling is over, and we can execute the default action for the event type on the target element, if it has one **6**.

Note that during the event-bubbling activity, we make sure that propagation hasn't been stopped **2**, and before executing any default action, we also check that it hasn't been disabled **3**. Also, note that we disable our event dispatcher **5** while executing the default action, because we've already triggered the handlers ourselves and don't want to risk double execution.

To trigger the default browser action, we use the appropriate method on the original target element. For example, if we trigger a focus event, we check to see if the original target element has a `.focus()` method **4** and execute it.

The ability to trigger events under script control is really useful in its own right, but we'll also find that it implicitly allows custom events to just work.

Custom events?

13.4.1 *Custom events*

Haven't you ever fervently desired the ability to trigger your own custom events?

Imagine a scenario where you want to perform an action, but you want to trigger it under a variety of conditions from different pieces of code, perhaps even from code that's in shared script files.

The novice would repeat the code everywhere it's needed. The intermediate would create a global function and call it from everywhere it's needed. The ninja uses custom events.

Let's chat a bit about why we'd want to consider that.

LOOSE COUPLING

Picture the scenario where we're doing operations from shared code, and we want to let page code know when it's time to react to some condition. If we use the global function approach, we introduce the disadvantage that our shared code needs to define a fixed name for the function, and all pages that use the shared code need to define such a function.

Moreover, what if there are multiple things to do when the triggering condition occurs? Making allowances for multiple notifications would be arduous and necessarily messy.

These disadvantages that we're seeing are a result of *close coupling*, in which the code that detects the conditions has to know the details of the code that will react to that condition.

Loose coupling, on the other hand, occurs when the code that triggers the condition doesn't know anything about the code that will react to the condition, or even if there's anything that will react to it at all.

One of the advantages of event handlers is that we can establish as many as we want, and these handlers are completely independent. So event handling is a good example of loose coupling. When a button click event is triggered, the code triggering the event has no knowledge of what handlers we've established on the page, or even if there are any. Rather, the click event is simply pushed onto the event queue by the browser (see chapter 3 for a refresher, if needed), and whatever caused the event to trigger could care less what happens after that. If handlers have been established for the click event, they will eventually be individually invoked in a completely independent fashion.

There's much to be said for loose coupling. In our scenario, the shared code, when it detects an interesting condition, simply triggers a signal of some sort that says, "this interesting thing has happened; anyone interested can deal with it," and it couldn't give a darn if anyone's interested or not.

Rather than invent our own signaling system, we can use the code that we've already developed in this chapter to leverage event handling as our signaling mechanism.

Let's examine a concrete example.

AN AJAX-Y EXAMPLE

Let's pretend that we've written some shared code that will be performing an Ajax request for us. The pages that this code will be used on want to be notified when an Ajax request begins and when it ends; each page has its own things that it needs to do when these "events" occur.

For example, on one page using this package, we want to display an animated GIF of a spinning pinwheel when an Ajax request starts, and we want to hide it when the request completes, in order to give the user some visual feedback that a request is being processed.

If we imagine the start condition as an event named `ajax-start`, and the stop condition as `ajax-complete`, wouldn't it be grand if we could simply establish event handlers on the page for these events that show and hide the image as appropriate?

Consider this:

```
var body = document.getElementsByTagName('body')[0];

addEvent(body, 'ajax-start', function(e){
  document.getElementById('whirlyThing').style.display = 'inline-block';
});

addEvent(body, 'ajax-complete', function(e){
  document.getElementById('whirlyThing').style.display = 'none';
});
```

Sadly, these events don't really exist.

But we've developed the code to add event handlers and code to mimic the triggering of handlers, so we can use that code to simulate custom events that don't rely upon the browser understanding our custom event types.

TRIGGERING CUSTOM EVENTS

Custom events are a way of simulating (for the user of our shared code) the experience of a real event without having to use the browser's underlying event support. We've already done some work to support cross-browser events, and supporting custom events turns out to be something that we've already implemented!

We don't need to change anything in the code we've already written for `addEvent()`, `removeEvent()`, and `triggerEvent()`to support custom events. Functionally, there's no difference between a real browser event that will be fired by the browser and an event that doesn't really exist that will only fire when triggered manually.

The following listing shows an example of triggering a custom event.

Listing 13.10 Using custom events

```
<!DOCTYPE html>
<html>
  <head>
    <title>Listing 13.10</title>
    <meta charset="utf-8">
    <script type="text/javascript" src="data.js"></script>
    <script type="text/javascript" src="fixup.js"></script>
    <script type="text/javascript" src="events.js"></script>
    <script type="text/javascript" src="trigger.js"></script>
    <style type="text/css">
      #whirlyThing { display: none; }
    </style>

    <script type="text/javascript" src="ajaxy-operation.js"></script>

    <script type="text/javascript">
```

```
                 addEvent(window, 'load', function(){

                   var button = document.getElementById('clickMe');
                   addEvent(button, 'click', function(){
                     performAjaxOperation(this);
                   });

                   var body = document.getElementsByTagName('body')[0];

                   addEvent(body, 'ajax-start', function(e){
                     document.getElementById('whirlyThing')
                       .style.display = 'inline-block';
                   });

                   addEvent(body, 'ajax-complete', function(e){
                     document.getElementById('whirlyThing')
                       .style.display = 'none';
                   });

                 });

             </script>
           </head>
           <body>

             <button type="button" id="clickMe">Start</button>

             <img id="whirlyThing" src="whirly-thing.gif" />

           </body>
         </html>
```

Establishes a handler for a custom event named ajax-complete on the body element that will cause the image to be hidden. No coupling here either. **3**

Adds a click handler to the button that will trigger a 5-second Ajax operation. This handler knows nothing about the pinwheel image. **1**

Establishes the handler for a custom event named ajax-start on the body element that will cause the image to be displayed. There is no coupling with the code that reacts to the button click. **2**

Creates the button to click on **4**

Defines the pinwheel image that should only be shown while an Ajax operation is under way **5**

In this manual test, we cursorily check custom events by establishing the scenario that we described in the previous section: an animated pinwheel image **5** will be displayed while an Ajax operation is under way. The operation is triggered by the click **1** of a button **4**.

In a completely decoupled fashion, a handler for a custom event named ajax-start is established **2**, as is one for the ajax-complete custom event **3**. The handlers for these events show and hide the pinwheel image **5** respectively.

Note how the three handlers know nothing of each other's existence. In particular, the button click handler has no responsibilities with respect to showing and hiding the image.

The Ajax operation itself is simulated with the following code:

```
function performAjaxOperation(target) {

  triggerEvent(target, 'ajax-start');

  window.setTimeout(function(){
    triggerEvent(target, 'ajax-complete');
  },5000);

}
```

The function triggers the ajax-start event, pretending that an Ajax request is about to be made. The choice of the button as the initial target of the event is arbitrary.

Because the handlers are established in the body (a customary location), all events will eventually bubble up to the body, and the handler will be triggered.

The function then issues a five-second timeout, simulating an Ajax request that spans five seconds. When the timer expires, we pretend that the response has been returned and trigger an `ajax-complete` event to signify that the Ajax operation has completed.

The displays are shown in figure 13.5.

Notice the high degree of decoupling throughout this example. The shared Ajax operation code has no knowledge of what the page code is going to do when the events are triggered, or even if there's page code to trigger at all. The page code is modularized into small handlers that don't know about each other. Furthermore, the page code has no idea how the shared code is doing its thing; it just reacts to events that may or may not be triggered.

This level of decoupling helps to keep code modular, easier to write, and a lot easier to debug when something goes wrong. It also makes it easy to share portions of code and to move them around without fear of violating some coupled dependency between the code fragments. Decoupling is a fundamental advantage when using custom events in our code, and it allows us to develop applications in a much more expressive and flexible manner.

Even though you may not have realized it yet, the code in this section was not only a good example of decoupling, it was also a good example of *delegation*.

Figure 13.5 Custom events can be used to cause code to trigger in a decoupled manner.

13.5 Bubbling and delegation

Simply put, *delegation* is the act of establishing event handlers at higher levels in the DOM than the items of interest.

Recall that even though the image buried within the DOM was the element that we wanted to be affected by the custom events, we established handlers on the body element to cause the image's visibility to be affected. This was an example of delegating authority over the image to an ancestor element, in this case, the body element.

But limited to custom tags, or even the body element. Let's imagine a scenario using more mundane event types and elements.

13.5.1 Delegating events to an ancestor

Let's say that we wanted to visually indicate whether a cell within a table had been clicked on by the user by initially displaying a white background for each cell, and changing the background color to yellow once the cell was clicked upon. Sounds easy enough. We can just iterate through all the cells and establish a handler on each one that changes the background color property:

```
var cells = document.getElementsByTagName('td');

for (var n = 0; n < cells.length; n++) {
  addEvent(cells[n], 'click', function(){
    this.style.backgroundColor = 'yellow';
  });
}
```

Sure this works, but is it elegant? Not very. We're establishing the exact same event handler on potentially hundreds of elements, and they all do *the exact same thing*.

A much more elegant approach is to establish a single handler at a level higher than the cells that can handle all the events using the event bubbling provided by the browser. We know that all the cells will be descendants of their enclosing table, and we know that we can get a reference to the element that was clicked upon via event.target. It's much more suave to *delegate* the event-handling to the table, as follows:

```
var table = document.getElementById('#someTable');

addEvent(table, 'click', function(event){
  if (event.target.tagName.toLowerCase() == 'td')
    event.target.style.backgroundColor = 'yellow';
});
```

Here, we establish one handler that easily handles the work of changing the background color for all cells clicked in the table. This is much more efficient and elegant.

Event delegation is one of the best techniques available for developing high-performance, scalable web applications.

Because event *bubbling* is the only technique available across all browsers (event *capturing* doesn't work in IE versions prior to IE 9), it's important to make sure that event delegation is applied to elements that are ancestors of the elements that are the event targets. That way, we're sure that the events will eventually bubble up to the element to which the handler has been delegated.

That all seems logical and easy enough, but... There always seems to be a "but," doesn't there?

13.5.2 *Working around browser deficiencies*

Unfortunately the submit, change, focus, and blur events all have serious problems with their bubbling implementations in various browsers. If we want to employ event delegation—and we do—we must figure out how these deficiencies can be worked around.

To start, the submit and change events don't bubble at all in legacy Internet Explorer, but the W3C DOM-capable browsers implement bubbling consistently. So, as we've done throughout this book, we'll use a technique that's capable of gracefully determining if the problem exists and needs to be worked around. In this case, we need to determine if an event is capable of bubbling up to a parent element.

One such piece of detection code, shown in the following listing, was written by Juriy Zaytsev (as described in his *Perfection Kills* blog at http://perfectionkills.com/detecting-event-support-without-browser-sniffing/).

Listing 13.11   Event-bubbling detection code originally written by Juriy Zaytsev

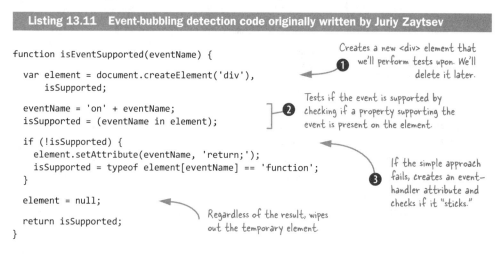

```
function isEventSupported(eventName) {

    var element = document.createElement('div'),        ← Creates a new <div> element that
        isSupported;                                       ❶  we'll perform tests upon. We'll
                                                              delete it later.
    eventName = 'on' + eventName;                       ❷ Tests if the event is supported by
    isSupported = (eventName in element);                 checking if a property supporting the
                                                          event is present on the element.
    if (!isSupported) {
        element.setAttribute(eventName, 'return;');
        isSupported = typeof element[eventName] == 'function';    If the simple approach
    }                                                             ❸ fails, creates an event-
                                                                  handler attribute and
    element = null;        ←  Regardless of the result, wipes     checks if it "sticks."
                              out the temporary element.
    return isSupported;
}
```

The bubbling-detection technique works by checking to see if an existing ontype (where *type* is the type of the event) property exists on a <div> element ❷. A <div> element is used because those elements typically have the most diverse types of events bubbled up to them (including change and submit).

We can't count on a <div> element already existing in the page—and even if we could, we don't really want to start sticking our fingers in someone else's element—so we create a temporary element to play around with ❶.

If this quick and simple test fails, we have a more invasive one we can try ❸. If the ontype property doesn't exist, we create an ontype attribute, giving it a bit of code, and check to see if the element knows how to translate that into a function. If it does, then it's a pretty good indicator that it knows how to interpret that particular event upon bubbling.

Now let's use this detection code as the basis for implementing properly working event bubbling across all browsers.

BUBBLING SUBMIT EVENTS

The submit event is one of the few that doesn't bubble in legacy Internet Explorer, but thankfully, it's one of the easiest events to simulate.

A submit event can be triggered in one of two ways:

- By triggering an input or button element with type of submit, or an input element of type image. Such elements can be triggered with a click, or with the Enter or spacebar key when focused.
- By pressing Enter while inside a text or password input.

Knowing about these two cases, we can piggyback on the two triggering events, click and keypress, both of which bubble normally.

The approach we'll take (for now) is to create special functions to bind and unbind submit events. If we determine that submit events need to be handled specially because browser support is lacking, we'll establish the piggybacking; otherwise, we'll just bind and unbind the handler normally.

Listing 13.12   Piggybacking submit bubbling on click or keypress

```
<script type="text/javascript">

  (function(){

    var isSubmitEventSupported = isEventSupported("submit");

    function isInForm(elem) {
      var parent = elem.parentNode;
      while (parent) {
        if (parent.nodeName.toLowerCase() === "form") {
          return true;
        }
        parent = parent.parentNode;
      }
      return false;
    }

    function triggerSubmitOnClick(e) {
      var type = e.target.type;
      if ((type === "submit" || type === "image") &&
          isInForm(e.target)) {
        return triggerEvent(this,"submit");
      }
    }

    function triggerSubmitOnKey(e) {
      var type = e.target.type;
      if ((type === "text" || type === "password") &&
          isInForm(e.target) && e.keyCode === 13) {
        return triggerEvent(this,"submit");
      }
    }
```

① Defines a utility function that we'll use to check if the passed element is within a form or not

② Predefines a handler for clicks that will check to see if the submit event should piggyback on this event, and triggers one if so

③ Predefines a handler for keypresses that will check to see if a submit event should piggyback on this event, and triggers one if so

Creates a special function for binding submit events **4**

```
this.addSubmit = function (elem, fn) {

    addEvent(elem, "submit", fn);
    if (isSubmitEventSupported) return;

    // But we need to add extra handlers if we're not on a form
    // Only add the handlers for the first handler bound
    if (elem.nodeName.toLowerCase() !== "form" &&
        getData(elem).handlers.submit.length === 1) {
      addEvent(elem, "click", triggerSubmitOnClick);
      addEvent(elem, "keypress", triggerSubmitOnKey);
    }
};
```

5 Binds the submit handler normally, and short-circuits the rest of the function if browser support is adequate

6 If not a form and is the first submit handler, establishes handlers for click and keypress piggybacking

Creates a special function for unbinding submit events **7**

```
this.removeSubmit = function (elem, fn) {

    removeEvent(elem, "submit", fn);
    if (isEventSupported("submit")) return;

    var data = getData(elem);

    if (elem.nodeName.toLowerCase() !== "form" &&
        !data || !data.events || !data.events.submit) {
      removeEvent(elem, "click", triggerSubmitOnClick);
      removeEvent(elem, "keypress", triggerSubmitOnKey);
    }
};
```

8 Unbinds the handler normally, and exits if browser support is adequate

9 If not a form and is the last handler to be unbound, removes the piggybacking handlers

```
  })();

</script>
```

First of all, we're using the immediate function technique, which should be familiar by now, to create a self-contained environment for our code. But before we get into the meat of adding special support for submit events, we're going to define a few things up front that we'll need later.

First, we need to determine if an element is inside a form in a couple of locations, so we define a function named isInForm() **1** to do that for us. It simply traverses the ancestor tree of the element to determine if one of its ancestors is a form.

Then we define two functions that we'll use as event handlers: one for clicks, and one for keypresses. The first such function **2** triggers a submit event if the element is in a form and the target element has submit semantics (has a type of submit, or is an image input element). The second function **3** triggers a submit event if the keypress is the Enter key and the target element is in a form and is a text or password input element.

With those helpers defined, we're ready to write the bind and unbind functions.

The addSubmit() binding function **4** first establishes the submit handler as normal, using the addEvent() function **5**, and then returns if the browser properly supports submit bubbling. If not, we check to make sure we're not binding to a form (in which case bubbling isn't a problem) and whether this is the first submit handler being bound **6**. If submit bubbling is supported, we establish the piggybacking handlers for clicks and keypresses.

The removeSubmit() unbinding function ❼ works in a similar fashion. We unbind the submit event as normal and exit if the browser adequately supports submit bubbling ❽. If it doesn't, we unbind the piggybacking handlers if the target isn't a form and this is the last of the submit handlers being unbound ❾.

> **NOTE** We created this logic as separate functions that use the services of add-Event() to make it easier to focus on the code necessary to handle submit events. But having separate functions is obviously not very caller-friendly. What we should really do is put this logic inside addEvent() so that all this would happen automatically and invisibly for the caller of our code. How would you go about merging this capability into addEvent()?

This approach tends to apply well to fixing other DOM bubbling events, such as the change event.

BUBBLING CHANGE EVENTS

The change event is another event that doesn't bubble properly in the legacy IE Model. Unfortunately, it's significantly harder to implement properly than the submit event. In order to implement the bubbling change event, we must bind to a number of different events:

- The focusout event for checking the value after moving away from the form element
- The click and keydown events for checking the value the instant it's been changed
- The beforeactivate event for getting the previous value before a new one is set

The following listing shows an implementation of special functions that bind and unbind change handlers by piggybacking on all of the preceding events.

Listing 13.13 An implementation of a cross-browser bubbling change event

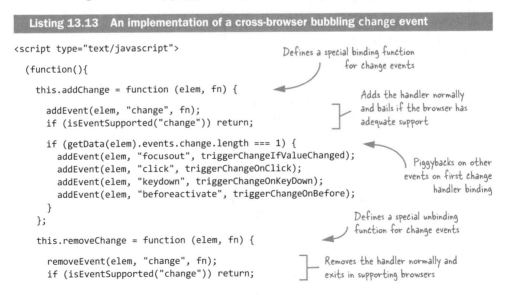

```
<script type="text/javascript">

  (function(){

    this.addChange = function (elem, fn) {          ◄─── Defines a special binding function for change events

      addEvent(elem, "change", fn);                 ┐ Adds the handler normally
      if (isEventSupported("change")) return;       ┘ and bails if the browser has
                                                      adequate support

      if (getData(elem).events.change.length === 1) {
        addEvent(elem, "focusout", triggerChangeIfValueChanged);
        addEvent(elem, "click", triggerChangeOnClick);         ◄─── Piggybacks on other
        addEvent(elem, "keydown", triggerChangeOnKeyDown);          events on first change
        addEvent(elem, "beforeactivate", triggerChangeOnBefore);    handler binding
      }
    };
                                                    Defines a special unbinding
    this.removeChange = function (elem, fn) {   ◄─── function for change events

      removeEvent(elem, "change", fn);              ┐ Removes the handler normally and
      if (isEventSupported("change")) return;       ┘ exits in supporting browsers
```

```
    var data = getData(elem);
    if (!data || !data.events || !data.events.submit) {
      addEvent(elem, "focusout", triggerChangeIfValueChanged);
      addEvent(elem, "click", triggerChangeOnClick);
      addEvent(elem, "keydown", triggerChangeOnKeyDown);
      addEvent(elem, "beforeactivate", triggerChangeOnBefore);
    }
};

function triggerChangeOnClick(e) {
  var type = e.target.type;
  if (type === "radio" || type === "checkbox" ||
      e.target.nodeName.toLowerCase() === "select") {
    return triggerChangeIfValueChanged.call(this, e);
  }
}

function triggerChangeOnKeyDown(e) {
  var type = e.target.type,
      key = e.keyCode;
  if (key === 13 && e.target.nodeName.toLowerCase() !== "textarea" ||
      key === 32 && (type === "checkbox" || type === "radio") ||
      type === "select-multiple") {
    return triggerChangeIfValueChanged.call(this, e);
  }
}

function triggerChangeOnBefore(e) {
  getData(e.target)._change_data = getVal(e.target);
}

function getVal(elem) {
  var type = elem.type,
      val = elem.value;
  if (type === "radio" || type === "checkbox") {
    val = elem.checked;
  } else if (type === "select-multiple") {
    val = "";
    if (elem.selectedIndex > -1) {
      for (var i = 0; i < elem.options.length; i++) {
        val += "-" + elem.options[i].selected;
      }
    }
  } else if (elem.nodeName.toLowerCase() === "select") {
    val = elem.selectedIndex;
  }
  return val;
}

function triggerChangeIfValueChanged(e) {
  var elem = e.target, data, val;
  var formElems = /textarea|input|select/i;
  if (!formElems.test(elem.nodeName) || elem.readOnly) {
    return;
  }
  data = getData(elem)._change_data;
  val = getVal(elem);
  if (e.type !== "focusout" || elem.type !== "radio") {
    getData(elem)._change_data = val;
```

Removes piggybacks if the last unbinding of change handlers

Piggyback handler for click events

Piggyback handler for keydown events

Piggyback handler for beforeactivate events; stores value of element for upcoming focusout event

Utility function that fetches the value of the passed element

Piggyback handler for the focusout event; triggers if the value of the element has changed

```
      }
      if (data === undefined || val === data) {
        return;
      }
      if (data != null || val) {
        return triggerEvent(elem, "change");
      }
    }
  }

})();
```

```
</script>
```

A lot of this code is similar to the approach taken in listing 13.12, so we won't go over it in detail; there's just more of it because there are more event types to handle. The code specific to this example is mostly found within the getVal() and triggerChange-IfValueChanged() functions.

The getVal() method returns a serialized version of the state of the passed form element. This value will be stored by any beforeactivate events in the _change_data property within the element's data object for later use.

The triggerChangeIfValueChanged() function is responsible for determining if an actual change has occurred between the previously stored value and the newly set value, and for triggering the change event if they differ.

In addition to checking to see if a change has occurred after a focusout (blur), we also check to see if the Enter key was pressed on something that wasn't a textarea element, or if the spacebar was pressed on a check box or radio button. We also check to see if a click occurred on a check box, radio button, or select element, because those will also trigger a change to occur.

All told, there's a lot of code here for something that should be tackled natively by the browser. It'll be greatly appreciated when those legacy versions of IE have fallen by the wayside and this code doesn't need to exist.

IMPLEMENTING FOCUSIN AND FOCUSOUT EVENTS

The focusin and focusout events are proprietary events introduced by Internet Explorer that detect when a standard focus or blur event has occurred on any element, or any descendant of that element. These events occur before the focus or blur takes place, making them equivalent to capturing events rather than bubbling events.

The reason that these nonstandard events are worthy of our consideration is that the focus and blur events don't bubble, as dictated by the W3C DOM recommendation and as implemented by all browsers. It ends up being far easier to implement focusin and focusout clones across all browsers than trying to circumvent the intentions of the browser standards and getting the events to bubble.

The best way to implement the focusin and focusout events is to modify the existing addEvent() function to handle the event types inline, as follows:

```
if (document.addEventListener) {
  elem.addEventListener(
    type === "focusin" ? "focus" :
```

```
      type === "focusout" ? "blur" : type,
    data.handler, type === "focusin" || type === "focusout");
}
else if (document.attachEvent) {
  elem.attachEvent("on" + type, data.handler);
}
```

Then we modify the removeEvent() function to unbind the events again properly:

```
if (document.removeEventListener) {
  elem.removeEventListener(
    type === "focusin" ? "focus" :
      type === "focusout" ? "blur" : type,
    data.handler, type === "focusin" || type === "focusout");
}
else if (document.detachEvent) {
  elem.detachEvent("on" + type, data.handler);
}
```

The end result is support for the nonstandard focusin and focusout events in all browsers. Naturally, we might want to keep our event-specific logic separate from our addEvent and removeEvent internals. In that case, we could implement some form of extensibility to override the native binding and unbinding mechanisms provided by the browser for specific event types.

More information about cross-browser focus and blur events can be found on the QuirksMode blog: http://www.quirksmode.org/blog/archives/2008/04/delegating_the.html.

There's another set of nonstandard, but useful, event types to consider.

IMPLEMENTING MOUSEENTER AND MOUSELEAVE EVENTS

The mouseenter and mouseleave events are two more custom events introduced by Internet Explorer to simplify the process of determining when the mouse is currently positioned within or outside an element.

Usually we'd interact with the standard mouseover and mouseout events provided by the browser, but frequently they don't really provide what we're looking for. The problem is that they fire the event when you move between child elements in addition to the parent element itself. This is typical of the event bubbling model, but it's frequently a problem when implementing things like menus and other interaction elements, when all we care about is if we're still within an element; we don't want to be told we've left it just because we've entered a child element.

Figure 13.6 illustrates this issue.

When the mouse cursor moves over the boundary from the parent to the child element, a mouseout event is triggered, even though we might consider the cursor to still be within the bounds of the parent element. Likewise, a mouseover event will be triggered when we leave the child element.

This situation is where the mouseenter and mouseleave events are quite handy. They'll only fire on the main element upon which we've bound them, and they'll only tell us we've left if the cursor actually leaves the parent element. As Internet Explorer

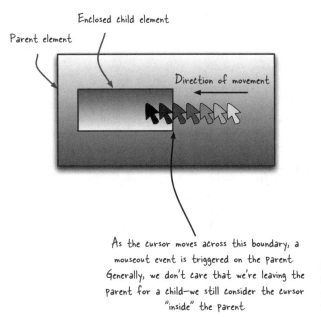

Parent element

Enclosed child element

Direction of movement

As the cursor moves across this boundary, a mouseout event is triggered on the parent. Generally, we don't care that we're leaving the parent for a child—we still consider the cursor "inside" the parent.

Figure 13.6   When crossing the boundary from a parent to a child element, do we really consider that to be "leaving" the parent?

is the only browser that currently implements these useful events, we need to simulate the full event interaction for other browsers as well.

The following listing shows the implementation of a function named hover() that adds support for the mouseenter and mouseleave events in all browsers.

Listing 13.14   Adding support for mouseenter and mouseleave to all browsers

```
<script>
  (function() {

    if (isEventSupported("mouseenter")) {

      this.hover = function (elem, fn) {
        addEvent(elem, "mouseenter", function () {
          fn.call(elem, "mouseenter");
        });

        addEvent(elem, "mouseleave", function () {
          fn.call(elem, "mouseleave");
        });
      };

    }
    else {

      this.hover = function (elem, fn) {
        addEvent(elem, "mouseover", function (e) {
          withinElement(this, e, "mouseenter", fn);
        });
```

Tests if the browser natively supports mouseenter (and hence, mouseleave) events

Adds handlers that invoke the handler for browsers that support the events

In nonsupporting browsers, handle mouseover and mouseout using a handler that detects whether the handler should fire or not

```
      addEvent(elem, "mouseout", function (e) {
        withinElement(this, e, "mouseleave", fn);
      });
    };
  }

  function withinElement(elem, event, type, handle) {

    var parent = event.relatedTarget;

    while (parent && parent != elem) {
      try {
        parent = parent.parentNode;
      }
      catch (e) {
        break;
      }
    }
    if (parent != elem) {
      handle.call(elem, type);
    }
  }

})();
</script>
```

Internal handler that fires the original handler to mimic the nonstandard behavior

Gets the element we're entering from, or exiting to

Traverses upward until it hits the top of the DOM or the hovered element

In case of error, assumes we're done (can happen with Firefox XUL elements)

If not exiting or entering the hovered element, triggers the handler

Most of the smarts for handling the mouseenter and mouseleave events lie inside the withinElement() function, which we establish as the handler for mouseover and mouseout events in browsers that don't support the nonstandard events. This function checks the relatedTarget of the event, which will be the element being entered for mouseout events and the element being left for mouseover events. In either case, if the related element is within the hovered element, we ignore it. Otherwise, we know that it's the hovered element that's being left or entered, and we trigger the handler.

Speaking of leaving, before we exit this chapter on events, there's one more event that's mighty handy to have around. Let's take a look at it.

13.6 *The document ready event*

The final event that we'll consider is called the "ready" event, and it's implemented as DOMContentLoaded in W3C DOM-capable browsers.

This ready event fires as soon as the entire DOM document has been loaded, indicating that it's ready to be traversed and manipulated. This event has become an integral part of many modern frameworks, allowing code to be layered unobtrusively. It executes before the page is displayed and without waiting for other resources to load—resources that can delay the firing of the load event.

Doing this in a cross-browser fashion is once again complicated by the need to support legacy versions of IE (those prior to IE 9).

The W3C browsers make it easy by triggering a DOMContentLoaded event when the DOM is ready. But for legacy IE, we need to rely on a multi-pronged attack to be notified as soon as the DOM is ready.

One of these techniques will use a trick developed by Diego Perini and described at http://javascript.nwbox.com/IEContentLoaded/, in which we attempt to scroll the document to the extreme left (its natural position). This attempt will fail until the document is loaded, so if we continually try to perform the operation (using a timer to make sure we don't block the event loop) we'll know the DOM is ready when the operation stops failing.

A second prong of our attack on legacy IE is listening for the onreadystatechange event on the document. This particular event is less consistent than the doScroll technique— it'll always fire after the DOM is ready, but it'll sometimes fire quite a while afterwards (but always before the final window load event). Even so, it serves as a good backup for IE, making sure that at least *something* will fire before the window load event.

The third prong is examining the document.readyState property. This property, available in all browsers, records how fully loaded the DOM document is at that point. We want to know when it reaches "complete" status. Long delays in loading, especially in Internet Explorer, may cause the readyState to report "complete" too early, which is why we aren't solely relying upon it. But checking this property on load can help us avoid unnecessary event binding if the DOM is already in a ready-to-use state.

NOTE For more info on document status, see the Mozilla documentation at https://developer.mozilla.org/en-US/docs/DOM/document.readyState.

Let's look at an implementation of the ready event, using the preceding techniques.

Listing 13.15 Implementing a cross-browser DOM ready event

```
<script type="text/javascript">

  (function () {

    var isReady = false,
        contentLoadedHandler;

    function ready() {
      if (!isReady) {
        triggerEvent(document, "ready");
        isReady = true;
      }
    }

     if (document.readyState === "complete") {
      ready();
     }

     if (document.addEventListener) {
       contentLoadedHandler = function () {
         document.removeEventListener(
            "DOMContentLoaded", contentLoadedHandler, false);
         ready();
       };

       document.addEventListener(
           "DOMContentLoaded", contentLoadedHandler, false);
     }
```

Starts off assuming that we're not ready

Defines a function that triggers the ready handler only once; subsequent calls will do nothing

If the DOM is ready by the time we get here, just fire the handler

For W3C browsers, creates a handler for DOMContentLoaded event that fires off the ready handler and removes itself

Establishes the just-created handler for the DOMContentLoaded event

```
    else if (document.attachEvent) {
      contentLoadedHandler = function () {
        if (document.readyState === "complete") {
          document.detachEvent(
              "onreadystatechange", contentLoadedHandler);
          ready();
        }
      };
      document.attachEvent(
          "onreadystatechange", contentLoadedHandler);

      var toplevel = false;
      try {
        toplevel = window.frameElement == null;
      }
      catch (e) {
      }
      if (document.documentElement.doScroll && toplevel) {
        doScrollCheck();
      }
    }
    function doScrollCheck() {
      if (isReady) return;
      try {
        document.documentElement.doScroll("left");
      }
      catch (error) {
        setTimeout(doScrollCheck, 1);
        return;
      }
      ready();
    }
  })();
</script>
```

For the IE Model, creates a handler that removes itself and fires the ready handler if the document readyState is complete

Establishes the previous handler for onreadystatechange event. Will likely fire late, but is iframe-safe

If not in an iframe, performs scroll check

Defines the scroll check function, which keeps trying to scroll until success

With a complete ready event implementation, we now have all the tools in place for a complete DOM event-handling system. It's high time to treat ourselves to a lovely beverage.

13.7   Summary

In this chapter, we've seen that a complete DOM event-handling system is anything but simple. The IE Model in legacy versions of IE, which will likely need to be supported for quite a few years to come, causes a great deal of mayhem that we need to circumvent. But it's not all IE's fault; even the W3C browsers lack extensibility in the native API, meaning that we still have to circumvent, and improve upon, most of the event system in order to arrive at a solution that's universally applicable.

Here's what we learned and did in this chapter:

- There are three event-handling models in the browsers that we're likely required to support:
  - DOM Level 0 is probably the most familiar, but it's unsuitable for robust event management.

- DOM Level 2 is the W3C standard, but it lacks many features that we need to create a full management suite.
- The IE Model is proprietary and has fewer features than DOM Level 2, but it's what we must use in legacy versions of IE.

- One of the problems with the IE Model is the lack of proper context in the handlers. We developed a handful of event binding and unbinding functions to normalize this.

- Another issue was the difference in the event information between DOM Level 2 and the IE Model, so we developed a function that "repairs" event instances to be consistent across platforms.

- We needed a means to store information regarding individual elements without resorting to global storage, so we developed a way to tack data onto elements. While we ended up using this to store event-handling information, it's a general facility that could be used for many purposes.

- We enhanced our event binding and unbinding routines to use the data storage facility to keep track of handlers for all event types for any element.

- One of the more important features that we added to our event-management suite was the ability to trigger events under script control. Although it's useful in its own right, we found that it enabled a bunch of really useful capabilities, such as the ability to create and trigger custom events.

- Creating and triggering custom events allowed us to bring loose coupling into almost anything we want to do within a page. This makes creating independent modular components a breeze.

- We also learned how delegating event handling to ancestors of a target object can be an efficient and elegant way to minimize the amount of code we need to create and establish.

- Focusing on browser deficiencies, we then developed ways to do the following:
  - Cause submit events to bubble like other events
  - Cause change events to bubble like other events
  - Implement focusin and focusout events in all browsers
  - Implement mouseenter and mouseleave events in all browsers

- We developed a document ready handler that fires across all browsers to let us know when the DOM is ready to be manipulated in advance of the browser load event.

All told, we now have the knowledge necessary to implement a complete and useful DOM event-management system that's capable of tackling even the greatest challenge presented to us by the browsers' event models.

We're not done with browser headaches yet—manipulating the DOM itself also holds its share of browser frustrations. The next chapter will confront those issues head on.

Manipulating the DOM

14

If we were to open up a JavaScript library, we'd certainly notice (most likely with some surprise) the length and complexity of the code behind simple DOM operations. Even presumably simple code, like cloning or removing a node (which both have simple DOM counterparts, like cloneNode() and removeChild()), have relatively complex implementations.

This raises two questions:

- Why is this code so complex?
- Why do I need to understand how it works if the library will take care of it for me?

The most compelling reason is *performance*. Understanding how DOM modification works in libraries can allow you to write better and faster code that uses the library or, alternatively, enable you to use those techniques in your own code.

There are two points that will likely be surprising to most people who are using a library: not only do libraries handle more cross-browser inconsistencies than typical handwritten code, but they frequently run faster as well. The reason for the performance improvement isn't all that surprising—the library developers keep on top of the latest browser additions. Libraries are thus using the best-possible techniques for creating the most performant code.

For example, when injecting HTML fragments into a page, libraries are using *document fragments* or `createContextualFragment()` to inject HTML. Neither of these techniques is commonly used in everyday development, and yet they both allow you to insert elements into a page in ways that are even faster than most better known methods (such as `createElement()`).

Another possibility for performance improvement is in the area of memory management. It's relatively safe to say that most developers rarely think of the memory usage of their web applications. This isn't the case for a JavaScript library; it must take into account memory usage and make sure that duplicate resources aren't created needlessly. The examples provided in this chapter will reveal many techniques that you can use to help reduce memory consumption in your own applications.

This chapter will talk about all those nasty cross-browser issues prevalent in DOM modification code and also the areas in which extra performance can be squeezed out. Understanding how those performance improvements have been made will allow you to write web applications that run faster than what you'd normally be able to create.

Here are some resources for further reading that you might enjoy:

- `range.createContextualFragment()` is the new hotness, although it's not in jQuery yet: https://developer.mozilla.org/en/DOM/range.createContextualFragment.
- metamorph.js is a DOM manipulation implementation that's worthy of citing: https://github.com/tomhuda/metamorph.js/blob/master/lib/metamorph.js.

Enough talk. Let's push up our sleeves and dive into manipulating the DOM.

14.1   *Injecting HTML into the DOM*

In this chapter, we'll start by looking at an efficient way to insert HTML into a document at any location, given that HTML in string form. We're looking at this particular technique because it's frequently used in a few ways:

- Injecting arbitrary HTML into a page and manipulating and inserting client-side templates
- Retrieving and injecting HTML sent from a server

It's somewhat technically challenging to implement this functionality correctly, especially when compared to building an object-oriented-style DOM construction API (which is certainly easier to implement, but it requires an extra layer of abstraction than injecting the HTML does).

There's already an API method for injecting arbitrary HTML strings; it was introduced by Internet Explorer, and it's now part of the W3C HTML 5 specification. This method exists on all HTML DOM elements and is named `insertAdjacentHTML()`. See www.w3.org/TR/html5/apis-in-html-documents.html#insertadjacenthtml. This method is fairly straightforward to use; somewhat easier-to-digest documentation on it can be found here: https://developer.mozilla.org/en/DOM/element.insertAdjacentHTML.

The problem is that we can't rely on this API across the entire suite of browsers that we're likely to support. Even though this method is broadly available in all modern browsers, it's a recent addition to most, and it's likely that some legacy browsers in your support matrix won't support this method. Even IE's implementation in its older versions was incredibly buggy, only working on a subset of all available elements.

And even if we had the luxury of supporting only the latest and greatest versions of the browsers, knowing how to do HTML injection is a skill that a JavaScript ninja should have tucked into his belt right next to his or her wakizashi.

For these reasons, we're going to implement a clean DOM-manipulation API from scratch. The implementation will involve a number of steps:

1 Convert an arbitrary but valid HTML/XHTML string into a DOM structure.
2 Inject that DOM structure into any location in the DOM as efficiently as possible.
3 Execute any inline scripts that were in the source string.

All together, these three steps will provide a page author with a smart API for injecting HTML into a document.

Let's get started.

14.1.1 *Converting HTML to DOM*

Converting an HTML string to a DOM structure doesn't involve a whole lot of magic. In fact, it uses a tool that you're most likely already very familiar with: the `innerHTML` property of DOM elements.

Using it is a multi-step process:

1 Make sure that the HTML string contains valid HTML/XHTML (or, to be friendly, tweak it so that it's closer to valid).
2 Wrap the string in any enclosing markup that's required by browser rules.
3 Insert the HTML string, using `innerHTML`, into a dummy DOM element.
4 Extract the DOM nodes back out.

The steps aren't overly complex, but the actual insertion has some gotchas that we'll need to take into account. Let's take a look at each step in detail.

PREPROCESSING THE **XML/HTML** SOURCE STRING

To start, we'll need to clean up the source HTML to meet our needs. Exactly what's involved in this first step will depend upon the product needs and context; for example, for the construction of jQuery, it became important to be able to support XML-style, self-closing elements such as `"<table/>"`.

These self-closing elements only work for a small subset of HTML elements; attempting to use that syntax in other cases is likely to cause problems in browsers like Internet Explorer.

We can do a quick preparse on the HTML string to convert elements like "<table/>" to "<table></table>" (which will be handled uniformly in all browsers), as shown in the next listing.

> **Listing 14.1   Making sure that self-closing elements are interpreted correctly**

```
<script type="text/javascript">

  var tags =
    /^(abbr|br|col|img|input|link|meta|param|hr|area|embed)$/i;
  function convert(html) {
    return html.replace(/(<(\w+)[^>]*?)\/>/g, function (all, front, tag) {
      return tags.test(tag) ?
          all :
          front + "></" + tag + ">";
    });
  }

  assert(convert("<a/>") === "<a></a>", "Check anchor conversion.");
  assert(convert("<hr/>") === "<hr/>", "Check hr conversion.");

</script>
```

Use a regular expression to match the tag name of any elements we don't need to be concerned about

A function that uses regular expressions to convert self-closing tags to "normal" form

As always, test!

With that accomplished, we need to determine whether the new elements need to be wrapped or not.

HTML WRAPPING

We now have the start of an HTML string, but there's another step we need to take before injecting it into the page. A number of HTML elements must be within certain container elements before they can be injected. For example, an <option> element must be within a <select>.

There are two approaches to solving this problem, both of which require constructing a mapping between problematic elements and their containers:

- The string could be injected directly into a specific parent using innerHTML, where the parent has been previously constructed using createElement. Although this may work in some cases in some browsers, it isn't universally guaranteed to work.

- The string could be wrapped with the appropriate required markup and then injected directly into any container element (such as a <div>). This is more foolproof, but it's also more work.

The second technique is preferred; it involves very little browser-specific code in contrast to the first approach, which would require a fair amount of mostly browser-specific code.

The set of problematic elements that need to be wrapped in specific container elements is fortunately a rather manageable seven. In the following list, the ellipses (...) indicates where the elements need to be injected:

- `<option>` and `<optgroup>` need to be contained in a `<select multiple="multiple">`...`</select>`.
- `<legend>` needs to be contained in a `<fieldset>`...`</fieldset>`.
- `<thead>`, `<tbody>`, `<tfoot>`, `<colgroup>`, and `<caption>` need to be contained in a `<table>`...`</table>`.
- `<tr>` needs to be in a `<table><thead>`...`</thead></table>`, `<table><tbody>`...`</tbody></table>`, or `<table><tfoot>`...`</tfoot></table>`.
- `<td>` and `<th>` need to be in a `<table><tbody><tr>`...`</tr></tbody></table>`.
- `<col>` must be in a `<table><tbody></tbody><colgroup>`...`</colgroup></table>`.
- `<link>` and `<script>` need to be in a `<div></div><div>`...`</div>`.

Nearly all of these are straightforward, save for the following points, which require a bit of explanation:

- A `<select>` element with the `multiple` attribute is used (as opposed to a non-multiple select) because it won't automatically check any of the options that are placed inside of it (whereas a single select will autocheck the first option).
- The `<col>` fix includes an extra `<tbody>`, without which the `<colgroup>` won't be generated properly.
- The `<link>` and `<script>` fix is a weird one: Internet Explorer is unable to generate `<link>` and `<script>` elements via `innerHTML` unless they're both contained within another element and there's an adjacent node.

With the elements properly mapped to their wrapping requirements, let's start generating.

GENERATING THE DOM

Using the map of containers from the previous section, we now have enough information to generate the HTML that we need to insert into a DOM element.

Listing 14.2   Generating a list of DOM nodes from some markup

```
<script type="text/javascript">

  function getNodes(htmlString, doc) {

    var map = {
      "<td":[3,"<table><tbody><tr>","</tr></tbody></table>"],
      "<th":[3,"<table><tbody><tr>","</tr></tbody></table>"],
      "<tr":[2,"<table><thead>","</thead></table>"],
      "<option":[1,"<select multiple='multiple'>","</select>"],
      "<optgroup":[1,"<select multiple='multiple'>","</select>"],
      "<legend":[1,"<fieldset>","</fieldset>"],
```

Map of element types that need special parent containers. Each entry has the depth of the new node, opening HTML for the parents, and closing HTML for the parents. ❶

Uses a regular expression to match the opening bracket and tag name of the element to be inserted **2**

If it's in the map, grab the entry; otherwise construct a faux entry with empty "parent" markup and a depth of zero. **3**

```
        "<thead":[1,"<table>","</table>"],
        "<tbody":[1,"<table>","</table>"],
        "<tfoot":[1,"<table>","</table>"],
        "<colgroup":[1,"<table>","</table>"],
        "<caption":[1,"<table>","</table>"],
        "<col":[2,"<table><tbody></tbody><colgroup>","</colgroup></table>"],
        "<link":[3,"<div></div><div>","</div>"]
    };

    var tagName = htmlString.match(/<\w+/),
        mapEntry = tagName ? map[tagName[0]] : null;
            if  (!mapEntry) mapEntry = [0, " ". " " ];

    var div = (doc || document).createElement("div");

    div.innerHTML = mapEntry[1] + htmlString + mapEntry[2];

    while (mapEntry[0]--) div = div.lastChild;

    return div.childNodes;
}

assert(getNodes("<td>test</td><td>test2</td>").length === 2,
        "Get two nodes back from the method.");
assert(getNodes("<td>test</td>")[0].nodeName === "TD",
        "Verify that we're getting the right node.");

</script>
```

Create a <div> element in which to create the new nodes. Note that we use a passed document if it exists, or default to the current document if not. **4**

Wrap the incoming markup with the parents from the map entry, and inject it as the inner HTML of the newly created <div>. **5**

Return the newly created element. **7**

Walk down the just-created tree to the depth indicated by the map entry. This should be the parent of the desired node created from the markup. **6**

There are two browser bugs that we'll need to work around before we return our node set, both in Internet Explorer. The first is that IE adds a <tbody> element inside an empty table: checking to see if an empty table was intended and removing any child nodes is a sufficient fix. The second is that IE trims all leading whitespace from the string passed to innerHTML—remember that HTML doesn't care about whitespace, and it's usually not taken into account when browsers render the document. This can be remedied by checking to see if the first generated node is a text and contains leading whitespace; if not, create a new text node and fill it with the whitespace explicitly.

After all of this, we have a set of DOM nodes that we can begin to insert into the document.

14.1.2 *Inserting into the document*

Once we have the actual DOM nodes, it's time to insert them into the document. There are a couple of steps involved, and we'll work through them in this section.

As we have an array of elements that we need to insert—potentially into any number of locations within the document—we'd like to try and keep the number of operations that are performed to a minimum.

We can do this by using *DOM fragments*. DOM fragments are part of the W3C DOM specification and are supported in all browsers. This useful facility gives us a container that we can use to hold a collection of DOM nodes.

This in itself is quite useful, but it also has the advantage that the fragment can be injected and cloned in a single operation instead of us having to inject and clone each individual node over and over again. This has the potential to dramatically reduce the number of operations required for a page.

Before we use this mechanism in our code, let's revisit the getNodes() code of listing 14.2 and adjust it a tad to make use of DOM fragments. The changes are minor and consist of adding a fragment parameter to the function's parameter list, as follows:

```
function getNodes(htmlString, doc, fragment) {
```

This parameter, if it's passed, is expected to be a DOM fragment that we want the nodes to be injected into for later use.

To do so, we simply add the following fragment just before the return statement of the function to add the nodes to the passed fragment:

```
if (fragment) {
  while (div.firstChild) {
    fragment.appendChild(div.firstChild);
  }
}
```

Now, let's see it in use.

In the following listing, derived from the code in jQuery, which assumes that the updated getNodes() function is in scope, a fragment is created and passed in to that function (which, you may recall, converts the incoming HTML string into DOM elements). This DOM is now appended to the fragment.

Listing 14.3 Inserting a DOM fragment into multiple locations in the DOM

```
<div id="test"><b>Hello</b>, I'm a ninja!</div>
<div id="test2"></div>

<script type="text/javascript">

  window.onload = function () {
    function insert(elems, args, callback) {
      if (elems.length) {
        var doc = elems[0].ownerDocument || elems[0],
            fragment = doc.createDocumentFragment(),
            scripts = getNodes(args, doc, fragment),
            first = fragment.firstChild;

        if (first) {
          for (var i = 0; elems[i]; i++) {
            callback.call(root(elems[i], first),
                i > 0 ? fragment.cloneNode(true) : fragment);
          }
        }
      }
    }

    var divs = document.getElementsByTagName("div");

    insert(divs, ["<b>Name:</b>"], function (fragment) {
      this.appendChild(fragment);
    });

    insert(divs, ["<span>First</span> <span>Last</span>"],
        function (fragment) {
```

```
        this.parentNode.insertBefore(fragment, this);
    });
};
</script>
```

There's another important point here: if we're inserting this element into more than one location in the document, we're going to need to clone this fragment again and again. If we weren't using a fragment, we'd have to clone each individual node every time, instead of the whole fragment at once.

There's one final point that we'll need to take care of, albeit a relatively minor one. When page authors attempt to inject a table row directly into a table element, they normally mean to insert the row directly into the <tbody> that's in the table. We can write a simple mapping function to take care of that for us.

Listing 14.4   Figure out the insertion point of an element

```
<script type="text/javascript">

    function root(elem, cur) {
      return elem.nodeName.toLowerCase() === "table" &&
         cur.nodeName.toLowerCase() === "tr" ?
         (elem.getElementsByTagName("tbody")[0] ||
            elem.appendChild(elem.ownerDocument.createElement("tbody"))) :
         elem;
    }

</script>
```

Altogether, we now have a way to both generate and insert arbitrary DOM elements in an intuitive manner. But what about scripting elements that are embedded in the source string?

14.1.3   *Script execution*

In addition to the insertion of structural HTML into a document, a common requirement is the execution of inline script elements. This scenario is quite common when an HTML fragment is returned as an Ajax response from a server and there's script that needs to be executed along with the HTML itself.

Usually the best way to handle inline scripts is to strip them out of the DOM structure before they're inserted into the document. In the function that's used to convert the HTML into a DOM node, we could use something like the following code from jQuery.

Listing 14.5   Collecting the scripts

```
for (var i = 0; ret[i]; i++) {
  if (jQuery.nodeName(ret[i], "script") &&
      (!ret[i].type ||
          ret[i].type.toLowerCase() === "text/javascript")) {
    scripts.push(ret[i].parentNode ?
        ret[i].parentNode.removeChild(ret[i]) :
        ret[i]);
```

```
    } else if (ret[i].nodeType === 1) {
      ret.splice.apply(ret, [i + 1, 0].concat(
          jQuery.makeArray(ret[i].getElementsByTagName("script"))));
    }
  }
}
```

The code in this listing deals with two arrays: `ret`, which holds all the DOM nodes that have been generated, and `scripts`, which becomes populated with all the scripts in this fragment, in document order. Additionally, the code takes care to only remove scripts that are normally executed as JavaScript (those without an explicit `type` or those with a `type` of `text/javascript`). Then, after the DOM structure is inserted into the document, the code takes the contents of `scripts` and evaluates it. It's more about shuffling things around than intricate code, but it does lead us to a tricky part.

GLOBAL CODE EVALUATION

When inline scripts are included for execution, it's expected that they will be evaluated within the global context. This means that if a variable is defined, it should become a global variable; the same applies to any functions.

The standard methods for code evaluation are spotty, at best. The one foolproof way to execute code in the global scope, across all browsers, is to create a fresh script element, inject the code you wish to execute inside the script, and then quickly inject and remove the script from the document. This is a technique that we discussed back in section 9.1. This will cause the browser to execute the inner contents of the script element within the global scope.

The following listing shows a part of the global evaluation code that's in jQuery.

Listing 14.6 Evaluate a script within the global scope

```
<script type="text/javascript">

  function globalEval(data) {
    data = data.replace(/^\s+|\s+$/g, "");

    if (data) {
      var head = document.getElementsByTagName("head")[0] ||
            document.documentElement,
          script = document.createElement("script");

      script.type = "text/javascript";
      script.text = data;

      head.insertBefore(script, head.firstChild);
      head.removeChild(script);
    }
  }

</script>
```

Using this method, it becomes easy to rig up a generic way to evaluate a script element. We can even add in some simple code for dynamically loading in a script (if it references an external URL) and evaluating that as well.

Listing 14.7   A method for evaluating a script (even if it's remotely located)

```
<script type="text/javascript">

  function evalScript(elem) {
    if (elem.src)
      jQuery.ajax({
        url:elem.src,
        async:false,
        dataType:"script"
      });

    else
      jQuery.globalEval(elem.text || "");

    if (elem.parentNode)
      elem.parentNode.removeChild(elem);
  }

</script>
```

After we're done evaluating the script, we remove it from the DOM. We did the same thing earlier when we removed the script element before it was injected into the document. We do this so that scripts won't accidentally be doubly executed (appending a script to a document, which ends up recursively calling itself, for example).

To our ninja toolkit we've added the ability to add new elements to the DOM. Now let's see how we can copy new elements from previously existing ones.

14.2   *Cloning elements*

Cloning an element (using the DOM `cloneNode` method) is straightforward in all browsers, except legacy Internet Explorer. Legacy versions of IE have troubling behaviors that, when they occur in conjunction, result in a very frustrating scenario for handling cloning.

First, when cloning an element, IE copies over all event handlers to the cloned element. Additionally, any custom expandos attached to the element are also carried over. In jQuery, the following simple test determines if this is the case.

Listing 14.8   Determining if a browser copies event handlers on cloning

```
<script type="text/javascript">

  var div = document.createElement("div");

  if (div.attachEvent && div.fireEvent) {
    div.attachEvent("onclick", function () {
      jquery.support.noCloneEvent = false;
      div.detachEvent("onclick", arguments.callee);
    });
    div.cloneNode(true).fireEvent("onclick");
  }

</script>
```

Cloning a node shouldn't copy over any bound event handlers. (IE does this.)

Second, the obvious way to prevent this would be to remove the event handler from the cloned element. But in Internet Explorer, if you remove an event handler from a cloned element, it gets removed from the original element as well. Fun stuff!

Naturally, any attempts to remove custom expando properties on the clone will cause them to be removed on the original cloned element as well.

Finally, the solution to all of this might be to just clone the element, inject it into another element, read the innerHTML of the element, and convert that back into a DOM node. It's a multistep process, but one that'll result in an untainted cloned element. Except (sigh), there's another IE bug: the innerHTML (and outerHTML, for that matter) of an element doesn't always reflect the correct state of an element's attributes. One common place where this is seen is when the name attribute of an input element is changed dynamically. The new value isn't represented in innerHTML.

This solution has another caveat: innerHTML doesn't exist on XML DOM elements, so we're forced to go with the traditional cloneNode call (thankfully, though, event listeners on XML DOM elements are pretty rare).

The final solution for Internet Explorer ends up being quite circuitous. Instead of a quick call to cloneNode, it's instead serialized by innerHTML, extracted again as a DOM node, and then monkey-patched for any particular attributes that didn't carry over. How much monkeying you want to do with the attributes is really up to you.

Listing 14.9 A portion of the element clone code from jQuery

```javascript
<script type="text/javascript">

  function clone() {
    var ret = this.map(function () {
      if (!jQuery.support.noCloneEvent && !jQuery.isXMLDoc(this)) {
        var clone = this.cloneNode(true),
            container = document.createElement("div");
        container.appendChild(clone);
        return jQuery.clean([container.innerHTML])[0];
      }
      else
        return this.cloneNode(true);
    });

    var clone = ret.find("*").andSelf().each(function () {
      if (this[ expando ] !== undefined)
        this[ expando ] = null;
    });

    return ret;
  }

</script>
```

Note that the preceding code uses jQuery's jQuery.clean method, which converts an HTML string into a DOM structure (as was discussed previously).

OK, we've added new elements and copied elements. How do we get rid of them?

14.3   Removing elements

Removing an element from the DOM *should* be simple (a quick call to removeChild()), but of course it isn't. We have to do a lot of preliminary cleaning up before we can actually remove an element from the DOM.

There are usually two steps of cleanup that need to occur on a DOM element before it can be removed from the DOM.

The first things to clean up are any bound event handlers by removing them from the element. If a framework is designed well, it should only be binding a single handler for an element at a time, so the cleanup shouldn't be any harder than removing that one function. This is exactly how we set up our event management framework in chapter 13. This step is very important because Internet Explorer will leak memory should the handler function reference any DOM elements.

The second step in the cleanup is removing any external data associated with the element. Just as we discussed in chapter 13, a framework needs a good way to associate pieces of data with an element *without* directly attaching the data as an expando property. It's a good idea to clean up this data so that it doesn't consume any more memory.

Both of these points need to be done on the element that's being removed, as well as on all descendant elements, because all the descendant elements are also being removed.

The following listing shows the relevant code from jQuery.

Listing 14.10   The remove element function from jQuery

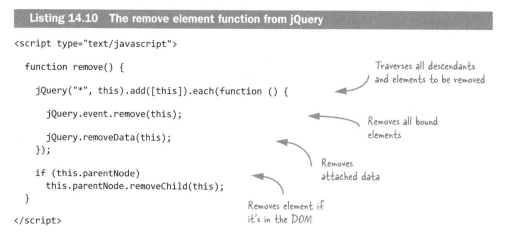

```html
<script type="text/javascript">

  function remove() {                                    Traverses all descendants
                                                         and elements to be removed
    jQuery("*", this).add([this]).each(function () {

      jQuery.event.remove(this);                         Removes all bound
                                                         elements
      jQuery.removeData(this);
    });                                                  Removes
                                                         attached data
    if (this.parentNode)
      this.parentNode.removeChild(this);
  }                                                      Removes element if
                                                         it's in the DOM
</script>
```

The next thing to consider, after all the cleaning up is done, is the actual removal of the element from the DOM. Most browsers are perfectly fine with the removal of the element from the page (with the exception of Internet Explorer, as described previously).

In IE, every single element removed from the page fails to reclaim some portion of its used memory, until the page is finally left. This means that long-running pages that remove a lot of elements from the page will find themselves using considerably more memory in Internet Explorer as time goes on.

There's one partial solution that seems to work quite well. IE has a proprietary property called outerHTML that gives us an HTML string representation of an element. For whatever reason, outerHTML is also a setter in addition to a getter. As it turns out, if we execute the following,

```
outerHTML = "";
```

it will wipe out the element from IE's memory more completely than simply doing removeChild().

We can do this step in addition to the normal removeChild() call.

Listing 14.11   Setting outerHTML in an attempt to reclaim more memory in Internet Explorer

```
if (this.parentNode)
  this.parentNode.removeChild(this);              ◄——   Removes element if
                                                         it's in the DOM
if (typeof this.outerHTML !== "undefined")
  this.outerHTML = "";
```

It should be noted that outerHTML isn't successful in reclaiming *all* of the memory that was used by the element, but it reclaims most of it (which is a start).

It's important to remember that whenever an element is removed from the page, you should go through the preceding three steps, at the very least. This includes emptying out the contents of an element, replacing the contents of an element (with either HTML or text), and replacing an element directly. Remember to always keep your DOM tidy, and you won't have to worry so much about memory issues later on.

That covers HTML elements pretty well, but a page consists of more than just elements. We also need to consider page text.

14.4   *Text contents*

Working with text tends to be much easier than working with HTML elements, especially as there are built-in methods that work in all browsers for text content. But as usual, there are all sorts of browser bugs that we end up having to work around, so these APIs aren't the complete solution we'd like them to be.

When it comes to dealing with text, there are two common scenarios:

- Getting the text content of an element
- Setting the text content of an element

W3C-compliant browsers conveniently provide a textContent property on their DOM elements. Accessing the contents of this property gives you the textual contents of the element, including its direct children and descendant nodes.

Legacy Internet Explorer has its own property, innerText, for performing the same behavior as textContent. (Just to be nice, some browsers, such as WebKit-based browsers, also support innerText.)

Consider the following code.

Listing 14.12   Using textContent and innerText

```
<div id="test"><b>Hello</b>, I'm a ninja!</div>

<script type="text/javascript">

  window.onload = function () {
    var b = document.getElementById("test");
    var text = b.textContent || b.innerText;

    assert(text === "Hello, I'm a ninja!",
        "Examine the text contents of an element.");
    assert(b.childNodes.length === 2,
        "An element and a text node exist.");

    if (typeof b.textContent !== "undefined") {
      b.textContent = "Some new text";
    }
    else {
      b.innerText = "Some new text";
    }

    text = b.textContent || b.innerText;

    assert(text === "Some new text", "Set a new text value.");
    assert(b.childNodes.length === 1,
        "Only one text node exists now.");
  };

</script>
```

Note that when we set the textContent/innerText properties, the original element structure is removed. So while both of these properties are very useful, there are a certain number of gotchas.

First, as we discussed while removing elements from the page, not having any sort of special consideration for element memory leaks will come back to bite us later on. Additionally, the cross-browser handling of whitespace is absolutely abysmal in these properties. No browser appears capable of returning consistent results.

If you don't care about preserving whitespace (especially end lines), feel free to use textContent/innerText for accessing the element's text value. For setting the value though, we'll need to devise an alternative solution.

14.4.1 *Setting text*

Setting a text value involves two steps:

1 Emptying out the contents of the element
2 Inserting the new text contents in its place

Emptying out the contents is straightforward; we've already devised a solution in listing 14.10.

To insert the new text contents, we'll need to use a method that'll properly escape the string we're about to insert. An important difference between inserting HTML and inserting text is that the inserted text will need to have any problematic HTML-specific characters escaped. For example < must appear as the HTML entity <.

Luckily, we can use the built-in `createTextNode()` method, available on DOM documents, to do precisely that, as shown in the next listing.

Listing 14.13 Setting the text contents of an element

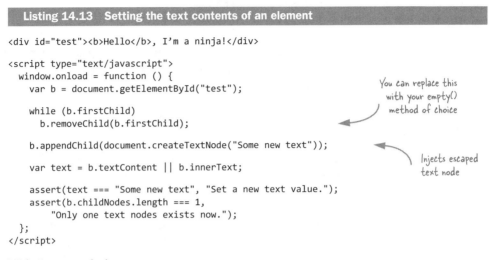

```
<div id="test"><b>Hello</b>, I'm a ninja!</div>

<script type="text/javascript">
  window.onload = function () {
    var b = document.getElementById("test");

    while (b.firstChild)
      b.removeChild(b.firstChild);

    b.appendChild(document.createTextNode("Some new text"));

    var text = b.textContent || b.innerText;

    assert(text === "Some new text", "Set a new text value.");
    assert(b.childNodes.length === 1,
        "Only one text nodes exists now.");
  };
</script>
```

You can replace this with your empty() method of choice

Injects escaped text node

We've *set*; now let's *get*.

14.4.2 Getting text

To get the *accurate* text value of an element, we have to ignore the results from `text-Content` and `innerText`. The most common problem with these properties is related to end lines being unnecessarily stripped from the returned result. Instead we must collect all the text node values manually to get an accurate result.

The following code is a possible solution that makes good use of recursion.

Listing 14.14 Getting the text contents of an element

```
<div id="test"><b>Hello</b>, I'm a ninja!</div>

<script>
  window.onload = function () {
    function getText(elem) {
      var text = "";

      for (var i = 0; i < elem.childNodes.length; i++) {
        var cur = elem.childNodes[i];

        if (cur.nodeType === 3)
          text += cur.nodeValue;

        else if (cur.nodeType === 1)
          text += getText(cur);
      }

      return text;
    }

    var b = document.getElementById("test");
    var text = getText(b);
```

Text nodes have a nodeType of 3

We need to recurse further if it's an element

```
    assert(text === "Hello, I'm a ninja!",
        "Examine the text contents of an element.");
    assert(b.childNodes.length === 2,
        "An element and a text node exist.");
  };
</script>
```

In our applications, when we can get away with not worrying about whitespace, we should definitely stick with the textContent/innerText properties, as they make our lives so much simpler. But it's nice to have a fallback for when those properties don't cut the mustard.

14.5 *Summary*

We've taken a comprehensive look at the best ways to tackle the difficult problems surrounding DOM manipulation. While modern browsers give us some newer options for DOM manipulation, knowing how to do it "by hand" is important to provide support for legacy browsers and improve performance.

These problems should be easier to overcome than they are, but cross-browser issues make implementing solutions much more difficult than it should be. With a little bit of extra work, we can have a unified solution that will work well in all major browsers, which is exactly what we should strive for.

Let's review what we've learned in this chapter:

- Using regular expressions, a handy tool we mastered in chapter 7, we can cajole HTML snippets into a well-formed syntax that we can parse.
- Injecting a fragment of HTML text into a temporary element's innerHTML property is a quick and easy way to convert a string of HTML text into DOM elements.
- Some elements, such as table component elements, need to be wrapped with certain other container elements in order for them to be properly created.
- Script elements in HTML fragments can be executed in the global scope using the techniques that we examined in chapter 9 on code evaluation.
- Legacy versions of Internet Explorer cause headaches when cloning nodes because they copy too *much*, including event handlers and expandos.
- We need to be mindful of memory management needs when removing elements from the DOM, especially when creating long-lived pages.

In this chapter, we've created, cloned, and removed elements. What about finding them? In the next chapter we'll consider the final subject in your ninja training: locating elements via CSS selectors.

CSS selector engines

This chapter covers

- The current status of browser selector support
- Strategies for selector engine construction
- Using the W3C API
- Some info on XPath
- Building a DOM selector engine

The good news is that we, as web development professionals, are well into the age in which the W3C Selectors API exists in all modern browsers. This API (which has two levels: Level 1 and Level 2) provides us with the querySelectorAll() and query-Selector() methods, along with other goodies that we can use in our applications to write very fast DOM traversals in relatively cross-browser ways.

> **NOTE** Want more info on this API? See the W3C pages for Level 1 (www.w3 .org/TR/selectors-api/) and Level 2 (www.w3.org/TR/selectors-api2/).

You might ask, as the W3C Selectors API has been implemented in virtually all modern browsers, why do we need to spend time discussing how a pure JavaScript CSS selector engine is implemented?

Although the addition of the standard API is a good thing, the implementation of the W3C Selectors API in most browsers (at least in their mid-2012 state) is rather a shoe-horning of existing internal CSS selector engines into the standardized JavaScript/DOM realm. To make this happen, a number of niceties that one would typically associate with a good API were set aside. For example, the methods don't make use of already-constructed DOM caches, they don't provide good error reporting, and they're unable to handle any form of extensibility.

The CSS selector engines in popular JavaScript libraries have taken into account all of these factors. They use DOM caches to provide faster performance, they provide extra levels of error reporting, and they're highly extensible.

> **TIP** If you're wondering what a "CSS selector engine" is, it's simply a grandi-ose term for functionality that matches a set of DOM elements given a CSS selector expression. For example, all elements that have the class ninja can be collected with the selector expression .ninja.

All this being said, the question remains: why should you understand how a pure JavaScript CSS selector engine works? The answer is that understanding how a pure-JavaScript CSS selector engine works can yield some rather astonishing performance gains. Not only will we be able to write better traversal implementations, allowing us to search through a DOM tree even faster, but we'll also learn to sculpt our CSS selectors to adapt to how the CSS selector engines work, giving us even more performant selectors.

CSS selector engines are a part of everyday development in this day and age, and understanding how they work, and how to make them work even faster, will give us a fundamental leg up in our development. After all, if you think about the types of things that we need to do in on-page scripts, a lot of it follows this pattern:

1 Find DOM elements.
2 Do something to or with them.

Excepting the new Selectors API, finding DOM elements has never been a strong point of in-browser JavaScript; the methods available to locate elements were pretty much limited to finding elements by ID values and tag names. Anything we can do to make that first step easier will let us focus on the more interesting "do something" step.

It's standard, at this point in time, for selector engines to implement CSS3 selectors, as defined by the W3C and shown at www.w3.org/TR/css3-selectors/.

With regard to approach, there are three primary ways of implementing a CSS selector engine:

- Using the previously mentioned W3C Selectors API, as implemented in most modern browsers
- Using XPath, a DOM-querying language built into a variety of modern browsers
- Using pure DOM, a staple of CSS selector engines, which allows for graceful deg-radation if either of the first two mechanisms doesn't exist

This chapter will explore all of these strategies in depth, allowing us to make some educated decisions about implementing, or at least understanding, a JavaScript CSS selector engine.

We'll start with the W3C approach.

15.1 *The W3C Selectors API*

The W3C Selectors API is a comparatively new API that's designed to reduce much of the work that it takes to implement a full CSS selector engine in JavaScript.

Browser vendors have pounced on this new API, and it's implemented in all major modern browsers (starting in Safari 3, Firefox 3.1, Internet Explorer 8, Chrome (pretty much since inception), and Opera 10). Implementations of the API generally support all selectors implemented by the browser's CSS engine, so if a browser has full CSS3 support, its Selectors API implementation will reflect that.

This API provides a number of useful methods, two of which are implemented in modern browsers:

- querySelector() accepts a CSS selector string and returns the first element found, or null if no matching element is found.
- querySelectorAll() accepts a CSS selector string and returns a static NodeList of all elements found by the selector.

These two methods exist on all DOM elements, DOM documents, and DOM fragments.

The following listing shows a couple of examples of how it could be used.

Listing 15.1 Examples of the Selectors API in action

```
<div id="test">
  <b>Hello</b>, I'm a ninja!
</div>
<div id="test2"></div>

<script type="text/javascript">

  window.onload = function () {
    var divs = document.querySelectorAll("body > div");      ← Finds <div> elements that are children of the body
    assert(divs.length === 2, "Two divs found using a CSS selector.");

    var b = document.getElementById("test")
      .querySelector("b:only-child");                        ← Finds only children who are bold!
    assert(b,
      "The bold element was found relative to another element.");
  };

</script>
```

Perhaps the one gotcha that exists with the current W3C Selectors API is that it's limited to supporting CSS selectors that are supported by the browser, rather than the wider-ranging implementations that were first created by JavaScript libraries. This can be seen in the matching rules of element-rooted queries (calling either querySelector() or querySelectorAll() relative to an element).

Listing 15.2   Element-rooted queries

```
<div id="test">
  <b>Hello</b>, I'm a ninja!
</div>

<script type="text/javascript">
  window.onload = function () {
    var b = document.getElementById("test").querySelector("div b");
    assert(b, "Only the last part of the selector matters.");
  };
</script>
```

Note the issue here: when performing an element-rooted query, the selector only checks to see if the final portion of the selector is contained within the element. This will probably seem counterintuitive. In listing 15.2, we can verify that there are no <div> elements within the element with an id of test, even though that's what the selector looks like it's verifying.

This runs counter to how most users expect a CSS selector engine to work, so we'll have to provide a workaround. The most common solution is to add a new id to the rooted element to enforce its context.

Listing 15.3   Enforcing the element root

```
<div id="test">
  <b>Hello</b>, I'm a ninja!
</div>

<script type="text/javascript">
  (function() {

    var count = 1;

    this.rootedQuerySelectorAll = function (elem, query) {
      var oldID = elem.id;
      elem.id = "rooted" + (count++);

      try {
        return elem.querySelectorAll("#" + elem.id + " " + query);
      }
      catch (e) {
        throw e;
      }
      finally {
        elem.id = oldID;
      }
    };
  })();

  window.onload = function () {
    var b = rootedQuerySelectorAll(
        document.getElementById("test"), "div b");
    assert(b.length === 0, "The selector is now rooted properly.");
  };
</script>
```

Immediate function binds count variable to rootedQuerySelectorAll() function

Defines function in global context

Remembers the original id; we'll be putting it back later

Assigns a uniquely generated temporary id value

Restores the original id in a finally block so that there's no way it can be circumvented

There are a couple of important points in listing 15.3.

To start, we must assign a unique `id` to the element and restore the old `id` later. This will ensure that there are no collisions in our final result when we build the selector. We then prepend this `id` (in the form of an `"#id "` selector, where `id` is the uniquely generated value) to the selector.

Normally this process would be as simple as removing the `id` and returning the result from the query, but there's a catch: Selectors API methods can throw exceptions (most commonly seen for selector syntax issues or unsupported selectors). Because of this, we'll want to wrap our selection in a `try/catch` block. But because we want to restore the `id`, we can add an extra `finally` block. This is an interesting feature of the language: even though we're returning a value in the `try`, or throwing an exception in the `catch`, the code in the `finally` block will always execute after both of them are done executing (but before the value is returned from the function). In this manner we can verify that the `id` will always be restored properly.

The Selectors API is absolutely one of the most promising APIs to come out of the W3C in recent history. It has the potential to completely replace a large portion of most JavaScript libraries with a simple method, after the supporting browsers gain a dominant market share and support the totality (or at least majority) of CSS3.

Let's now turn our attention to a more XML-centric way of approaching the issue.

15.2 Using XPath to find elements

A unified alternative to using the Selectors API (for browsers that don't support it) is the use of XPath querying.

XPath is a querying language used to find nodes in a DOM document. It's significantly more powerful than traditional CSS selectors, and most popular browsers (Firefox, Safari 3+, Opera 9+, Chrome) provide some implementation of XPath that can be used against HTML-based DOM documents. Internet Explorer 6 and onward provide XPath support for XML documents (but not for HTML documents—the most common target).

If there's one thing that can be said for utilizing XPath expressions, it's that they're quite fast for complicated expressions. When implementing a pure-DOM implementation of a selector engine, we're constantly at odds with the ability of a browser to scale all the JavaScript and DOM operations. On the other hand, XPath loses out for simple expressions.

There's a certain indeterminate threshold at which it becomes more beneficial to use XPath expressions instead of pure DOM operations. While this threshold might be determined programmatically, there are a few givens: finding elements by `id` and simple tag-based selectors (`<div>`) will always be faster with pure-DOM code (using `getElementById()` and `getElementsByTagName()`).

If our intended audience is comfortable using XPath expressions (and is happy limiting themselves to the modern browsers that support it) then we can utilize the method shown in the following listing (from the Prototype library) and completely ignore everything else about building a CSS selector engine.

Listing 15.4   A method for executing an XPath expression on an HTML document

```
if (typeof document.evaluate === "function") {
  function getElementsByXPath(expression, parentElement) {
    var results = [];
    var query = document.evaluate(expression,
        parentElement || document,
        null, XPathResult.ORDERED_NODE_SNAPSHOT_TYPE, null);
    for (var i = 0, length = query.snapshotLength; i < length; i++)
      results.push(query.snapshotItem(i));
    return results;
  }
}
```

But while it would be nice to use XPath for everything, it simply isn't feasible. XPath, while feature-packed, is designed to be used by developers and is prohibitively complex in comparison to the expressions that CSS selectors make easy. We can't look at the entirety of XPath here, but table 15.1 offers a quick look at some of the most common XPath expressions and how they map to CSS selectors.

Table 15.1   CSS selectors and their equivalent XPath expressions

Goal	XPath	CSS3
All elements	`//*`	`*`
All elements named p	`//p`	`p`
All immediate child elements of p	`//p/*`	`p > *`
Element by ID	`//*[@id='foo']`	`#foo`
Element by Class	`//*[contains(concat(" ", @class, ""),"  foo ")]`	`.foo`
Element with attribute	`//*[@title]`	`*[title]`
First child of all p	`//p/*[0]`	`p > *:first-child`
All p with an a descendant	`//p[a]`	Not possible
Next element	`//p/following-sibling::*[0]`	`p + *`

We could use XPath expressions to create a selector engine, rather than constructing a pure-DOM selector engine, by parsing the selector using regular expressions. The important difference is that the resulting CSS selector portions would get mapped to their associated XPath expressions and executed.

This approach doesn't hold many advantages because the result is, code-wise, about as large as a normal pure-DOM CSS selector engine implementation. Many developers opt to not utilize an XPath engine simply to reduce the complexity of their resulting engines. You'll need to weigh the performance benefits of an XPath engine (especially taking into consideration the competition from the Selectors API) against the inherent code size that it will exhibit.

And now for the "rolling up our sleeves" approach...

15.3 *The pure-DOM implementation*

At the core of every CSS selector engine is a pure-DOM implementation. This entails parsing the CSS selectors and using the existing DOM methods (such as getElement-ById() and getElementsByTagName()) to find the corresponding elements.

> **TIP** HTML5 adds getElementsByClassName() to the set of available standard methods.

It's important to have a DOM implementation of a CSS selector engine for a number of reasons:

- *Internet Explorer 6 and 7*—While Internet Explorer 8 and 9 have support for query-SelectorAll(), the lack of XPath or Selectors API support in IE 6 and 7 make a DOM implementation necessary.
- *Backwards compatibility*—If you want your code to degrade in a graceful manner and support browsers that don't support the Selectors API or XPath (like Safari 2), you'll need some form of DOM implementation.
- *Speed*—There are a number of selectors that a pure-DOM implementation can do faster (such as finding elements by ID).
- *Complete coverage*—Not all browsers support the same set of CSS3 selectors. If we want to support the complete set—or at least a common subset—of supported selectors across all browsers, we need to roll our own.

With that in mind, we can take a look at the two possible CSS selector engine implementations: top down and bottom up.

A top-down engine works by parsing a CSS selector from left to right, matching elements in a document as it goes, working relatively for each additional selector segment. This type of engine can be found in most modern JavaScript libraries and is, generally, the preferred means of finding elements on a page.

Let's take a simple example. Consider this markup:

```
<body>

  <div></div>
  <div class="ninja">
    <span>Please </span><a href="/ninja"><span>Click me!</span></a>
  </div>

</body>
```

If we wished to select the `<span>` element containing the text "Click me!", we could do so with this selector:

```
div.ninja a span
```

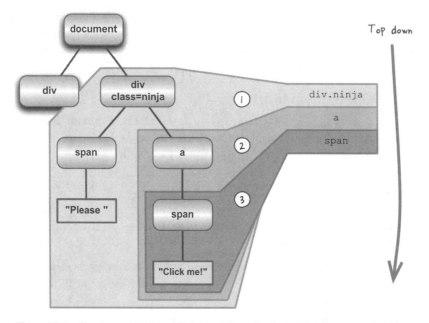

Figure 15.1   Top-down selector engines work from the top of the document, locating sub-trees matching the terms of the selector

The top-down approach to applying this selector to the DOM is depicted in figure 15.1.

The first term, div.ninja, identifies a subtree within the document ①. Within that subtree, the next term, a, is applied, identifying the subtree rooted at the anchor element ②. Finally, the span term identifies the target node ③. Note that this is a simplified example. Multiple subtrees can be identified at any stage.

There are two important considerations to take into account when developing a selector engine:

- The results should be in document order (the order in which they've been defined).
- The results should be unique (no duplicate elements should be returned).

Because of these gotchas, developing a top-down engine can be rather tricky.

Let's take a look at a simplified, top-down implementation, limited to finding elements by their tag names.

Listing 15.5   A limited, top-down selector engine

```
<div>
  <div>
    <span>Span</span>
  </div>
</div>

<script type="text/javascript">
```

```
window.onload = function(){
  function find(selector, root){

    root = root || document;

    var parts = selector.split(" "),
        query = parts[0],
        rest = parts.slice(1).join(" "),
        elems = root.getElementsByTagName(query),
        results = [];

    for (var i = 0; i < elems.length; i++) {
      if (rest) {
        results = results.concat(find(rest, elems[i]));
      }
      else {
        results.push(elems[i]);
      }
    }

    return results;
  };

  var divs = find("div");
  assert(divs.length === 2, "Correct number of divs found.");

  var divs = find("div", document.body);
  assert(divs.length === 2,
      "Correct number of divs found in body.");

  var divs = find("body div");
  assert(divs.length === 2,
      "Correct number of divs found in body.");

  var spans = find("div span");
  assert(spans.length === 2, "A duplicate span was found.");
};
```

If no root provided, starts at the top of the document

Splits the selector on spaces, grabs the first term, collects the remainder, finds the element matching the first term, and initializes an array to gather the results within

Calls find() recursively until all the selectors are consumed

Pushes found elements onto results array

Returns list of matched elements

```
</script>
```

In this listing we implemented a limited, top-down selector engine that's only capable of finding elements by tag name. The engine breaks down into a few parts: parsing the selector, finding the elements, filtering, and recursing and merging the results.

We'll take a closer look at each task in turn.

15.3.1 Parsing the selector

In our simplified example, our parsing was limited to converting a trivial CSS selector composed of tag names, such as "div span", into an array of strings, with this result: ["div", "span"].

This example simply broke the string apart on space delimiters, but CSS2 and 3 introduced the ability to find elements by attribute or attribute values, so it's possible to have additional spaces in most selectors. This makes our tactic of splitting the selector on spaces too simplistic.

For a full implementation, we'd want to have a solid series of parsing rules to handle any expressions that may be thrown at us; these rules would most likely take the form of regular expressions. The following example shows a more robust parser using a regular expression that's capable of capturing portions of a selector and breaking it into pieces (and splitting on commas, if need be).

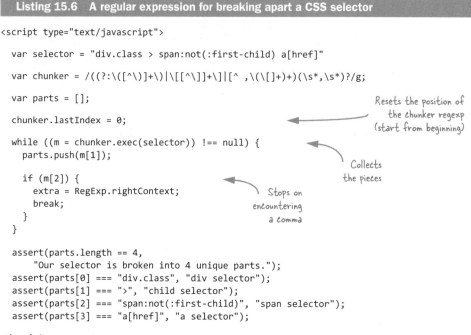

> **Listing 15.6   A regular expression for breaking apart a CSS selector**

```
<script type="text/javascript">

  var selector = "div.class > span:not(:first-child) a[href]"

  var chunker = /((?:\([^\)]+\)|\[[^\]]+\]|[^ ,\(\[]+)+)(\s*,\s*)?/g;

  var parts = [];

  chunker.lastIndex = 0;                                         Resets the position of
                                                                 the chunker regexp
                                                                 (start from beginning)
  while ((m = chunker.exec(selector)) !== null) {
    parts.push(m[1]);
                                                                 Collects
    if (m[2]) {                                                  the pieces
      extra = RegExp.rightContext;
      break;                                                Stops on
    }                                                    encountering
  }                                                        a comma
}

  assert(parts.length == 4,
      "Our selector is broken into 4 unique parts.");
  assert(parts[0] === "div.class", "div selector");
  assert(parts[1] === ">", "child selector");
  assert(parts[2] === "span:not(:first-child)", "span selector");
  assert(parts[3] === "a[href]", "a selector");

</script>
```

Obviously, this chunking selector is only one piece of the puzzle. We'll need to have additional parsing rules for each type of expression that we want to support. Most selector engines end up containing a map of regular expressions to functions; when a match is made on the selector portion, the associated function is executed.

Going over such expressions in detail would take far too long here. If you really want to dig into how it's done, we encourage you to grab the source code of jQuery or your favorite library and look though the selector-parsing code.

Next, we need to find the elements that match the parsed expression.

15.3.2   *Finding the elements*

Finding the correct elements on the page is a piece of the puzzle that has many solutions. Which techniques are used depends a lot on which selectors are being supported and what is available from the browser. There are a number of obvious approaches, though.

Consider `getElementById()`. Only available on the root node of HTML documents, this method finds the first element on the page that has the specified id (of which there should only be one); it is therefore useful for the ID CSS selector: `#id`. Internet Explorer and Opera infuriatingly will also find the first element on the page that has the same specified name. If we only wish to find elements by id, we'll need an extra verification step to exclude elements selected by this "helpful" feature.

If we wish to find *all* elements that match a specific id (as is customary in CSS selectors, even though HTML documents are generally only permitted one specific id per page), we'll need to either traverse all elements looking for the ones that have the correct id, or use document.all["id"], which returns an array of all elements that match an id in the browsers that support it (namely Internet Explorer, Opera, and Safari).

The getElementsByTagName() method performs the obvious operation: finding elements that match a specific tag name. It has another purpose, however: finding all elements within a document or element by using the * tag name. This is especially useful for handling attribute-based selectors that don't provide a specific tag name, such as .class or [attr].

There's one caveat when finding element comments using *; Internet Explorer will also return comment nodes in addition to element nodes (for whatever reason, in Internet Explorer, comment nodes have a tag name of ! and are thus returned). A basic level of filtering will need to be done to make sure that the comment nodes are excluded.

getElementsByName() is a well-implemented method that serves a single purpose: finding all elements that have a specific name (such as <input> elements and other form-control elements that have a name attribute). It's really useful for implementing the single selector [name=*name*].

The getElementsByClassName() method is a new HTML5 method that's being implemented by the browsers. It finds elements based upon the contents of their class attribute. This method tremendously speeds up class-selection code.

Although there are a variety of techniques that can be used for selection, the preceding methods are the primary tools used to find what we're looking for on a page.

Using the results from these methods, we can move on to filtering.

15.3.3 Filtering the set

A CSS expression is generally made up of a number of individual pieces. For example, the expression div.class[id] has three parts: it will find all div elements that have a class name of class and have an attribute named id.

The first step is to identify the root selector we want to begin with. For example, we can see that div is used, so we can immediately use getElementsByTagName() to retrieve all <div> elements on the page. We must, then, filter those results down to only include those that have the specified class and that have an id attribute specified.

This filtering process is a common feature of most selector implementations. The contents of these filters primarily deal with attributes or the position of the element relative to its siblings and other relations:

- *Attribute filtering*—This approach is used for accessing the DOM attributes (generally using the getAttribute() method) and verifying their values. Class filtering (.class) is a subset of this behavior (accessing the className attribute and checking its value).

- *Position filtering*—For selectors like :nth-child(even) or :last-child, a combination of methods is used on the parent element. In browsers that support it, children is used (IE, Safari, Chrome, Opera, and Firefox 3.1), which contains a list of all child elements. All browsers have childNodes, which contains a list of child nodes, including text nodes and comments. By using these two methods, it becomes possible to do all forms of element position filtering.

Constructing a filtering function serves a dual purpose: we can provide it to the user as a simple method for testing their elements, and we can quickly check to see if an element matches a specific selector.

Let's now focus on tools to refine our results.

15.3.4 *Recursing and merging*

As was shown in listing 15.1, selector engines require the ability to recurse (find descendant elements) and merge the results together. But our initial implementation was far too simple. We ended up receiving two <span> elements in our results instead of just one. We need to introduce an additional check to make sure the returned array of elements contains unique results. Most top-down selector implementations possess some means of enforcing this uniqueness.

Unfortunately, there's no simple way to determine the uniqueness of a DOM element, so we need to figure out a way to do it ourselves. The approach we'll take is to go through the elements and assign temporary identifying values to them, so that we can verify whether we've already encountered them.

Listing 15.7   Finding the unique elements in an array

```
<div id="test">
  <b>Hello</b>, I'm a ninja!
</div>
<div id="test2"></div>

<script type="text/javascript">

  (function(){

    var run = 0;

    this.unique = function(array) {
      var ret = [];

      run++;

      for (var i = 0, length = array.length; i < length; i++) {
        var elem = array[i];

        if (elem.uniqueID !== run) {
          elem.uniqueID = run;
          ret.push(array[i]);
        }
      }
    }
```

Sets up our willing test subjects.

Defines the unique() function inside an immediate function to create a closure that will include the run variable but hide it from the outside world.

Accepts an array of elements and returns a new array containing only unique elements from the original array.

Keeps track of which run we're on. By incrementing this value each time the function is called, a unique identifier value will be used for testing for uniqueness.

Runs through the original array, copying elements that we haven't "seen" yet, and marking them so that we'll know whether we've "seen" them or not.

```
      return ret;
  };
})();
```
← Returns the resulting array, containing only references to unique elements.

```
window.onload = function(){
  var divs = unique(document.getElementsByTagName("div"));
  assert(divs.length === 2, "No duplicates removed.");

  var body = unique([document.body, document.body]);
  assert(body.length === 1, "body duplicate removed.");
};
```
← Tests it! The first test shouldn't result in any removals (as there are no duplicates passed), but the second should collapse down to a single element.

```
</script>
```

This unique() method adds an expando property to all the elements in the array as it inspects them, marking them as having been "seen." By the time a complete run-through is finished, only unique elements will have been copied into the resulting array. Variations on this technique can be found in almost all libraries.

For a longer discussion on the intricacies of attaching properties to DOM nodes, revisit chapter 13 on events.

The problem we solved with this function specifically resulted from the top-down approach we employed. Let's briefly consider an alternative.

15.3.5 Bottom-up selector engine

If you prefer not to have to think about uniquely identifying elements, there's an alternative style of CSS selector engine that doesn't require it. A bottom-up selector engine works in the opposite direction of a top-down one.

For example, given the selector div span, a bottom-up selector engine will first find all <span> elements, and then, for each element, will navigate up the ancestor elements to find an ancestor <div> element. This style of selector engine construction matches the style found in most browser engines.

This engine style isn't as popular as the top-down approach. Although it works well for simple selectors (and child selectors), the ancestor travels end up being quite costly, and it doesn't scale very well. But the simplicity that this engine style provides can end up making for a nice trade-off.

The construction of the engine is simple. We start by finding the last expression in the CSS selector and then retrieve the appropriate elements (just like with a top-down engine, but using the last expression rather than the first). From here on, all operations are performed as a series of filter operations, removing elements as the operations progress (see the following listing).

Listing 15.8   A simple bottom-up selector engine

```
<div>
  <div>
    <span>Span</span>
  </div>
</div>
```

```
<script type="text/javascript">

  window.onload = function(){
    function find(selector, root){
      root = root || document;

      var parts = selector.split(" "),
          query = parts[parts.length - 1],
          rest = parts.slice(0,-1).join(""),
          elems = root.getElementsByTagName(query),
          results = [];

      for (var i = 0; i < elems.length; i++) {
        if (rest) {
          var parent = elems[i].parentNode;
          while (parent && parent.nodeName != rest) {
            parent = parent.parentNode;
          }

          if (parent) {
            results.push(elems[i]);
          }
        } else {
          results.push(elems[i]);
        }
      }

      return results;
    };

    var divs = find("div");
    assert(divs.length === 2, "Correct number of divs found.");

    var divs = find("div", document.body);
    assert(divs.length === 2,
        "Correct number of divs found in body.");

    var divs = find("body div");
    assert(divs.length === 2,
        "Correct number of divs found in body.");

    var spans = find("div span");
    assert(spans.length === 1, "No duplicate span was found.");
  };

</script>
```

Listing 15.8 shows the construction of a simple bottom-up selector engine. Note that it only works one ancestor level deep. In order to work more than one level deep, the state of the current level would need to be tracked. This would result in two state arrays: the array of elements that are going to be returned (with some elements being set to undefined because they don't match the results), and an array of elements that correspond to the currently tested ancestor element.

As mentioned before, this extra ancestor-verification process does end up being slightly less scalable than the top-down method, but it completely avoids having to use a unique method for producing non-repetitive output, which some may see as an advantage.

15.4 *Summary*

JavaScript-based CSS selector engines are incredibly powerful tools. They give us the ability to easily locate virtually any DOM element on a page with a trivial amount of selector syntax. There are many nuances to implementing a full selector engine, but the situation is rapidly improving as the browsers improve, and there's no shortage of tools to help.

Here's what we learned in this chapter:

- Modern browsers are implementing the W3C APIs for element selection, but they've got a long way to go.
- It still behooves us to create selector engines ourselves, if for no reason other than performance.
- To create a selector engine, we can
  - Leverage the W3C APIs
  - Use XPath
  - Traverse the DOM ourselves for optimum performance
- The top-down approach is most popular, but it requires some cleanup operations, such as to ensure the uniqueness of elements.
- A bottom-up approach avoids these operations, but it comes with its own bag of problems with respect to performance and scalability.

With modern browsers implementing the W3C Selector API, having to worry about the finer points of selector implementation may soon be a thing of the past. For many developers, that day can't come soon enough.

index